The Problem of Proof

Second Edition

The Problem of Proof

Complete and Unabridged

Especially as Exemplified
in
Disputed Document Trials

A Discussion of the Proof of the Facts in Courts of Law, with Some General Comments on the Conduct of Trials

Second Edition

by

Albert S. Osborn

Author of *Questioned Documents*

Introduction by
Professor John Henry Wigmore
Author of *Wigmore on Evidence*

A Facsimile Edition
With an Introduction by
Daniel Vander Werf, Jr.
Director
World Association of Document Examiners

Professional/Technical Series

Nelson-Hall Inc. nh Chicago

Library of Congress Cataloging in Publication Data

Osborn, Albert Sherman, 1858-1946.
The problem of proof, especially as exemplified in disputed document trials.

(Professional/technical series)
Photoreprint of the 2d ed. published by Essex Press, Newark, N.J.
Bibliography: p.
Includes index.
1. Evidence, Documentary—United States. 2. Forgery—United States. 3. Writing—Identification. 4. Trial practice—United States. I. Title.
KF8947.08 1976a 347.'.73'64 75-20212

ISBN 0-88229-300-1

Manufactured in the United States of America

INTRODUCTION TO THE FACSIMILE EDITION

I was delighted and felt privileged to write the introduction to the Nelson-Hall reissue of Osborn's *Questioned Documents.* Now I can again express my pleasure in being asked to introduce the new Nelson-Hall publication of Osborn's *The Problem of Proof,* which, like *Questioned Documents,* is a faithful and unabridged reproduction of the complete work.

While *Questioned Documents* is the basic source book for the technical aspects of document investigation, *The Problem of Proof* is the definitive work for the legal procedures connected with documents cases. In *The Problem of Proof* we go from the laboratory into the courtroom, where we are introduced to all the legal technicalities and psychological snares that await the document examiner called to the stand as an expert witness.

Who would dispute Dean Roscoe Pound's opinion that Osborn *created* the profession of examiner of questioned documents in this country? Among present-day document professionals, it is axiomatic that Osborn's insight into the requirements of scientific investigation and demonstration was equalled by his foresight in anticipating developments in our field.

Here we find the rules of evidence as they apply to expert testimony explained in detail, and the psychological atmosphere of a trial described clearly. Not everyone in our field is aware that Osborn was not only the "dean" of document technicians but also a legal expert highly respected by lawyers and judges. In his original introduction to *The Problem of Proof,* Dean Wigmore of Northwestern University, the noted authority on evidence, stated that Osborn's chapter on Advocacy was one he wished he had written himself. "It should be read aloud every year before law classes."

But what is especially instructive in this book, from the standpoint of document specialists, is the practical advice and briefing Mr. Osborn provides for the expert witness in dealing with the very real problem of proving the factual truth of the evidence gathered in his investigation.

No matter how much court experience a document examiner has had, he can learn from *The Problem of Proof*. One measure of the soundness of this work is that Osborn seemed to anticipate the various revisions in evidentiary law that have taken place since original publication of the book. He took into account almost every situation that could arise involving document litigation, and these situations apply today just as much as they did when the book was first published. The reasons for this are Osborn's firm grounding in the principles and rules of law and his insight into all aspects of persuasion and practical psychology, which have not changed at all down the years.

It should also be noted that while *The Problem of Proof* deals primarily with the relationship between lawyer and document examiner and their cooperation in a court trial, the book is fascinating and instructive reading for professionals and businessmen, technical specialists, and, indeed, countless people in all walks of life who may find themselves called into court as expert witnesses.

As Osborn says, "Though renowned as a specialist, a man may be a pitiful failure as a witness. To be effective as a witness the specialist must not only know, but must be able to explain, to convince, and to undergo cross-examination. . . . Much language as spoken suggests that man is, to a considerable degree, a dumb animal and only feebly hints at much he would express. The thoughtful and practiced technical witness fully realizes this difficulty of conveying an idea to another. . . . A man is at once suspected who stumbles in talking about what he is supposed to know."

How is one to overcome this difficulty? Here we find Osborn instructing us not only as a technical document expert and a legal counsel, but also as a shrewd expert in the art of verbal communication. He shows us how to organize our technical knowledge, how to collect the terminology of our specialty—all the modifying and descriptive terms, and how to practice and use them until we are confident we can contend successfully with the most searching cross-examination in court. And he forearms us to deal with the wide variety of tricky questions that opposing counsel may use to weaken our testimony on the witness stand.

The technical witness, Osborn stresses, should never go into court relying on nothing but his expertise. The basic problem of proof, he indicates, is that the *proof* of a fact in court is a much more difficult operation than the *discovery* of that fact. "A relatively inexperienced document examiner must become aware before appearing in court that while his exhibits may seem conclusive, he will still have to contend with the psychological elements of sympathy, prejudice, perjury, and skillful opposition."

Any document examiner with court experience is aware that the mere fact of presenting himself in court as an "expert" may get him off on the wrong foot. "The word itself," Osborn says, "suggests a certain superiority that may produce in the mind of the inexperienced hearer an immediate feeling of antagonism aroused by the thought that the name is not given to the witness, but is assumed by him."

This is only one of the pitfalls Osborn calls to our attention while providing us with effective means of avoiding such pitfalls. These measures, obviously, should be planned before any court appearance. So, pre-trial cooperation between attorney and expert witness is of the utmost importance. The witness is not a lawyer, and he may believe that a bare recital of facts is all that is necessary to win a suit. A skilled lawyer, however, can show him that evidence, even in a good case, may fail to win a favorable verdict if it is presented without regard to order of statement, tone, emphasis, or general effect on the judge and jury. The lawyer does not have to "coach the witness," but he must instruct the witness in proper preparation of the case consistent with the rules of evidence and court procedure. He should also instruct the witness in proper demeanor to counteract possible dangerous prejudice in the mind of judge or juror.

Prejudice may arise because the witness presents himself too strongly as an "expert" or because he talks down to the jury or tends to be argumentative under cross-examination. He must be briefed by the lawyer to avoid making a statement or giving an answer that will be "stricken from the record" after objection by opposing counsel.

In this connection, Osborn advises the lawyer in the case to learn as much as he can about the technical aspects of the testimony his witness will present. The lawyer cannot hope to become an expert on every subject, but he should be ready to support key technical points at issue. Too often, lawyers are not effective in disputed document cases because they do not bother to examine the real basis of the evidence and lean entirely on the witness, rather than being able to assist with illuminating incidental arguments.

Every document examiner on the witness stand has been forced at some time or other to run the gauntlet of questions by opposing counsel which attempt to discredit his testimony. He will be asked, for example, if it is not true that handwriting experts often disagree. Or he will be asked if he receives pay for his services, with the inference that his fee is a sort of bribe to provide the kind of evidence his attorney wants. Osborn demonstrates how to turn this line of questioning to the witness's advantage.

While, by its nature, a book of this kind is mainly concerned with document cases in an adversary system of justice, the professional role of the document examiner out of court is not neglected.

The document examiner may often make a valuable social contribution by persuading contesting parties to avoid litigation. As a consultant, he can give an expert opinion on any document or handwriting exhibit in question and can make whatever laboratory or photographic tests might be required. By rendering this professional service he often discourages foolhardy or fraudulent claimants. As a result, many claims without merit are withdrawn or dubious claims are compromised out of court. Osborn observes that when dishonest people know there is a competent document examiner available in the community, they hesitate to make use of fraudulent documents in their operations.

So, as Director of the World Association of Document Examiners, I share the gratitude of all members of my profession that *The Problem of Proof* is once more in print and readily available to aid us in our specialized field of criminal justice.

Daniel Vander Werf, Jr.

The Problem of Proof

The Problem of Proof

ESPECIALLY AS EXEMPLIFIED

IN

DISPUTED DOCUMENT TRIALS

A DISCUSSION OF THE PROOF OF THE FACTS IN COURTS OF LAW, WITH SOME GENERAL COMMENTS ON THE CONDUCT OF TRIALS

SECOND EDITION

BY

ALBERT S. OSBORN

AUTHOR OF "QUESTIONED DOCUMENTS"

INTRODUCTION BY

PROFESSOR JOHN HENRY WIGMORE

AUTHOR OF

"WIGMORE ON EVIDENCE"

NEWARK, N. J.

THE ESSEX PRESS

1926

Fourth Printing—Second Edition.

THE ESSEX PRESS, PRINTERS
NEWARK, N. J.

INTRODUCTION

This volume is a worthy successor of "Questioned Documents". There is wisdom on every page. It is far more than a book of advice on Document Trials; its ripe wisdom ranges over a wide scope of the practitioner's field. Its emphasis on the study of facts in preparation for trial is pervasive. It contains varied and valuable warnings for both counsel and witness. Chapter XV on Court Rooms, and Chapter XVIII on Judges, are samples of original and candid comments, which deserve the widest circulation. But Chapter V, on Advocacy, is my favorite. It is the climax of the book. The rest *could* not surpass that mark. I would like to have written that chapter myself,—only I could not. It should be read aloud every year before every law class.

JOHN HENRY WIGMORE.

Northwestern University
School of Law,
Chicago, Ill.

The league between virtue and nature engages all things to assume a hostile front to vice. The beautiful laws and substances of the world persecute and whip the traitor. He finds that things are arranged for truth and benefit, but there is no den in the world to hide a rogue. Commit a crime, and the world is made of glass. Commit a crime and it seems as if a coat of snow fell on the ground, such as reveals in the woods the track of every partridge and fox and squirrel and mole. You cannot recall the spoken word, you cannot wipe out the foot-track, you cannot draw up the ladder, so as to leave no inlet or clew. Some damning circumstance always transpires. The laws and substances of nature — water, snow, wind, gravitation — become penalties to the thief.

EMERSON.

TABLE OF CONTENTS

''The testimony of attesting witnesses to a will may be overcome by any competent evidence. Such evidence may be direct, or it may be circumstantial; and expert and opinion evidence is just as competent as any other evidence. Indeed, where the signature to a will is a forgery, and where the attesting witnesses have the hardihood to commit perjury, it is difficult to see how the bogus will can be overthrown, except by expert and competent opinion evidence tending to show that the pretended signature is not that of the testator, but spurious. The rule contended for by appellants would frequently baffle justice and give judicial countenance to many a high-handed fraud.'' Baird v. Shaffer, Kansas Supreme Court, 168 Pacific 836 (1918).

''In the use of demonstrative evidence one relies upon the evidence of his own senses. It is therefore evidence of the highest rank. . . . The questioned signatures and photographs of them are before the court, as well as signatures admittedly genuine and photographs of them, some enlarged for convenience of comparison; and the means were at hand for measurement and other comparisons embracing the whole field of examination. So that the facts to which the expert witness testified concerning the characteristics and construction of the signatures are matters within the field of demonstrative evidence.'' Boyd v. Gosser, 82 Southern Reporter, 758, Florida Supreme Court (1919).

''The controlling question for determination is the sufficiency of the evidence to sustain the finding that the instrument offered for probate is the will of decedent. . . . If the subscribing witnesses told the truth the will offered for probate was executed in the manner outlined. . . . The story of John O'Connor's signature told by the experts who testified on behalf of contestants, when considered in the light of corroborating circumstances, is better evidence of the truth than the testimony of subscribing witnesses in controlling issue of fact. . . . The evidence as a whole shows that the will is a forgery, that the judgment of the County Court denying the probate is free from error and that the judgment of the District Court sustaining the will is clearly wrong.'' In re O'Connor's Estate, Supreme Court of Nebraska, 179 Northwestern 401 (1920).

TO

WILLIAM JOSEPH KINSLEY

AN INSPIRING CO-WORKER, A LOYAL FRIEND,

A GOOD MAN.

Lawsuits are rare and catastrophic experiences for the vast majority of men, and even when the catastrophe ensues, the controversy relates most often not to the law, but to the facts. Cardozo's *The Nature of the Judicial Process,* (1921).

This science, the principles of proof, to be sure, may as yet be imperfectly formulated or even incapable of formulation. But all the more need is there to begin in earnest to investigate and develop it. Furthermore, this process of Proof is the more important of the two,—indeed, is the ultimate purpose in every judicial investigation. The procedural rules for Admissibility are merely a preliminary aid to the main activity, viz., the persuasion of the tribunal's mind to a correct conclusion by safe materials. This main process is that for which the jury are there, and on which the counsel's duty is focused. Wigmore's *Principles of Judicial Proof,* (1913).

He who denies or doubts the evidence of his own proper senses will, of course, deny or doubt the existence of matter, and be an universal sceptic; and to such a mind there can be no such thing as *proof;* for if he distrusts his own senses, he will be much more distrustful of the testimony of others as to the evidence of *their* senses. Hence *autopsy,* or the evidence of one's own senses, furnishes the strongest probability, and, indeed the only perfect and indubitable certainty, of the existence of any sensible fact.

But we are compelled to depend on an inferior grade of evidence — the testimony of others — respecting facts of which we have no personal knowledge. And jurors, selected and sworn to try facts litigated in court, are generally in this condition. But when they decide altogether on the testimony of others, they do so only because the fact to be tried is unsusceptible of any better proof. Chief Justice Robertson in *Gentry v. McMinnis,* 3 Dana, 33 Ky. 382, (1835).

FOREWORD

TO

SECOND EDITION

The necessity having arisen for another printing of this book, the fourth since the book was issued late in 1922, the opportunity is taken to change the order of the matter and add a brief new chapter on Thought and Reasoning.

The book was originally intended to be a technical work discussing only the various phases of the preparation and trial of a disputed document case and their relation to the subject of proof. The manuscript, which was in hand for some time, gradually expanded up to the time the work was published, when with surprise it was found that more than half of the book could perhaps be described as general rather than technical matter relating to this important subject of proof in courts of law and this general matter seems to have aroused unusual interest. In the book as published these various parts were left as they had been developed in the manuscript.

In response to certain helpful suggestions by reviewers and readers a rearrangement of the matter is now made with the general matter in the first part of the book and the technical matter arranged continuously in the later chapters. This new arrangement will no doubt make the book more useful, especially to student readers who have manifested much interest in the work.

The new chapter, it is hoped, will supplement in a useful way, some similar suggestions in the other chapters.

It is gratifying at this time to have this opportunity to record the fact that the welcome to the book has demonstrated that the legal profession does not resent constructive criticism, an attitude that always is a symptom of health and virility in a profession as well as in an individual.

ALBERT S. OSBORN.

New York,
July 1, 1926.

PREFACE TO FIRST EDITION

It is usually possible to discover the purpose of a book from the book itself without the aid of the preface, but these customary explanations do at least serve as a warning to those who do not care for what is promised so they need go no further than the portal.

One is not likely to add to the great number of books unless he at least thinks he has some message to deliver, but not until he makes the attempt does he fully understand how difficult it is for mind to communicate with mind by means of printed words. It is altogether probable that many of those who have failed really had a message but did not deliver it. Language, with all of its complications, is finally a language only of signs that but feebly expresses thought, and every frank man who writes a book is inclined to apologize when he compares the result with the intention. In some measure we are all dumb—some of us more than others—and are all bound to be misunderstood to some extent when the attempt is made to put ideas into words. A preface would serve a really useful purpose if it led the gentle reader to add to what is said that which the writer aimed to say.

When one thinks back over the controlling influences of life, memory recalls, along with lost opportunities and foolish mistakes, certain vivid hours and minutes of inspiration through the written and the spoken word. These memories furnish the impulse to give advice, warnings, and suggestions to others in spite of the fact that the great bulk of them produce no result. If one could tell another how to do a thing, so that the other could go out and do it, then skill and ability would be passed on from generation to generation, but each of us must begin almost at zero. Each one must burn his own fingers, but to learn the lesson it is not always necessary to cripple the hand for life.

But it is incomparably harder to take advice than to give it. To be able even to recognize a new idea, or appreciate a new emphasis, among the great mass of ideas of high and low degree that flow by in the stream of thought, is a clear proof of intelligence, and to adopt an idea and make it our own is a distinct achievement. The test of ability is to recognize it and to see genius is a sign of genius.

The advice of a friend, or of a book, can do for us but little more than the sign-board does, that is point the way, and then we ourselves must go; but many, if not most, poor humans grope and stumble without even seeing the sign-boards. But few things in the life of a man are more important than the developing of a constant, consuming desire to find the sign-boards though he knows full well how little they can do for him.

The main purpose of this book is to help the lawyer who has a case to try in which it becomes necessary to prove the facts relating to a disputed document. Either directly or indirectly, the matter presented has application to the general problem of proof, which may give the work a somewhat wider use.

The task of the advocate is to convince a judge, or a jury, that his client is entitled to a favorable verdict. He works with facts, ideas, law, testimony, and argument. All of his preparation and all of his efforts finally focus on the central question of proof, and only when he is prepared to prove his case is he ready for trial. The attempt is made in these chapters to show the necessity for adequate general, as well as technical, preparation and also the importance of certain special study and training that apparently has been overlooked by many who are called upon as attorneys to protect the rights and interests of others.

Certain tendencies in legal procedure and, what are here considered to be, certain common faults of method and weaknesses of presentation in law practice are pointed out with an emphasis which it is thought the conditions justify. Emphasis is also laid on the fact that a trial at law is more than a narrow, abstract, intellectual task and requires not only study of many puzzling questions of law and of fact but also study of puzzling variations of human personality.

The scientific investigations necessary to the discovery and illustration of the physical evidence in disputed document cases are treated here only incidentally as an extended discussion of those subjects has been attempted in a previous book. The subject of technical law is considered only in connection with certain phases of law reform, and, although there are included discussions of tendencies of legal procedure and of a number of general questions that arise in the practice of law, the book does not aim to be a general treatise on the practice of law.

In considerable part the book is a report of direct observations of the work of able, as well as of stupid, attorneys in courts of high and low degree in widely separated fields. Parts of many of the chapters have been written in court-rooms, and if the book does not possess the right atmosphere the fault is in execution and not because it did not come from the right surroundings. This matter has been combined with the results of study and experimentation relating to the problem of how to prepare and present a technical subject to a court and jury. A book would be required for a complete treatment of some of the topics which are briefly discussed, and they are considered only because of their bearings upon other questions that are treated more fully.

Portions of this book have appeared in certain law journals, and a small part of the matter has been read to law classes, to bar association meetings, and to general audiences under various titles, all relating to some special phase of the problem of proof. This matter has been rearranged and put in connected form, its scope has been extended, and new matter has been added.

Unlike much other litigation, in a case involving the genuineness of a document one side is right and the other wrong. There is no middle ground and one party is in court through error, or through fraud and perjury. To decide whether or not to assist a litigant in a case of this kind often affords a test of the credulity as well as the integrity of the attorney. This book definitely aims to assist those who are endeavoring to prove the facts. Some legal treatises, reflecting a phase of the spirit of advocacy, apparently are as willing to help those to win who may seek to defeat justice as those who are attempting to establish it. Definite directions are given for destroying the correct testimony of honest witnesses, and it is related with what appears to be a kind of glee that by some subterfuge, or by what in effect was a piece of sharp practice, the "difficult case" was won; or, to state it more bluntly, the case was won against the facts. This too frequent neutrality lessens respect for the honorable profession of the law. Although fraud may appropriate the weapons and tools of right, fortunately they are not all adapted to this improper use and certainly direct and definite aids should not be prepared and put into the hands of those whose business is the assisting of fraud to win. Methods and procedure which test alleged facts in the most thorough manner need no defense, but obstructive, unfair, and confusing tactics, designed to prevent the proof of the facts, at least should not be encouraged. True law reform aims to make it easier not only to free the innocent, but to convict the guilty; to help the just cause towards success, and to make it more difficult for the evil cause to win.

The surprising credulity of certain members of the legal profession who have had intensive training in certain phases of advocacy, is an idea discussed in a number of connections in this book. The thought is naturally presented with some hesitation. The contention is somewhat novel and, to those who have not carefully considered the question, may seem to be unwarranted. If the contention is true it does explain certain phases of advocacy that are sometimes assailed in a much harsher manner, and the thought is offered, not so much as a criticism as an explanation. If only to a limited extent the contention is correct, a knowledge of it may contribute to the interests of justice. This excessive credulity is probably not mainly an inherent quality but is a result developed by conditions. An eager desire to believe, as William James has so clearly pointed out, develops the ability to believe and that is the thought here presented. One whose training has mainly been that of a proponent, or a defense attorney in criminal cases, has a tendency eagerly to reach out with the mind in every direction for confirmation of strange tales and claims.

This condition of credulity partly explains the surprising connection of certain men with certain cases; it explains to some extent incredible arguments; it tends to explain the presentation of ridiculously incredible testimony, and it no doubt in some measure accounts for certain surprising judgments. Strange as it may seem, it is probable that attorneys sometimes do really believe the fantastic stories told to them by clients and actually give some credence to the incredible testimony of the witnesses they call. Zealous advocates have now and then been charged with dishonesty and insincerity, when perhaps they should only have been accused of possessing a childlike credulity. Their "will to believe" had been developed to an abnormal and dangerous degree.

During the early history of the law and even down nearly to the present day, the scientific investigation of disputed documents made but little progress for the reason that the subject was so hedged about by restrictions that many facts were not allowed to be proved in court even if discovered. As a result of the progress of science many of the facts in these investigations can now be discovered that in the old days remained effectively hidden, and the modernizing of legal procedure gives the opportunity to the client and his attorney to go into court and effectively present the proof of the facts on the point at issue. The modern methods have gradually tended to make a disputed document trial a legally supervised, scientific investigation by a court and jury. Hundreds of just cases are now tried and won that under the ancient rules were summarily disposed of by one sustained objection. Under the old rules this book would have been of little use as many of the methods here outlined would have been "contrary to law".

It seems strange that the law itself should thus ever be the actual means of hiding the truth and defeating justice, but unfortunately this has been the fact, and much of what is called law reform has consisted in getting what has been the law out of the way so that an investigation could be taken up in a sensible manner, taken into court, and the facts proved. There are many persons who do not seem fully to understand that this opportunity to prove the facts in a court of law is the means by which justice is maintained in civilized communities, and that the progress of civilization is marked by the halting steps by which this proceeding has been made more easy and certain. When attention is fixed on a brief space of time the advance seems cruelly slow, but as the time perspective is lengthened, the evidence of progress becomes more apparent.

These various law reforms as a rule have been instituted by the profession itself, but never by all the members of the profession. There have been members of the bench and bar who have disturbed the placidity of their unprogressive associates and who have dared to think and to say not only what the law was but what it ought to be. Some of the self-styled practical lawyers, with whom the profession is only a business, have been and are particularly bitter in their criticism of certain judges, law writers, and "theoretical professors" who have attacked the worst of the ancient practices and precedents. Those who are the victims of the outgrown procedure help these progressive critics, and now and then a step forward is taken. A dissenting opinion may not show just what the law is, but it sometimes shows quite clearly what the law is going to be.

It is hardly necessary to say that the following chapters do not presume to instruct the seasoned veteran who on the field of conflict has himself worked out and demonstrated whatever there is of merit in the suggestions here offered. The work is instead designed to assist those just enlisted who aim to make themselves worthy successors of the leaders who have gone before, or to help those who already do well but are ambitious to do better. Much of that here offered is not altogether new but may have a somewhat new setting and a new emphasis. Some of it may seem quite elementary, but if so then there is need for the elementary. The book is mainly a collection of suggestions and cautions that, it is hoped, will have, not merely a critical, but a constructive value. It obviously is very difficult in a work of this kind to avoid the didactic tone. The danger has been recognized and the attempt has been made to avoid it without at the same time sacrificing the practical purpose of the book.

It also has been difficult to discuss some of these quite closely related subjects fully and clearly without a repetition of at least certain thoughts. It is hoped that some of these ideas may warrant this emphasis which has grown out of the attempt to make each division of the work more complete and useful in itself. The book will not answer the purpose for which it was written if in some way it cannot at once be applied to a practical problem actually in hand.

These discussions relate principally to a phase of law practice of growing importance that, as now conducted, is comparatively new in many courts, and for this reason there is more necessity for aid and suggestions in this special field. It is hoped that the discussions are sufficiently general to apply in some measure to other classes of legal proof and that they will contribute something to the slow-moving reform of all legal procedure which seeks to insure that every court of law shall also be a court of justice.

ALBERT S. OSBORN

New York City,
September, 1922.

If any person shall falsely forge, or make, or cause or assent to be falsely forged or made, any false deed, charter, or writing sealed . . . court-roll or will in writing . . . and shall be convicted . . . he shall pay to the party aggrieved double costs and damages to be assessed by the court . . . and shall be set on the pillory, and there have his ears cut off, and his nostrils slit and cut, and seared with a hot iron; he shall also forfeit to the queen the profits of his lands during life, and suffer perpetual imprisonment. 5 Eliz. c. 14 (1563).

All persons invoking any evil spirit, or consulting, covenanting with, entertaining, employing, feeding, or rewarding any evil spirit . . . to be used in any witchcraft, sorcery, charm, or inchantment . . . should be guilty of felony without benefit of clergy, and suffer death. 1 Jac. I. c. 12 (1603).

No prosecution shall for the future be carried on against any person for conjuration, witchcraft, sorcery, or enchantment. 9 Geo. II. c. 5 (1736).

CHAPTER I.

PREPARATION ON THE FACTS.

Relevant facts, when clearly illustrated and properly interpreted, become the strongest witnesses that appear in a court of law; they stand silent but unassailable. They are not injured by cross-examination. No one in any field is better able to appreciate their well-known stubbornness than the trial attorney. If favorable, they point the way to success; if adverse, they block the road to victory.

It is customary to refer to the two divisions of a case as "the law" and "the facts". What is called "the law" is quite definite and well understood, while the term "the facts" is a somewhat elastic term which covers nearly everything in the case which is not included under the term "the law".

Facts that have a bearing on the case, when found, are bound to assist the attorney whose contention is correct, for the reason that they are always consistent with each other. They need no reconciliation; they match and confirm each other simply by being facts. The matter of finding, understanding, arranging, and presenting them is the important part of the attorney's business. There may come to the unprepared attorney a tense moment when, to paraphrase the sorely beset Richard, he will be inclined to cry, A fact! A fact! My Kingdom for a fact!

Many disputed document cases are prepared and tried with an inefficiency that is almost criminal. Hundreds of thousands of dollars are jeopardized, or actually lost, and reputation, liberty, and even life are imperiled because of lack of preparation and through bungling methods. Important evidence is not found and even the very theory upon which a case is tried is sometimes wrong from the beginning and dooms it to failure. Many lawyers are unaware how thoroughly other lawyers prepare their cases. The unprepared are inclined to think that the difference in result is due to the quality of the case rather than to the quality of the preparation.

There are those who acquire knowledge of the history and principles of the law simply as a part of a comprehensive general education, but most students take up the subject with a view of becoming lawyers. They are preparing for a profession in which they will seek to apply their knowledge to practical affairs. This application may be mainly advisory in which the principles of the law are applied to the relations of men and affairs through counsel, advice, and consultation. These practitioners who know the law and its application are known as advisory, corporation, or business lawyers. They are called upon to give advice on matters of the most momentous character and far-reaching effect and their work is highly important and often very lucrative.

A quite different class of lawyers are those who try cases in court and are known as trial lawyers. Many men practice somewhat in both fields, but there are these two general classes. The trial lawyer contends in court as an advocate. He seeks to promote a client's interests through a trial that will lead to a favorable decision by a judge, or a favorable verdict by a jury. It is probably true that the majority of students of the law have an ambition to become trial lawyers, and nearly all lawyers do try cases now and then. The great lawyer is usually thought of as one who contends in court.

It is obvious that at least a portion of the desirable training for these two classes of lawyers is not just the same. The lawyer in the first class seeks results mainly through the application to the problem of the principles of the law, while the lawyer in the other class seeks through evidence and argument to persuade those who are to decide a case that a certain contention should prevail. The advisory lawyer works with legal precedents, statutes, and the history and the principles of the law in their direct and varied applications to the affairs of men. The work of the trial lawyer has direct application to the problem of proof. With facts and law he works with and through the minds and emotions of people. He is engaged with evidence of events, and must be able to examine, understand, and report on a great variety of tangible things. Success with him depends not only on his knowledge of the law, but on his knowledge of men and of facts.

A point of law alone has won many a case, and it is not to be inferred from what is here said regarding the importance of knowing other things that the lawyer does not need to know the principles of the law and their application to his case, but that this knowledge is only a part of his necessary preparation. Law study naturally emphasizes the importance of knowing the law, but law practice undoubtedly emphasizes the necessity of knowing the facts. In the preliminary study of law the facts of a case are necessarily assumed, but in actual practice a law suit consists mainly, not in applying the law to the facts, but in proving the facts to which the law then applies.

In some law suits the questions in controversy are comparatively simple, and the trial attorney can perhaps sufficiently inform himself by a discussion of the matter with his client and by the interviewing of his witnesses. In a case, however, involving any unusual technical question special study and investigation are usually necessary. Even in the simpler cases it is many times desirable that a more thorough study be made of all the facts of the case in all their bearings. A clear understanding of all the technical points at issue is desirable in any case, for without this knowledge one cannot properly appreciate the significance of evidence, a qualification which necessarily is a vital part of the trial lawyer's equipment. Thorough preparation on the facts is also necessary in order that the attorney may be prepared to make the necessary arguments and conduct in an effective manner his direct examinations of witnesses. The force of testimony depends in considerable measure upon the kind of questions asked, and one cannot ask questions that go to the heart of a subject which he does not fully understand. Adequate preparation in a law suit is forcibly shown by apt, intelligent questions which tend to elicit the correct degree of emphasis and the right shade of meaning.

An understanding of the facts is also necessary as part of that preparation by which the attorney becomes qualified to cross-examine adverse witnesses with intelligence and skill. Attorneys often damage their own cases by attempting to cross-examine on subjects they do not understand. No other phase of the practice of law affords an attorney so great an opportunity to bring his ignorance of the facts of a case out into the broad light of day as cross-examination. Lacking this essential knowledge he is helpless when he faces stupidity or perjury in the witnesses against him. Efforts to assist an unprepared attorney in his attempt to show the error, or the worse than error, of opposing testimony often end in failure because suggestions are mutilated and rendered ineffective by one who attempts to use them without understanding them.

It is a distressing sight to see an unprepared attorney struggle helplessly in a case he does not understand. He often is unfamiliar with the use and meaning of the common terms which apply to the questions involved, and yet he attempts to argue and to cross-examine and exposes his ignorance every time he speaks. If opposed by even weak perjury, or by mistaken or charlatan expert testimony, he may lose when he ought to win. Some of his errors of law are corrected by courts of appeal, but there is no court of appeal to correct his errors of fact, they are made at the expense of his poor client and the interests of justice.

A lawyer who comes into court with more law books than one man can carry, but with a knowledge of the facts of his case that can be written out on a visiting card, is quite sure to find that his lack of preparation will be exposed sooner or later. A jury is at once suspicious of a lawyer who does not understand his own case. The alert jurymen soon see that he does not understand what he is trying to talk about and discount all that he says on any subject. This knowledge of the facts is especially desirable in order that, by his incidental discussions in connection with the examination of witnesses, the offering and the answering of objections, and in all direct and incidental argument, he may create a favorable atmosphere surrounding his case by making it more and more clearly understood, as the case progresses, what his contention in the matter is and why it should prevail. In their inaccuracies and their weaknesses many so-called arguments on technical questions are simply pitiful. They abound in errors, overstatements, and understatements, and naturally often fail to persuade.

The proof of the forgery of a will, representing hundreds of thousands of dollars, may depend in large measure upon the correct analysis and interpretation of the qualities of a disputed signature, and the attorney who is attacking it in argument and on cross-examination cannot himself tell the disputed signature from the genuine signatures in the case, or correctly state how they differ. If he clearly shows that he knows little or nothing about the principles underlying the identification of handwriting, then anything he says on that subject will have but little weight. A juryman is excusably indifferent about learning what the lawyer has not himself learned.

It would be a great help to the trial attorney if he could have a training from within the jury box. He would find it enlightening if he could observe law practice and for a time hear and weigh evidence from the effect side instead of from the cause side alone. Some of this benefit he can obtain by the careful reviewing of the case after the trial, but the difficulty is that it may be impossible for him to discover, and no one may be frank enough to tell him, what the weaknesses were in his preparation and presentation of the case.

There are attorneys who approach these technical questions with a condescending air of superiority implying that their time is too valuable to give to questions other than those relating to the "basic principles of jurisprudence and the foundations upon which civilization rests and nations are founded". Law with these men is always "jurisprudence" with a long drawn out emphasis, and they pose as the defenders of the basic principles of something or other. The plain truth is that they too often are cheap and shallow actors who have never learned anything thoroughly. Their main reliance is upon rhetoric and oratory, and to them the practice of law consists chiefly in a fervid closing speech to a jury. Books are not written for these men for they do not read them.

In an important case all the machinery of a great law office often is set in motion combing the decisions back to the days of Blackstone for everything on the technical law of the case, but not one associate counsel or clerk is set to work on the task of preparing a brief on the facts, with reference to methods of discovery and proof. It is inevitable that vital questions entirely outside the law will arise, and prudence suggests that at least one man be set to work on this phase of the case.

The usual method followed makes it necessary to say that in studying the facts it is not sufficient to read only ancient legal opinions. In science, age does not add force to any statement, and every alleged authority is tested by the latest researches. It is a well-established principle in the scientific world that any scientific work twenty-five years old, for that reason alone, may not be an authority, and when the law investigates or discusses scientific subjects accuracy demands that the rules of science be followed. A scientific investigation of anything relating to physical facts is not properly completed by simply looking into some old law book and seeing what was said in some old opinion, written perhaps by an unscientific writer many years ago.

When a lawyer is engaged on a case involving a disputed document he sets about preparing to prove that the contention of his client is correct. The whole controversy may centre around the one important question as to whether a certain decedent actually signed a certain will. Complete preparation for trial of a case of this kind must, of course, include attention to both "the law" and "the facts", but the thought here emphasized is that the facts do not usually receive sufficient attention.

The most important part of this preparation for trial, as in any case, is the formulating of the underlying theory of the case with its main emphasis, its supporting claims, and the method of proof. This theory must, of course, be based on the evidence and must grow out of "the facts" that are to be proved. If inadequate knowledge of the case, or haste, or carelessness, leads to an incorrect theory, or even a wrong emphasis, then disaster is probable, if not inevitable.

It is important, not only to know what can be proved, but to know what to admit and what to anticipate. There is great need in the practice of law of what Professor Tyndall calls the scientific imagination.

The first of the facts is, of course, the main point at issue in a controversy. In a case involving a disputed will, or disputed contract, the will or the contract is the main "fact". In addition to the claim paper itself there may be a confirmatory document and perhaps an alleged oral understanding, or agreement, and in addition there often are many alleged "eye-witnesses" and circumstances which tend to attack, or to support, the genuineness of the disputed paper. The facts of the case, of course, include all this alleged incidental information relating to the disputed instrument itself.

Naturally, the most important group of facts in cases of this class are the physical attributes of the disputed document itself. Among these elements and features are the handwriting, the paper or printed form, the ink, the cover and binding, the qualities, age, and kind of typewriting if any is included, the seal, pen-ruling, erasures, interlineations, crossed lines, offsets, blots, folding, writing over folds, continuity, arrangement, margins, spacing, paper cutting, paper color, paper ruling, and size, pencil marks, stains, perforations, filing marks, wax, tape, paper fasteners, composition and language. Every alleged or actual circumstance leading up to and connected with the preparation, custody, and discovery of the document is also part of the facts.

In a trial of this kind one party attempts to prove that the document in controversy is not genuine, and also usually endeavors to show that it is not in harmony with the circumstances out of which it came. Those opposed endeavor to prove that the contrary view is correct. This testimony is all addressed to the facts of the case.

A thorough study of the facts requires that all this alleged or actual history of the matter be carefully considered in connection with every circumstance that bears upon the probability or improbability of the act. Light is also sometimes thrown on an inquiry of this kind by studying the stories of similar cases as recorded in the books. Human nature reacts in much the same manner under similar conditions and it is surprising how cases of actual forgery duplicate each other in many striking ways. Through experience and close study it is sometimes possible to anticipate what confirmatory evidence will appear, what apologies and explanations of the document will be made, and even what other documents will be produced.

In the event that the disputed document is genuine, a thorough investigation will almost certainly disclose valuable confirmatory evidence, but this evidence does not often become visible or vocal unless it is sought for. As an investigation proceeds it often becomes more and more clear that a disputed document is undoubtedly genuine. Circumstances, both remote and immediate, when brought to light, so interlace and confirm the claim that it is altogether reasonable to conclude that it was the intention of the decedent to execute a paper of the character of the one in controversy, and the physical and other facts in combination, when clearly illustrated and properly interpreted, prove that he did so. The cumulative evidence of genuineness in many instances amounts to a practical demonstration. It is necessary to keep in mind in any investigation that a document is not spurious simply because it is violently attacked.

Part of the trial attorney's information on the facts in a technical case will necessarily be obtained from a competent specialist, and this matter of investigating specialists is another phase of preparation that sometimes has an important bearing on the result. Proper inquiry will disclose that there are specialists available, in some communities at least, who can be hired to do whatever is wanted of them and that there are others who make investigations and report the facts as they find them. Too late, sometimes, the attorney learns that he has secured a witness with a shady reputation, or with limited ability, who casts a shadow over his whole case. Advance information on an important subject like this can be obtained, and the failure to obtain it is another evidence of the slipshod manner in which cases are prepared.

Another fatal error is sometimes made in the trial of a disputed document case by bringing in new trial counsel at the last moment. These men, often able and distinguished, may bungle a case in a hopeless manner. Experience in the trial of cases is, of course, an almost indispensable requisite to success, but even the experienced trial attorney in a technical case should have time and opportunity to learn the facts of the case in all their bearings. The mistake is made, not in getting the assistance, but in getting it too late for neither brilliant parts nor experience will serve as a satisfactory substitute for ready and accurate technical knowledge.

Briefs on some of the relevant questions outlined below will almost certainly be of use in a trial. If prepared by the trial attorney himself, or under his personal direction, he will know what they contain. Even a carefully prepared brief, prepared by an assistant and put into the trial attorney's brief-case the morning of the trial is not likely to be of much use to him. Some of these questions are:

What are some of the natural inferences from the circumstances of the case in hand indicating that the document is genuine or not genuine? What is the strongest favorable point of fact in the case and what is the strongest adverse fact? What are the adverse elements of sympathy or prejudice in the case in hand and how may they be counteracted or minimized?

How is handwriting proved? What are the most common indications of forgery? What are inherent evidences of genuineness in writing? What are some inherent evidences of forgery? What are the most significant characteristics in writing? To what extent must proof go to justify a positive opinion? In what ways is handwriting personality shown? What are some of the more common errors that may be made in identifying handwritings? What bearing will systems of writing and national characteristics have on the problem of handwriting identification?

To what extent and how may typewriting be identified? What are the most significant evidences of credibility in human testimony? From what facts or physical conditions can the age of a document be determined? What are the usual or common methods of forgery? How can a traced forgery be best attacked? How will a traced forgery be likely to differ from a simulated forgery? What other elements than form should be considered in examining a questioned writing? What are some of the common misconceptions and prejudices regarding handwriting identification? What conditions make forgery easy or difficult? What are the usual defenses of, or excuses for, actual forgery?

What are the most important technical books and text-book discussions on the subject of disputed documents? What are the most important modern disputed document trials? Who are the leading specialists on disputed documents and what is their reputation for honesty and ability? What recent changes have been made in the law relating to disputed document trials? What is the law in your state relating to (a) The admission and proof of standards, (b) The use of enlarged photographs, instruments, blackboard or chart, and illustrations, (c) The giving of reasons for opinions.

In an important case involving a technical question like forgery, or any controverted question regarding a document, the careful trial attorney will, of course, find and consult the special books on the technical question at issue. The unscientific quality of much of so-called preparation for trial is shown by the failure to find anything bearing upon the subject under investigation outside of law books. The unprepared attorney does not know that anything has been printed on the subject outside of law reports, and when he sees for the first time on the counsel table of the opposing attorney the technical works that discuss the very questions at issue in the case, it will then perhaps be too late for him to learn what he ought to have known before the trial began. A man who tries a forgery case ought to know something about the subject. A thorough study of the facts in a technical case includes attention, not only to the special books on the subject, but to general books and articles in which the subject is considered. The greatest collection of general information on all kinds of technical questions is, of course, that stored away in the great mass of printed books and pamphlets in the great libraries, and complete preparation on the facts in a case of importance will be likely to take the thorough trial attorney, at least once, to a general library.

Naturally one of the first steps in this search for information on any question is the study of indexes of all kinds. Many times it seems to be forgotten that their purpose is to tell where information can be found. This suggestion may appear to be unnecessary but indexing is now carried to an extent wholly unknown to many persons. In addition to the general index in a library, familiar to all, there are comprehensive indexes to all leading periodicals, to technical literature, including law, and, in some places, even to daily newspapers.

Much valuable information is also buried away in thousands of pamphlets that, with proper diligence, can also be found. Regular files of old newspapers, going back many years, often contain just the information desired. There are also available in many libraries the many kinds of directories, even including those for farmers and business men in small towns, in addition to the great variety of directories available in a city.

Even old almanacs have assisted to win law suits and an authentic weather report of a particular date is sometimes a very valuable piece of evidence. It is often of vital importance, especially in cross-examination, to know just what day of the week a certain remote date came upon. There are available tables in the almanacs where this information can quickly be obtained. The business history of any man in these later years is recorded in city directories, in business directories, and in the modern telephone books. If, for example, it is desirable to know where a man's office was, or what his business was, five, ten, fifteen or twenty years ago, this information can often be found in these books which are on file at the office of the publisher if not in the public library. Foreign directories are also at the libraries and even at some leading hotels. All these sources of information should be known and used when necessary.

Finally, in every considerable city there are men who possess unusual knowledge relating to almost any technical question, and always an important means of securing information is to find these men who know. They often can give, or at least can tell where to obtain, information of great value on the most unusual subjects. There is the man who knows all about pencils, another one knows all about ink, and others who know about pens, paper, stamps, erasers, typewriters, engraving, paper fasteners, paper ruling, ink eradicators, paste, mucilage, punches, wax, tapes, printing, printers' type, account books, diaries, memorandum books, or almost anything on earth. These men sometimes furnish the one fact that wins a law suit.

The conduct of trials generally suggests the desirability of fuller consideration of this question of finding, interpreting, and proving facts as a definite part of the lawyer's preparation for his important work. Perhaps it would be possible to establish something equivalent to a Chair of Facts in the law school with lectures on the facts of representative trials, with special reference to this question of preparation for trial on this important phase of a law case. This work perhaps might be supplemented by study of, and lectures on, the scientific method, the five senses, memory, observation and report, visible evidence, scientific investigation, weight and significance of testimony, credulity and belief, and certain other practical phases of psychology. Perhaps in this same course could in some way also be included some attention to, or formal or informal study of phases of, that old and important, but little understood, subject called human nature, itself a stupendous fact in this world of differing personalities.

CHAPTER II.

SIFTING THE EVIDENCE.

Much as he may desire it, the trial attorney cannot choose from the community his witnesses by which to prove his case. He must cut his garment from the cloth brought to him, but he can refuse to put in a rotten piece.

By a careful examination and analysis of the evidence available, the attorney can often suggest how to find corroboration and, in cases where an issue involves the proof of a tangible thing, like a handwriting or a typewriting, the experienced attorney can do much to assist in finding and developing the evidence by which the facts are finally proved. With living witnesses, however, it is not alone a question of finding the evidence, but of testing it.

The astonishing amount of perjury in courts of law is a sad commentary on human veracity. In spite of the oath, more untruths are probably uttered in court than anywhere else. This deviation from veracity ranges from mere exaggeration all the way to vicious perjury. Much of this untrue testimony grows directly out of human nature under unusual stress and is not an accurate measure of truth-speaking in general. In order to shield a friend, or help one to win in what is thought to be a just cause, or because of sympathy for one in trouble, many members of the frail human family are inclined to violate the truth in a court of law as they will not do elsewhere. There are many persons who are not criminals, some of them women, who if asked whether it is not the duty of one to help a friend by testifying falsely, will promptly answer by their acts that it certainly is. Like cheating corporations, this is a performance not covered by all codes of ethics.

If prepared to try law suits the trial attorney will clearly understand these phases of human nature. He will be aware of these natural human tendencies in order effectively to meet the evidence by which he may be defeated and also in order judiciously to sift the evidence by which he hopes to win. Through experience and this knowledge of human nature, and by a careful study of the relation of each witness to the controversy, and the relations of the witnesses to each other, and a study and comparison of their stories, he is able many times to make a correct estimate of the truth or falsity of proposed testimony.

In order to insure success an unwise client, whose main contention is true, sometimes brings into a case not only perjury but forgery. The alert attorney scrutinizes every piece of evidence produced by his client with a thoroughness and intensity that will prevent unfortunate surprises in the midst of the trial. It is sometimes highly important to sift out of a case an alleged evidential scrap of ragged, wrinkled, folded paper, having about it an apparent appearance of age, but which, when attacked, cannot be successfully defended, and becomes a hated, repulsive thing that casts a shadow over the whole case.

Two dangers from perjury beset the attorney's path: perjury by those against him, and perjury by his own witnesses. Opposing testimony may not be so damaging as stupid testimony by one's own witnesses that is shown to be untrue. It is often a most unfortunate act of friendship to commit unskilful perjury for a friend. The cross-examination of witnesses in advance is a means of preventing these disasters. Some of the most useful cross-examination in the practice of law is that of a lawyer's own witnesses before trial in the seclusion of his own office.

In these preparatory interviews and later amid the white heat of controversy, it is the business of the attorney firmly and skilfully to keep his witnesses in hand and to sort out and keep out of their testimony exaggeration and untruth. By this study and experience he also qualifies himself to detect and expose this same sort of exaggeration and untruth in the witnesses against him. One witness successfully attacked on the ground of veracity may throw a shadow over a whole case, and woe unto the case of that attorney whose own client is caught with a lie on his lips.

Cautions and warnings, of course, may be carried too far. Witnesses are useless who become timid and hesitating and so qualify an entirely true story that it has no force as testimony. Cases are not won by tepid and uncertain testimony, presented in a mild and apologetic manner, and witnesses can usually be led to relate clearly and positively what they know and be impressed with the importance of sticking to a story that they know is true. They also can usually be made to understand that they are not truthful when they qualify and limit statements more than the facts warrant. Some witnesses by their weakening admissions are guilty of what in effect amounts to perjury.

It is not improper for witnesses to know that the attempt will be made to weaken their testimony either by asking them to modify what they have said and thus break its force, or by leading them, by tantalizing methods, into exaggeration or actual untruth. In discussing the sifting of evidence, emphasis naturally is laid on the latter danger. Witnesses are made more self-confident by being made to understand that the best preparation for cross-examination is to tell the exact truth.

There is one definite direction that the experienced attorney sometimes gives to witnesses, and that is that they are not to hesitate to say that they do not know when they do not know. There are numerous witnesses who in some way get the notion that on the witness-stand they must know everything, or remember everything, or they will appear to be either unintelligent or dishonest. They will try to answer every question and apparently would be humiliated to admit that they could not explain the theory of relativity or give the exact amount of salt in the sea. Always and everywhere one of the sure marks of truth, as well as of wisdom, is the admission of ignorance.

It is obvious that all of these suggestions will hardly fit into the plans of one who sets out with the purpose of defeating justice and whose only hope of winning is by perjury and sharp practice. Even this practitioner, however, often learns by bitter experience that but few members of the human family are skilful liars and that truth has most unexpected ways of proclaiming itself. Unfortunately it is true that perjury, especially when aided by prejudice and sympathy, does sometimes defeat justice. This is a glaring fact in many cases in those states where the rules are over-technical and arbitrary, or where the presiding judge is debarred from rendering any assistance in interpreting the evidence.

Unscrupulous attorneys of actual criminals and of criminal grafters and fraudulent claimants of all kinds, naturally do not exercise a nice discrimination regarding the testimony they present excepting to be sure to make it strong enough; they are inclined to employ what they think will be useful without regard to its source or its ethical quality. In opposing these advocates there is no doubt sometimes a strong inclination "to fight the Devil with fire" in order to promote justice, but even on the low ground of policy this procedure is not wise. When one with a just cause succumbs to the temptation and attempts to meet perjury with perjury, then a trial becomes a sorry spectacle with no advantage to the just cause because it is just. The other alternative is to make it appear by every proper means that right and justice is being assailed by unfair and dishonest methods. There are skilful attorneys who when opposed by obvious perjury and questionable methods are over-scrupulous and fair and thus create as great a contrast as possible in the two courses of procedure before the court.

It often happens that after a few witnesses have committed obvious perjury for an over-zealous, unfair attorney, the intelligent members of the jury will give little further attention to the witnesses on that side of the case. There are in every community shrewd men, sometimes not highly educated, described by their neighbors as "hard men to fool", who fortunately are often drawn on juries. As they sit in the jury-box they are all the time aware of what is going on and seem to have an almost uncanny ability to recognize deception. These men are the stumbling-blocks in the path of the glib advocate who thinks that, to one whom he calls the common man, he can make black look almost white. These wise villagers have "seen through" his shallow deception from the very beginning. They are constantly sifting the evidence.

A part of this operation of sifting testimony on the part of the attorney is the study of inherent improbability. It is well known that there are contentions that when tested by ordinary experience and intelligence, without comparison with anything, appear so improbable that they do not make good evidence. This faculty of discovering the relation to each other of facts and of ideas is of great value to the attorney and is the important part of the process of weighing testimony. This ability is, of course, a phase of natural intelligence, but can be cultivated, at least in some measure, by study, observation, and experience.

There are many hearers and observers who are unable readily to understand the real significance of facts until they are brought close together in thought and their real relation pointed out. "Oh! I see", they say, "and how did you think of that?" When this inability is too marked we describe it as stupidity. In a lawyer it is a fatal defect. The essential qualification of the cross-examiner is the ability instantly to recognize the lack of harmony between an alleged new fact and one already under consideration. This special ability in many examiners becomes so trained and sharpened that the attorney puts his question, like a keen dissecting tool, exactly on the inconsistent, quivering point of adverse testimony. This test he applies to his own witnesses before they are attacked by an alert opposing attorney.

This examination of the inherent qualities of evidence the attorney first applies to the subject-matter or content of testimony, as it would appear in a printed record, and then, as far as possible, studies it in connection with the personality and probable manner of delivery of the evidence by the living witness. This double test he applies because it is impossible accurately to measure the force of testimony before it is given.

As scrutinized by the experienced and able attorney, there are evidences of truth and of untruth in appearance, in voice, in attitude, in manner, as well as in the matter of testimony as it comes from living witnesses in court. In the seclusion of his office, however, the attorney listens to the proposed testimony without this restraint, excitement, and inspiration of actual court surroundings. When under these quiet conditions the story is closely scrutinized, some estimate can, however, be made of how the force of the tale will be affected by the manner and personality of the witness in actual delivery. Experienced attorneys know that it is always dangerous to talk to witnesses about testimony to be given, but it can be done in a proper way and the inexperienced witness can thus be given suggestions that may prevent disaster. This is a delicate, dangerous, but important part of preparation for trial.

With a sinking heart the attorney sometimes hears from the witness-stand a story that is so different in effect from that he heard in his own office that he hardly recognizes it. Sometimes, alas! too much is said, and then again the witness is not sure of anything. On the other hand, a witness is sometimes called who produces an unexpected effect, and by clearness, frankness, and above all by the indefinable qualities of personality, makes an astonishing impression and almost, if not quite, wins the case. The shrewd attorney sometimes calls one who will thus probably be a good witness even to prove a comparatively unimportant fact, or on the contrary, sacrifices evidence, not absolutely essential, in order to keep from the witness-stand a garrulous gossip who will be likely to say too much. Some witnesses of this latter class that must be called are cautioned and, in some cases, plainly told some of the things that must not be done.

Skilled practitioners know that with a bright witness who has a pleasing personality it is often advisable to make no suggestions whatever in order that the testimony may have as unstudied a quality as possible, emphasized perhaps by infractions of minor rules and by an obvious lack of familiarity with the surroundings. It is better to err in interviewing witnesses too little rather than too much. Witnesses sometimes are so thoroughly and so unwisely coached that they become almost dumb with apprehension and self-consciousness and give the impression that they have been cautioned that if they are not very careful it will be discovered that they are lying. The preparatory methods of some attorneys suggest that they have forgotten that in addition to giving testimony fully and accurately it is important that a witness give it in such a manner that it will be believed.

Students of the subject know that one of the inherent evidences of lack of truth in a narrative is a wealth of detail regarding unimportant matters, and the careful attorney applies this test to the testimony of every witness, favorable as well as adverse. One who remembers too much is immediately suspected. A witness should, of course, know the main facts, but when, for example, testimony is given regarding the execution of a document dated many years before, and it is related just what was said, who spoke first, where each party sat, how long the interview lasted, what was said before and after the writing, and who went out first and who last, it is obvious that the witness is reporting from imagination, is confusing memory with inference, or is committing outright perjury. In an important patent litigation a witness claimed to remember just what she ate at a restaurant twenty years before where it was stated an important document was signed and dated. The careful attorney severely applies the recollection test to the testimony of his own witnesses before they get into court and endeavors to sift out the improbabilities. An adverse witness who presumes to possess this faculty of "total recall" is effectively cross-examined by still further cautiously drawing out the witness to a ridiculous extreme until everyone is aware of the fact that the story is not true.

Another common inherent evidence of lack of truth in testimony is too close harmony in detail between the stories of two or more witnesses regarding the same event. If they pretend to remember exactly the same things in detail, in exactly the same order of occurrence and of importance, it is certain that one of the witnesses is furnishing the details which all the others have adopted, or that they all are lying.

In the scientific world one of the evidences of lack of collusion in minute measuring is a slight divergence in results by two operators, due to the uncontrollable personal equation of each, and the same is true of the report of two observers who are called upon to describe in detail what they have seen. Unskilful advocacy sometimes drills witnesses until testimony might almost be recited in concert and apparently without understanding that its credibility is thus impaired. In the process of sifting testimony the discreet lawyer interviews his various witnesses separately and cautions them not to discuss their testimony with each other.

Where it is suspected that adverse witnesses are prepared to commit perjury, caution suggests the advisability of not allowing them to hear each other's testimony, and in this way perhaps be led to disagree on some of the main facts in the testimony or on matters brought out on cross-examination. Skilful cross-examination of untruthful witnesses of this class who must, at least on cross-examination, make up part of the story on the impulse of the moment, often demonstrates the absolute unreliability of the testimony. A superficial study of this question of the reliability of evidence may, however, fail to distinguish this gross divergence in material facts that shows perjury from a natural divergence in unessential details that shows honesty and lack of collusion. It is by a sort of intuition that one suspects the truth of a tale too highly embellished. Without analysis of any kind we sometimes say that a story of this kind does not sound right. In a recent opinion of a high court this statement is made, "This testimony bears the unmistakable stamp of truth". There is no business of the trial attorney more important than learning just what this "stamp" consists of.

Many stories related in court in the form of testimony do not contain this desirable "stamp" but, on the contrary, are subjects for the study of inherent improbability. One class of stories of this kind are those relating to "foundling wills" which make a tardy appearance and, in effect at least, are left on the doorstep of the administrator, or executor, of an estate. When these peculiar papers, many of which are spurious, are brought into court they must, of course, be accounted for in some way. The stories designed to explain the long delay, the unusual appearance, and the startling contents of these documents furnish most interesting studies.

When analyzed these stories often are inherently improbable. This improbability is accentuated when they are compared with the stories relating to similar papers in other cases. One of the common similarities in the alleged life histories of these misplaced documents is the utter indifference with which a very valuable paper was handled and kept by those in whose hands it was left and in whose interest it was drawn. It apparently was tossed about from pillar to post with the utmost unconcern. It was thrown into some old box or basket, or shoved into some old book, or almanac, or handed over to a witness, who is almost a stranger, and then entirely forgotten. After the death of the testator, and sometimes long after, it all at once turns up "accidentally and providentially". The accounts of the hiding places of some of these forgotten wills develop some occasional and striking originality, but in numerous ways the stories are strangely alike.

Another of the common improbabilities of these stories is that the active party in the transaction, the testator himself, takes no particular interest in his own will and, like the alleged custodians, gives no thought to the care of perhaps the most important document that he ever signed. It is solemnly related, frequently with the utmost detail, that after signing, he said, "You keep this and if anything happens to me, etc." and then ignores the whole matter.

In a recent important case, tried twice, one of these "found" wills did not appear until eleven years after the death of the alleged testator. In this case an itinerant, clumsy stenographer, with a shady past, remembered she wrote it, the only paper, she admitted, that she ever wrote for the testator. Fortunately alleged finders, who are usually partners in the fraud, often overplay the part. In some instances, however, these discoverers are innocent, but gullible participants, who have been cleverly led to look where a document has been carefully planted. The perusal of a collection of these stories of foundling wills would be sufficient in many cases to cast grave doubt on a new and similar story. A complete collection of these strange tales should be printed for the guidance and warning of credulous trial attorneys.

In one case an important document of this sort, according to the story, was delivered to a total stranger by an old Mexican woman, who came out of a hovel out on the western plains, and asked a passer-by if he would send it to a lawyer up in Colorado. He sent it and it led to a long and expensive trial, but it did not get the estate. In another case a man saw a rat run under a board in an old house down in "Arkansaw", so the story was told in court, and in pulling off the board to catch the rat a will fell out that was the basis of two protracted trials in the state of Texas. This rat's-nest will was finally declared to be a forgery. In another case an alleged will was written under two stamps on a letter received by mail from the West Indies and was finally probated as a genuine document.

Another peculiar thing about many of these foundlings is that witnesses, if not long since dead, are chauffeurs, manicurists, ignorant workmen, teamsters, or anybody but business men, bankers, or those whose signatures would forcefully verify and lend dignity to such a document. As a rule, however, one of the witnesses is a dear friend of the claimant, usually a woman, who at the trial possesses what amounts to a photographic memory of the minutest details of the preparation and signing of the lost paper. She sometimes relates how she "entirely forgot all about it until the will was found"; then, she adds, "it all comes back just as plain as day."

In those states where holograph wills require no witnesses these foundlings are more easily proved, and a dim pencil entry in any old memorandum book, or on an ancient postal card, or almost any scrawl on a wall, becomes a "last will and testament". The dangerous doctrine of holograph wills and codicils furnishes an open invitation to loot an estate and more than one of these invitations has been accepted. It should be a legal requirement that a holograph will should contain at least one hundred words and be written in ink.

Although produced not in a wilderness nor out on a prairie, but in a civilized community, another common characteristic of these surprising documents is that they are written on some old derelict scrap of paper unfitted for the purpose, but having a desirable ancient appearance. In one case in Canada one of these stray wills was written on a piece of transparent, oiled butterpaper, and in another case a will of nine words, covering a large estate, was all written with a pencil on thin tracing paper which purported to be of a kind, according to the testimony, "always carried by the testator in his pocket in which to take home dog-meat". In many cases the ancient and unusual material upon which these tardy testaments are written is utterly inconsistent with the practices and surroundings of the testator.

Strange to say, these cases go on repeating each other all over the land and are being soberly tried from day to day, and, sad to say, by the aid of perjury and prejudice, and the old restrictive procedure in some courts, and also in some measure because of the strange credulity of certain members of the legal profession, some of the rat's-nest, dog-meat wills are probated. The stories are not received with peals of laughter, as might be expected, but are listened to without a smile. A sense of humor in a court of law would sometimes promote justice.

The curious credulity of numerous lawyers in these matters, as well as their estimate of the credulity of others, is an interesting study in psychology and is a condition that it is difficult to explain. It may be that one can become so accustomed to perjury that a little more does not attract notice. One cannot but wonder whether a story could be made so incredible that a lawyer could not be found to defend it and witnesses found to support it.

If it should be related by a waiter in a restaurant, "where", as the learned brief would state, "an alleged testator had been accustomed to eat", that he, the waiter, opened a hard-boiled egg and a tiny, folded will fell out, it would not be surprising to find an attorney who would say, "Well, of course, that is unusual but—" and would then proceed to explain how it might have occurred. It apparently would not occur to him that the waiter is not telling the truth.

The curious estimate of human credulity, often observed in courts of law, has perhaps grown out of that phase of advocacy which contends, in at least partial good faith, that an advocate should be prepared to defend or attack either side of any proposition. There are those who are inclined seriously to argue that it is the duty of the lawyer to make the best of whatever disagreeable task may come to him. His weapons are sophistry, subterfuge, plausibility, violent assertion, and that quality of language that conceals thought. But the strangest thing about the performance is that this insincere pleader has himself become a victim of childish credulity. He partly convinces himself that a ridiculous proposition is possibly true. Of all men it is natural to think that the lawyer would have developed the keenest critical sense, but with many members of the profession this is not the fact. They are not qualified to decide what is credible and what is not, and are totally disqualified as scientific investigators. These men have become experts in excuses, apologies, and explanations, and in the process of acquiring their skill they seem to have dulled their judgments as well as their consciences.

If this "Egg Will Case", referred to above, should come to trial, some "Mrs. Cluppins", like her namesake in the celebrated Pickwick Case, would no doubt appear and testify in great detail that she saw the will fall out, and a "Mr. Fogg", of the same quality as the attorney in the above-named action, could probably be found, and he would proceed to argue at great length that this egg incident was not only possible, but so common an occurrence that it had become almost a habit for waiters to pick wills out of eggs, and the rare "Mr. Stareleigh", of the same celebrated case, would perhaps learnedly remark that, "Strange things, indeed, come out of eggs and there is good authority for the statement that no man, person, individual, or party, can tell positively, certainly, and surely, what may come out of an egg", and so the case goes to the jury.

Fortunately for the interests of justice there are

lawyers in every community who are entirely sane, who have a sense of humor, who are not intoxicated by the spirit of advocacy, and who have overcome the tendency to look upon any grotesque, ridiculous narrative as possibly true. They have trained their common-sense, their perceptions, and their critical faculties until unerringly they can fix their intelligence, like a steel-trap, on the weakest point in an incredible story and almost rudely expose perjury and pretension. Training in this critical ability is a most important part of a lawyer's preparation and this training he can secure to some extent in every case by carefully sifting the evidence.

The amount of the evidence that it is advisable to present, as well as its quality as determined by the "sifting" process, is a question that the advocate must carefully consider. Close observation of the processes of the law cannot fail to recognize in not a few legal minds a kind of fatalistic idea that the ascertainment of the facts in any case is an almost, if not quite, impossible task and that testimony is a kind of voting contest in which every vote has a count and the truth is shown by a "preponderance" of the evidence when the whole mass is considered irrespective of its quality. The fact is, incredible as it may seem, that testimony, sworn to and offered in a formal way, receives some consideration and apparently produces some effect on some minds no matter how ridiculous and incredible it may be. There are legal opinions that practically say this and in effect apparently contend that there is no such thing as inherent improbability in evidence. It is solemnly argued that testimony, no matter what its quality, must be given "due weight". Rank and obvious perjury anywhere outside of a court of law would be dismissed as perjury, but in court it seems to receive a sort of unconscious and unexplainable consideration that it does not deserve.

It is plain that this condition, if it exists, has a practical bearing on the actual conduct of a trial. Because of this attitude toward formal testimony, no matter what its quality may be, the careful attorney usually, if not always, considers the volume of the testimony offered and the number of the witnesses called, as well as the quality of the testimony given. If the decision in a lawsuit could always be made by a Solomon then the number of the witnesses and the volume of testimony need be given no consideration whatever, but with the unknown conditions within the human cranium, especially the craniums of some of those trained in advocacy, and the uncontrollable effect of possible sympathy and prejudice, it is not safe to ignore the question of mass in testimony.

Not juries alone are influenced by that which is not evidence, and with probable, or even possible, prejudice, or sympathy, surrounding a case it is thus often advisable deliberately to over-prove the facts. Proof in some cases must be presented and then confirmed and enforced and emphasized until to decide against it is a flagrant and obvious disregard of the proved facts. While it is reasonably argued in opinions and in legal treatises that testimony is not properly weighed by counting the witnesses, this method is sometimes actually followed where a case is decided against the facts. With a good case, the facts of which are clearly proved, and in effect demonstrated, by one reliable technical witness, it may seem unnecessary to enforce this proof, but where there may be a temptation and a desire to do what is called "substantial justice" by deciding against the facts, it is sometimes a matter of safety to make the proof overwhelming by adding to its mass.

The testimony of the additional witnesses need not be extended and in effect will be only corroboration, but the mere unconscious influence and moral effect of numbers tends to prevent that contemptuous waving aside of reasonable testimony that if given proper consideration would not permit a decision prompted by unconscious sympathy or prejudice. There actually are decisions rendered, in cases with no jury, in which it is said in a helpless sort of way, "An equal number of witnesses testified on each side", with the apparent inference that, like an election, there was no choice, and therefore the decision must be based upon other grounds. This statement would be justified if all the witnesses gave merely bare opinions, but scientific, illustrated, rational testimony is not an appeal to the credulity of the hearer, but to his intelligence, and if the hearer will not apply his intelligence to the problem then he is ignoring the evidence.

Justice is sometimes defeated by the unconscious or the deliberate disregard of the distinction between a "verdict" in a criminal case and a "decision" in a civil case. The verdict "not guilty" in a criminal case, when it is admitted that the defendant committed a certain act, is often misinterpreted by those unfamiliar with the law. This verdict does not mean, as some critics seem to think, that the accused did not commit the act, but that the act did not constitute the crime charged. As is well known, self-defense, or certain kinds of justification, or actual insanity, renders one actually "not guilty" of a particular crime.

In a civil case, however, involving the genuineness of a document, it should not be overlooked that the question to be determined is simply a question of fact and not the possible justification of that fact as in a criminal case. If a will is a forgery, then it is a forgery, and cannot be properly described as anything else no matter what the "justification" for the forgery may be. If a decision, by any tribunal, states that "on all the evidence it is found" that a document is genuine when it is not genuine, then the decision is not correct no matter how strong a "moral right" the claimant may have for reward or compensation. To speak the exact truth a judgment or decision should sometimes say that "on all the evidence it is found that the claimant, in our opinion, ought to have the money". If in such a case the triers could simply render a decision "in favor of the plaintiff" on all the "circumstances" and facts of the case, then possibly it could honestly be done and a verdict would then be "interpreting the facts" instead of registering a finding that is at least under suspicion.

These occasional decisions against the facts, based on so-called rights of the party to that which is sought, are conspicuous encouragements to fraud. They render crime and perjury profitable. The fact that a claimant is poor, or is a woman, or because an estate is large and can spare the money, does not make a forgery genuine. A decision of this kind is all the more to be criticized if supported by the specious argument that the "testimony was conflicting" when it is clearly evident in some cases that the "conflicting testimony" brought into the case against the facts was obvious perjury that could not have been believed by those called upon to decide the case, but merely served as an excuse for deciding against the facts. Fortunately most men will not resort to sophistry in order to reach a desired result, but, as already said, there are cases in which safety requires that the facts be shown so overwhelmingly that the inclination to decide against them is overcome.

CHAPTER III.

THE ATMOSPHERE OF A TRIAL.

The atmosphere of a trial grows out of the nature of the controversy and the character and conduct of the participants. To a considerable extent this intangible but important phase of a legal controversy is the inevitable effect of the conditions, but the advocate who is qualified can do something to shape it to his will. If he is sufficiently skilful he can give to a proceeding such an atmosphere as he chooses, or at least can prevent it from becoming unfavorable to his contention. The shaping and control of this delicate phase of a trial is the advocate's most important task, for to do this well everything must be done well. Every statement, every objection, every word spoken by the skilled attorney, and almost every look and gesture, is made to bear upon this question. This phase of law practice affords the opportunity to show the essence of the skill of the great trial lawyer.

As a trial progresses there are attorneys who in some way gradually gain an almost unexplainable advantage, which is felt rather than understood. This advantage, in large measure, grows out of this matter of atmosphere. Sufficiently keen observation and analysis would no doubt show that the condition always is the effect of definite causes which, however, are too subtle and too elusive for the superficial practitioner who gives little thought to tact and to human nature.

The prepared attorney goes into court with a clear conception of his case based on the facts, the evidence he will present, and the law applying to it. He is qualified and ready to take advantage of every opportunity and not only proves his case, but does it with a skill that is constantly creating a favorable atmosphere.

The lawyer who plans to qualify himself on any of these important phases of the case after the trial begins will probably have plenty of time to study the questions in the seclusion of his own office after he is defeated. He probably will never know the causes of all the unfavorable conditions that led to the unfortunate result. It is true that the unprepared bungler sometimes wins, but not because of his own skill, but because his opponent's work was even worse. There are men in every profession who believe in the doctrine of luck, and thus attempt to excuse their own failures. They are at a great disadvantage when arrayed against an opponent who believes in the doctrine of cause and effect.

One who goes from court to court cannot but observe the varying quality of law practice, a variation wider perhaps than in any other profession. It ranges from the delicate, masterly skill of the legal artist down to the work of the ignorant bungler who knows but little of the facts or of the law of the cases he tries and even less of human nature. A law suit in many courts is not the scientific work of trained and skilful specialists, but too often is the crude performance of the inexperienced and the unfitted. As a rule the surgical clinic shows the skilled work of trained men; but the court-house often shows the bungling efforts of the unskilled. For every lawyer now and then to try important cases in the law courts is as if every doctor attempted on rare occasions to perform major operations. The legal operating room shows many mangled legal corpses.

As in other fields, this variation in skill in the practice of the law naturally results from many causes. Some of these are beyond control but all are not. There are lawyers who try cases who never fully understand that the trial of a suit at law is an intricate, difficult intellectual performance, while those who pay the bills are no better judges of the quality of law practice than they would be of the comparative merits of ancient Greek Art. Lawyers are praised for fatal errors, and blamed for doing what should have been done. Litigation with the average citizen is only occasional—happy for him that it is—which perhaps partly accounts for his inability to judge of its quality.

In the usual legal controversy there is a main contention, which must be proved by evidence and which is attacked by opposing evidence. The able attorney, with a clear view of the whole case, will of course take advantage of every proper opportunity to enforce his own contention, directly and indirectly, and, if possible, weaken the adverse contention. If the verdict he seeks must mainly be based upon a certain class of evidence, this will receive indirect favorable consideration as early and as often as conditions warrant. If adverse evidence is mainly of a particular class he naturally will endeavor to surround it by as unfavorable an atmosphere as can be produced.

As some trials progress the impression is gradually developed that one attorney is trying to prove the facts and that the opposing attorney is attempting to keep proper evidence out of the case. This impression grows out of the unwise zeal of one attorney who too obviously seeks to exclude everything unfavorable to his contention. This he usually does on the plea that it is "incompetent, irrelevant, and immaterial", but, in fact, because it is damaging to his case. Even if not admissible, it is sometimes wiser to admit evidence than constantly to appear to be keeping facts from the jury. The discreet attorney does not object unless he has some well-defined purpose in view, and then many times does so in an unobtrusive, inquiring manner.

The value of a favorable atmosphere is, of course, known to the unskilful practitioner, but he does not know how to produce it. He is naturally the last to realize that his own personality, reputation, and conduct, may be handicaps that must be overcome in every trial, and of course he does not understand that his obviously partisan efforts to overreach and gain advantage all throw an unfavorable light on everything that he does. Frantic efforts to produce favorable atmosphere sometimes are so palpably crude and obvious that they produce the opposite effect. Favorable atmosphere is not produced with a club and an axe, but is the skilful, indirect, and inconspicuous work of the adept.

The clumsy and transparent tactics often employed to win favor suggest that those employing them look upon the jury as only the equals of unsuspecting children. It is dangerous to assume that all of the twelve members of a jury are stupid and gullible. It is, for example, a serious error for the well-groomed attorney, talking to a farmer jury, to try to talk to them as a farmer. A man's words should be adapted to his audience, but if a jury suspects that he is "talking down" to them, his case is in grave danger. The competent pleader uses appropriate illustrations but does not assume an unnatural part that is perfectly transparent and that aims to mislead and deceive. By these acts he is producing the wrong kind of atmosphere.

Courtesy and good manners are powerful creators of atmosphere and are among the desirable, if not the essential, qualifications of the trial attorney, but in attempting to lead others to his point of view any unctious and obvious attempt to please and to curry favor by an affected cordiality, and an insincere, artificial manner, is worse than a gruff and seemingly somewhat discourteous exterior that, however, has about it the high quality of sincerity. It is at once suspected that one who indulges in blarney is about to make an attempt to deceive. The man who endeavors to "cultivate" us often repels us more than the man who swears at us. The forced, continuous smile, seen too often in court, and designed only as a mask for deception, does not often deceive. This facial contortion not only identifies Shakespeare's villain, but is the badge of the insincere pleader.

A common error of the trial attorney is a too great reliance on the force of his own unsupported statements. He often acts on the theory that favorable atmosphere can be created, mistakes corrected, lack of preparation made up, blundering methods hidden, and damaging adverse testimony destroyed, by loud, long continued, and insincere assertion. His final argument is to be the panacea that is to cure all the ills of the trial and win success. The value of shallow talk as a part of law practice is greatly overestimated. If there is not back of it a knowledge, skill, and sincerity that at least changes assertion into argument, if not argument into eloquence, then mere talk vanishes without effect into thin air.

One who is able to produce the atmosphere of belief understands the comparative force of inference from suggestion and of dogmatic statement. The skill of some advocates is due in no small degree to their ability to lead others to a desired point of view by suggestion rather than by assertion. In effect they say, with Antony, "I tell you that which you yourselves do know". An atmosphere of confidence, skilfully created in an unobstrusive way, is often almost irresistible. It may be impossible to go back and point out all the definite causes that led to the result, but always there were causes. One of the common weaknesses of advocacy is its direct, insistent demand upon the belief of those to whom it appeals. It does not adroitly lead and persuade but attempts to force and to drive.

The careful student of the law considers every fact, every statement, and piece of evidence in two ways, first, their direct bearing upon the controversy, and their effect upon this question of atmosphere. The sagacious attorney knows that it is sometimes advisable to sacrifice testimony in order to exclude its unfavorable secondary effect. Decisions of this kind necessarily require thoughtful attention to every point which directly or indirectly affects proof. Like the skilled chess player, he is always planning the second, or third, or fourth move ahead.

The able and experienced attorney does not, of course, neglect or overlook his main proof in thinking of atmosphere or of incidental matters. He keeps in mind all the time that the main question in the case is the proving of the facts. He knows that if he is to succeed that he must make his main contention clearly understood. He has an intellectual grasp of the controlling points of the whole case and keeps these in the foreground in the right manner, in the right order, and with the right emphasis. Every word is selected with care and every act has a purpose.

The calling of one witness who is discredited on cross-examination sometimes throws a cloud of suspicion over a whole case. A dangerous risk is thus sometimes taken by an attorney with a good case who seeks to bolster up his contention by a witness whose testimony is of a doubtful character. As outlined in a previous chapter, the careful attorney sifts the testimony in advance and carefully estimates the honesty and general desirability of every witness. If a discredited witness has testified on the main point in controversy, as an expert for example, his appearance is indeed a disaster. Carelessness, or what may be an unwise parsimony, is thus punished when an attempt has been made to prove the important fact in a controversy by one weak, unprepared technical witness, sometimes directed and supervised by a whole troop of attorneys.

The unattractive qualities in a client sometimes unfavorably affect the atmosphere of a trial. When his reputation is bad, or his habits under suspicion, or his personal appearance forbidding, even if his contention is correct, he sometimes damages his own case. One of the important duties of his attorney under such circumstances is to keep him in the background. This is an instance where the play of Hamlet is improved by keeping the Prince of Denmark off the stage, or giving him a very brief part.

The order of proof also affects atmosphere. A jury can be prepared for testimony which otherwise would be unfavorably received, or that would not produce its full effect. Attorneys usually prefer to follow rather than lead in proof, but with a strong case a decided advantage is sometimes gained by leading. When a strong first impression is produced the case of the opposition is surrounded by an atmosphere of suspicion from the start. In some cases it is thus advantageous to take the lead even when not compelled to do so by the procedure.

CHAPTER IV.

INCIDENTAL ARGUMENT AND THE LAWYER'S WORDS.

Evidence is merely information. A law suit, with all its details, is simply a contest in court where two parties lay what purports to be information before those who are to decide between them. It is always in conflict, and in order to avoid error one who is to decide must be able to determine whether or not the "information" is true, and then by reasoning must be able to decide what conclusion is justified by the information. Error may result because a hearer may not understand the evidence, or because he is unable to interpret the evidence correctly.

To the advocate who seeks to prove the facts is given the task of making this hearer, for this occasion, an observing, intelligent, and reasoning man. This he must do through evidence and argument. It is easy to understand that the task, in many instances, is too difficult for any mere human being to perform and an attorney should not always be disbarred because he fails to prove his case.

Many persons do not connect the operation of what is known as logic with the task of convincing another by evidence, or by argument. Like Moliere's rustic, who without knowing it had to his own delight for so long been talking prose, we all also, in a lame or skilful way, have long been using logic. The common understanding of a logical conclusion is one justified by the evidence as it is understood. If a witness convinces us that he is qualified, and we believe he is truthful, and the evidence is sufficient to prove the fact, then a conclusion logically follows. A hearer may, however, reach a wrong conclusion in spite of credible evidence. The opposing advocate is there to see that he does. A case is not won when the evidence is simply laid before the court. It is necessary to show what it means and what conclusion it justifies. That is the task of the advocate.

For several generations European law concluded that witchcraft was a proved fact and thousands of victims were executed, and America had a short but sad experience with the same delusion. Even Blackstone said the legal proof in these cases was absolutely conclusive. These unfortunate conclusions, now admittedly erroneous, at the time were entirely logical as based upon the interpretation of the alleged evidence of that day. The error was an intellectual error, an error of interpretation, and the whole pitiable delusion was based upon superstition and ignorance. The real or imaginary suffering of the witnesses was not caused by those who were accused of being witches. The conclusion reached was not justified by the evidence.

Failure to appreciate the significance of a fact, or to "see the point" often leads to erroneous conclusions on many subjects. It is not only necessary to make the facts stand out with the utmost clearness, but illuminating arguments must show the meaning of the facts. This is the most difficult phase of the problem of proof for the reason that to see the relations of things is one of the severest tests of intelligence. There are many who cannot, without assistance, draw correct inferences from separated facts and it is at just this point that the opportunity is given the advocate to show his greatest power.

Footprints clearly impressed in soft earth indicate the direction of a walker. This inference even a stupid observer would draw. If, however, the tracks on the right were lighter than those on the left, and there was the regular impressions of the tip of a blunt cane on the right-hand side, there are many observers who would never infer that the walker was lame. When, however, evidence of this kind is interpreted, then even the dull and the unintelligent are able to draw the proper inference. No phase of the work of the advocate is more important than this business of interpreting facts and ideas. There are puzzling "footprints" in the evidence of every trial.

A trial at law is often a long drawn out, tiresome performance, in which the participants become not only weary but irritable, impatient, and critical. These changing conditions have an important bearing on the question of order of proof and also powerfully affect the force and value of arguments. With the fresh interest and the natural curiosity at the beginning of an inquiry a few ideas in well-chosen words sometimes make a permanent favorable impression. At this critical time a good sentence may be worth more than a whole speech later.

Throughout the course of a trial opportunities constantly arise for incidental arguments by which the significance of the evidence is made clear. These opportunities arise in connection with the examination of jurymen, the offering and answering of objections, the arguing of points of law, and the conducting of direct examinations and cross-examinations. The skilful lawyer unobtrusively, but effectively, utilizes these opportunities, always in an entirely proper way, and as the trial progresses makes it more and more clear just what his contention is, and why it should prevail. Convincing discussions of this kind necessarily result from a thorough understanding of the facts of the case and the evidence by which they are to be proved. Weak arguments often result from a weak knowledge of the facts for even an intelligent man cannot discuss intelligently a subject he does not understand.

The definition of argument, as reasons offered for or against an opinion which tend to produce belief, shows the importance of the subject to a trial attorney. The matter of producing belief is a part of the lawyer's business that certainly deserves careful consideration. The argument in a trial at law is usually thought of only as the set speech to the jury at the close of the trial, but if all argument is so long postponed it oftentimes is just as well to omit it entirely for the reason that the opponent will already have his case won. Long before the closing speech the able attorney presents much that has the effect of argument. From the time he makes his opening statement and examines the first juryman, up to the end of the trial he is "producing belief".

Incidental argument is of special importance in connection with technical testimony relating to a disputed document. Evidence of this class, an opinion with reasons, strikingly differs from ordinary evidence, and the giving of reasons for an opinion in cases of this kind is the vital part of the testimony. Lawyers who present this testimony sometimes are not fully aware of the extent to which this matter of giving reasons should be carried in order to make testimony effective and there are courts where the question is not correctly understood.

In accordance with a well-known rule of evidence, a witness is not permitted to give testimony in the form of argument, but, by well-established precedents, a scientific witness who gives an opinion is permitted to give reasons therefor. When he does this he is doing that which the ordinary witness is not permitted to do, and a confusion of mind often exists in court and counsel on this point. In some courts, dominated by the older practice, effective testimony with reasons cannot be given. Opposing counsel at once objects that a witness is making an argument, especially when the testimony is effective, whereupon the ruling is made that argument of any kind is not permissible. By this means the important part of the evidence is excluded.

As an example, this proper question may be asked, "Will you explain to the jury the reasons why you reached the conclusion that these five signatures are not genuine signatures?" In answering this question fully it is necessary to describe the process of reasoning by which all the facts in combination have appealed to the mind of the witness. If the witness merely points out the physical evidence, without interpretation of it, or any estimate of its comparative and cumulative force, it is as though he were a dumb witness. Freely interpreted, the ruling on the question sometimes is that testimony with reasons can be given if it is not given very convincingly.

The vital part of the evidence which assists one in reaching a correct conclusion regarding it is the rational interpretation of the facts. The special knowledge and the experience of the qualified witness enable him to say what the physical evidence really indicates. Without this reason-giving part of the testimony the bare facts are before the court and jury, and the testimony of the witness is only an opinion.

It is also important to understand that reasons are desirable, not alone to enforce the testimony, but sometimes to show its weakness and the inadequate basis upon which it rests. The insincerity and futility of certain "conflicting testimony" is sometimes conclusively shown by insisting that reasons be given for the opinion expressed. Unless the basis for the opinion and the reasoning leading to it are given, court and jury are of course unable to weigh the evidence and determine whether or not the conclusion is warranted. In most courts in these days when a witness is asked to give reasons and an objection is made, the court simply asks, "Are you giving the reasons which have led you to the opinion you have here given?" If the answer is yes, then the testimony is considered not only admissible, but desirable.

As more specifically pointed out in a previous chapter, effective presentation of evidence of this class is difficult in the absence of properly framed questions which specifically ask for the reasons and principles upon which the opinion is based. If only general questions are asked and the inevitable objection is made, the testimony is often excluded as not responsive, but if the question says, "Why do you say, etc., etc." the answer is then responsive and is usually admitted. Weak and colorless testimony naturally will not be objected to, but as soon as it tends to become effective and convincing an opposing attorney naturally at once tries to interfere. Failure to make a good argument just at this point often leads to defeat as the controlling evidence may be practically excluded, and a forceful incidental argument at this psychological moment, that gains admission for the testimony, may almost win a verdict. Narrow and technical rulings sometimes practically destroy the testimony of the capable witness of this class and as a rule there is no remedy except a possible point for appeal.

If objection is made to the giving of reasons, as is inevitable if the evidence is effective, the door is opened for an argument along the lines given below. This argument is adapted from numerous arguments and opinions, and if made at once will strongly enforce the testimony. This is an example of incidental argument on the facts of the case:

"If Your Honor please, we have now reached in the presentation of our case what we consider a vital part of the testimony. If I understand my learned opponent correctly, he contends that this witness should not be permitted to give the reasons for the opinion he has here expressed.

"There is some excusable confusion on this point, due to the fact that an ordinary witness is not permitted to give reasons. We are not asking this witness to do what is legally improper, but we call him here, as one who is experienced and qualified on this subject, and we ask him as an expert for an opinion. We then ask him why he gives this opinion and to give us the benefit of the reasons that have led him to reach the conclusion that he expresses. It is just here that the confusion arises. Reasons for an opinion of any kind necessarily amount to what may be described as an argument and this simply cannot be avoided. If our opponent was entirely sincere, his objection would be, not that this witness is making an argument, but that he is showing this jury in a convincing way that his conclusion in this matter is fully justified by the facts before him. He is simply interpreting these facts and that is exactly what we ask that he be permitted to do. If he fails and his reasons are not good reasons, then my opponent has the opportunity to destroy his testimony on cross-examination, and if my opponent can tell us how he, or I, or this witness, can give reasons for an opinion without making what he here sees fit to call an argument, I should like to have him do so."

"There are in fact the highest authorities for this procedure. The best modern practice permits exactly what we are asking this witness to do. There was a time in the history of the law when a bare opinion was the only thing asked of a witness in cases of this kind, but that is no longer the fact where subjects are investigated and reported on in a scientific manner. In the well-known New York case of Johnson Service Co. v. MacLernon, 127 N. Y. Supp. 431, a 1911 decision, the court says, 'In this state the practice of permitting experts to give the reasons for their opinion, and even to illustrate upon a blackboard, has been distinctly approved. The reasons for the expert's opinion, if he had been permitted to give them, might, and probably would, have added great force to his testimony, for the expression of opinion, standing alone, has little probative force.'

"This well reasoned statement by the court, it will be seen, is exactly in point. We bring in here not a mere opinion to be blindly followed, but an opinion with definite reasons by which it can be tested. We do not ask that it be taken and followed unless it is reasonable and appeals to ordinary intelligence. The procedure for which we plead certainly is based not only on good law, but on good sense.

"Moreover, this same court here quoted has gone even further than this in a most significant way in a later case, Venuto v. Lizzo, 148 (N. Y.) App. Div. 164, 132 N. Y. Supp. 1066. The verdict of a jury was reversed because opposing counsel in that case persistently did exactly what opposing counsel in this case is doing. The attempt was made in that case, as the attempt is made in this case, to make the expert's testimony valueless by constant, improper interruptions. These are the significant words of the court: 'The conclusion of a handwriting expert as to the genuineness of a signature, standing alone, would be of little or no value; but, supported by sufficiently cogent reasons, his testimony might amount almost to a demonstration. While the court in this case did not directly refuse to allow the experts to state their reasons, as was done in the case of Johnson Service Co. v. MacLernon, the effect of allowing constant, trivial objections, and of the erroneous rulings, was virtually equivalent to such a denial.'

"That, we contend, is the hope of those opposed to us in this case, and we respectfully ask that this witness be permitted to give in full the reasons for the opinion he has expressed here without constant interruptions and trivial objections, which, we contend, are not primarily designed to keep this case within the rules of the law but actually to prevent effective testimony from being given."

It will, of course, not often be advisable to make this extended argument all at once, but with the numerous objections usually offered opportunities will arise to cover all the points thoroughly. As occasion offers these various ideas can be put into the lawyer's own language.

The outlines of arguments which follow are of a somewhat more general character, but occasion for the presentation of the ideas contained in them will almost certainly arise in an extended disputed document trial in answer to general objections to the testimony offered. In substance these arguments have been made many times, but this phase of law practice, under the new laws and decisions, is still somewhat novel in many courts, and these paragraphs may furnish some ideas that will lead to a procedure and understanding that will assist in proving the facts:

"We also desire to be heard in answer to the unwarranted contention made here that this testimony is inherently weak and unreliable, and for that reason should not be presented before this court. The contention is first made that the testimony is necessarily weak and valueless and then a procedure is insisted upon that will make it so. As with many subjects in law, conflicting precedents can be found, and the question then arises as to which of the authorities are most reasonable and most likely to promote justice.

"In the case of Strong v. Brewer, 17 Ala. 706, quoted with approval in the American and English Encyclopedia of Law, Vol. XV, 283, the court says: 'Upon principle, therefore, as well as from the necessity of the case, proof of handwriting, under proper restrictions, is, as has been seen, everywhere admitted. Moreover, as has been well said, it seems that this kind of evidence, like all probable evidence, admits of every degree of certainty, from the lowest presumption to the highest moral certainty.'

"Now, if Your Honor please, we urgently contend that if full and explicit reasons are given for any opinions expressed on this subject, on our side of the case, or on the other side, it will then be possible for this court and jury to determine whether the testimony is of the 'lowest presumption' or of the 'highest moral certainty'. All we ask is that the jury be permitted to hear the testimony and decide for themselves regarding its quality. We think our contention is based on good law and also on good common sense that can be understood by any intelligent man."

The advocate who attempts to destroy the force of convincing testimony by constant interruptions and restrictions can be effectively silenced by arguments of this kind and the testimony materially strengthened. It is also obvious that court and jury will become instructed on the theory and important points of the case and be better able to understand the real significance of the technical testimony.

It is not to be expected that the attorney will become an expert on every subject, but in the trial of a disputed document case he may win when he otherwise would have lost because he has qualified himself to assist by illuminating incidental arguments in bringing out the testimony in the most effective manner. The informed attorney and the competent witness by co-operation can present the real basis of the evidence, and thus counteract possible dangerous prejudice in the mind of judge or juror, and successfully combat erroneous argument and opposing testimony that is mistaken or corrupt.

The capable technical witness will be able to put into well chosen words the principles of handwriting identification and connect them directly with the case, but, as with the general question of giving reasons, this cannot be done without the assistance of examining counsel. If proper connection is not made, by question as well as by answer, this vital part of the evidence, the explanation of the principles, may be excluded as not relevant.

The following paragraphs contain a condensed discussion of some of the main principles underlying the question of the identification of handwriting and furnish additional material to the trial attorney for incidental and indirect argument. They also supply some ideas by which he can test in advance the testimony of his own witnesses, or later attack incorrect adverse testimony. Some of these principles are here outlined:

The identification of a signature, as to its genuineness or lack of genuineness, or a decision as to whether a continued writing was written by a certain writer is based upon the fact that handwriting embodies qualities and characteristics which in combination are sufficiently personal to serve as a basis of identification. These attributes are of many kinds and of varying degrees of force as evidence of identity, depending upon their character and their number. When they combine in sufficient number they form the basis for a conclusion.

The problem of identification of any kind has two principal phases: first, accurate observation and mental recognition or perception of the evidence; and second and more important, correct interpretation of the meaning or significance of the evidence.

The problem of identifying handwriting presents two main difficulties. In the first place there is some inevitable variation in genuine writing, as written by the same writer on different occasions, and second, it is to be expected that an imitation of a handwriting will resemble in some measure the writing imitated.

The process of identification therefore must include the determination of the extent, character, and significance of the resemblance, as well as of the variation. It becomes necessary to determine whether the variation is due to the operation of a different personality, or is only the expected and inevitable variation found in genuine writing. It is also necessary to decide whether the resemblance is the result of a more or less skilful imitation, or is the habitual and characteristic resemblance which naturally appears in a genuine writing. When these two questions are correctly answered the whole problem is solved. The unskilled lay witness, as a rule, is manifestly not qualified to consider and weigh these elements that affect the problem, and unless these things are given proper consideration it is plain that an opinion on the question is little more than a guess. When the question is properly illustrated and intelligently discussed even the untrained observer, who is fairly intelligent, is able to understand and weigh the testimony.

If error is to be avoided it must also be understood that the attributes and qualities of handwriting include much more than the mere outline or forms of the letters. The forming of letters by hand is a mental as well as a physical act, but finally becomes nearly automatic and unconscious. Handwriting has many of these physical and psychological qualities outside of, or in addition to, the shapes of the letters that are not seen by the ordinary observer. Superficial and untrained observers see in a writing only its superficial qualities and if the designs are approximately correct the writing is considered genuine, or, on the other hand, if they appear to diverge in any way, or any degree, from the usual forms made by the alleged writer, the writing is thought to be a forgery.

One who has studied the subject sees in a handwriting the degree of speed with which it was written, the pen position, the degree of skill of the writer, artistic qualities, proportions, slant, arrangement of words, size of writing, evidences of culture or of illiteracy in the forms, shading and pen-pressure, pen-lifts, flourishes or decorations, foreign qualities, evidences of nationality, occupation, sex, and many other things.

One of the most distinctive qualities of writing is its line quality, which indicates that it was freely and unconsciously written, or was produced in a constrained and unnatural manner. Unconscious writing is not necessarily skilfully written, but it is produced with a lack of care and attention to the act or process of writing which its quality discloses. If unconscious, careless writing at the same time embodies the significant individual habits shown in a genuine standard writing, this combination of qualities is proof of genuineness. The most common indications of forgery are shown by this particular attribute of writing that is perhaps best described as "line quality".

Handwriting contains many of these inherent evidences of genuineness, or, on the other hand, shows inherent evidences of lack of genuineness without comparison with any standard writing whatever. Carelessness, freedom, and evidence of unconsciousness of the operation point toward genuineness in writing without comparison with any standard writing, and the opposite conditions, undue care, attention to detail, hesitation indicating, not lack of muscular control, but attention to the process, and also delicate unnecessary repairs and overwriting, are all suspicious qualities that often point toward lack of genuineness without comparison with any standard writing.

Correct identification of handwriting depends upon an analysis of the standard writing with accurate estimation of the identifying value of all of its elements and qualities, and a similar analysis of the disputed writing, followed by a rational comparison of the two writings and a weighing of all the evidence.

An exhaustive study of a standard writing discloses what is to be expected in a writing by the same writer. A study of the disputed writing should answer the question as to whether it does contain what is to be expected in a writing by the alleged writer, and also whether it contains other qualities foreign to it. A writing that is not genuine may fail in both particulars, as not containing that which it should contain and having in it what it ought not to have in it. If the writing under investigation is genuine then it should contain the elements and attributes of the genuine writing, and, furthermore, should not contain divergent qualities, the presence of which cannot reasonably be explained.

It will thus be seen that the process of reasoning enters into all phases of the problem and one not qualified to reason on the subject is not qualified to assist another in reaching a conclusion on the subject. It is at just this phase of the process that the deficiency of the ordinary lay witness appears. The weighing of the significance of the various qualities is the necessary and difficult part of the problem of handwriting identification. Many look at things and never see what they contain because they have no power to interpret what is before them. Things seen that are not understood are seen with the eyes only and not with the brain. It is obvious that one cannot reason correctly regarding a thing until it is mentally perceived. As the old Greek adage says, "Mind sees and mind hears; all things else are deaf and blind".

A disputed writing sometimes contains a general fundamental divergent quality of design or execution, which alone is very significant as indicating that the writing is not genuine, but as a rule, an opinion must be based upon a number of divergent qualities in combination so that it is unreasonable to conclude they would all accidentally combine in one genuine writing. When even a few qualities are distinctly foreign to the genuine writing, or are violations of fixed habits shown in the genuine writing, and cannot be explained in any reasonable manner, then the conclusion based upon these divergencies must be that the writing is not genuine.

On the other hand a disputed writing or series of writings may contain so many delicate, unconscious, inconspicuous attributes, qualities, and characteristics that are found in the genuine writings with which it is compared, that it is altogether unreasonable to reach any other conclusion than that the writing is genuine. It is often possible to prove, against the most positive denials by the writer himself, that a writing is undoubtedly a genuine writing.

Certain comparatively trivial and unimportant divergencies can be pointed out when any two genuine writings or signatures by the same writers are compared with each other. These writings will differ somewhat in size, as well as in certain unimportant particulars in design and execution, because of the fact that the human writing mechanism is not an entirely accurate reproducing instrument like a copper plate, but produces an inevitable variation within a certain field. The degree of this variation varies with different writers and its degree is to be determined, not by any general rule, but by an examination of the genuine writing in the particular case. One of the common fallacies in considering the subject is the contention that because genuine writing varies it is therefore proper to assume that any variation whatever in a disputed writing is thus sufficiently explained. This is the usual defense of actual forgery. If the truth is to be discovered and shown it becomes necessary to determine the amount, extent, and exact quality of the variation.

As suggested above, the most common error in the identification of handwriting is undoubtedly due to the fact that evidence of actual forgery is excused on the ground that there is variation in genuine writing. No correct reasoning is applied to the problem and all variation is construed as of the same significance. Forgery is thus excused in some legal opinions with no attempt to interpret variation. Many undoubtedly fraudulent wills have been accepted as genuine for the reason that the proper study would not be given to the subject. With what amounts to a kind of perversity that it is difficult to understand, clearly illustrated, detailed testimony with logical reasons is referred to as "merely opinion testimony". In too many instances those called upon to pass upon the question either cannot or will not distinguish between "opinions" and "reasons for opinions".

Fortunately more and more there are courts (vide Baird v. Shaffer (Kansas), 168 Pac. 836 (1918); Pratte v. Voisard (Canada Sup. Ct.), 44 D. L. R. 157 (1918); Boyd v. Gosser (Florida), 82 So. 758 (1919); In re O'Connor's Estate (Nebraska), 179 N. W. 401 (1920); Gordon's Case (New Jersey), 26 Atl. 268) that can see and reason on the subject and make the distinction between mere opinions and testimony that appeals "not to the credulity, but to the intelligence of the hearer".

If it is true, as quoted above, that "This kind of evidence, like all other probable evidence, admits of every degree of certainty, from the lowest presumption to the highest moral certainty", it follows, therefore, that it is incorrect to assume its quality without careful examination. Weak and inconclusive testimony should not be followed nor should conclusive testimony be ignored. The facts of the testimony in the particular case under examination should always be taken into account.

Because of the conflicting evidence in the writing itself or its limited quantity, there are conditions under which it is impossible to reach any positive conclusion as to the genuineness of a disputed writing. While, on the contrary, there are other cases in which there can be no reasonable doubt by an intelligent observer as to the significance of the physical evidence upon which an opinion is based.

The discreet attorney will of course understand that these arguments, the outlines of which are here given, are naturally not all to be made in succession and under no circumstances are they to be "lugged in" at inopportune times, but the particular point is to be discussed during the trial when the door is opened by the opposition, or in the final argument. Many of these ideas can properly be presented in incidental argument and when so presented are doubly effective.

The effective use of language, a subject discussed briefly in other connections, is so important in the lawyer's business that it deserves constant emphasis and is especially important in connection with this whole matter of direct and incidental argument. It can almost be said of a lawyer that by his language is he known. He is at once a marked man in court who has a ready, forceful, pleasing command of language. There are many ways of saying a thing, and all of the varieties, from the best to the worst, are illustrated from day to day in courts of law. All who speak there are not qualified to speak; many lack ideas and many lack words. The many failures serve to emphasize the more infrequent successes.

From the opening statement of the case, and the examination of the first prospective juryman, up to the final argument, the lawyer, as is well understood, has opportunities to be heard in a trial at law. It is by his words that he shows why he is there. His appearance and his manners contribute to the total effect, but it is mainly by his ability to put ideas into words that he succeeds as an attorney. All of his preparation and ability is exemplified in the knowing what to say and when and how to say it. Long and laborious study is necessary that one may know what to say, but that study may never ripen into results if in the end the man is dumb.

Intelligent observers are naturally inclined to think that skill in the use of language as one of the qualifications for law practice has been over-emphasized, and it must be admitted that even brief experience in courts of law discloses that empty declamation and pseudo oratory are frequent and ineffective accompaniments of law practice. The shallow have been led to believe that the only necessary qualification of a lawyer is the ability to talk. It is true that when this dangerous gift has been developed independently of the ability to think, the possessor may be sought for as a Fourth of July orator, but desirable clients will not be likely to make a beaten pathway to his door. The lawyer who assumes and maintains a shallow oratorical pose throughout his career may not have time to qualify himself in those solid parts that are necessary to any considerable success.

In the old days the court houses of America were famed for much cheap, ear-splitting, insincere oratory, and the country people came for miles to hear the lawyers "sum up". Law practice has not deteriorated, but in many jurisdictions results are now obtained with less noise. Words, however, still furnish the principal medium by which mind communicates with mind, but they are now used in court rather to persuade than to thrill; and to inform rather than to impress. There was a time in the old days when the lawyer adorned his discourse, even when addressing an ordinary jury, with high-sounding Latin phrases, which, of course, he used, not to convey ideas, but to impress his auditors. By a few advocates and by certain vain specialists, this grandiloquent use is still made of certain high-sounding words, but happily the practice is declining.

Certain old-style practitioners looked upon these pet terms as part of the robes and banners of their profession and at every opportunity they flaunted them with lively satisfaction. The skilful trial lawyer who must talk in court, and the able specialist who testifies, both learn all the big words relating to the business, and then studiously avoid using them. Professional men and specialists of all kinds are naturally under a constant temptation to use terms not generally understood. This temptation should be guarded against, as one who would convince must first be understood. The intelligent lawyer who has opportunity to enforce his contention during the trial does not waste his opportunity in vain personal display of his oratorical powers.

When, however, everything has been said as to the futility of mere empty words, it remains true that the skilful use of language is one of the lawyer's greatest assets. The use of words as a means of producing results is one of the important parts of his business. But it must be language timed, controlled, and saturated with ideas. When thus timed and saturated, words may strike like a hammer, pierce like a stiletto, or soothe like a mother's lullaby. Words are more important as a part of a lawyer's equipment than his diploma, or his library. To him language is both a weapon and a shield. Ideas naturally must come first, but words are his tools. It is only by them that he can give his ideas life, and it is through them that he achieves success. Words represent ideas, and even the beginner knows that the planting of ideas is the important part of the lawyer's business. There is in fact no other kind of planting that he can do that is so sure to bring valuable returns.

This is a phase of his qualifications in which he can constantly improve himself, and the lawyer with the student spirit develops a keen interest in words, in idioms, and in phrases. His eye and his ear are constantly being trained, and all the time he adds to his stock of words from which on occasion he can instantly draw. The command of a new word is an addition to his equipment and carries him nearer to what he, like other mortals, never quite achieves—perfect expression.

CHAPTER V.

ADVOCACY.

There is no other relation in human affairs exactly analogous to that of attorney and client. It is a relation that in its intimacy and responsibility is an example of supreme trust and confidence. By it we ask another for the time and the occasion to be ourselves. It is as if for the time being we transfer our individuality to another who then becomes our mind, our voice, and even in a degree, our conscience. It is not strange that this relation from the earliest times has been most closely guarded, and that there are inseparably connected with it certain rules of honor which to disregard puts the brand of infamy upon the transgressor. To violate this sacred trust and be disloyal to a client is deservedly the unpardonable sin of an attorney. By this betrayal he sinks lower than by any other act of dishonor.

In the early history of advocacy this relation of advocate and client was not one of ordinary humdrum affairs. It was a noble service of honor and, if need be, of self-sacrifice of the strong for the weak, of the able for those who could not protect themselves. It was a kind of service for which, for many generations in human history, one who represented another would scorn the offer of any pay for the service rendered. Even to this day the barrister in England cannot collect by process of law a bill for services as a barrister. The debt is still a debt of honor.

In the course of time and as a result of the complications of civilization, the attorney's acts became, not occasional altruistic efforts, but a kind of service which merited a return that at first, however, was somewhat disguised under the term of honorarium. In the course of time a profession was developed which in modern times retains some of the ancient qualities, but which has taken on characteristics quite in contrast with some of those that existed during its early history.

Certain rules and practices were gradually developed and certain precedents established that were necessary to stability. It was found that a trial at law must necessarily be conducted in accordance with certain rules, and it became the business of the lawyer to see to it that the interests he represented were not endangered by the violation of these rules. At any time he could object to what he considered improper, and as time went by, certain rules of procedure were developed. Rules of some kind were, of course, absolutely necessary, but one of the weaknesses of the administration of the law from the beginning has been that the rules have tended to take on an almost unchangeable, if not sacred, character, and too many times have themselves defeated the very ends they were designed to promote.

Objections, exclusions, and exceptions are no doubt necessary, and at any rate are inevitable, in a trial at law, but the proper control of this phase of law practice is one of its greatest problems. One unfamiliar with the practice of the law is astounded to learn that certain things cannot be done in court that common sense would suggest ought to be permitted. Obstructive tactics within the law may be wisely employed, but often are used in a manner that only tends to delay and to defeat justice. These tactics often at once arouse the suspicion of a juryman, or indeed of anyone not familiar with law practice. There are many thoughtful men in the legal profession who are even coming to think that many of the revered rules of evidence should be radically changed, if not abolished altogether.

There is a type of advocate who, in his use of these various rules, is properly described as the negative or obstructing advocate. His business is not the proving of anything, but the prevention of proof. He succeeds if he prevents the facts from becoming known. While thus engaged he tries to make it appear that he is defending the eternal principles of justice and the very foundations of civilization and incidentally, of course, his client. His fighting methods are many times similar to those of the cuttlefish which, by discoloring or muddying the water and thus preventing anything from being seen, defends itself. Some of the ancient rules are often of great assistance to these men.

An advocate of this kind usually will be against the facts, a defender of a guilty man, or a representative of a fraudulent claim. He accepts employment to win the case for his client. This end he will attain fairly, if possible, but if he cannot win fairly then he will employ other means. His methods are tinged, if not saturated, with insincerity and unfairness, and his final resource is perjury. He objects strenuously to everything that tends to injure his chance of success, and viciously attacks all opposing witnesses. And all the time, he who protects fraud and crime and cheats justice, poses as the zealous guardian of the ancient and revered rules and precedents.

Certain of these common abuses of advocacy can hardly be condemned with too great severity. They are flagrant, cruel, and shocking to the moral sense of all whose sensibilities have not become dulled by familiarity with them. They should not be excused and condoned, but should be repudiated by the great respectable majority of an honorable profession.

In connection with some of these abuses, openly practiced, a moral tone is exhibited which would be looked upon with scorn in any other field of human activity. Boasts are made of winning cases against the facts! It is thought to be commendably clever to destroy the effect of honest adverse testimony and thus defeat the ends of justice. Crime is thus encouraged and fraud made profitable. This conduct, at least tacitly, is often praised in discussions of the practice of law. This would be paralleled if a business man should be praised for his skill in cheating his neighbor across the way. As civilization advances this law practice, which openly defeats justice, will come to be looked upon with the scorn that it deserves.

Certain books on advocacy will also become obsolete, or will be revised so they are not in effect manuals teaching how to defeat justice. Their chapters on methods and tactics will be not simply directions as to the most effective ways of destroying the opponent's case and the testimony of honest witnesses. One would not gather from certain parts of certain books of this class that the purpose of courts of law is to establish justice. Think of a discussion of the practice of medicine with only a secondary or remote thought of the life of the patient!

There are lawyers who at once get purple with rage at any criticism of the law or of legal procedure of this character, especially if criticism is made by one who is not a lawyer. These men apparently look upon the law as something finished by certain more or less wise men many years ago for their use as a business. They resent criticism as a kind of interference with what they consider to be their own private affairs. To them the law is not a profession but a trade. The lawyers of the type described in Jarndyce and Jarndyce found no fault with the administration of the law of their day because it served their purposes, but there were those who saw its faults and corrected them. There still are Jarndyce cases, but their numbers are growing less through the efforts of judges, lawyers, and legal authors who, like the creator of the Jarndyce case, see the faults and gradually correct them.

There can hardly be a more responsible and important duty than that of the attorney called upon to plead the cause and protect the rights, or even the life, of another. As in the old days he still is the brain and the voice of his client. He becomes a defender and an advocate of the rights of him for whom he speaks. As his ability in furthering the interests of his client is the measure of his success as a lawyer, the business of advocacy in all its bearings must naturally be a subject of great interest to him. So important is it and so great is his interest that he is constantly tempted to overdo it. The undue emphasis of advocacy is one of its common weaknesses.

One of the most important things that the lawyer must do in order to be successful is to lead others to his own point of view, and his unwise overemphasis of the spirit of advocacy may become the enemy of persuasion. The sagacious trial lawyer seeks to protect his client's interests, but in doing so does not make of himself a prejudiced, unfair partisan. Many lawyers defeat the ends for which they strive by unwittingly trying too hard to protect a client's interests. If they appear for the defense, their excessive zeal and obvious bias gives the impression that by every means, fair or unfair, they will endeavor to prevent the guilt of their client from becoming known.

These advocates will not grant in any case, civil or criminal, that the opposition has even a shadow of a leg to stand upon. In court they object on the slightest provocation, and as a result of these constant objections and their partisan attitude, the effect of everything they say is lessened. Their violent contentions, with equal effect, might as well be whispered in the words of some dead language instead of being spoken in the loud, rasping, disagreeable tone too often heard in court rooms. These men appear to be very active and busy attorneys, but because of their unwise zeal they give the impression that they are on the wrong side of the case. By their activity and intensity they lead a jury to think that they really would do quite well if they could only get on the right side of some good case.

The attorney whose too frequent objections are constantly being overruled also gives the impression to the untrained juryman that he does not know what the law is and therefore is constantly being ruled against by the court. The too zealous advocate, by his whole conduct, finally arouses a permanent suspicion as to the sincerity of everything he says and does. The force of his incidental arguments and his final argument is greatly diminished, if not wholly nullified, because his manner and methods throughout the trial have been unfair and insincere. This advocate who is habitually insincere often possesses no more personal magnetism than a phonograph and is utterly devoid of ordinary human sympathy. He is a mere legal machine. This habitual mental attitude not only dulls the keen edge of conscience, but benumbs the higher judgment and makes impossible the highest efficiency.

By his unwise activity, his venom, his unfairness, and his vociferous defense of his client's interests, the advocate may win the applause of the shallow and unthinking, but at too high a price. By these tactics he is at the same time laying the foundation for defeat and, what is more unfortunate, for a reputation as one of that class of undesirable citizens in certain communities known as shysters. These men, often more dangerous and undesirable in a community than burglars and highwaymen, debase and disgrace an honorable profession. They can still be found at many county seats, but the vigorous activity of bar association vigilance committees is gradually lessening their activities in many communities.

The uncontrolled spirit of advocacy also has a tendency to deaden, if not to destroy, that delicate, elusive, but most important of qualifications which we call tact, which has tremendous force in achieving success. It is a misfortune for a young lawyer to train himself in insincerity by advocating causes in which he does not believe. There are those who wisely advise that even in friendly debate it is not a good practice to take either side of any question. Mental agility is thus acquired at the expense of sincerity. This sort of training is good for the mind, but bad for the soul.

Undue emphasis on the spirit of advocacy also leads an entirely conscientious attorney to overload his case with evidence, to overtry it in every way, and to overemphasize everything that he presents or discusses. The important and the trivial are with him both apt to be put into the superlative degree, and his whole conduct is governed by a partisan intensity which prevents him from applying ordinary sane judgment to many things. Many trial attorneys of this class apparently sit on springs in court and jump into the air at every provocation, with objections to everything unfavorable to their own contention and intense arguments on every point until all are weary and nobody is convinced. The most trivial point is argued with the same intensity that is given to the vital issue in the case, and as a result nothing is emphasized because everything is emphasized.

There is also another important ethical phase of this question of advocacy that deserves consideration. The unforgiveable sin in an attorney is the betrayal of a client's interests. This relation of attorney and client is of so confidential and intimate a character that custom and law have properly thrown around it the utmost protection. The relation is, however, sometimes interpreted and acted upon in a way that leads directly away from the interests of justice as well as of morals. Loyalty to a client is a plea which, too often it is assumed, will cover almost any sin from deception up to bribery.

The spirit of advocacy in too many instances develops a peculiar code of ethics which permits an advocate to do for a client what he would not, without some hesitation at least, do for himself. This strange code permits him, in the interest of his client, to misrepresent, deceive, lie, and suborn perjury. All of these acts in any other relation than that of attorney and client he would condemn. Stranger still, he even may think it improper for the client to do things for himself that he, his lawyer, does not hesitate to do for him as his representative. This illustrates a strange sort of moral blindness which grows out of excessive and unwise advocacy. There are men who, perhaps because of familiarity with it, defend conduct of this kind who ought not to defend it.

The advocate is in duty bound to protect the interests of his client in every proper way, but for a fee he is not called upon to sell his own soul. Temptations are sure to come to the attorney that test the quality of his conscience and the strength of his character. There are unworthy clients who for money seek to buy not simply the experience and ability of an advocate, but also his reputation and his honor. The man who is disloyal to his own higher self in order to be loyal to a client is not only paying too high a price for success, but is disqualifying himself for the highest success.

Those who resist the temptations deserve praise and honor in proportion to the severity of the test.

Most litigation grows out of controversy over certain alleged facts. In many cases the lawyer cannot know and may never know what the truth of the matter really is. It is also true that in some classes of cases each side may be partly right and partly wrong, but a careful distinction is drawn by the conscientious advocate between civil and criminal cases. Although the guilty man is entitled to counsel in order that his rights may be protected, it does not follow that a self-respecting lawyer should become in effect a partner of a party in a civil case who obviously is attempting to perpetrate a fraud. Just at this point comes the great temptation in the practice of law. No sophistry ever really convinces the lawyer that he has a right to smother his intelligence and say that he is not called upon to decide upon the merits of any case in advance. If he does not decide some cases in advance he will soon come to be known as a partner in fraud and in crime.

Like other professional men, lawyers are surrounded by certain conditions that hamper and limit their development. One of the greatest of differences in workers in all fields is the degree of their inspiration by the student spirit, that attitude of mind that makes practical life a constant course of study. The education of men of this latter class is only finished when life is finished. But with many professional men the deadly routine and the making of the profession a business and only a business, tends to kill the learning spirit. They become mere machines going through a fixed routine.

There is a very wide distinction between the men who in some measure live for a profession and the men who simply live on it. Of professional men as a class but few attend conventions, but few read technical magazines or books, and it is a rare man who does the first stroke of work in any field of original research! There are many professional men, not all of whom are lawyers, who pay less for general technical books and magazines, and for memberships in societies, and traveling expenses to meetings, than they do for tobacco. The total number of members in the American Bar Association is about the same as the number of lawyers in one American city.

Experience with the unprogressive man develops simply a kind of manual and mental facility in the humdrum things and nearly all improvement stops. And strange to say, the man of this class, who has entirely finished his study, boasts that he is a practical man and looks with some contempt upon the progressive man who attacks the ancient theories with some new and improved ideas. There was a time when the learned doctor at once took some of the life out of a sick man by bleeding him. There was a time when solemn, bewigged doctors of the law condemned poor women to be hanged as witches. There still are abuses to correct and reforms to promote; and, figuratively speaking, the bleeding and the hanging are still going on.

The desirable, if not necessary, qualities that go to make a great lawyer are so numerous that it is discouraging to a beginner to catalogue them. There is, however, some value in a catalogue for one who is perhaps deficient in one quality can make it up by emphasizing others that are a part of the desirable equipment. It is easy to specify some of the essential qualities.

Before making this catalogue of the desirable qualities, and for the purposes of contrast, a passing glimpse is taken of the other side of the shield. It is well known that there are men, even in quite civilized communities, whose ideal of a great lawyer is a forceful, rather coarse, if not somewhat brutal, personality, unhampered by fine sensibilities or a too active conscience, and willing to take up any task without too close a scrutiny of its merits. It is hardly necessary to say that this conception of the profession as a whole is a base slander. The men who answer these requirements unfortunately do exist, but they are not the great lawyers, but rather the scavengers of a great profession.

The first requirements of the great lawyer are a good working conscience and a strong personality. Added to these in the great advocate is what, for a better description, we call a ready, working knowledge of human nature. Other important, if not essential, qualities are the ability to understand facts, an analytical, alert mind, and a forceful command of language.

The great lawyer is a student of his fellow man. At no time in a trial does the skilful attorney forget the variations in the personalities with which he must deal. He understands the danger of weakening his case simply by a careless manner of dealing with those who must participate in the proceeding. He knows that people cannot with safety all be treated alike. He constantly realizes that he cannot retrace a false step, nor recall an unwise word that has given offense. By experience he knows how easily a friendly witness may be antagonized, or the court may be offended, or adverse witnesses made more dangerous by oversight, by carelessness, by bad manners, or by any unfortunate error of speech or of conduct.

Either by instinct or by experience he has learned that even a disagreeable voice may contribute to defeat, and to him it is obvious that any conduct that naturally leads to aversion or dislike lowers efficiency in one who seeks to lead others to his own point of view. The wise attorney has learned in the school of experience that we are always more easily persuaded by one with an attractive personality, and that a man's logic may fail to convince because we do not like his manners. This wise and discriminating lawyer does not make the mistake of treating an adverse party too severely, even where severity is justified, and he has learned from the unwise actions of others as well as by bitter defeat that the testimony of adverse witnesses is often strengthened because the sympathy of jury and spectators has been aroused in their behalf.

The partly unconscious effect of personality is an important part of law practice and deserves careful study. We are born as we are, but our conduct is what we make it. It is certainly desirable to discover, if possible, why and how one unconsciously offends and this knowledge is of practical value to the attorney. It is well said that he knows best how to be a gentleman who knows best how not to give offense. There is no doubt that one of the qualities of the great lawyer is that of being a gentleman.

The greatest "verdict getters" with all their other qualities, have intelligence, force, and charm, and charm is not always the least of these. That law school would soon be marked that made of all its students attractive, pleasing personalities; that added to knowledge, wisdom; to information, tact; and to intelligence, courtesy. The inherent gentleman carries with him something that gives him instant advantage wherever he may be. He receives a consideration and commands an attention that it is somewhat difficult to analyze and to understand. A man of this kind has back of him and with him to speak for him the influence of the gentlemen of all time.

Those who lack this high quality at once acknowledge their inferiority by their acts and their attitude and are immediately at a disadvantage in a contest with a personality that is instinctively respected and admired. This valuable quality of charm is not simply a matter of birth, of education, of clothes, of family, of race, or of sex, but of conduct and of a right relation to other people. More than from anything else it grows out of thoughtfulness, good manners, and friendliness. Courtesy begets courtesy, and he is liked who himself likes others. The indispensable price of friendship is to be a friend.

The three qualities of personality, reputation, and professional ability are fused in an attorney and naturally are the main elements that constitute his ability as a lawyer. It is not always easy to estimate their comparative force as a means of winning success and their values may vary in different fields and in different cases. It is undoubtedly true that technical professional ability alone, however valuable it may be, does not always command success, and, as in other professions and in other fields, the race is not always to the swift, nor the battle to the strong. Industry and thoroughness are in many instances more than a match for brilliant, but careless and lazy genius.

In every city and at nearly every county seat representatives of the various classes of lawyers can be found. One of the number is the lawyer to whom the right side of the most important case is likely to go. There is also the advocate who is naturally called upon to help fraud to win. These men have made their places in the community. The man with a shady reputation takes that, as well as his trial brief, into court, and the man who is known to the judge, to his fellow citizens, and to the jury for honesty and fairness begins every trial with a distinct advantage over an opponent without this reputation. These men of high character and ability are not only the leaders of their profession, but the trusted leaders of their fellowmen. They share with a type of family physician the unlimited confidence and trust of the community and their advice and assistance is sought on many questions outside of the strict field of the law.

The practice of law, like that of medicine, is much concerned with the abnormal. One profession has much to do with disease and suffering, and the other with injustice and crime, but this contact need not develop a narrowing pessimism that tends to make of this world mainly a place of anguish and of sin. The correct and wider view makes work in both fields a service of help and of rescue in lessening suffering and combatting evil. The lawyer is the natural champion to be called upon to defend right, promote justice, protect the weak, and guard those priceless heritages of the ages that we inadequately describe as freedom and civilization. Through all the stress and strain the great physician and the great advocate both come to realize more and more that honesty and health are the normal conditions and that the high task given to them is that of making these conditions more nearly universal.

In conclusion, to summarize briefly what is discussed elsewhere, the great trial lawyer, though not necessarily a great orator, must be able to use language to produce results as a skilled craftsman uses a delicate and complicated tool. He must have sympathy, tact and courtesy, and must know men and their ways. By study, experience, and a trained intuition, he will also have acquired an instant appreciation of the significance and force of evidence and will have learned its correct order of presentation. He must be able to control his temper and maintain his poise under trying conditions, and it will steady him and keep him sane if he has a sense of humor, which, however, he can hold in proper subjection. Finally, he must know the law.

CHAPTER VI.

PERSUASION AND PRACTICAL PSYCHOLOGY IN COURTS OF LAW.

A trial at law is simply a competition in persuasion. It is a contest where many influences are brought to bear to persuade a judge or a jury to take certain action. Law is administered through the minds, the consciences, the emotions, and the prejudices of men. It is the task of the attorney to consider all these matters and endeavor to discover and utilize all the various influences that have a bearing on the problem. If he learns the law, but fails to give attention to something else that causes defeat, his unsupported technical knowledge is of but little value to a client.

The judge and the jury, the lawyers, the litigants, and the witnesses, all gather in a court room in order that a judgment may be reached, or a verdict rendered, regarding some controversy. On each side of the case is a man who has prepared himself as a lawyer in order that he may assist a client in a proceeding of this kind. The success of each of these men in the undertaking depends on his ability, using the various means at his command, to lead a judge or a jury up to a decision favorable to the client he represents. One of the qualifications of a lawyer that affects his success in this important task is his power to persuade.

This ability to influence others is of priceless value in many fields. With it, as Emerson says of perfect manners, all doors open. Its importance to the lawyer can hardly be overestimated. There are persons, lawyers and others, who are more successful than others in this business of persuading and, unless it is wholly a mystery past finding out, it should be of interest to the attorney to discover the causes of this varying ability. Some of the causes of failure and some of the aids to success are discussed in this chapter.

It is not presumed to formulate even one infallible rule of persuasion, but to offer some warnings and suggestions that can perhaps be developed and applied by the earnest student. It is difficult even to analyze the subject, and no attempt is made to outline any definite course of study. The somewhat empirical survey here sketched directs attention to certain outstanding phases of the subject and perhaps will furnish a few working ideas. The mere developing of an interest in the matter has value for, with an inquiring mind, much can be learned by intelligent observation. In many fields of human activity this important subject of persuasion can be studied with profit through ordinary experience as guided by that uncommon quality described as common sense.

As is well known, many of the lessons growing out of problems regarding the relations of people and their influence on each other begin in earliest childhood and continue through life. When understood and applied, they have a bearing on this power to persuade. Something of that appreciation of what is fit and proper, called tact, can do doubt in some degree be consciously developed. This precious personal quality furnishes a first long step toward persuasion. These valuable intuitions relative to conduct, that everybody inevitably develops to some extent through life experience, the student of persuasion endeavors to apply more directly to his practical problems.

A discriminating and practical study of the habits, tendencies and prejudices of the human mind as it functions in a practical world might well form a part of courses of study leading up to various professions, and especially that of the law. All who are to do business successfully through, or with, people must in some manner, either by intelligent study and observation, or by costly experience based upon a crude rule of thumb, learn what to expect of them and how they will act and react under varying conditions. It is certainly important to learn, as far as it is possible to learn, why people think as they think and do as they do. One must necessarily learn something of this subject, vaguely called human nature, in order to avoid getting into constant trouble with other human beings. There are people who never learn. A large part of this discipline must no doubt be acquired in the severe school of experience, but intelligent attention to the subject reduces the severity of the lessons of a practical world.

It is hardly necessary to call attention to the fact that one of the most forceful influences in the process of persuading is the known character and reputation of the one who seeks to persuade. This influence always powerfully supplements all other forces. There are men in every community, lawyers as well as others, whose statements alone go a long way towards carrying conviction. Back of their words is their reputation for honesty and sincerity and their plain statements are often more persuasive than the polished effort of the pleader who is himself under suspicion.

Although it must be admitted that there is an interesting mystery about certain phases of persuasion, there is no mystery about some of its essential elements. One goes to school, and studies, and listens to instruction, and reads books, and burns the midnight oil, that he may be qualified to consider intelligently and discuss persuasively matters that he must consider. Patient, industrious, intelligent labor in acquiring accurate knowledge and in training the intellect is the first price a man must pay for skill in influencing his fellowmen. It can be stated with much positiveness that one of the greatest obstacles to success in persuasion is ignorance. A hearer is not often persuaded by one who shows that he does not know what he is talking about. If we are inclined to dispute his alleged facts he has made a poor start toward persuasion.

It is the trained intellect, as guided by knowledge, that from first to last controls the performance of persuasion. It sometimes even decides that the appeal must not be to the intellect alone. Knowledge and intellectual power are both essential in the operation, but knowledge is the secondary force. Knowledge is power only when it can be intelligently applied. To think and not simply to know is the prime requisite to success in most human endeavors and is the essential element in persuasion. Education more often fails in developing the ability to reason than in imparting knowledge, and persuasion often fails because the real significance and relations of the known facts are not discussed and are not presented in the proper manner, in the proper order, and with the proper emphasis. Live thoughts are the most interesting things in the whole world, as well as the rarest, and they are the keys to persuasion.

While all this direct, thorough preparation on the principles and details of a subject, and the fusing of this material into thought, are the primary steps in the preparation for influencing others, there are numerous important incidental influences that cannot safely be disregarded. Many an industrious young attorney who has been bitterly disappointed by a defeat in a legal controversy, later learns that the result was due to a prejudice to which he had given no attention whatever. He had proved his case, but it was decided against him. These uncertainties in the administration of justice are the cause of much severe criticism, but the fault is not in the law alone, but in the frailties of human nature.

It is helpful to examine this process of persuasion somewhat in detail and endeavor to discover just what it is. Definitions tell us that we are convinced by evidence addressed to the intellect, but are persuaded by that addressed, not to the intellect alone, but also to the will and to the emotions. To convince is to lead one to believe; to persuade is to lead one to act. The two operations merge into each other, however, and to convince is usually the first step toward persuasion, but our purpose in convincing is to get a man to do something. A man may be convinced that life insurance is a wise provision for the future, but he is not persuaded until his name is on the "dotted line". The preparation for a law suit necessarily gives its principal attention to the presenting of evidence and arguments addressed to the intellect and designed to prove the facts. If the performance is carried through with the assumption that one is always persuaded when he is convinced, the effort may end in failure.

There are certain of these indirect influences that have so important a bearing on the operation of persuading that they deserve special consideration. One of the first of these is the power of personality. There is no doubt a vague, ever-present, human quality, that is thus described, that has much to do with the influence of men in human affairs. It is always an element in the act of persuasion. This somewhat mysterious power that under certain conditions enables one, almost without effort, to influence another is no doubt, in large measure, a gift of the gods. It is difficult to say definitely from just what qualities all of the power arises, but it is no doubt the total effect of numerous human attributes. For most of them the possessor perhaps deserves but little praise; others come through patient, toiling effort and are personal achievements. Some of these elements are a kindly, human sympathy, combined with directness, frankness, general intelligence, pleasing manners, unaffectedness, and a practical knowledge of people. The best teacher in the whole world of this rare quality is a wise and loving mother. Of some phases of it she is the only teacher.

Fakirs of various kinds advertise and in effect offer to supply this priceless human quality; they undertake to teach others how to acquire it in a few easy lessons, although they themselves do not possess it. It is not to be learned from the hypnotist, the phrenologist, the graphologist, the character delineator, nor from any kind of a fortune-teller. Advertising pages show that there are those who need to be told that it cannot easily be learned all at once by correspondence, nor is it transmitted by the laying on of hands, nor does its force arise from any mere formula, incantation, superficial trick, or device.

There is here and there, sometimes in the big city and then again in a little town, a lawyer who possesses the persuasive quality. What he says carries conviction and what he asks people to do they are inclined to do. He is always a most dangerous opponent, but not principally because he is highly educated, nor because he knows all the law. In the first place he is a dangerous antagonist because he knows the controlling points of his case and, in the second place, because he knows his fellowmen, and knows how to talk to them persuasively. He speaks their own language and they understand. He has a way, as it is figuratively described, of "getting over into the jury box", and often his opponents wonder how it was that he won. Many of them will never quite understand. Whatever his methods, it can reasonably be asserted that those he persuaded understood him and did not dislike him nor suspect him.

It is hopeless to attempt to weigh the comparative force of all the important qualities that combine to produce this valuable personal quality that attracts and, because of its power, that is well described as personal charm, but no doubt pleasing manners often is one of the forceful elements. This phase of personality is one of the indirect influences that many times assists men in leading others to agree with them. We like to agree with some men because we like them and we are inclined to oppose others even when they are right. As a part of training for ordinary practical affairs pleasing manners are usually thought of as desirable rather than necessary, but if the lawyer who seeks to persuade takes with him into court, besides his brief and his law books, the attractive manners of a gentleman, he begins this persuading contest with a marked advantage over an opponent not thus equipped. When some men enter a court-room the tone of the proceedings is at once raised to a higher plane. There are many judges whose influence at once unconsciously develops courtesy and earnestness in those who appear before them. Men of this type in any field are listened to when they speak and hearers are glad to agree with them.

There are persons who are not lawyers, and unfortunately there are lawyers themselves, whose conception of a qualified attorney, or what is thought of as a "smart lawyer", is not a cultured gentleman but a disagreeable, belligerent individual who in a trial is constantly on fighting edge, and who gives the impression that he is liable to bite a piece out of anyone who opposes him. It is difficult for those who have this ideal of a lawyer to understand how courtesy has any value as part of the equipment of an attorney at law. They evidently do not understand that courtesy is not a synonym for weakness, nor good manners the equivalent of cowardice. The rough bully often finds himself weak and almost powerless, and in some way strangely handicapped, before his courteous adversary whose weapon is the keen-edged rapier of intellect that runs him through, with a bow and a wave of the hand, before he can bring his own coarse weapons into play.

If the intelligent and receptive mind of a listener could be free from all prejudice and preconceived, and perhaps incorrect, notions on a subject under consideration, the problem of persuasion would be much simplified. Belief is produced and persuasion is reached only when the hearer understands and is without opposed definite impressions, or prejudice, or when the quality of the evidence presented is sufficiently forceful to counteract any opposed belief. It is sometimes said that certain evidence, or certain arguments, are of a quality that will inevitably produce belief, but this is not necessarily true unless the receiving mind is at least neutral on the subject.

It is impossible for one to say that to another evidence will be conclusive for the reason that the other may mix with the ideas presented some adverse ideas he already possesses. Out of just this condition arises the uncertainty of a verdict of a jury or the judgment of a court. All of the evidence upon which the decision was actually based is not known. It is obvious that one who would persuade must diligently endeavor to learn what these adverse ideas probably are. Here is an opportunity to utilize the scientific imagination. A part of preparation to persuade always should include an intensive study of what is now popularly termed "the psychology of the question and of the situation". We must endeavor to learn what is already in the other mind.

This unknown and disturbing element, already in the mind of the hearer, may be misinformation, or it may be what we mildly call pre-disposition, or more emphatically denounce as prejudice. All these tendencies for or against any contention are largely unconscious to the possessor and for that reason are all the more dangerous. They must always be reckoned with, and if possible counteracted, in the attempt to persuade.

Success in persuasion largely depends upon the unconscious estimate by the hearer of the qualities of sincerity and of accuracy in the speaker. These tests are usually applied almost unconsciously as a result of experience and by a more or less trained intuition. The estimates are sometimes inaccurate, but close study of the question discloses some of the reasons why we suspect some speakers and believe others.

Among the influences that affect our estimate of sincerity are directness, frankness, fairness, unaffectedness, properly qualified statements, absence of egotism, and a kind of unconventionality and simplicity that tend to disarm suspicion. We are also somewhat influenced by general appearance, manner, quality of voice, inflection, self-control, and, if the speaker is a witness under questioning, the promptness of his replies, and if he is a lawyer making an argument, his attitude as to fairness. The first step in successful persuasion is this inspiring of confidence, as without this element all else fails. With the witness, as with the lawyer, the greatest enemy of persuasion is any kind of suspicion of the speaker, and until this is removed mere words are vain and useless sounds and become as a tinkling cymbal. Many distressing discords of this kind are heard in courts of law.

This belief in a speaker is sometimes partly the unconscious effect of personality, already referred to, and it is sometimes partly the effect of definite causes deliberately employed. A jury is sometimes misled by perjury, or an individual by deception or false statements. Unfortunately these various powers to affect decisions can be employed for base uses. In all ages the weaknesses of the human family have enabled certain of its members to prey upon their fellowmen. In this nation of intelligence and education, hundreds of millions of dollars are paid each year for "blue sky" stocks, and notwithstanding Franklin's sage advice, many a man "has paid dear, very dear, for his whistle". These unfortunate results illustrate a misuse of the power of persuasion, and part of the necessary study of the important subject from youth to old age is a practical study of its false appeals and an attempt to discover the proper defenses against them. This knowledge has value for all. Even if one cannot by study learn how to persuade, he can learn why some fail who attempt it. There is some value in this negative knowledge if one thus learns to protect himself and in his own efforts to persuade he thus learns to avoid the faults seen in others.

One of the common indications of insincerity in a speaker is a forced and unnatural manner. If we are led to think that a speaker is "making a speech" instead of simply saying something to us, he has already partly failed as a persuader. To be successful he must wisely conceal his method. Naturalness and frankness dispel suspicion, and sincerity carries its own stamp of genuineness. All human beings to some degree have developed these more or less subtle instincts by which affectation and insincerity are recognized by sight and by sound. It is never safe, for example, for the zealous advocate to assume that the members of a jury are unintelligent and easily deceived. Many times they know exactly what he is trying to do.

There are some speakers who have given some superficial attention to the question of manner in speaking, who act on the notion that it is easy to play a part and anywhere and anytime make things appear to be what they are not. These speakers, with their shallow elocution and their obvious insincerity, usually deceive only themselves. Their set gestures, forced tone, and simulated emotions are all too evident. One reason why they fail to persuade is because it is so apparent that they are seeking to persuade. One of the fundamental weaknesses of advocacy in general is its manifest insincerity, and there are few evidences of it that are more palpable than cheap, forced, artificial oratory. We at once suspect the sincerity of a speaker if he too directly and unskilfully appeals to our prejudice or to our sympathy. If we are led to think that he appeals to our prejudice we are unconsciously offended that he should thus accuse us of prejudice, and if he appeals directly to our sympathy we are offended as this tends at least to accuse us of weakness.

To some minds this whole operation of persuading at once suggests a sort of fawning, wheedling attempt to curry favor in some improper and humiliating way and the methods pursued by these persons in attempting to persuade suggests that what they are doing is not quite respectable. Between equals this menial method and mental attitude usually at once defeats the end aimed at. The motives for performing an act are of the widest range of variation. It is true that we are persuaded to act because of pity or revenge, because of self-interest or of charity, because of prejudice, or, on the other hand, because of a controlling sense of right and justice. The persuasive appeal may be of a high order or of a low order.

Evidence is presented and arguments are made in court in order to show that a certain contention or proposition should prevail and, at least in form, the basis for persuasion in a court of law is an intellectual appeal that seeks to prove a state of facts out of which naturally grows an action that is in harmony with right and justice. It follows from this condition that direct and open appeals to motives entirely outside of the proof are improper, but they are being made everywhere all the time and must be met. It is a rare case the decision of which is not influenced to some extent by these outside matters that are not recorded in the reporter's note book but most certainly are in the case.

One of the common sources of suspicion of the legal pleader is his unskilful and improper attempt to employ sympathy and emotion as a force in persuasion. These human qualities often play highly important parts in trials at law, but to be effective they must be used with skill and not too obviously. The tear-shedding attorney becomes well known in the community and his emotional appeals are apt to be discounted in advance. If, however, emotion is tactfully and skilfully employed it is a powerful aid to persuasion. Where human rights and liberty are at stake, cold, accurate logic is not a match for live, moving emotion. The lawyer, however, who quotes Scripture and sheds tears over every "cow case" that comes to him, is soon a joke in the court-house, and even jurymen from the back districts come to recognize his cheap acting for exactly what it is. Sympathy and emotion when properly employed sometimes win against the fact, but when fictitious and insincere they often arouse a suspicion that can hardly be overcome. We instinctively resent the attempt to deceive us.

The second test of persuasion is our conscious, or unconscious, estimate of the intelligence and accuracy of the speaker. Some of the qualities that at once affect our estimate of the intelligence of a speaker are his clearness and brevity of statement, his selection of words, especially his descriptive terms, his pronunciation, his control of emphasis, and finally, as far as we are able to judge, the extent and accuracy of his knowledge of the subject on which he speaks. It is well understood how unconsciously we are at once affected by certain errors of speech by which we inevitably measure education and culture, and it is also true that we are, consciously or unconsciously, also affected by certain accuracies which instantly appeal to us and lead us to have confidence in the statements of a speaker.

One of the arch enemies of persuasion is lack of clearness. We assume that a speaker understands and can explain a thing he really believes in. A rambling, incoherent statement may fail to convince, not alone because the facts are not brought to our apprehension, but because we unconsciously are led to suspect the speaker is not himself a believer in his own contention. It is, of course, difficult, if not impossible, for a man to speak clearly on a subject he does not clearly understand and many arguments do not reach the point of persuasion for the simple reason that they do not get below the surface of the subject they attempt to discuss. They are defective in reasoning because they contain no discussion of the principles out of which the facts arose.

The thorough trial attorney who seeks to persuade his fellowmen learns the facts of his case and gets assistance from every possible source of information and his search is not confined to matter found between the old sheepskin, or even the modern buckram, covers of law books. If he is to discuss a collision at sea he should know something of winds, currents and signals; if he is to discuss forgery he should know something of forgery and of the psychology, qualities, tendencies, and characteristics of handwriting.

Those qualified to speak on the subject say that this same lack of thoroughness that renders arguments on the facts of the case weak and inconclusive, is also shown in arguments on the law. Those who have been made lawyers by a narrow, exclusive, and "practical" study of the subject may have acquired a facility that has an immediate practical value, but they may have altogether missed the soul of the law in their diligent search for its body. There are students of the law who have studied results with little attention to causes and the underlying principles upon which the precedents themselves are based. There are many of these men who at least do law business and who are known as lawyers, who do not own and rarely read text-books, and who have no interest whatever in discussions of the history, principles, and tendencies of the law. They cite precedents but cannot weigh and analyze them; they quote law without knowing what it means. They do not seem to understand that an argument based on a precedent has power to persuade in proportion as it correctly interprets and directly applies the precedent to the problem to be solved. To win on a law point it is not only necessary to find the law, but to be able to recognize it and understand it when it is found.

Another important factor in persuasion by means of spoken words that deserves attention is a desirable quality of virility that secures and holds attention. This element of strength is the joint effect of vigorous thought and distinct utterance. Effective virility is something more than the saying of unimportant things in an important way. The vigor must mainly grow out of the thought itself which, because of its importance, seems to compel the speaker to say earnestly and distinctly that which deserves serious attention. We soon recognize and grow weary of emphasis on the commonplace, and when we begin to suspect that a speaker is attempting to put gold plate on his pewter spoons of thought his effectiveness as a speaker is ended.

High thoughts, however, in spoken words often die in their flight because of lack of vigor and of lung power. Lack of energy often completely masks and renders ineffective high intellectual qualities. It is sad indeed to see a gifted speaker fail for lack of this secondary and comparatively unimportant quality. He who seeks to persuade must speak intelligently, and at the same time must speak clearly and forcefully. It is naturally assumed that one who has something important to say will say it so that it can be heard and understood.

Public speakers trained in England, especially those who have had experience as political speakers, are generally superior to American speakers in this quality of making themselves understood. The peculiar English custom of heckling—often highly discourteous—it is reasonably claimed is an element of training that has made these public speakers superior in some ways to speakers of some other countries. The mumbler who swallows his terminals and attempts to secure emphasis by lowering his voice to a whisper is not tolerated by English political audiences. The speaker who is assailed from the back seats with the discourteous cry, "Louder and funnier", will probably make himself heard or sit down. When one of these foreign trained speakers undertakes to speak in public you will probably hear what he says, even if you are not convinced; when an American speaks you may hear and understand and you may not.

There are many who speak in court in America who would be benefited by a severe course in heckling. Lacking this, they would do well to train themselves in the back fields, with pebbles in their mouths, speaking to the flocks and the trees until they can be understood by their fellowmen. It is a discourtesy to an audience to speak in public in a way that puts a burden upon a hearer, and if one seeks to persuade who cannot be understood his words are as the wind that blows.

The strange variation in the opinions of people on all subjects is one of the unaccountable things regarding the human family and must be considered in this operation of persuading. It is well known that people of equal intelligence, born in the same town and living on the same street, differ widely in their views on many subjects. On questions of politics, government, social questions, estimates of public characters, interpretations of history and events, schools of medicine, and notably on religious questions, the opinions of friends and neighbors are in hopeless conflict. The condition would suggest that accurate information was not available for all, or that in some way one group of those who differ have been misled or deceived, but this is not the fact. The truth of the matter is that the ideas and opinions of human beings are, in large degree, controlled by inheritance, by habit, and by prejudice. This fact necessarily has a most important bearing on this whole question of persuasion.

If we contemplate changing, or even modifying, the opinions of others, it is important to discover some of the reasons for the strange differences. Some of the reasons why people do not all think alike are because of:

1. The accident of birthplace.
2. Differences in home training.
3. Differences in formal education.
4. Association with differing strong personalities.
5. Permanent mental and spiritual influence of certain personalities in history and in literature.

6. Association of certain subjects or ideas, especially in youth, with a deep, heart-stirring emotion.

7. The wide variation in the "authorities" that affect our judgment.

8. The difference in the evidence from (a) printed words, (b) from intimate association with those holding certain views.

9. The natural, continued intensity of attention and memory regarding the things we approve.

10. Our constant, unconscious acceptance of alleged confirmations of our own views, or unconscious rejection of evidence that is in conflict with our opinions.

11. Our predisposition, prejudice, and whims as affected by, and growing out of, sex, disposition, race, color, social status, occupation, governmental surroundings, social conditions, health, physical characteristics.

12. Obstinacy, hypocrisy, self-deception or intellectual insincerity.

13. Ignorance.

When we consider all these varied influences on the mind of man, caution teaches that arguments should be made with a recognition of the fact that every hearer is uncontrolably a bundle of prejudices, and that the entrances to his mind on many questions are partially, if not altogether, closed. Before new ideas can be put in, it is necessary to get old ideas out.

Sincere differences of opinion by those of equal intelligence and who have access to the same information, are partially accounted for by the principle underlying the somewhat surprising contention that the intellect is subordinate to the will and the emotions. If this contention is correct then those who differ from us may be neither ignorant nor dishonest, and we, who differ from them, may also be sincere even if we are in error. Whether or not we admit it, we all are strongly inclined to put intellect in a subordinate position in many of our supposed rational judgments.

Man has a most extraordinary capacity for believing what he wants to believe. The fact is that any argument as presented to others or to us is at once either weakened or enforced by memories, experiences, emotions, or prejudices that often are entirely beyond control. The will at once modifies belief by the interpretation and emphasis it puts upon testimony of any kind on any subject. What in others may seem to us, or in us may seem to them, to be mere unreasoning prejudice is a mixture of information, sentiment, tradition, and emotion, which in combination powerfully affects judgment. We must all frankly confess that many of our opinions are what they are simply because we were born at a certain place at a certain time.

By a course of training the intellect can thus in considerable degree be brought under the control of the will. This is the kind of training in intensive advocacy that tends to develop marked credulity in certain members of the legal profession. Because their desire to believe develops their ability to believe, their minds unconsciously become warped. Many of these men become at least partially disqualified to recognize inherent improbability in any statement of alleged facts or occurrences. Arguments by men with this weakness usually consist only of unsupported assertions and their powers of persuasion are of a very low order.

Effective persuasion anticipates these various possible existing adverse ideas and illogical objections, and not only presents the facts upon which belief is to be based, but, to some extent, also answers the unconscious objections arrayed against the contention that are already in the mind of the hearer. The skilful advocate remembers that man is only partially rational.

The citadel of the mind may be captured in more ways than one, but an entrance is not often gained without a proper approach. The first sentence of an argument is often the most important sentence because it is the first. By it interest is kindled, suspicion removed, and confidence awakened; or, on the other hand, antagonism is aroused and a prejudice created that it is difficult to overcome. The mind opens or shuts according to the hailing signs given, and the truth itself may be told in such a way that it is not believed.

A familiar acquaintance with Plato, and that famous old teacher of his, has helped many who would learn to persuade and to reason about things; and full of wise suggestions is Franklin's quaint recital in his autobiography of how he improved himself in the art of leading others to his way of thinking. These men teach that often the most effective part of an argument is a skilful inquiry, a Socratic question, that penetrates to the heart of a subject and puts in operation the receiving mind that is being worked upon; then a definite statement with just the proper emphasis gains admission almost unawares, and an idea is planted in the mind of another.

The skilful pleader does not often find it advisable to attempt to force an idea full grown and complete into the mind of another. He plants it by skilful suggestion and then nurtures it with rich words until it develops into a mature thought in the mind of the hearer. Antony's funeral oration is a masterpiece of suggestion and persuasion. The other extreme of undue caution is sometimes fatal to success, and the mental fort is not captured because a too long and circuitous line of attack was followed.

The speaker who is to carry conviction must also correctly adjust the emphasis of his language to the topic he is discussing and to the capacity of his hearers. Belief and unbelief are no doubt greatly affected by control and by excess of emphasis. One of the common indications of insincerity in the salesman and the legal pleader is undue and improperly placed emphasis. The successful speaker is earnest when earnestness is proper, but we at once recognize the weakness in one who "doth protest too much." If, however, the conditions warrant emphasis and strong statement, then the absence of these qualities is unnatural and suspicious. When a man's character is impugned and he answers as he would if asked the time of day, we are inclined to infer that there is some basis for suspicion as to his past.

Another obstacle to success in persuasion and one of the conspicuous faults of advocacy is the leaving in the mind of the hearer the suspicion that the evidence is not all in, that there is in fact something vital yet to be said on the other side of the question. In order to be conclusive an argument must take some account of the opposition. As long as the hearer suspects that there is information not supplied he is in a state of doubt and thus is partly prepared to be convinced that the contention of the opposition is correct.

Some consideration of the claims of the opposition also is necessary in order that an argument, especially the argument of the advocate, should not lack the important elements of frankness and fairness. Lacking these two qualities an otherwise quite perfect argument will often fail to persuade. If it appears that one does not dare to consider an opponent's point of view, the necessary inference is that he has some doubt about the strength of his own contention. The quality and force of an argument on any question can be measured quite accurately by the character of the consideration given to opposing evidence. The tendency of narrow-minded advocacy is to ignore, belittle, or deny the value of all opposing testimony. This is not usually good generalship on any field, unless the antagonist actually deserves such treatment and this can be made apparent. Opposition is not often made contemptuous by merely calling it so.

Even though it may be erroneous, or even corrupt, opposing testimony, or argument, that has made an impression must be met in some way, and, as a rule, it must be discounted by something more than the mere statement of a partisan advocate, no matter how loud, or long, or violent the statement is. One of the common fallacies of advocacy is the notion that strong testimony can be destroyed by weak argument. This exaggeration of the force of an advocate's mere statements often is one of the contributing causes of defeat. He cannot persuade a jury that they have not heard certain testimony.

An argument may now and then persuade a jury that their view of the case already formed is incorrect, but not often, and many cases are lost because vital matters are "left for argument" that should have received earlier and more effective attention. If damaging testimony could be destroyed by simply saying loudly that it is not true, the trial of a case would be very much simplified. If an argument can be made which shows clearly the inherent weakness of opposing testimony, or shows its contradications, and especially if this argument is made by an attorney who has not himself weakened the force of his own statements by his constant exhibition of partisanship and insincerity, then opposing weak, erroneous, or corrupt testimony can be successfully attacked by argument.

Unless the facts warrant the statement, it is unwise to contend that there is practically no opposing testimony that deserves consideration. According to some advocates all opposing testimony in every case is "a tissue of lies without a scintilla of truth". This word "scintilla" is another word without which some men would find it difficult to practice law. These pleaders "challenge the opposition" to do this and do that and "demand a verdict", and, no matter what the opposing testimony has been, ask for "a rebuke of unwarranted and unblushing perjury". Unfortunately verdicts in some jurisdictions are occasionally jammed through and won by these methods, but they certainly are often lost.

The natural effect of this ultra partisan attitude is the opposite of persuasion, and jurors are led to put no credit whatever in the statements of an attorney who is obviously unfair if not actually dishonest. With an intelligent jury, or even with a jury made up only in part of intelligent men, it is best in attempting to persuade them to assume that they are at least fairly intelligent instead of treating them as though they could not see, could not hear, could not remember, and could not reason.

It is ridiculous to attempt to bring a hearer to the point of persuasion by compulsion and it is not an intelligent act by one who seeks to lead another to his own point of view to attempt to ram arguments down the throat of his unwilling victim. The attorney who is sure of his own ground often finds it advisable not to approach opposing testimony by assuming that all adverse witnesses are either scoundrels who have committed perjury, or feeble-minded babblers. Plain words should be spoken when they are justified, but one who uses "blunderbus" abuse is quite sure to get somewhat spattered himself. The most persuasive argument on any subject, in which the one making the argument has a clear and sound basis for his own contention, includes a proper consideration of the claims of the opposition followed by a strong argument for his own contention. If a lawyer has no case, and is against both the law and the facts, he naturally is inclined to admit nothing and claim everything, but fortunately he is not thus likely to deceive many.

CHAPTER VII.

"OFF THE RECORD" INFLUENCES IN TRIALS AT LAW AND VERDICTS, COMPROMISES AND SETTLEMENTS.

A frequent occurrence in the closing of estates that undoubtedly encourages fraud is the immediate secret compromising of fraudulent claims. The crude quality of many forgeries indicates quite conclusively that the claimant had anticipated that the case would be "settled out of court". When investigated and illustrated, many documents in these cases are shown to be so palpably fraudulent that it is surprising that anyone would have had the audacity to bring them out into the light, and it is clearly evident that they were not prepared for a trial, but for a settlement.

The conditions surrounding a claim against an estate, the sympathy and prejudice that it may be possible to enlist in behalf of a fraudulent claimant, as well as the nature of the claim itself, must, of course, all be taken into account if a settlement is under consideration. In some cases there is indirect and ingenious suggestion of blackmail, sometimes amounting to an attack, not only on the living, but upon the memory of the honored dead, all looking toward quick settlement of the fraudulent claim behind closed doors.

Under some conditions the mere bringing of a claim into court by a certain claimant has in effect a suggestion of blackmail. Frantic efforts are sometimes made to keep a matter of this kind hidden, and the tendency of some relatives is to offer money at once. There are also selfish heirs in nearly every will case who are anxious to have fraudulent claims of almost any kind promptly paid in order to prevent any delay in getting the great or small bequest that is coming to them. In some instances this compromising with fraud, which is practically known to be fraud, almost amounts to a participation in it, a performance known to the law as the compounding of a felony. These hasty and unwise settlements are an encouragement to other fraudulent claimants of all kinds to go and do likewise.

Prompt and vigorous opposition to what is no doubt fraudulent is in the end almost always the best method of procedure. Nothing so terrorizes fraudulent claimants, who bring forward a forged claim paper, as the demand for immediate, careful examination and thorough photographic illustration of the document. They who know a document is fraudulent are its most severe critics, and with a criminal fear no doubt imagine that enlarged photographs will be even more effective in exposing fraud than they possibly can be. A just claim should of course be paid, but the paying of fraudulent claims is nearly always an unwise proceeding especially if the purpose is to hide the fact that a claim has been made. In the end nothing is usually hidden, and whispered gossip regarding what is apparently suppressed is many times worse than open publication.

The ordeal of a trial is sometimes naturally dreaded even by the party who will probably win. Those with even a little experience know that a trial at law is not always a calm, friendly, judicial proceeding devoted entirely to the mere discovery and proof of the facts, but is sometimes an undertaking where prejudice, venom, family jealousy and envy are given free play. In a law suit over an estate, relatives, friends, and neighbors often are arrayed in two warring camps, actuated by selfish interests and bitter prejudice. Under these circumstances when disputed documents represent claims against estates, and prejudice and sympathy are with the fraudulent claimant, it often becomes necessary to show the facts with the utmost clearness and force, for the reason that in the background there are influences outside of the evidence that strongly tend to affect a verdict. These outside influences are often skilfully arrayed in order to force an immediate settlement and under some circumstances settlement is no doubt advisable.

The cautious attorney in any case carefully considers the question of all "off the record" influences. Mr. Prejudice and Miss Sympathy are the names of two witnesses whose testimony is not recorded, but nevertheless must often be reckoned with in a trial at law. The influence of these two silent, but powerful forces unfortunately affects not alone the witness stand, but the counsel table, the jury box, and the bench. There are really few trials in which elements do not enter that have a tendency to affect the decision in some measure which certainly are not evidence. The lawyer should learn what they are and prepare to meet them, or see to it that his case does not reach the stage of actual trial.

In some of these cases there is sympathy for the claimant who is a relative, friend, or old employee. In other cases it is some poor woman, or needy man, who presents a claim paper against a rich estate and it can sometimes be shown that there is some moral justification for the claim. Sometimes also, because of the parsimony, neglect, or partiality of a decedent, there is strong prejudice against his wishes, and this feeling has potent influence upon those who must render a verdict. The faithful old servant, or hardworking relative, forgotten or ignored, sometimes finds it comparatively easy to collect a claim based on a written document which should be looked at only in dim twilight. All these influences make it more difficult to prove the facts. In connection with many of these cases, although the contention is not openly made, there is prevalent a strong undercurrent of feeling and whispered talk that the claimant "ought to have the money". These powerful forces in some unknown way often seep through the walls of a court-house and reach a jury.

Then again, it is the poor man against the rich corporation, or the individual against his wealthy relatives. In cases of this kind it may, as suggested, sometimes be advisable to compromise the matter, but if the claim is actually fraudulent, thorough investigation many times discloses the most surprising and conclusive evidences of fraud that at first were entirely hidden. It is practically impossible to make presumptuous fraud both invisible and consistent with known facts. Many claims by caretakers, nurses, doctors, and distant relatives, based on written contracts, are ridiculously excessive, and when carefully investigated are often shown to be palpably fraudulent.

The mere appearance of a claimant sometimes has a bearing on the result of litigation. The weeping woman, and also the attractive woman who does not weep, often are most effective "exhibits", stronger than any opposing testimony, and the weeping and the smiling acts are sometimes very skilfully staged. There are jurisdictions where an important preliminary detail of a law suit is the arranging of matters so that a case will, or will not, be brought before a particular tribunal. All these indirect influences have force and bearing depending somewhat upon whether the case is to go before an experienced, capable judge or an ordinary jury.

It is usually the desire of a fraudulent claimant and his attorney to get a case before a jury, and it is often with a sinking heart that a litigant with a good case looks at a jury that has been selected to decide a matter of almost life and death importance to him. Those who are against the facts and seek to deceive and mislead endeavor to excuse every capable juryman that by any means can be eliminated, until in some cases the jury is made up of men who are not qualified. The certainty of a just decision in many cases requires the ability to understand, interpret, and weigh conflicting testimony, which can be done only by those with intelligence and experience.

The successful administration of justice in jury trials depends upon the joint activity of the judge, the jury, and the advocate, and a weakness in any one of the three elements often destroys the effectiveness of all. If an unqualified jury is called upon to decide a case, then, for that case at least, the value of all legal experience, the aid of libraries, the benefits of law courses and law reforms may all come to nought, and knowledge, skill, and long and careful preparation may all be as if they were not.

In many important cases the only standard required for jury duty is that jurymen should not know certain things. If justice is to be promoted by the aid of juries, there should not simply be a standard of ignorance, but a standard of intelligence. A reform in this matter should go back to the initial selection of candidates and all should be excused who do not come up to a certain required standard of intelligence and experience. If candidates for jury duty are selected because their services are worth nothing anywhere else, their services as jurymen will be of about the same value, with the danger of doing serious and permanent injustice. There are cities where notoriously poor juries are called upon to decide cases, and other cities and courts where juries are qualified to assist in promoting justice. In spite of all the difficulties, however, juries usually decide cases right, but sometimes the problem is too difficult for them, especially if made still more difficult by an unfair advocate whose constant effort is to deceive and mislead. It is fortunate that on every jury there are likely to be at least a few fair, practical, hard-headed men, unfamiliar with the niceties of hair-splitting legal excuses and explanations, not warped by the sort of credulity developed in many instances by that phase of law practice which in an eager manner seeks some remote excuse, or incredible explanation, to stand against the most obvious condition of facts.

As heretofore pointed out, a disputed document trial is of the nature of a scientific investigation carried on in court, and to rely upon a jury, as sometimes made up in a case of this kind, is but little more than an uncertain lottery. These twelve men of a jury may possess any of the possible varying strengths and weaknesses of human nature. It is upon this twelve-keyed instrument that those who have to do with courts play with varying skill and somewhat uncertain results. It is well known that this instrument of justice is a decidedly human tribunal and many strange incidents are related regarding the methods employed in the jury room in reaching a verdict.

There are several classes of complicated cases involving technical details, books and accounts that are wisely put into the hands of qualified, experienced referees who hear the evidence, carefully study the subject, and make a finding. Many times it would be in the interest of justice if important disputed document cases could be disposed of in this manner, or by three judges sitting as a trial court. This latter procedure has been followed in some important cases with most satisfactory results.

If a case is to be taken before a jury, it is then, of course, necessary to consider the nature and quality of the jury that will probably be selected and to determine, if possible, how they will be likely to be affected by the nature of the claim and the character and personality of the claimant. The intelligent and cautious attorney thinks of all these varied influences that are to be brought to bear, and prepares for trial accordingly, or seeks the most favorable settlement he can obtain.

Unconscious prejudice against a claimant may arise simply because of his appearance or nationality. Even some peculiar mannerism in speech, attitude, or gesture arouses a prejudice that affects a verdict. Many an honest client with a good case has lost through the unfortunate and unintended effect of his own testimony that was not frank and convincing. Prejudice also sometimes arises because an attorney himself is under suspicion and bears an unsavory reputation in the community in which he lives. It is sometimes suspected with good reason that he goes out and procures in some manner, either good or bad, what testimony he needs, and under these conditions entirely honest testimony naturally is weakened when presented by an attorney of this kind. It is obvious that part of the client's preparation for trial is the selection of an attorney who will not bring discredit upon a good case.

One argument actually advanced for the continuance of the jury system is that juries will consider conditions and circumstances outside of the evidence and base decisions thereon. This is, of course, always a dangerous tendency, and yet, as long as human nature remains as it is, these "off the record" influences will undoubtedly continue to affect court judgments. And there are, no doubt, some cases where a decision based strictly upon the facts and evidence alone is perhaps too severe, even if in accordance with the facts and the strict rules of law. Some of the unfortunate precedents, as recorded in opinions, have resulted from cases in which the judgment was, no doubt in some measure, based on sympathy and matters "off the record". Unfortunately general principles are sometimes distorted to serve a particular end. Unwise precedents of this kind may serve as obstructions in the path of justice for many years and be quoted hundreds of times by those who defend error.

Successful appeals are sometimes made to what is called the "higher law" with most disgraceful results, emphasizing, however, the fact that court decisions, which must come through human agencies, are subject to influences of many kinds which cannot be ignored by the careful attorney. The great book of human nature deserves the constant and careful study of the lawyer who would fully prepare himself for his important work.

Especially with certain claimants strong and unmistakable proof and confirmation are necessary in order to restrain sympathetic and susceptible triers of the facts from "doing substantial justice" in spite of the facts. The uncertainty of a verdict grows out of all of these surrounding conditions, more or less hidden and unknown, which have a most forceful bearing upon the result of the trial. Jurymen may sometimes look one side and, in effect at least, "make a will for the decedent in the jury room", and distribute the property as they think it ought to be distributed.

A highly important part of the preparation of a good case by lawyer and client is to anticipate, carefully weigh, and definitely prepare for every one of these "off the record" influences that may affect the verdict. One way of meeting the question in certain cases is to make an open, frank avowal of the danger. When the door is thus opened it may then be possible to meet sympathy with sympathy and thus weaken or nullify an adverse influence. It is sometimes unsafe to ignore the whole subject and to try for a verdict on the cold facts alone when opposed, it may be, by powerful sympathy. If the questions of sympathy and prejudice are to be considered at any time it is usually advisable to bring out the fact in connection with the evidence.

It may be too late to wait until his final argument to warn against the danger of these various influences. The challenge is sometimes thrown down with effect at the very beginning of the case by the experienced attorney, who even in his first examination of prospective jurymen, admits by the nature of his questions that two of his invisible and powerful opponents in the case are prejudice and sympathy. By this stand he is sometimes able to counteract in some measure the effect of that which the opposition had been confidently depending upon, but intended to bring into the case by indirect and stealthy methods.

The lawyer who is fully aware of all the conditions sometimes says in argument:

"I would be stupid indeed if I did not recognize some of the indirect influences at work and relied upon by the opposition in this case, but I ask that this case be decided on the evidence. I know what it is easy to think and what one at first may possibly be inclined to think, but I ask you as honest men to cast all indirect and improper influences aside and do justice. I ask you to overcome what may be natural tendencies and decide this case on its merits. It often takes courage to do right, but I have confidence that justice will be done here. I thus speak plainly that I may be correctly understood."

There are conditions when it may be unwise to refer

in this way directly to the matter. Some things cannot be talked about. Although these adverse influences that tend to affect a verdict are often weakened in force by open discussion, this brave act requires delicate skill and an exact appreciation of the atmosphere of the trial. The uttering of one bungling sentence, or even the placing of one wrong emphasis, may lead to defeat.

In effect, these words have been said in cases where indirect forces were being relied upon by the opposition:

"Many arguments have been made attacking the system of trial by jury on the ground that juries are swayed by other matters than evidence and that the interests of justice are not safe in their hands. As is well understood, evidence is presented in a court of law in order that the truth may be proved and in order that justice may prevail for the protection of society and the guarding of human rights. This source of danger from outside influences creeps stealthily into trials when, by indirect and ingenious methods and misleading arguments, appeals are made to the feelings instead of to the judgment of a jury. Now and then these methods succeed. If they succeeded generally then it were just as well to close the courthouses, and when a verdict is against the evidence then a court of justice is closed.

Some matters are in this case, and have been brought into this case, *that do not grow out of the evidence.* They were brought in here with the hope that you men can be led to do what ought not to be done. These outside influences are appeals to weaknesses and not to intelligence and judgment, and they will not prevail when their purpose and its significance are clearly understood."

In some disputed document trials one of the allies of sympathy and prejudice is erroneous, or corrupt, expert testimony. As pointed out in a previous chapter, this testimony is not usually put into a case to prove the point at issue, but simply to furnish an excuse for disregarding opposing correct testimony. When this is the fact it should be made clear to court and jury. The condition has thus been discussed:

"We have in this case a disagreement in the expert testimony. Some of this testimony must be either erroneous or dishonest and is here either through incompetence or perjury. That last word must be spoken, for it is clearly dishonest to call dishonesty the truth. The effort has been made to lead you to think that this astonishing expert testimony opposed to our contention has been put into this case to prove something, but that is not the fact. You should clearly know that this is not its purpose, but it is hoped, and we think vainly hoped, that by this dishonest conflict you will be led, not to consider the expert testimony in any way and will then decide the case, not on the evidence, but on certain timidly but ingeniously suggested reasons that those opposed to us do not put into plain words and put before you. This appeal to possible hidden motives is simply bolstered up in a weak and vicious way by this alleged expert testimony that it would be too magnanimous to call only erroneous. We ask you to examine and consider all of this so-called "conflicting testimony" for yourselves and when you do we are sure you will understand why this "conflict" has been brought about. You will find the real conflict is one merely of opinions and not of the reasons for the opinions, for those against us have given no reasons that are worthy of serious consideration".

CHAPTER VIII.

SYSTEM, METHODS, AND TENDENCIES.

Always in a criminal trial, and often in an ordinary law suit, it is necessary for one party to prove a fact, or series of facts, upon which a verdict or judgment is to be based, while the principal efforts of the opposition are directed, not to the proving of anything, but to the prevention of proof. Among the weapons of those who would prevent proof are confusion, complications, and delay.

Even limited experience shows how those arrayed against the facts are greatly assisted in their efforts to befog and confuse when methods and details of presentation of a case are not carefully arranged. Some lawyers spend a large part of their time in court on things that should have been done before coming there, and often acquire a hectic, worried, and petulant manner that lowers their own efficiency as well as that of all who work with them. While great issues are not won simply by attention to unimportant details, it is a fact that defeat is sometimes partly due to lack of attention to certain comparatively unimportant matters. The loss of the traditional horseshoe nail often leads to a loss of greater consequence.

Many lawyers are unnecessarily handicapped because they never have learned how to keep documents and memoranda so they can be found quickly. The care, custody, and filing of papers is an incidental but necessary part of all law practice. Lawyers' office desks and their counsel tables at a trial are often veritable rats' nests. Much valuable time in court and elsewhere is spent in looking for things, and their own time and the time and patience of the court and jury are thus wasted, and then often that which is sought is not found, or is found too late to be of service. Astute opponents sometimes take advantage of this unfortunate failing in an adversary and keep him looking for things much of the time.

In an important case the filing and custody of papers should be put into the hands of a trained clerk who should be responsible for them. The system followed should not be so complicated that the system itself wastes time, but there should be a system and it should be followed. The mere employment of suitable strong envelopes for exhibits, properly indexed, numbered, and arranged, in which papers may all be kept unfolded, may save hours of time in a trial involving many documents. Time is saved wherever they are to be handled if documents are all filed unfolded. There should be a law requiring that all public record documents should be filed unfolded.

For some unknown reason, lawyers seem to have a natural impulse to pile things up so that they hide each other until all is confusion and chaos. Their papers often are filed in heaps. Naturally, the papers in the latest matter are thus filed on the top of the heap, and if someone inadvertently turns the pile over it almost becomes necessary to adjourn court. There are many offices that are examples of how an office should not be kept. A good system of filing for any office will save time and vital energy to be devoted to more important things than the looking for that which is lost. Simple and effective filing systems are available, and those who sell the filing cases will willingly give valuable assistance. This matter is deemed of sufficient importance so that a committee of the Illinois Bar Association has been appointed to report on suitable business systems for law offices.

An important detail in a trial, by which time is saved and confusion avoided, is the correct marking of exhibits. It is unfortunate and unnecessary for lawyers and witnesses to lose time and patience in court looking for illegible numbers of exhibits placed at diverse and inappropriate places on papers. Some stenographers use a big, clumsy rubber stamp for marking exhibits, which defaces every paper upon which it is used. If a stamp is to be used it should be not larger than about one inch by three-fourths of an inch in size. The trial attorney should superintend this whole operation of marking exhibits so that the marks are legible and easily found and so that when papers are numerous the marking itself tends to avoid confusion and error.

It saves much time if exhibits, as far as possible, are all marked at the same place on the sheet; on the lower left-hand corner of the face of the first page, or on the upper right-hand or left-hand side of the same page, but in some fixed position, always avoiding, of course, the defacing of a signature or writing with the exhibit number. The marking should be small and perfectly legible. If a stenographer cannot make legible letters and figures he should learn to make them and then should always take time enough to make them. Many stenographers grab a paper offered as an exhibit and scrawl with a pencil a few illegible letters and figures on it that causes a loss of ten times as much time as it would have taken to mark the paper legibly in the right place.

It is often a great help in an important and complicated case to number the plaintiff's exhibits from one upward, for example, and the defendant's exhibits beginning with two hundred or five hundred, depending upon how many the plaintiff offers. If this method is followed the number alone at once distinguishes an exhibit as plaintiff's or defendant's, and all are then easily identified and assorted. Numbers are better than letters as they are not exhausted no matter how many exhibits are admitted.

In an important trial involving many exhibits the trial attorney saves much time and greatly adds to his own efficiency by learning the numbers of all the frequently used exhibits. Some attorneys fumble over every paper referred to through a long trial, even "Exhibit A", looking for the exhibit number, when these few important numbers could be memorized in a few minutes of close attention.

. . . . . .

The fact that the law is based upon matters connected with the past may perhaps partly account for the accumulation of old junk in law offices. It often appears in material things, as well as in legal matters, that the place itself is related to ancient days. This connection with times gone by perhaps gives a sense of permanence and reliability that otherwise might be absent, but it also suggests bankruptcy and the sheriff. Unfortunately current affairs and live issues may be hindered and hidden by old dead things that are strewn about, as well as by some of the old dead matters in the books on the shelves.

Even in a modern building, and in an otherwise well-furnished office, the old useless things sometimes abound. Old framed certificates and dusty pictures with straggling wires lean against the wall, an old battered papier-mache court exhibit that resembles a broken leg, a pitcher with handle broken off, and an old soiled dictionary with one cover gone, are grouped on a corner table. An old chair with one weak leg holds a blackened heap of worthless old magazines and papers; old bottles with faded labels, rickety boxes, useless old catalogues and ancient calendars with agricultural views, all links to the past, are on every side. An old pigeon-hole frame stuffed with ancient debris is in the corner, and rows of dust-covered, broken-backed old books lean in a weary sort of way upon each other on the sagging shelves, and appear to have been unopened for years. The whole combination is suggestive of a garret rather than a modern laboratory where live questions are given scientific, careful attention.

Lack of order in material things may not indicate that the same qualities will appear in other things, but a brief in its disorder and incompleteness may be much like the cluttered office from which it came. Where cobwebs cover things they are also likely to cover ideas. There are law offices where, in some ways at least, a fire would not be altogether a calamity.

. . . .

The proof of the facts in a disputed document case is made more difficult if documents to be compared with each other are fastened together permanently, as they often are in signed depositions. But few observers can properly compare two things which cannot be put close together and looked at at the same time. If disputed exhibits and standards are scattered through a series of depositions in which the sheets are all fastened together, it sometimes is impossible to prove the facts for the reason that their real significance cannot be seen and understood. In cases of this kind permission should be obtained to take out the various exhibits and mark them appropriately so that they can be grouped, arranged, and compared in an effective manner. In some of these cases it is helpful, where photographs cannot be made, to arrange and fasten the various papers on a small drawing board with the signatures to be examined all close together in order of dates.

In arranging signatures of this kind for study, or to be photographed, the paper should be folded *above* the signature instead of below it. If the signature of the earliest date is put at the top and then the paper is folded just above the next signature it can be put close to, and directly under the first one, and so on until they are all arranged. It is usually best not to fold a disputed document in any new way, or trim, or mark, or cut, or pin, or paste it, or change it in any manner whatever. It should be kept flat between celluloid covers where it will be properly protected at all times.

. . . . . .

Where a great number of standard signatures are available confusion may result if too many are put in evidence. A sufficient number, nearest in date to the disputed documents, should be used to show the characteristics of the writing examined and the extent of its variation. It is seldom desirable to use more than from twenty to fifty signatures, excepting in certain unusual cases where it may be desirable to make a historical study of a handwriting. In many cases a few good signatures of the right date, a dozen or even less, are all that are necessary.

It is proper to photograph with signatures the dates they bear, or a brief description of what they are, but it is objectionable to put on the photographs a written or typewritten description of their purpose, or a designation, by marks or otherwise, of what it is claimed they prove. Photographs of this kind, improperly marked, if objected to may be excluded as prejudicial. It is permissible to photograph signatures under ruled squares to show damaging identity of traced signatures with each other or with a model, or make prints on transparent films, so they can be superimposed.

Illustrative photographs are more useful when properly grouped and arranged for easy comparison, so that they will not become cumbersome and unwieldy and thus cause confusion. Where a disputed signature is to be compared in natural size and in enlarged form with a number of photographed signatures, the disputed signature may appear in permanent form in connection with the standard signatures in a properly arranged album, and duplicate photographs of the disputed signature, in natural size and enlarged, can be printed on separate, loose prints so that they can be moved from place to place and compared side by side with any of the other signatures. These separate photographs can be kept in an envelope or pocket attached to the inside of the cover of the album.

. . . . . .

The whole subject of investigation, with its methods and its emphasis, is an important part of preparation for law practice. Old Samuel Johnson's wise remark about knowledge has some bearing on the matter. He said, "There are two kinds of knowledge; actual knowledge and potential knowledge; actual knowledge is the knowing of a thing; potential knowledge is knowing where you can find out about it". Even those with but little experience know that law suits have been lost because of undiscovered favorable evidence and even of helpful law not found. Although these aids lay only just beyond the horizon of the attorney's narrow field of inquiry, for all practical purposes they were as far away as if hidden in Timbuctoo. As a rule, success in these various quests is more the result of industry than of intuition or of genius, although there are practitioners who seem to have developed a kind of second sight that enables them to find the facts and the law that are necessary to success. Thorough investigation usually discloses, however, that their trained intuition is the result of intense thought, patient effort, and long experience.

Success in all these phases of investigation is promoted by setting down in black and white a systematic, detailed list of every probable and possible source of information. It is then often helpful to discuss all these subjects with those who possibly may throw even the faintest light upon the matter. When we talk about a subject to another we ourselves often think of things that never would have arisen in our minds if we had remained silent. Silence may sometimes be golden, but it is also sometimes stupid.

An attorney's study of this matter of intelligent and systematic investigation may also enable him to discover the shortcomings of, or perhaps stimulate a special investigator who, of course, ought to be an adept in the matter, but who often is not. In this special field many otherwise intelligent persons are not brilliant; they, like some who pose as detectives, can hardly find the post-office. Incompetent investigators often hopelessly bungle cases. A part of the attorney's business is to find out first whether or not they are honest and then whether or not they know anything

This subject of scientific investigation is connected with the practice of law in many ways, and it would be well if it could receive some attention in connection with the lawyer's preparation. The attorney who aims to become a real scientific student of his subject will be helped by reading at least the first part of the little book, "Thomson's Introduction to Science", and some of the chapters written by the great scientists with a view of learning how the real searchers after truth go about the task.

For the purpose of stimulating the faculties of observation, as well as for the study of methods by which correct inferences are drawn from the most obscure facts, some benefit, as well as entertainment, can be obtained by the reading of good detective stories. This latter suggestion should, however, be accompanied with the warning of the danger of developing that superficial detective state of mind which tends to make everything the basis of suspicion.

. . . . . .

In a trial at law it is impossible for one always to gauge accurately the weight and significance of evidence, or of prejudice, on another's mind, and the only safe method is to underestimate one's own appeals and all the time recognize and appreciate to the full the efforts of the opposition and the possible force of unknown influences. The alert tactitian is not satisfied with a mere preponderance of proof, but endeavors to overwhelm opposition; nor does he count the victory won until the end of the conflict. It is well to remember the ancient admonition, "Let not him that girdeth on his harness boast himself as he that putteth it off". When it is seen that an adversary is leaving nothing undone, is providing for every possible contingency, this thoroughness itself has a tendency to disconcert and weaken those against whom it is aimed. Fortune not only favors the brave, but also the prepared.

The careful attorney does not forget that a condition, in the practice of the law as well as in athletics, that sometimes contributes to disaster, is an over-confidence that relaxes vigilance and weakens effort. When a contest seems to be entirely won is the time the great general brings up the reserves and makes assurance doubly sure. Unwise praise, or little successes along the way, sometimes tend to develop an unwise optimism and encourage a mental attitude unfitted to resist the final attack of a vigilant and prepared opponent who takes advantage of every opportunity and to the end puts his whole weight into the contest.

There is, however, now and then a good case that cannot be won. There are guilty defendants that juries will not convict and there are civil cases in which it is almost impossible to secure a verdict in harmony with the facts. Defeat in these cases should not lead to pessimism or melancholy. Nor, on the contrary, should failure be too quickly excused and forgotten. A valuable lesson of experience is that gained through the discipline of defeat. A wise man knows that he cannot always be successful, but when he fails, he stares the fact full in the face and tries to learn its lesson. There are those who learn nothing from defeat, while with others a defeat is a preparation for a greater victory. To the strong defeat often is a wholesome stimulus, a challenge to greater effort, but to the weak it is sometimes only a bitter discouragement leading to futile excuses and weakening pessimism. When defeat leads even to partial belief in the existence of that ill-starred goddess called luck, it is indeed a disaster.

The strong man's attitude toward defeat is first one of inquiry as to the causes, direct and indirect, and then the seeking out of every means to prevent its recurrence. With the brave and the virile the matter is taken up in almost an impersonal manner. The purpose of the inquiry is not to find excuses, but to prepare more fully for the next encounter. Out of the depths of bitter disappointment may arise qualities that in the end command the highest success. Man is often admonished not to believe too much in himself, but a too limited belief is almost a death warrant.

Without self-respect, and a justified pride, and a reasonable measure of self-confidence, a man is unfitted to meet the stern realities of life. There are weak souls, apparently fitted only to take orders and work under direction, to whom defeat is deadening. The brave soul is sometimes cast down, but is not in despair. It is even possible for him to be of that number who, as Emerson says, "rises refreshed at a threat".

. . . . . .

The excitement, the strain, and the importance of the questions involved, often render it difficult in the midst of a trial to reach a calm, reasoned conclusion regarding some important matter that must be decided. The question may be one as to trial policy, as to the settlement of the case, as to the advisability of calling a particular witness, as to the wisdom of raising some fundamental objection, or making some fundamental admission, and an error in judgment may be a disaster. The strenuous atmosphere of a trial is not conducive to rational judgments on all questions, especially when infused with the spirit of contest. One who is called upon to make such a decision does well, if possible, to seek advice and seclusion and consider the question calmly from every possible standpoint. Looking back at a trial it is too often necessary to say, "We made a mistake at that point". No one is infallible, but there are certain conditions that tend toward error and one of these conditions is this atmosphere of strain and excitement. Sometimes a decision must be made at once, but often there is time for conference and careful review of the whole evidence. The advice of one entirely outside the controversy, who is in no degree influenced by the surrounding conditions, may be of great value.

There are many public offices, especially district attorney's offices and offices of certain other officials and special committees, where, on account of the confusion, the noise, the lack of system, the hurry, the insistent telephone, and the petty details, it is simply impossible to apply to a subject consecutive, effective thought. It is not surprising that in these places work is done in a slipshod manner; that plans, policies, and methods are often wrong; that important matters are neglected or never discovered, and that defeat is the frequent, if not the natural, result. There seems to be something in human nature that makes it difficult, if not impossible, to conduct public business as efficiently as private business.

. . . . . .

Many disputed document questions, as well as other classes of litigation, arise in regard to books and papers connected with the subject of bookkeeping. This is a subject so frequently considered in general litigation that a trial attorney does well to acquire a knowledge of it as a part of his general preparation for law practice. If he does not understand the principles of bookkeeping he can go to night school, if necessary, until he acquires that knowledge. One who has seen the experiment tried knows that even with a skilful accountant at his elbow he cannot properly try a case involving accountancy problems if he is ignorant of the principles of the subject. Questions of fact frequently arise involving the principles of accountancy that the attorney cannot discuss, or even consider, until he deliberately informs himself on the technical subject. He must know what a "trial balance" is, and debit and credit must have accurate and definite meaning to him. A knowledge of the general principles of the subject can be acquired in a short time and will certainly assist a trial attorney in many cases.

. . . . . .

The subject of note taking in court is a matter of sufficient importance to warrant some attention by a law student. With many attorneys the unskilful effort to make voluminous notes prevents them from hearing the testimony and learning what is being done. The poorest note taker usually is the one who makes the fullest notes. One cannot listen intently and grasp the essential ideas and delicate qualities of any discourse while frantically trying to write down in illegible long hand what a speaker says. Another objection to note taking is that it prevents a hearer from looking at a speaker. It is surprising how much of the real meaning and significance of spoken language is lost if the speaker cannot be seen.

A lawyer who is to cross-examine a witness should perhaps now and then write down a few words, but hardly more than that. These words merely suggest ideas that should receive attention. Many of the best cross-examiners do not make a mark on a piece of paper, but are able to go back and review every significant part of the testimony. The human memory can be trained to an almost unlimited extent and one way to weaken it is to make it depend upon incomplete, illegible and incorrect notes.

. . . . . .

One of the common weaknesses in cross-examination is the failure to appreciate the importance of climaxes. If a crucial question covering an essential point comes at the end of a series of inquiries, all of which lead up to the final inquiry, the effect is not only heightened, but the witness finds it impossible to evade the question. The correct method is that followed in the Socratic Dialogues in which all the arguments which prove the final statement to be elicited from the witness himself are obtained from the witness step by step by admissions. If the witness makes every admission except the final one, which is the inevitable conclusion from the previous successive admissions, then his testimony is much weakened, if not entirely discredited. Of course, this kind of cross-examination requires careful thought and thorough preparation, and a knowledge of the subject that goes all the way through and is in direct contrast with the frequent inane "fishing excursions" that have no plan and no goal.

. . . . . .

One man on an island might have need for a technical engineer, but he would have no use for a lawyer. In many vocations relations with people are only occasional and incidental, but with the lawyer it is constant. His work, in contrast with that in many fields, with that of the engineer, for example, is largely with men and women. Their acts, their rights, their duties, their crimes, and their relations to each other, are the matters on which his business depends. Certainly with the lawyer an important part of his proper study is a study of mankind. With too many lawyers this important part of preparation apparently does not begin until the diploma is hung and the swivel-chair is bought. It should be begun sooner and should be diligently considered and studied in every possible way.

The value of experience, in some professions at least, does not depend so much on the fact that it supplies added technical knowledge, as that it furnishes opportunities for a testing of knowledge and a study of the "humanities", so-called, that develops a philosophy of life and this necessary knowledge of human nature, already referred to, that gives balance, sanity, and wisdom. Its value, therefore, depends not so much on increase in knowledge as on the weighing and appraisal of the knowledge already obtained and its application to humanity and to affairs. The highest act of wisdom is determining what is important and what is unimportant. The recent graduate would perhaps be better qualified for a technical examination on some phases of his profession than the experienced practitioner and seasoned veteran, but he lacks that testing and measuring of knowledge as applied to human affairs that only experience supplies. Knowledge of these facts regarding experience develops in the beginner that caution and appreciation of advice that tends toward avoidance of errors that may lead to humiliation and defeat.

. . . . . .

A large majority of the problems that arise in regard to disputed documents, at least ten to one, are connected with civil cases, but now and then the facts regarding a disputed document form part of the evidence in a criminal trial. Methods and proof are the same in both classes of cases, but the administration of the criminal law in the United States of America has developed certain conditions that often make it impossible to prove in a criminal case what can positively be proved in a civil case.

There are certain tendencies in this matter of the relation of law to crime that are looked upon with grave concern by all thoughtful men. A problem as old as history and as new as yesterday in all communities of the world is this problem of crime and of punishment. From the beginning it necessarily has been closely connected with the administration of the law, and much deserved criticism of the law has grown out of the error and ignorance of humanity in relation to the question, and the crude, cruel, and ineffective methods employed in dealing with this subject of crime. It always has been, and still is, a sad, disagreeable, and difficult problem of all government. The practical question is what is to be done in a practical world with those who do not play the game of life fairly, but who cheat, defraud, rob, waylay, and kill? A more fundamental and still more important problem is to learn how best to prevent or lessen crime and deter or restrain the possible criminal.

Modern civilization has come fully to realize that its first duty in the matter is to prevent, as far as is humanly possible, the development of the criminally minded by conditions of inheritance and environment. All are agreed that the most important work is this work of prevention. Whether or not crime is inherent in some individuals, it is more and more coming to be insisted upon that there must be no breeding places for crime and also fewer imported, ready-made criminals.

These are problems deserving the earnest attention of every thinking, forward-looking, loyal citizen.

It is a deplorable fact that crime exists, but unfortunately it does. Last night a brutal murder was committed on our streets, and to-night an innocent victim of the highwayman will be brutally stricken down. To-morrow's paper will give the details of blackmail and robbery. Last week these things were done and next week the work will go on, and the cool and calculating cheat, the forger, and the confidence man will take their toll of the provident and the honest. As the fact cannot be ignored that crime exists, the practical question is what is to be done about it. The answer of the past has been a sad story of savage punishments and brutal revenge by torture, branding, and maiming that is so horrible that it can hardly be believed.

Punishment is now thought of, by the enlightened at least, mainly as a deterrent effect upon others, as a means of reform of the individual, and as a protection for society. A comparatively new science of criminology is gradually being developed in the civilized world in these latter days, and the savage methods of the past not only have disappeared, but, in contrast, there has been developed in this country a maudlin sentimentality, and a legal procedure in the administration of criminal laws, that excuses, frees, and encourages the criminal and develops crime.

Partly, no doubt, as a reaction against the ancient savagery in punishment, the law in the old days specifying more than thirty crimes in England punishable by death, and also no doubt because of what Professor Pound describes as the "frontier spirit" in our comparatively new land, the administration of the criminal law in this country, in its delays, its uncertainty, and its ineffectiveness, does not deter, does not punish, and does not protect. Our able Chief Justice in a notable address of a few years ago quoted in *The Reform of Legal Procedure,* by Moorfield Storey, said:

"It is not too much to say that the administration of criminal law in this country is a disgrace to our civilization, and that the prevalence of crime and fraud, which here is greatly in excess of that in European countries, is due largely to the failure of the law and its administration to bring criminals to justice."

The facts regarding the prevalence of crime in this free and enlightened country are so astounding that they can hardly be believed. It does not tend to make the American bosom swell with pride to realize that there are more murders committed in some single cities of this land each year than in all England, Wales, and Scotland, and that fraud and crime of all kinds are safer under our flag than in any other civilized land. The gruesome details and statistics regarding the prevalence of crime and the escape of the guilty in the United States of America are easily available in the official bulletins.

The following startling comparisons by Mr. Raymond B. Fosdick, the distinguished author of *European Police Systems,* are made in his later book, *American Police Systems* (The Century Company, New York, 1920). The quotation follows:

"As to the fact of our excessive criminality, the statistics furnish startling evidence. London in 1916, with a population of seven millions and a quarter, had nine premeditated murders. Chicago, one-third the size of London, in the same period had 105, nearly twelve times London's total. In the year 1916, indeed—and it was not an exceptional year—Chicago with its 2,500,000 people had twenty more murders than the whole of England and Wales put together with their 38,000,000 people. The Chicago murders during this year total one more than London had during the five year period from 1910 to 1914 inclusive. In 1917 Chicago had ten more murders than the whole of England and Wales and four more murders than all England, Wales, and Scotland. In 1918 Chicago had fourteen more murders than England and Wales. In 1919 the number of murders in Chicago was almost exactly six times the number committed in London."

"But Chicago is not exceptional. Other American cities suffer equally from comparison with crime conditions abroad. New York City in 1916 had exactly six times the number of homicides (murder and manslaughter) that London had for the same year, and only ten less homicides than all of England and Wales. In 1917 New York had six times more homicides than London and exceeded the total homicides of England and Wales by 56. In 1918 New York again had six times more homicides than London, and exceeded the total homicides of England and Wales by 67. This contrast cannot be attributed to the peculiar conditions in London induced by the war. In each of the years from 1914 to 1918 inclusive New York had more homicides than occurred in London during any three year period previous to the outbreak of the war in 1914."

"Statistics of this kind could be multiplied at length. In the three-year period, 1916-1918, inclusive, Glasgow had 38 homicides; Philadelphia, which is only a trifle larger, had during this same period 281. Liverpool and St. Louis are approximately the same size; in 1915 St. Louis had eleven times the number of homicides that Liverpool had, and in 1916 eight times the number. Los Angeles, one-twentieth the size of London, had two more homicides in 1916 than London had for the same period; in 1917 she had ten more than London had. Cleveland, Ohio, one-tenth the size of London, had more than three times the number of homicides in 1917 and approximately twice the number in 1918.

"Equally significant is the comparison of burglary statistics between Great Britain and the United States. In 1915, for example, New York City had approximately eight times as many burglaries as London had in the same period, and nearly twice the number of burglaries reported in all England and Wales. In 1917 New York had four times as many burglaries as London, and approximately the same number as occurred in England and Wales. In 1918 the burglaries which the police reported in New York were approximately two and a half times those in London. While war conditions undoubtedly served to heighten this contrast, they were by no means entirely responsible for it; in 1915 New York City had more burglaries than occurred in all England and Wales in 1911, 1912, or 1913. Chicago in 1916 had 532 more burglaries than London, in 1917, 3459 more, in 1918, 866 more, and in 1919, 2146 more. Detroit and Cleveland generally report several hundred more burglaries per annum than London, although London is seven or eight times larger. The annual burglaries in St. Louis always exceed those in London."

"Even more startling are the statistics of robbery. New York City in 1915 reported 838 robberies and assaults with intent to rob where London had 20, and England, Wales and Scotland together had 102. In 1916 New York had 886 such crimes to London's nineteen, and England, Wales and Scotland's 227. In 1917 New York reported 864 to London's 38, while England, Wales and Scotland reported 233. In 1918 New York had 849, while London had 63, and England and Wales had 100."

"Practically the same proportion exists between Chicago's

robberies and those in Great Britain. In 1918, for example, Chicago had 22 robberies for every one robbery in London and 14 robberies for every one robbery in England and Wales. Washington, D. C., in 1916 had four times the number of robberies that London reported; in 1917 three times the number; and in 1918 one and one-half times the number. Los Angeles in 1916 had 64 more robberies than all of England, Wales and Scotland put together; in 1917 she had 126 more than these three countries. Cities like St. Louis and Detroit, in their statistics of robbery and assault with intent to rob, frequently show annual totals varying from three times to five times greater than the number of such crimes reported for the whole of Great Britain."

"America's crime rate is greatly augmented by the presence of unassimilated or poorly assimilated races. It must not be supposed, however, that our foreign and colored population is the sole cause of our excessive crime rate. If the offences of our foreign and colored races were stricken from the calculation, our crime record will still greatly exceed the record of Western Europe. With all its kindliness and good nature, the temper of our communities contains a strong strain of violence. We condone violence and shirk its punishment.

Those best qualified to speak say without hesitation that the important reason for this deplorable prevalence of crime is the failure of the criminal law. That would be an unwarranted, if not foolish, optimism that hoped to abolish all crime by the most perfect administration of the law, but it is a still more unfortunate pessimism that contends that prompt, humane, and just, but vigorous and effective criminal law administration would not at once decrease the evil. The courts alone cannot correct the abuse, but it is through them, no doubt, that reforms must come that will tend to remedy the evil. A necessary step towards reform is a full realization by the public of the awful facts.

A recent report of a Committee of the American Bar Association on the administration of criminal law says on a phase of the subject, "The prevalence of an abnormal volume of crime in our cities is the result of years of mollycoddling and sympathy by misinformed and unwise meddlers". The courts can hardly be entirely relieved of responsibility in the matter, but they certainly are not altogether to blame. It is no doubt true that many of the conditions in the courts are direct reflections of a shallow public sentiment largely based upon misinformation.

There are certain widely believed fallacies that are contributing factors. One of these is the false idea that many innocent victims are all the time being convicted of crime, and not that guilty criminals are all the time escaping deserved punishment. The common argument is that it is "Better that one hundred guilty should go free than that one innocent person should be punished", and no one would favor a procedure that tended to convict the innocent, but few either would approve the contention, "Better that one hundred innocent victims should be murdered because of the laxity of the law than that one person should be unjustly punished". The error in the reasoning and the unfortunate shallow view of the question is the ignoring of the thousands of victims of crime and fraud, with pity only for the guilty criminal, to whom too often flowers are sent and who, upon acquittal, is often welcomed home as a conquering hero.

It is no doubt well within the facts to say that in this

country there are hundreds of innocent victims of the murderer, who were in some measure actually made victims because of the failure of the law to punish, to even one innocent victim of the law. It will thus be seen that the problem is a practical one that should be considered in a practical way. It is also undoubtedly true that many of these criminals were actually led into a career of crime because it has been so difficult in America to convict anyone of crime, especially a murderer.

Criminologists generally agree, and history and experience prove, that it is the *certainty and promptness* of punishment, and not its severity, that has the greatest deterrent effect upon crime. It is a notorious fact that punishment in this country is not certain and is not prompt. The whole machinery of the law, as controlled by public opinion, in its delays, its technicalities, its restrictions, and its assumptions, makes it difficult, and often impossible, to convict the criminal except the man with no friends and no money. To convict a noted criminal of the crime of murder in this land is a rare and distinctive achievement.

Our American current literature, and much of our more permanent literature, is permeated with this misrepresentation of the facts regarding the administration of criminal law. The central idea in much of this printed matter is this widely disseminated, erroneous contention, just referred to, that innocent men and women are constantly in danger of being convicted of crime, when the awful fact is that innocent men and women are constantly in danger of being defrauded, waylaid, and murdered by the criminals who have not been convicted. Some new stories should be written emphasizing the danger to the innocent.

The whole subject in this country is surrounded by a short-sighted sentimentalism and this mistaken conception of the conditions, which sees only the accused criminal and not that greater number who suffer because of the prevalence of crime. Nor, as stated above, should the members of the legal profession receive all the blame for the awful conditions. They also have reacted to this common public sentiment, but in the end they will no doubt be called upon to inform and educate the public on the question and bring about reform. Upon them rests a great responsibility. The whole problem is to make the machinery of justice more accurate, and more prompt, in its action. It is not a simple problem, but after a time, let us hope not too long, it will be solved.

. . . . . .

It finally comes to be understood that there is nothing in the whole realm of the administration of the law—nor the administration of anything, for that matter—more fundamental or more important in furthering justice than correct reasoning regarding the comparative force and significance of testimony. Miscarriages of justice are due to a misunderstanding of facts, a deliberate ignoring of facts, or incorrect reasoning regarding facts, but the real problem is not so often a question of hearing, or seeing, the evidence, as of interpreting it. All else necessarily fails if finally the interpretation of testimony is wrong.

The ultimate purpose of the law is, of course, to establish justice, and the basis of justice always is truth, but in all controverted questions it not only becomes necessary to learn what the truth is, but to determine what inference to draw from it, and this is reasoning. The basis of all correct reasoning is, of course, knowledge as assisted by experience and controlled and directed by general intelligence. Twelve men listen to conflicting evidence and sometimes disagree. Although the causes of these disagreements are many and various, the most common cause is no doubt this failure to reason accurately. The result, when incorrect, may of course be due to dishonesty, or it may result from ignorance, but more often it results from this inability to draw correct inferences. Differences in this quality of reasoning also account for conflicts in opinions and reversals of judgments in all courts of high as well as of low degree. Error everywhere in everything is not so much due to lack of information as lack of intelligence.

There are but few questions presented in court where it becomes more important to exercise the faculty of reasoning than those relating to the genuineness or identity of disputed documents. This class of cases usually presents a variety of testimony, and in a trial, or a review, it becomes necessary first to consider and compare oral conflicting testimony, based on alleged direct knowledge, and it then becomes necessary to weigh this testimony against technical testimony based upon the controverted facts in the documents themselves, which testimony may also be conflicting, and finally, it becomes necessary to test all of this testimony by the judgment of the trier himself, who can himself make an examination of these technical facts as well as of the oral testimony of witnesses. This review of the facts is the distinctive feature of a disputed document trial.

The decision in some trials before one hearer, even when there is other evidence in the case, is sometimes admittedly based entirely upon the alleged facts stated by oral witnesses. In other cases the judgment is based only upon the comparison of the oral testimony of witnesses who purport to have positive knowledge, with the technical testimony based upon the physical evidence in the case, but without any personal examination by the trier of the visible, explained, and illustrated facts of the case. In these instances the examiner, by giving no attention to this third phase of the inquiry, apparently by his method admits that he is unable to apply his own powers of observation and reasoning to the problem, and takes only the evidence as presented and, what is more unfortunate, sometimes apparently takes only part of this evidence.

In the old days, where expert testimony consisted of mere opinions, and there was a conflict, all of this opinion testimony was summarily brushed aside, and this is still done now and then even where illustrated and reasoned testimony has been given. The trier refuses to test the conflicting testimony by his own intelligence as applied to the facts before him, and, by a sort of perversity, refuses to examine all the evidence.

In a thorough review of a case on appeal it also becomes necessary to examine all the evidence. The difficulty of accurately weighing conflicting oral testimony from a printed record is well understood, but where in connection with records of this kind the disputed document itself is present and enlarged illustrations of the very points in controversy, and testimony with full reasons and explanations regarding these questions is in the record, then it is clear that a court, of five or more men, called upon to reverse or confirm a judgment, perhaps by one man, would certainly be aided by an examination of the facts themselves which are before them. Some courts in some states, however, will not do this sensible thing; they only read the testimony.

When fifty or more opinions involving these questions are carefully analyzed and compared, it appears quite clearly that the decisions, especially as rendered in the old days, apparently were often based on only part of the evidence. Due and proper credit should, of course, be given to all testimony, including so-called fact testimony, but, in a printed record where oral testimony of this kind conflicts with reasoned, illustrated evidence *which can be seen and understood by an intelligent man,* if he will give attention to it, then plainly an ignoring of this evidence, which itself furnishes a tangible basis for reasoning, endangers the interests of justice. It is but natural to inquire why a reviewer should not examine and reason on the facts before him in order fully to test the reasoning made in the preceding examination and decision.

In every group of men there are some who are better qualified than others to investigate scientific questions and determine the comparative force of testimony on technical subjects, and the interests of justice require that a final report on problems of this kind should be made only by men who are qualified. There should at least be one man thus specially qualified in every group where legal opinions are written on these questions.

These same problems of reasoning are, of course, problems for the ordinary juror who, unaided, many times is not qualified to give them proper consideration, but with proper assistance from the judge, and an intelligent discussion in argument by a prepared attorney of all the evidence and its significance, even untrained jurors can usually be assisted to a right understanding of conflicting evidence in cases of this class.

CHAPTER IX.

THE AID OF THE SPECIALIST.

Although there are many versatile members of the profession, it cannot reasonably be expected that a lawyer will be qualified on all technical subjects, and in a case involving an unusual question he naturally will secure the assistance of a specialist. He finds and consults an expert on the subject. This he does in order to secure immediate information on the merits of the case he is asked to take into court, and also to secure the assistance of one who will be able to instruct him on the technical subject involved and testify on the controverted question.

The lawyer who investigates a disputed document case, with a view of taking it into court, will naturally enlist the services of one qualified and experienced in this special field. In an important case the matter will perhaps be submitted to more than one specialist and when this is done ordinary prudence will suggest that these submissions be made independently.

For his own instruction, and for use at the trial, the lawyer will obtain a written report from the specialist with a full discussion of the reasons for the opinion expressed. If a specialist cannot give to the friendly attorney logical reasons for a conclusion, he will not be likely to get a sudden inspiration under the restrictions surrounding the witness-stand that will enable him to present in an effective manner the basis for any opinion he gives. With a detailed report in hand the careful attorney is able to determine the value of the proposed evidence, and, if necessary, can cross-examine his own witness in advance or even dismiss him. This advance scrutiny of testimony of this class is an important phase of the sifting of evidence, discussed in a preceding chapter. The careful attorney does not risk damaging his case by calling as a witness a stupid, pretentious, or corrupt specialist even if he is described as an "expert".

The conscientious attorney, careful of his own reputation, will also secure the best advice obtainable on a technical matter in order that he may refuse to appear if he finds that the claim he is asked to present is a fraudulent one, or if he is asked to attack a genuine document. Contrary to the view of uninformed and pessimistic critics, many lawyers say frankly in presenting a case for investigation that they are not primarily seeking to obtain favorable testimony but accurate information on the disputed question. Many cases end abruptly before they get into court because reputable and intelligent attorneys will not take them there.

The lawyer also desires to learn whether the case, even if it has merit, is one that he is likely to win. In his own interest, as well as in the interest of his client, he tests in advance the strength of proposed testimony in order to decide whether the case should be tried or settled. The attorney is better qualified than a litigant to measure the probative value of proposed testimony and, after investigation, may advise against a trial. The investigation is, therefore, taken up in a manner that will furnish the most reliable information. The careful attorney does not allow himself to jump to a conclusion, nor will he be unduly influenced by any first impressions of others.

Although it is impossible in any investigation not to be somewhat influenced by first impressions, the proper control of these impressions is a measure of the thoroughness with which any investigation is conducted. A scientific inquiry proceeds by certain steps based upon preliminary working theories each of which is investigated and then rejected or adopted. The true scientific spirit is in control when each theory is as likely to be discarded as to be confirmed, in order that the conclusion shall be drawn from the evidence and not from any preconceptions. The advance of civilization has been due to the development of the scientific spirit in defiance of prejudice and of tradition.

The careful lawyer scrutinizes every step of an investigation, tests every claim and theory of client and of specialist, and especially reviews the basis of all testimony and the process of reasoning by which conclusions are reached. He knows that in all decisions error is avoided by giving every item of evidence its true evidential value and only its true value.

There are those in many fields who pride themselves on their ability to reach the truth at one leap by a kind of intuition. This danger surrounds every investigator and every investigation. The advocate is in danger of jumping to the conclusion that the contention of his client is correct and provable, and the specialist is in danger of being led to adopt the conclusion of an enthusiastic advocate. The careful lawyer tests every point of evidence in his case by his experience, his knowledge of the subject, and the application to it of common sense. In a trial in court a contention should always be able to withstand this latter important test.

Because of intense interest in a problem, an advocate often finds it difficult to interpret and weigh evidence accurately. He must constantly guard against an uncontrolled zeal that dims vision and cripples judgment. This weakness of both specialist and of advocate is well described in a homely way by saying that one is too close to a subject to see it whole and see it clearly. There are many intensely prejudiced litigants who acquire a mental blindness that renders their judgments almost valueless.

The technical enthusiast, misled by unscientific praise, often flatters himself that he has acquired a kind of occult power above reason. A writer on the so-called science of graphology says, "Is it not possible that some of those fine and acute touches may have been arrived at through some subtle transference of ideas beyond the concept of the senses. . . . This insight, this seer faculty, is not so rare as might be supposed, and under proper and controlling restrictions, is, I am confident, one of the highest qualities of which the soul is capable." These words exactly describe the mental condition of certain enthusiastic specialists whose ideas come "from beyond the concept of the senses". They often apparently are deficient in ordinary common sense and are unable to appreciate how ridiculous their metaphysical claims are to those who are still under the control of reason. This so-called "occult intuition" is many times accompanied by untrained reason even if not mixed with pretension, stupidity, and fraud. As already suggested, the careful lawyer does not wait till he gets into court to find that his witness cannot show to others what he himself claims to know and to see.

The careful scientific spirit does not necessarily develop an attitude of timidity in attorney or specialist, but it certainly develops an attitude of caution. Thorough knowledge and extended experience will develop the ability to draw correct inferences from what may seem to the unskilled and the inexperienced to be slight evidence, but the inference will still be drawn from evidence and experience which an intelligent man is able to understand.

In the examination of an alleged forgery one of two opposed conclusions must necessarily be correct; that the document either is forged or is genuine. There often are in writing certain inherent evidences of forgery as there are also in genuine writing certain inherent evidences of genuineness, but these evidences may run across and interlace in a zone of doubt and uncertainty which becomes the field of possible error. If the facts warrant it, the sincere and capable investigator does not hesitate to say that the case is in the zone of uncertainty and that he cannot reach a positive conclusion. The attorney who looks for the facts does not criticise but praises this sincerity.

There are two widely divergent attitudes of mind regarding the document specialist. There are those who think of him only as a shallow pretender who can do nothing, while there are others who, perhaps having read many overdrawn detective tales, think he has a sort of occult power that enables him to do the impossible. Naturally the truth lies somewhere between the two views. The general field of expert testimony, like that of the law, is an attractive one for pretenders and charlatans, and anyone has a difficult task who would defend all the members of either class, but there are competent and reputable men to be found in both fields. In a subsequent chapter the subject of erroneous and dishonest expert testimony and its relation to the practice of law and the interests of justice is discussed in plain words, and here and there in these chapters it is also suggested that there are those who practice law who do not always promote justice.

In connection with the investigation of an alleged forgery the prepared attorney gives some attention to the principles underlying the proof of handwriting, which is dependent upon accurate observation of its various characteristics and correct interpretation of them. This process of proof also includes the application to the problem of the principles underlying the general act of identification. A conclusion on any question is, of course, only justified when it results from a correct interpretation of sufficient evidence.

If brought together so they could be compared, a hundred forged documents would contain many common evidences of forgery. They could be grouped into a few general classes. Experience in the examination of documents enables the qualified examiner to make a mental comparison of a new document with all that he has before seen and studied. One thus qualified not only knows what to expect in the usual forgery, but also knows as well the earmarks of genuineness, and, in the absence of the one and the presence of the other, or the weighing of both, reaches his conclusion. His testimony explains how the result of his experience is applied to the problem. The inexperienced observer may interpret accidental variation incorrectly, or may entirely overlook fundamental divergences. The vigilant attorney endeavors to qualify himself to understand these matters, at least in a general way, so that he may be able correctly to estimate the value of the assistance he seeks, qualify himself to discuss the subject in court, and cross-examine those in error.

When two or more specialists are to be called as witnesses on the same side of the case it is usually advisable that they do not confer on the details of the testimony to be given nor see each other's reports. Prospective witnesses will report directly to the attorney who will then arrange the testimony for presentation in the most effective manner. Separate preparation encourages permissible and desirable variation and allows each witness to present the matter in his own manner and with such emphasis and order of statement as appears to him to be most effective. Testimony of any class is weakened if witnesses confer on details and then all testify just alike.

In order further to test the strength of his own case and the prospective witness at the same time, the attorney carefully considers the question of how best to present the matter to a specialist so as to get an unbiased opinion, and also so that, in the event that the specialist appears as a witness, it can be shown that he was not improperly influenced. Technical witnesses are often accused of always reaching the conclusion desired by those who consult them, which statement is not true. It is true, however, that some of the criticism of expert testimony arises from the initial methods employed by lawyers in securing this class of witnesses. The testimony of honest and competent witnesses is strengthened when it is relieved of the suspicion that they were consulted in a partisan manner.

Attorneys naturally desire to win cases, and, if success must be secured through expert testimony, the zealous and not excessively conscientious attorney will naturally use every effort to secure favorable expert testimony. The man with a good case is unwise to approach a witness in this way. It is natural that a lawyer should be inclined to discuss the merits of his case, and describe to a prospective witness the available evidence favorable to his contention, but it is bad policy for an attorney thus to outline to a prospective witness the character of the general evidence tending to prove his contention. If, after an improper opening of this kind, what are to be the exhibits in the case are shown, and the attorney points out everything favorable to his views that he can see in the documents, and gives all this information before any examination whatever is made by the specialist, then the case has been presented in an improper manner. An improper presentation of this kind naturally tends to insure a favorable opinion from the unscrupulous witness, but may embarrass the conscientious witness and weaken the force of his testimony if the fact is brought out on the trial.

Through inexperience, excessive zeal, or distrust of expert ability, a conscientious attorney with a good case sometimes seeks to insure a favorable opinion by this partisan method of presenting a problem to a competent and reliable expert. It is important that an attorney believe in his own witness, and by this improper procedure he may not give the witness the opportunity to give an opinion without knowing in advance whether it is favorable or unfavorable. 'It is often difficult, and sometimes impossible, to restrain an attorney, even when he has a good case, from giving information that is not necessary in presenting the problem to a specialist. The circumspect attorney restrains himself.

If a case has been properly presented to a witness and his testimony in court is fair and well reasoned, the judge, in most courts, will protect him from unfair attacks. Furthermore, numerous judges will assist, as far as is proper, in bringing out the evidence so it will be clearly understood. Unfortunately this participation of the court is not permitted in some jurisdictions. The informed judge can greatly assist a jury in understanding and weighing certain kinds of expert testimony. Much of the charlatan, presumptuous, "conflicting" testimony would not be heard in courts of law if judges had the power they ought to have. But few will contend that a fair, experienced judge cannot assist a jury in promoting justice by drawing the line between false and true testimony, and between the pretender and the qualified specialist. This subject is discussed more fully in a later chapter.

The non-partisan method of presenting a case, as suggested above, is welcomed by the competent technical witness, and is of decided disadvantage to the incompetent pretender who often must be told what is wanted of him. This testing of testimony in this manner also gives the attorney information at the outset of the inquiry as to the ease or difficulty with which his contention can be supported, and, most important of all, secures unbiased, honest opinions.

CHAPTER X.

THE SPECIALIST AS A WITNESS.

Theoretically it would seem possible to go into the laboratory or the library and bring any qualified specialist directly into the court room to prove as an expert some technical fact within his special field. The desired result could thus be reached if a mere opinion were all that is required; but when proof is necessary under the legal rules, and always against opposition, something more than technical knowledge is necessary. Though renowned as a specialist, a man may be a pitiful failure as a witness.

To be effective as a witness the specialist must not only know, but must be able to explain, to convince, and to undergo cross-examination. For his own protection, as well as to increase the effectiveness of his testimony, the special witness must know these things and understand what conditions and qualities strengthen or weaken the technical evidence of a specialist. The law does not require that he be thrown to the lions without any preparation for the ordeal. In the interest of justice it is desirable that he have knowledge of the facts here outlined.

The first essential qualification of a technical witness is, of course, that he understand his specialty. Many technically qualified men, however, fail as witnesses through lack of ability to use simple, understandable language; others are unable to make themselves heard in a court room; still others cannot control their tempers under provocation; while others, especially some experts, appear to have no knowledge of human nature whatever, and are unable to convince others of what they themselves perhaps understand. There also are technically qualified men so timid and inexperienced that a violent opponent nearly frightens them out of their wits; and, unfortunately, there are other men, technically able perhaps, who are so dogmatic and conceited that they fail to convince even when they do tell the truth.

The highest qualification of a witness is, of course, the ability to convince those who listen to his testimony. This matter of bringing about belief in the mind of another, however, is not always the simple process it may appear to be. This subject of persuasion is considered more fully in another chapter and is here discussed only as it relates directly to the specialist as a witness.

The first requirement in a witness who is to succeed in convincing a hearer is a clear and forceful presentation of the evidence supporting the fact to be proved, but the second requirement, the inspiring of confidence in the sincerity, as well as the ability, of the one making the proof, is often a matter given little, if any, thought by trial attorney or by specialist. It is possible that a series of facts may be presented in such a logical manner that belief will not depend in any way upon confidence in the one stating the facts. This result, however, can only be attained when the proof does not rest upon any unverified statement of the witness. It is perhaps more probable that a witness by his personality may inspire such confidence that his statements are presumed to be correct even in the absence of a clear demonstration; but this result is also exceptional.

Practically every one by the mere fact of having grown up in society has developed some natural skill by which truth and sincerity, in some measure, are constantly being tested. This test is usually applied unconsciously and we are not often able to say why we believe or do not believe, except that we do so by intuition, which is no answer. There are certain delicate indications of truth as well as of deception which we detect in a way that we cannot describe. Our act is no doubt the result of a sort of funded experience and our estimate may be correct or we may be deceived.

It may be difficult to teach one how to inspire confidence, but there are some things which can be avoided that certainly weaken confidence. It is highly important for the trial attorney, as well as the specialist, to know what they are. Some of these elements and qualities that affect belief and unbelief no doubt are beyond control, but all are not. In the first place the attorney who wishes testimony to be believed asks only truthful witnesses to testify. Emerson says, "What you are speaks so loud that I do not hear what you say", and this thought embodies a truth which has a direct bearing on the credibility of all testimony. The first requirement then, of one who would be believed, is that he speak the truth. One who speaks the truth freely and fully states a fact as a child states it, with that tone, emphasis, and manner which in combination proclaim that the truth is spoken.

The fully qualified trial attorney must be an expert

in discerning evidences of truth and of untruth. He clearly understands that the truth speaker is direct, fair, and frank, and not only admits, but volunteers the limitations of his knowledge, and considers the possibilities of error when there are such possibilities. He will encourage the witness to speak positively, but without excessive emphasis and well within the limit of fact. Too strong a statement is often at once a basis of suspicion, and we unconsciously may not believe because a speaker "doth protest too much". The essential elements of effective technical testimony are accuracy and clearness, and these qualities of fairness and frankness that tend to inspire confidence. It is part of the business of the attorney to assist in getting these valuable qualities into testimony. To insure its fullest effectiveness, evidence must be surrounded by conditions that produce this right atmosphere. The development of these modifying conditions is in some measure the duty of the witness, but he cannot do it alone. The unwise zeal of an advocate often creates an unfavorable air of incredulity surrounding testimony, and a witness may be made to appear to be an unfair partisan through the reflected influence of an overzealous advocate.

The general conduct of the witness naturally affects the force of his testimony. It is natural to expect that the demeanor of one about to give evidence in a court of law will be characterized by a dignity and self-control befitting the occasion. The frivolous witness is at once suspected either of shallowness or of insincerity. The technical specialist who testifies with the fullest effect avoids any word or act that suggests that he does not understand that he is performing an important duty. He maintains a serious manner throughout the examination. It is particularly important in a criminal case that the demeanor of a witness for the prosecution should be carefully guarded. He avoids anything indicating personal feeling, and makes his testimony positive, but impersonal and unimpassioned.

From the nature of the duty he is called upon to perform, a witness is the object of intense interest, and his every word and movement receive minute attention and may be the basis of favorable or unfavorable inferences. It is unfortunate if simply a forbidding demeanor subjects a witness to unwarranted suspicion which weakens his evidence. No matter how otherwise competent he may be, the evidence of a special witness is seriously weakened if he exhibits from his conspicuous position ill-temper, self-conceit, insolence, or unattractive manners.

The capable and experienced witness understands that under the provocation of severe cross-examination it is especially important that he should sit still and keep all his physical movements under control. He looks at his inquisitor constantly, and by his words, attitude, tone, and appearance endeavors to avoid just criticism; and, at the same time, by his manner and his well chosen words, makes it clear that he is there to give positive aid in proving a fact. To be an effective witness he must say the right things, at the right time, and in the right way.

Especially under cross-examination it is highly desirable that the witness maintain, as far as is humanly possible, an attitude of self-control, courtesy, and respect. One of the direct purposes of cross-examination is to irritate a witness and lead him to say something that will expose him to attack and thus weaken his testimony. The psychologists say that bodily activity and posture directly affect mental conditions, and therefore one who is to control his mind and his temper under trying conditions should keep himself under perfect physical control.

The capable witness does not give his own feelings first consideration, but endeavors so to conduct himself that the convincing quality of the testimony is not disturbed. This governing idea at once changes the attitude of the prudent witness who sometimes may be sorely tempted to indulge in ill-tempered and unfair retaliation. Under no circumstances does the good witness allow himself to be led into an exhibition of unfairness, exaggeration, or the slightest tendency toward untruth.

The qualified and experienced witness is attentive, but not eager; he does not indulge in levity of any kind, except under the most unusual conditions, and does not endeavor to respond in similar manner to innuendoes and slurs from the opposing attorney, unless the provocation is so great that the sympathy of court and jury will certainly be with him. The effect of a specialist's testimony is greatly weakened if he assumes a self-satisfied, bumptious air, which naturally invites criticism of any witness, and especially of an expert. Testimony is appreciably strengthened if the witness, even under the severest provocation, continues to exhibit the conduct of a gentleman.

Although the capable witness will not lose control of

his temper under any conditions, he will promptly respond to slurs and insults in an earnest and dignified manner. He need not be a silent, cringing martyr, but will not, in an effort to injure his tormentor, attempt to make his testimony more damaging than the facts warrant. The experienced witness understands, and it is helpful for every other witness to know, that, as far as the effect of testimony is concerned, there need be no fear of cross-examination if the truth is told and the witness knows what he says. One may dread the ordeal, but need have no fear of the result. There are a few coarse and brutal men practicing law who try to please their clients by insulting all opposing witnesses, but good lawyers know that this is bad law practice, and it becomes less frequent as human conduct improves with the advance of culture and the progress of civilization.

As pointed out in a previous chapter, it needs to be better understood that the specialist cannot easily do full justice to himself and his subject without the intelligent co-operation of the examining attorney. A series of prepared, carefully phrased technical questions will always greatly assist in bringing out the evidence with the right tone and emphasis. A wrong effect is sometimes produced by testimony because some of the necessary questions were not asked and evidence sometimes can only half be given because it is only half asked for.

An attorney's questions, when skilfully framed, will not all call for affirmative answers and will not give the impression that the witness will undertake to answer any question under the heavens. Evidence is always weakened if a long examination is made to appear like the glib reciting of what has been rehearsed. Testimony is also sometimes made less effective if the lawyer seems to be trying in a bungling manner unduly to emphasize the qualifications and importance of the witness. The questions can be so framed as to bring out the importance of the reasons given for the opinion expressed, and also arranged so as to bring out the evidence in the right order. Testimony is sometimes dumped into a case as potatoes are dumped into a barrel.

The force of the testimony of a technical witness may be weakened for the simple reason that he is referred to as an "expert". The word itself suggests a certain superiority that may produce in the mind of the inexperienced hearer an immediate feeling of antagonism aroused by the thought that the name is not given to the witness, but is assumed by him. The attorney can do something to correct this misunderstanding by bringing out the fact in some manner that the word is a legal term used to designate certain witnesses. Some of the criticism of expert testimony is undoubtedly due to this word, as well as to the manifest egotism of certain "expert" witnesses who, led on by the lawyer who seeks to emphasize their testimony, are inclined to claim or admit a degree of skill and intelligence that preferably is spoken of by others rather than by themselves, even if the extraordinary claims are true.

As with the lawyer, the forceful and accurate use of language is another matter of first importance to the technical witness. If he cannot say what he knows, then as a witness there is no value in his knowledge. He must be able to describe clearly and forcibly every phase of the subject regarding which he testifies, or the time of the court is used to no purpose. Effective technical testimony requires the use of the exact simple words that clearly express the ideas to be conveyed. To give the exact shade of meaning to an expression often makes, not simply the difference between clearness and obscurity, but the difference between belief and unbelief. Much language as spoken suggests that man is, to a considerable degree, a dumb animal and only feebly hints at much that he would express. The thoughtful and practiced technical witness fully realizes this difficulty of conveying an idea to another. He makes a collection of the simple technical terms and the modifying and descriptive words relating to his specialty, and then practices using them until he can express himself with accuracy, simplicity, and force. But few can do it. Most men cannot even give brief and intelligent directions as to the best road to take to the next village. A man is at once suspected who stumbles in talking about what he is supposed to know. Accuracy in language is not desirable primarily to please the grammarian, but to add force to a statement by making it better understood. Force and clearness are always necessary elements in the process of convincing.

Weakness of statement may be due to failure to use a strong enough word, and also may result from exaggeration. The competent witness does not give the impression of hesitation in stating his point of view, but, like the ordinary witness, he is more apt to fail in the opposite direction. A danger in all expert testimony is a tendency toward unwarranted emphasis, if not of assumption. Some witnesses of this class give the impression that wisdom will surely die with them. Technical testimony can be earnest and positive and at the same time avoid unwarranted assumption and overemphasis. The wise witness also avoids assuming the superior air of an instructor; and does not use strange technical words unnecessarily. High-flown language does not tend to convince those who listen, even if they do understand. It is always the shallow man who uses showy and unnecessarily big words.

There is an occasional technical speaker, however, who, in his endeavor to make things clear, has just the opposite fault and underestimates the intelligence of his hearers. He explains that circles are round, and defines his simplest terms to an extent that tends to make those who listen feel that they are being put into a primary class. This fault is much worse than that of talking above his audience, as listeners who do not understand at least will not be offended. The speaker who is least likely to convince is the intolerable bore who defies the obvious and explains the commonplace. On most subjects a speaker who himself understands can make himself understood without talking down to his hearers.

Although constantly tempted to indulge in it, the honest and competent specialist in any field avoids any kind of buncombe. He knows that with men in all the professions the temptation to be a pretender is constant and appealing. He is asked again and again to do what no one can do. With some who are tempted poor human nature is too weak to overcome the temptation. In no field does the real expert pretend and seek to impress, but to inform and to convince, and having ideas to communicate, he expresses them so that they will be understood, and then perhaps believed. He remembers also that the real purpose of language is its use as a tool, and not a means of personal display.

The principal cause of the common prejudice against expert testimony is the frequent disagreements of alleged experts, especially in the medical field on subjects not susceptible of illustration and of scientific proof. Probably nine-tenths of the expert testimony given in courts of law is that given, by a comparatively few witnesses, relating to some phase of the subject of medicine. This includes the disgusting exhibitions where insanity is put forward as a last desperate resort in murder cases, and also the hopelessly conflicting testimony in personal injury cases. There are witnesses available who will testify that any injured person can never recover and another set, around the corner, who will testify that persons so injured will make a rapid recovery and be stronger than ever before. When two witnesses of this class disagree, the hearer is helpless as one opinion practically offsets the other for the reason that no logical reasons are given that can be understood by the ordinary juror.

The force and value of expert testimony generally is much weakened by this abuse of mere opinion testimony in this class of cases because it is often incorrectly assumed that any expert testimony is a mere opinion because the great mass of it is. This erroneous reference to expert testimony as being a "mere opinion" is even made in some decisions in disputed document cases where clear, full, and explicit reasons were given and where every point was illustrated by accurate enlarged photographs. There are men who approach the subject with fixed prejudice, who seem to consider it a mark of wide knowledge and extended experience to exhibit narrow, unjudicial bias in considering any phase of expert testimony. They will not discriminate between testimony that is a mere opinion and testimony that is more. Attorneys and witnesses sometimes sadly realize that the attempt to convince the prejudiced is like talking to the deaf and showing to the blind.

Some of the possible prejudice in the minds of a jury the skilful attorney can dispel by timely and effective argument. The witness can also further this same end by his reasons, his illustrations, and his attitude of fairness. When lawyer and witness both emphasize the fact that it is not the opinion, but the reasons and illustrations leading to the opinion that are important, and the witness, when properly interrogated, shows that his opinion is justified by the facts, then testimony tends to allay prejudice. If the witness frankly points out and discusses any qualifying conditions and explains difficult points, he naturally will be given credit for fairness. In this way he may be able to modify, or partly remove, latent prejudice as well as meet in advance certain lines of attack on cross-examination by showing that the purpose of the testimony is to assist in reaching a correct conclusion.

The witness can specifically say, "I have recognized this possible source of error and have given it consideration". If an actual source of error exists, this he will of course frankly state, and to that extent will limit and qualify the testimony. Although it is sometimes difficult to induce an attorney under any conditions to consent to any limitations whatever in testimony, the conscientious witness, who is the one responsible for what he says, will not allow himself to be unduly controlled by any overzealous advocate. He will state the fact exactly as it is.

In order to avoid embarrassment and possible reproof, it is desirable that the special witness know something of the rules of evidence and understand in a general way the requirements and limitations of a witness. It is also important for him to know what his rights are and especially to understand that he is permitted to finish answers to questions asked him, and finally that he is permitted to appeal to the court for protection from any unfairness.

The experienced witness learns that the limitations placed upon his testimony vary greatly in different courts. He discovers that what is courteously welcomed in one place is ruled out in another. But no matter how severely his evidence is curtailed by the rulings, he must remember that the court is the almost absolute monarch of the situation. No matter what the case may be, nor how well qualified the attorney and the witness may be, there are courts where effective expert testimony simply cannot be given. Fortunately, however, there is a pronounced tendency toward a common sense, liberal procedure and in most courts the capable and conscientious witness is given full opportunity to present testimony in the most effective manner. It is obvious that in difficult cases, involving abstruse and unusual testimony, the informed and fair judge can render great aid in furthering justice by making it possible in every proper way to prove the facts.

Even at the risk of weakening his testimony in some degree, the experienced expert witness constantly guards against making any objectionable statement, or giving any answer, that will be "stricken from the record" upon request of an alert and eagle-eyed opposing counsel. A ruling of this kind is interpreted by the average juryman as a severe reprimand of the witness, unless his own attorney comes to his defense by an immediate and effective argument. As a matter of fact, matters are constantly "stricken" in nearly every trial because it is deemed they violate some rule of evidence. The court has wide latitude on some of these points and, no matter how sweeping they may be, the witness must keep within the requirements of the particular court.

Finally, the technical witness to be effective must be distinctly heard and clearly understood or there is no good reason why he should be in court. In theatrical parlance he must "get his message across the footlights", and his spoken words must be loud enough to be heard and his ideas clear enough to be understood. Lack of clearness is usually due to a lack of clear thinking, but may result from wrong order of statement, weak language, or improper emphasis. This proper control of emphasis is of vital importance if language is to be convincing, and is always a test of knowledge of any subject. Mature knowledge is not made up of a combination of isolated facts, but of facts in their proper relations to each other. A distinction between knowledge and wisdom is that wisdom knows what knowledge is of most importance. The statement of a fact without a proper estimate of its importance, or a correct interpretation of its relations, may be entirely unconvincing. There are witnesses, like other speakers, who think that their failure to convince was due to the stupidity of the hearers instead of to their own lack of clear thinking and clear expression.

CHAPTER XI.

CO-OPERATION OF ATTORNEY AND EXPERT WITNESS.

It is of course not proper for the attorney to instruct the witness as to the facts of the evidence he is to give, but it is not only proper, but highly important that, as far as possible, he assist the witness in securing the most desirable tone, emphasis, and order of presentation of testimony. These latter qualities are sometimes as important a part of the proof as the subject matter of the evidence. Cases are sometimes apparently conducted on the theory that a bare recital of the facts is all that is necessary to win a suit. If evidence, even in a good case, is presented without regard to order of statement, tone, emphasis, or general effect, it may fail to bring a favorable verdict.

Because of justified criticism of the reprehensible practice known as "the coaching of witnesses" the proper co-operation of the attorney and the technical specialist sometimes is misunderstood. In this relation of attorney and witness the attorney is not coaching the witness, but together they are arranging the necessary evidence so that it may be clearly understood and correctly interpreted. For some reason it sometimes is asserted that it is improper for an honest technical witness to assist an honest lawyer in preparing and presenting the facts in an honest case. According to this peculiar view the technical witness, called upon to help prove a controverted fact, must do it in a sort of offhand, unprepared manner, and is not to be permitted to furnish technical help nor make suggestions of any kind to a trial attorney regarding the preparation or conduct of a case.

The fact deserves frequent emphasis that it often takes the best combined efforts of a capable attorney and a skilled and experienced specialist to discover and expose in court ingenious and presumptuous fraud, especially when furthered by unscrupulous advocacy, aided perhaps by antiquated procedure, and supported by unblushing perjury. Critics of this proper preparation by attorney and specialist contend in effect that a lawyer must get all his help from lawyers and law books, or from some unknown source. They imply, if they do not dogmatically assert, that effective assistance in proving the facts, by one who is not a lawyer, and especially by one who is to testify, is for some reason improper. It is said in criticism that the technical witness is "actively engaged in assisting in the case like a lawyer".

It is, of course, not a fact that approved legal ethics allows the advocate to promote a contention with all his powers in which perhaps he only half believes, but criticises that procedure by which a specialist is asked to assist in preparing to prove and in proving a state of actual facts in which he implicitly believes and on which he has given a positive opinion. If the technical witness is assisting the attorney to prove the facts, discover error, and defeat fraud, he certainly is assisting in promoting justice. This performance ought not to be objectionable even in a court of law!

Even the technical witness who has had experience and knows his own powers and limitations can be greatly assisted by the attorney in presenting his testimony in the way that is most natural, easy, and effective for him to present it. This assistance can be given only when attorney and witness confer before the trial and understand each other's point of view on the questions involved. There is occasionally an attorney who hampers and annoys a witness by persisting in conducting a direct examination much like a cross-examination. These examiners are inclined to become petulant with their own witnesses. They sometimes even coerce and browbeat them in much the same manner as they treat all witnesses opposed to them. This conduct is often due to the fact that the lawyer only partly knows the facts, and naturally does not understand how to assist the witness. With the inexperienced witness it is, of course, necessary that the lawyer control the situation, but it is usually advisable that the competent specialist be allowed to testify in the manner that experience has shown him is most effective. If the competent specialist is not permitted to give his testimony in an effective manner, then naturally he will be relieved of responsibility as to the outcome.

The capable and experienced technical witness will sometimes actually give more effective testimony with an "assistant" counsel as an examiner than with a senior counsel who ignores all suggestions and insists on conducting the examination in a way that weakens the evidence. A technical witness, who apparently has given convincing testimony, may leave the stand knowing that his testimony has not been nearly so effective as it was possible to make it because he was not properly examined.

As is well known, many ordinary witnesses get the

erroneous idea that it is improper to confer in any way with an attorney for whom they may testify, and an attack upon such a witness often begins with the question, propounded in an accusing tone of voice, "You talked with the attorney about the evidence you were to give, didn't you?" Unfortunately a witness thus assailed will sometimes foolishly deny having had any conversation whatever with the attorney. Proper preparation of a case enables the witness to say truthfully, "Yes, I told him what I knew about the matter". There are attorneys who begin every first interview with witnesses with the frank statement, "I want you to tell the truth fully and clearly", and the witness in answer to indiscreet questions by the cross-examiner truthfully answers, "The attorney told me to tell the truth fully and clearly".

Proper preliminary questions relating to the technical qualifications and experience of the specialist always include a brief explanatory statement by the examining lawyer that it is legally necessary, before a witness is permitted to give opinion testimony, that it be shown that he is legally qualified to do so. This "qualifying" of the witness is always desirable even though opposing counsel promptly admits the expert qualification of the witness. With a capable and experienced witness this admission is often hastily made, really as a bit of sharp practice, in order to keep out of the record and to prevent the jury from being informed to what extent the witness is experienced and qualified.

When it is known that the admission will be made that the witness is qualified, the examiner at the outset of the examination sometimes says, "I have no doubt that my opponent will admit that this witness is qualified to testify as an expert, but for the purposes of the record and the information of court and jury I desire to ask him a few questions regarding his experience and preparation in his special technical field". It is usually important that this matter of qualification be brought before the jury and that it get into the record, but it is very desirable that it be done so that the jury will understand that it is a proper legal requirement and not simply an opportunity which the lawyer gives the witness to exploit his own importance. The getting of this information before the court in just the right manner is one of the important little matters which often affects the tone of a trial.

Successful objection to the discussion of general principles in technical testimony cannot usually be made if the evidence is given in direct response to a definite and proper question. If, however, evidence regarding even the controlling principles of a technical subject, is given by the witness in response to a general question, an objection is sometimes sustained to the evidence on the ground that it is not responsive and not directly connected with the case. A proper question by the attorney connects the discussion of the principle involved to the case and thus avoids the common objection that the witness is delivering an irrelevant lecture. A series of suitable questions will fully develop in proper order, and with the proper emphasis, the testimony to be given.

Questions can be so framed that the witness can state specifically at the beginning of the examination his conclusion covering all the disputed points on which he is to give an opinion. It is desirable that these comprehensive questions and answers come near the beginning of the testimony so that the witness in his detailed discussion, as well as his general explanations, will be permitted to cover the whole field of the investigation in all its relations.

It is just at this point that trial attorneys with firmly fixed habits sometimes unwisely insist that the witness shall take up one specific point at a time and cover that point alone, as in cross-examination. This method seriously hampers the witness and makes it impossible for him to present the evidence in a connected and forceful manner. The examiner's lack of knowledge of human nature, as well as his lack of preparation on the facts, are both uncovered by some of these unskilful direct examinations. It is a pity to see the interests of a client with a just cause seriously endangered simply because a lawyer does not know how to ask questions.

Failure is often due to the incorrect assumption that all witnesses are alike. Brief experience ought to teach the advocate that the personality of the witness must be taken into account if evidence is to be brought out in the most effective manner. With direct examinations conducted in a dictatorial, aggressive style, the evidence of the timid witness often is rendered almost valueless, and this unfortunate attitude also seems to suggest that the attorney's own witnesses are not above suspicion and must be kept well in hand. Where the evidence is quite evenly balanced, these apparently trivial matters sometimes turn the scales of justice.

The trial attorney can prepare the way for the special witness to illustrate testimony. It is often advisable, even when photographs are provided, to use chart and crayon during part of the examination and make off-hand illustrations of the various points involved as the evidence is being given. It is now a well established rule of law in most courts that a witness can illustrate his testimony on a chart, and this method gives the prepared witness an opportunity to present evidence in an interesting and convincing manner. Not only can facts thus be made clearer, but the attention of all the members of the jury can be secured and held at the beginning of testimony when important general principles are explained. As a preparation for this manner of testifying the examining counsel specifically asks the witness whether he can make his testimony clearer and better understood if illustrations are made as the testimony is being given. It is proper to state when illustrations are made that they do not purport to be facsimiles, but are general illustrations of the particular point under consideration.

Prepared examining counsel will know in advance the exact significance of each point of the evidence to be presented by a technical witness so that in answer to the inevitable objection an effective argument can be made on the exact point involved. An argument on an important point at just the right time is worth much more than if made at the end of the trial. The jury are present with the eyes and ears open on these occasions, and an argument, although addressed to the court, will not be for the court alone. For the prepared attorney these are the rare opportunities to enforce important testimony and thus assist in proving his case.

The competent and conscientious witness does not for a moment hesitate to correct his own counsel in any inadvertent exaggeration or statement in a question that is not justified by the facts. In every proper way the examination as it progresses develops an atmosphere of frankness, accuracy, and thoroughness. The fact is obvious that it is hardly worth the time to present evidence if it is brought out by examining counsel and by technical witness in a manner that leads the members of the jury to suspect that both parties are presenting a one-sided, unfair view of the case.

CHAPTER XII.

UNINFORMED "EXPERT" WITNESSES, ALSO PERJURERS AND CHARLATANS.

When two witnesses who are testifying as experts disagree, their contentions cannot both be correct, and it is reasonable to infer that at least one of them is either incompetent or corrupt. Although generally true, this assumption is not always exactly correct as there are some mooted technical questions that are so closely balanced that competent men may honestly reach different conclusions regarding them. It is unfortunately true, however, that most disagreements of experts cannot thus be explained, for the fact is that corrupt expert witnesses are among the tools with which certain lawyers practice law.

This abuse of expert testimony is a matter that deserves plain words. The temptation to bolster up a desperate case by corrupt expert testimony is too great for certain zealous advocates. They go out and diligently search until they find just the kind of testimony they need. The usual object of this search for corrupt testimony is the finding of someone who will disagree with qualified and reputable specialists who are to testify to the facts. This "conflict of expert testimony" many times has accomplished its evil purpose, and it has weakened confidence in all classes of expert testimony.

The abilities of certain members of certain professions have been prostituted to a disgraceful use by these efforts to defeat justice. In many cases for both participants, the advocate and the witness, the performance is distinctly a dishonorable, if not actually a criminal act. The questionable conduct of these legal practitioners in actually buying stupid or perjured testimony is too often lightly excused. When a lawyer goes out and hires a corrupt witness to give false testimony in court, his act in legal phrase is described as suborning perjury, and for this he can be punished. There is no good reason why he should be condemned for hiring an ordinary corrupt witness and should not be criticised for deliberately hiring a corrupt expert.

This improper use of expert testimony is a practice that has been gradually developed and has been tolerated so long that its serious character is not fully appreciated. A reputable attorney is sometimes led into this use of corrupt testimony without fully realizing in advance the actual nature of the performance. If, however, the accident becomes a habit, then the attorney can no longer be looked upon as entirely reputable. A man who knowingly and habitually uses perjury is not very different from a perjurer.

The insufficient excuse is sometimes advanced that the lawyer is not qualified in any case, at any time, on any subject, to distinguish between good and bad expert testimony. If he cannot draw the line he is, of course, not to be morally blamed, though in many cases if he cannot tell the true from the false, he should confess to plain stupidity. In some cases when he argues to himself, or to others, that he does not know that the testimony that he has industriously sought and brought into court is either corrupt or erroneous, he is simply not telling the truth.

When expert testimony is used to defeat justice it is true that the corrupt witness violates his oath and that the attorney does not directly commit perjury, but the attorney who has deliberately suborned perjury cannot throw about himself the mantle of innocence and virtue simply because he has not taken an oath. He who hires a thief to steal is more to be condemned than the thief himself, and one who hires an incendiary sinks lower in the moral scale than the man who burns the buildings. Not the tools alone but those also who develop and use them should be condemned.

It is a pitiable sight to see a member of an honorable profession sell his soul as a corrupt expert on the witness stand under the suggestion and direct leadership of a lawyer who knows the witness is not telling the truth and who is to pay him to commit perjury. It is not at all probable that these two performers often deceive each other, and the disgusting performance is viewed by the legal profession with a tolerance that can hardly be understood by those not familiar with the practice. It seems to be assumed that the use of perjury, if not its purchase, is a necessary part of the practice of law. As the great bulk of expert testimony is on medical subjects, the medical profession is also not altogether above criticism by its apparent condoning of questionable acts of its members.

Until human nature advances considerably beyond its present state, charlatans and fakirs will no doubt be found in many of the various fields of human endeavor. There are here and there these dishonorable doctors, some of them with honorable degrees, ready to swear that anyone is sick or well, incurable, crazy, or sane, as is desired; there are here and there chemists, who have been, or who actually are, professors, who can be hired to swear that there are impurities, if not poison, in anything examined, and there are alleged experts ready to swear that documents are forged, or are genuine, as may be desired.

As has been pointed out in certain modern discussions of the subject, a distinction should however be drawn between expert testimony in which the facts are not before the court and that testimony in which they are. In practically all medical testimony the witness not only testifies as to his opinion but to the very facts upon which his opinion is based. The phenomena which affected his judgment is not before the court and would have no significance to the ordinary observer if it were present. With a disputed document, or writing, however, the facts are before the court; their existence, or character, or quality does not depend upon the honesty, or accuracy of observation, or of statement, of the witness.

There are several grades and classes of these witnesses who are permitted to testify as experts against the facts. In one class are those who are uninformed, or who are misled and induced to appear against their own best judgment, and there are others who are actually stupid. In another class are those who are clearly corrupt and commit perjury for pay. The uninformed and inexperienced are sometimes prevailed upon to appear as alleged expert witnesses without fully realizing what they are doing; the corrupt, who sometimes are technically qualified, are simply employed to defeat justice. It cannot be too plainly and bluntly said that there are these witnesses who for pay can thus be hired to lie in court, and it cannot be too plainly and bluntly said that there are lawyers who deliberately hire and pay them to lie.

The worst charlatans in the expert field are those who pose as experts on many entirely unrelated subjects. They will certify to purity or detect impurities, or find, or fail to find, poison, or identify bullets, blood, hair, finger-prints, or typewriting, or even discover, or not discover, forgery, as may be desired by their employers. One super-expert in the West in formal testimony in court undertakes to give the exact proportion of the mixed nationality of a child by the examination of a tiny particle of blood, and one nearer the Atlantic, not to be outdone, undertakes to give an expert opinion, based upon a mere superficial examination of a letter-press copy of an agreement on flimsy paper, that the document is "just about" twenty-one years old, and also, that the metal eyelets in the document have been in the papers for "at least" the same length of time. In this twentieth century, and in more or less enlightened America, even gunmen have been found who for money have gone out and committed murder, and when men can be found for employment of this kind it is easy to understand how they can be found for any task.

Both of these two classes of witnesses who are against the facts, the charlatans and the uninformed, have been developed by advocacy and especially by advocates in civil actions who by the terms of their employment have practically become parties to an action. Dishonest, or misguided, expert witnesses are also the tools of zealous defense attorneys, striving for a reputation as "defenders", whose main business is the defending, by any and all means, of those who are actually guilty of crime.

As pointed out in connection with another topic, these mistaken or corrupt witnesses are not usually brought forward really to prove anything, but merely to bring about a "conflict" in the testimony. The attorney uses these witnesses simply to prevent the facts from being proved. The testimony of witnesses of this class is usually of the most vague, superficial, or even grotesque character. It is mainly the expression in a positive manner of a mere opinion on the question at issue. When the attorney has brought about a conflict, he then usually attacks and attempts to discredit all expert testimony, including that of his own witnesses. In effect he says they are all ignorant, or are all liars, and that testimony of that kind is "very dangerous". Of course, only the thick-skinned perjurer would allow himself to be used in this manner by his own employer.

The most frequent conflict in testimony in disputed document cases is, however, brought about, not by expert testifying against expert, but by the bringing in of uninformed lay witnesses who disagree with other lay witnesses or with experts. Strange to say, as has been pointed out elsewhere, the law allows anyone, who has seen a person write anything, anywhere, at any time, to give an opinion under oath regarding that person's handwriting. Diligence usually is rewarded by finding one or more of these lay witnesses who, when properly led, will testify, as is desired, that any genuine signature is a forgery, or that any forgery is a genuine signature. Witnesses of this class are not usually dishonest, but are not qualified to solve the problem submitted and simply answer as they are led to answer.

These unqualified witnesses give only bare opinions and their testimony seldom has but little if any technical or scientific value. Conflicts of this kind are not serious except when this merely opinion testimony, by the procedure, or the precedents followed, or the judge's charge, is given an importance which it does not deserve. It is a well established principle that testimony on any subject that is a mere opinion should always be received with caution, and this rule certainly should cover the testimony of untrained lay witnesses who, without giving reasons, testify as to the genuineness, or identity, of disputed handwriting. Under the old procedure, described in a preceding chapter, and the unscientific manner of presenting document expert testimony, erroneous or corrupt testimony could only be counteracted by the bare contrary opinion of opposing witnesses and not by the illustration and demonstration of the actual physical facts in the case. It was mere opinion against mere opinion.

It is not often that perjury in court can win by itself; but when coupled with prejudice and sympathy, it may prevail, even though testimony of this kind is weak and highly improbable. When, therefore, a lawyer puts perjury into a case, or stupid and erroneous testimony, either by lay witnesses or by experts, it is usually employed to assist prejudice and sympathy to win against the facts and furnish an excuse for an unjustified verdict. It sometimes succeeds. Corrupt testimony of this class permits one who must decide a case to justify, or excuse, to his own mind and conscience a decision against the facts. It allows him to say to himself, "The evidence was conflicting", and then he sometimes proceeds to decide, not according to the evidence, but according to his prejudice or his sympathy. This, of course, is an unethical act, but the act has been made easier because of the "conflicting testimony".

It is gratifying to know that attorneys who attempt to defeat the ends of justice in disputed document cases by the use of corrupt witnesses do not thrive so well in these latter days when adequate standards of comparison can be used, and when enlightened methods of illustration are permitted and full and explicit reasons for an opinion are allowed. One competent man on the right side will prevail against the perjured or erroneous testimony of an omnibus load of the uninformed and the vicious. In these days it is easier to show that one who has gone out and bought perjury has bought a worthless counterfeit. Nor can effective testimony now so easily be swept aside simply by abusing the witness, or by quoting some ancient opinion in which expert testimony was severely criticised. With the procedure now followed in most courts, if a case has been properly illustrated, the attorney who is qualified on the facts can also often cross-examine in a most effective manner the ignorant or the corrupt specialist.

The many ancient restrictions surrounding the proof of documents have been pointed out in a previous chapter. Among these restrictions was the unwise exclusion until yesterday of all standards of comparison. This procedure undoubtedly directly tended to develop a class of superficial and incompetent witnesses who, under suggestion, undertook to give positive and definite, but often wholly unscientific, opinions based upon a slender and uncertain foundation. In some cases only one ancient and undesirable standard signature was available because it "happened" to be in the case. Like too much of the present testimony on medical subjects and insanity, it usually amounted to little more than the giving of a bare opinion, which usually was so vague and indefinite that it could not be reviewed and directly attacked.

There is no doubt about the unreliability of expert testimony of this class, especially as presented under the old restrictions. It is of the same general class, though not quite so bad, as the ingeniously framed, hour-long, "hypothetical question" testimony, still used in medical and insanity cases, in which the witness, after listening, sometimes for an hour, simply says yes, or no. Expert testimony of this kind has brought contempt and ridicule upon the whole process of expert proof as a means of discovering and establishing the fact in a court of law.

To-day in many courts the trial of a properly prepared disputed document case does not involve a conflict of mere opinions, but a conflict of reasons for the opinions, which is a very different matter. Unfortunately there still are courts, some of them reviewing courts, conducted under the ancient regime, where it is impossible to demonstrate the facts in a disputed document case and there is a prevalent fallacy in many of the old legal opinions dealing with the subject of expert testimony in the form of an assumption that even an intelligent, experienced referee or judge, who can see as well as hear, is never able to distinguish between the different qualities of expert testimony. These old discussions, still occasionally followed, suggest that, even in a case susceptible of complete and conclusive illustration and demonstration, the trier of the case is blind, if not also deaf, and is as helpless as a child in the face of any conflict of expert testimony of any kind. This point of view undoubtedly grows out of the ordinary conception of all expert testimony as consisting of mere opinions on subjects that cannot be understood by the ordinary man.

The vital question with expert, as with other testimony, is not whether it has been conflicting, but whether it is true and convincing. Conflicts in testimony that cannot be reviewed in any way by the trier of the fact, or the reviewer of the fact, may, of course, nullify all the testimony and defeat the ends of justice, but the fallacy, as suggested, is to assume that this is true of all conflicts. When conflict is specifically brought about for the sole purpose of making the argument that all testimony on the subject is therefore nullified, and the judge, or referee, or reviewing court, takes this same view, then perjury and stupidity have accomplished their intended purpose and have succeeded in defeating the ends of justice. This view on the part of courts directly encourages zealous advocates to go out and buy perjury simply to discredit honest and accurate expert testimony.

If the hearer of thoroughly explained and illustrated evidence is so inexperienced, uninformed, or dull, that he must take the mere opinion of a witness, then the confession of inability is justifiable but unfortunate. When, however, testimony is on a subject within his knowledge and experience, and is clearly illustrated and given with logical reasons, the trier of the fact cannot honestly brush it all aside and render a verdict, or write an opinion, against the facts "because the testimony was conflicting". Neither can he, with entire fairness, adopt the finding and the reasoning of the expert testimony on the right side of the case and then bewail the conflict, as though both sides were wrong, and give no credit to the correct testimony which has actually been followed. *The conflict itself in these cases often illuminates and enforces the correct testimony* and when correct and honest testimony is thus condemned by a wholesale criticism of expert testimony in general, simply because it is in conflict with perjury, this procedure is unfair as well as unfortunate and tends to encourage the use of perjury.

Frank, intelligent, and fearless discussion during a trial, and in legal opinions, of palpably corrupt testimony would discourage the promoters of expert testimony of this class and would certainly further the interests of justice. The usefulness of certain lying witnesses would be reduced and their corrupt employing advocates would be less inclined to bolster up weak cases by perjury.

There is no doubt about the necessity for improvement in the methods and practices surrounding the use of expert testimony, but in defense of the professions from which experts are drawn, and in defense of the legal profession, it should also be said that, with all its defects, the abuse of expert testimony is not so bad as it appears on the surface. The great body of expert testimony is given by honest men for honest attorneys on the right side of honest cases. Naturally all of this testimony gets little if any notice in the newspapers, but the disagreements in sensational cases do get extraordinary publicity. The misconception on the subject, even among lawyers, arises because of this wide news exploitation in these sensational cases. There are, after all, comparatively few of the liars, and comparatively few of the purchasers of perjury, and, as with numerous other abuses, it is gratifying to know that it tends to correct itself. The lawyers, and still more surely the specialists, who attempt to profit by perjury, sooner or later come to be known for what they are and often bring discredit upon any matter with which they are connected, and thus directly defeat the very ends they aim at.

A large proportion of corrupt expert testimony has grown out of personal injury cases in which medical expert testimony has been used; will cases in which it has been alleged that testators have been of unsound mind; and murder cases in which, to support sympathy and prejudice the desperate defense has been brought forward that a murderer was insane at the time he committed the act. As already stated, some of these cases are very widely reported, and the conflict of expert testimony is thus heralded to the world. These cases, however, are comparatively rare. In the usual case there is no conflict, and the testimony is given by conscientious and capable witnesses and the testimony receives no publicity.

A tabulation of a large number of consecutive cases in which document expert testimony has been employed discloses the surprising fact that there was disagreement of expert testimony in these cases in not more than two to three cases out of twenty. When it is argued, therefore, as it often is, that such testimony is "always in conflict", the statement is not correct. Testimony of this class relating to documents is not in conflict as frequently as ordinary so-called fact or observation testimony.

Another error or omission in many of the discussions of this subject of reform is that no discrimination is made between the different kinds of expert testimony, but nearly all of the discussions, whether so stated or not, actually refer to testimony regarding medical questions and insanity with no distinction made of testimony that refers to matters that can be seen and understood when properly interpreted as is the fact in many disputed document cases. It is at once apparent to one who thinks on the subject that a distinction should be drawn in expert testimony between a mere opinion, that cannot in any way be reviewed by the trier of the facts, from an opinion with reasons and illustrations which can be understood and appreciated by an intelligent hearer.

Most of the abuses of expert testimony grow directly out of the nature of the legal controversy. There has been developed after centuries of growth the method in litigation in which two opposed advocates, representing two opposed parties, strive in court. The performance is admittedly for each contestant one-sided and partisan. One advocate contends for one party that one contention is correct, and the opposing advocate makes just the opposite contention. The theory underlying this method of ascertaining the truth is that out of the conflicting contentions the facts will become known. Expert testimony is brought into this performance, which is admittedly a fight, as a part of the partisan attempt to prove one contention without any regard to the claims of the opposition. It is not at all surprising, therefore, that in a controversial trial that this particular phase of the proceeding should not take on the characteristics of a scientific investigation. Only a few times in a lifetime will both advocates be inclined to allow a non-partisan scientific arbitration to determine a scientific fact regarding a vital phase of the case.

One of the principal criticisms of expert testimony is that it is one-sided and partisan, and in certain discussions of the subject the expert witness, who was brought in to take a part in a controversial proceeding, is criticised for being a witness on one side of the case as though he had invented and arranged the whole proceeding and was wilfully giving to it its controversial quality. It is obvious that he is simply one element in a controversy, selected by the advocate to take a part in a controversial proceeding and it must be admitted that where only opinions are given the testimony often is entitled to but little weight.

It is not at all certain that the contentious method is the best method of establishing justice, but it is quite securely fixed at the present time. In a more perfect society in the distant future undoubtedly some sort of a permanent scientific court of arbitration will be established. It is well known that the present contentious method in all kinds of legal controversies is an outgrowth of and a survival of a savage, belligerent type of society. In the early history of the law controversies were settled by "trial by battle" in which the parties, or their representatives, engaged in actual physical combat.

The question of importance to consider in connection with all of these proposed regulations, of course, is the ultimate bearing they will have upon the interests of justice. The question of reform should be considered entirely aside from the wishes or advantage of advocates or of experts. As testimony of this class when properly employed does assist in discovering and proving the facts, the interests of justice manifestly will be promoted by methods and procedure which insure the assistance to the courts of the ablest and most reliable specialists in all fields. Any proposed regulation that tends to repel and lessen the effectiveness of this aid is obviously undesirable. All proposed reforms should therefore have a positive as well as a negative phase. A procedure and a practice that tends to keep competent and honest men out of the courts will necessarily tend to defeat justice. It should be possible in every community to enlist, use, compensate, and protect the best technical and professional men of every kind who can assist in promoting justice.

Various methods have been suggested for the regulation of expert testimony, and these proposed reforms have mainly been aimed at medical and insanity expert testimony as employed in damage, murder, and contested will cases. As already suggested, many of these proposed regulations have not distinguished between the different classes of expert testimony, nor have they properly taken into account the conditions which have brought criticism upon the methods employed in using expert testimony, especially the activity and immunity of a certain limited class of legal practitioners who openly suborn perjury and profit thereby. Few legal writers on the subject even suggest the possible culpability of the advocate in connection with the abuses of expert testimony. Long articles are printed in the law magazines without one line suggesting that attorneys are at fault in any way.

Much of the discussion of the subject does not consider these real conditions surrounding the presentation of this testimony and many of the proposed changes would undoubtedly leave the matter in a worse condition than it is. These discussions of the question that utterly ignore the fact that the abuse mainly comes about through the action of these advocates who know they are presenting perjury, manifestly do not tell the whole story. Many of these discussions seem to imply that the advocate is an ignorant and innocent purveyor of expert testimony about which he knows nothing and can know nothing.

One of the unjust references made to testimony of this kind, even in some decisions, which in effect excuses or ignores the part taken by the advocate, states that the expert always "testifies in favor of the advocate who calls him". Of course he does, because those experts whose opinion was unfavorable were not "called" by the advocate. The plain and unjust implication from the statement is that any of these experts would have thus testified on either side of the case if they had been called, which is a cruel, unjustified statement. The advocate who has presented error or perjury diligently searched until he found just the testimony he wanted.

The restrictions in some of the proposed changes would make it difficult to get any self-respecting specialist to appear in court. It is difficult enough and disagreeable enough as it is, against dishonest advocacy and with all the complications and disagreeable features of court procedure, to prove a fact and defeat fraud and render error and perjury ineffective. A court room should be made more attractive to honest and competent technical men who can assist in proving facts, and, at the same time, should, if possible, be made a more uncomfortable place for the charlatan who is there to defeat justice. Some of the proposed changes are vicious and indiscriminate attacks upon expert witnesses of all kinds without any distinction whatever being drawn between the good and the bad, and with no criticism of this corrupt practitioner who with a bribe brings the lying witness into court. Some of the bitterest attacks upon expert testimony, both in arguments and in printed briefs, are made by the actual purchasers of perjury who have themselves thus brought about "a conflict in expert testimony". The charlatan and his conscienceless employer, under most of these proposed changes, would no doubt continue to act, while the work of the capable specialist, whose conscientious and skilful efforts are not differentiated from the work of the charlatan, would be diminished and weakened, if not ended altogether. Fortunately there are capable, experienced, and reliable men in all special fields, and, as suggested above, they should be encouraged in every proper way to assist in trials at law in discovering and proving technical facts.

One of the frequent suggestions looking toward reform is that of paying the expert like the ordinary witness for the actual time in court at the rate of about one dollar and twenty-five cents a day. The suggestion has not yet been made in any article on the subject so far found, that the advocate as well as the expert witness should appear in these cases "solely in the interest of justice" and be paid merely nominal fees in all cases requiring expert testimony. This change, that probably will not be made, would correct the abuses by ending the use of all expert testimony.

If only offhand, perfunctory opinions of experts, without special study or preparation, is all that is required, they could perhaps be obtained in this way, but as a rule the kind of assistance that would be available would be worth just about what it would cost. These experts would be in the class of those beginning attorneys who are "appointed by the court" to defend indigent defendants. It seems to be assumed by some of those who propose changes that a technical witness without any definite special preparation on the specific problem, without preparation of the matter with the trial attorney, and with little or no experience in court, will go directly into the court room now and then and give effective testimony. Even with a good case the attorney and the client who expect in this way to win against sharp practice, unfair cross-examination, and adverse, mistaken, or corrupt expert testimony, are quite certain to be disappointed.

A frequent change that is suggested is that the witness should be selected by the court or by some tribunal and should be a wholly non-partisan participant. Another proposal is that questions requiring expert testimony should be submitted to a jury of experts. There has been much ill considered discussion of these various phases of the subject. If some safe and practical method could be devised by which it would be possible to designate certain capable men as expert, but not exclusive, specialists in the various branches, this change would no doubt be desirable. There is, however, always danger of favoritism and political influences, by which means the conditions might easily be made much worse than they now are. There is also danger in appointing an exclusive "official expert" who in effect in a judicial capacity would be called upon to decide vital questions affecting human rights and liberty. No witness should be given the power to decide a question without being open to full and free attack on cross-examination in the event that his testimony is not correct. Most thorough students of the conditions and the subject agree that this official designation of the exclusive witness is dangerous and undesirable.

The fundamental objection to the selection of one non-partisan expert witness to whom problems of this sort are to be submitted is that it is opposed to the fundamental rights of a litigant who is permitted to call his own witnesses. A man accused of murder, in which case a piece of handwriting, or a laboratory chemical reaction, was the controlling evidence, would certainly properly object to the judicial, or state, selection of one man who would decide the vital question affecting his liberty or life. This practice would give the expert a judicial position by which he practically decides the case. A single specialist thus selected might be mistaken, but, if officially selected, his opinion would have great weight and it would be assumed to be correct and he could not be effectively cross-examined. It is easy to understand how under these circumstances the interests of justice might be imperiled. A law of this kind was declared unconstitutional in the State of Michigan for the reason that it practically gave a witness a judicial authority.

In certain foreign lands, where the judge has power and there also appears to be greater respect for the law than in this country, official experts testify on certain subjects and apparently with most satisfactory results. These specialists are selected with the utmost care and, under the control of, and co-operating with a qualified judge, are able to assist in a most effective manner in discovering and proving the facts in trials at law. Without the fullest participation of an able and just judge this practice manifestly would be dangerous.

Eventually there will perhaps be found an unobjectionable method by which judges of courts will be permitted to call experts "to assist the court" but not necessarily to be the exclusive witnesses on a special subject in any legal controversy. There would be violent objection even to this innovation, in many states, where the power of the judge is restricted, and it also might lead to abuses, but it is probably the least objectionable of the various proposed remedies. No doubt, the most effective reform or improvement in the use of expert testimony will eventually come through the presiding judge. Like many other reforms, however, they must perhaps await that day when all judges are appointed and confirmed by two-thirds vote of senates or other reviewing bodies; when they are given back the power taken from them; and the judicial office is everywhere given the dignity and honor it deserves. Advocates would not then so freely bring lying experts into courts if all judges were like those in certain courts who have the ability, the disposition, and *the power* to promote justice.

As discussed more at length in a later chapter, there is nothing that would so effectively assist in correcting the worst of the present abuses of expert testimony as a court procedure that thus permits the experienced, high-minded judge to co-operate to a greater extent in the trial of cases, as is permitted in the United States Federal Courts, the courts of New Jersey, and the courts of Canada. In these courts the fraudulent claimant, his conscienceless attorney, and his lying expert, do not have so free a field, and are not so immune from criticism and possible punishment as in the courts of some of our other free American commonwealths. In too many courts the judge must sit silent and powerless and see fraud and injustice triumph.

CHAPTER XIII.

MEMORY AND THE PROOF OF THE FACTS.

In practically every disputed document case part of the proof is based upon the alleged memory of some witness, or witnesses, who claim to have been present when the document was executed or who say they saw it afterwards. In one case (People v. Storrs, 207 N. Y.) six witnesses testified that they saw a document signed, and, notwithstanding this so-called "fact testimony", a jury decided on other evidence that the document was a forgery and that the six witnesses were mistaken or had committed perjury. As described in a previous chapter, many fantastic stories are told about the finding and the custody of forged documents, and the question of memory has an important bearing on the probable truth or falsity of many of these strange tales.

Although it often receives practically no specific attention, there is hardly any trial of importance in which the qualities and limitations of human memory should not carefully be considered. The subject bears so important a relation to the proof of facts by means of testimony that one who prepares a case for trial, examines a witness, or cross-examines a witness, needs to have a thorough knowledge of the matter in all its phases. One who listens attentively to testimony in courts of law soon comes to see that much litigation actually grows out of inaccuracies of human memory. Unfortunately there are litigants and witnesses who deliberately commit perjury, but most erroneous testimony is due to inaccuracies of memory, to unwarranted inference, and to imagination intensified by sympathy and prejudice. In many cases the parties to the controversy do not remember accurately what occurred. If all conflicts in testimony in courts were due to outright perjury, there certainly would be good cause for pessimism regarding the human race. As is well known, testimony growing out of observation and memory shows an almost unaccountable variation. It would almost seem that the average human observer could not see clearly, could not understand spoken words correctly, and could not report accurately.

To be completely prepared for his important task the lawyer must have a thorough knowledge of the subject of memory. He must know why one remembers and why one does not remember, and be able to discuss the subject with scientific accuracy, as a psychologist understands it, but in clear and simple language. One who is qualified to do so can often show that certain testimony has no proper basis. It is a rare closing argument in which memory in relation to testimony should not receive some careful discussion.

In the process of sifting the evidence the prudent attorney first tests the testimony of his own witnesses by the memory measure. They may remember altogether too much to make their testimony credible, and then again their stories, if true, can sometimes be greatly enforced by the recollection of, and association with, other occurrences. If the truthful witness is carefully taken over the matter in detail with all the attending conditions and circumstances recalled, some particular event or circumstance, that can itself be proved, sometimes positively fixes the time and greatly enforces the credibility of the testimony. It is, however, mainly in dealing with the inaccuracies and conscious perjury in adverse testimony that it is helpful to apply to it a knowledge of the various conditions affecting memory.

By a series of carefully prepared questions it is sometimes possible for the trial attorney to bring out by admissions that none of the necessary conditions upon which accurate memory depends were present in connection with an alleged recollection of a past occurrence. These questions will, of course, not disclose in advance the purpose of the admissions and will not at first refer to the subject of memory. For example, it became desirable to show in a criminal trial that a certain paper had been in existence for several years, and a defense witness testified that five years before he had seen in the hands of an alleged signer the unimportant document which later became the basis of the criminal trial. This paper was a prosaic document, of no interest in itself, and was written on ordinary writing paper and had nothing whatever about it of an unusual nature that would attract attention. Upon being properly interrogated, the witness readily made these admissions: "I took no interest whatever in the matter at the time. I merely happened to be present". "I was at the same place on numerous other occasions and saw many other papers and other things there at different times". "I do not remember any special thing that occurred at this particular time except that I was there and saw the paper". "Neither party interested in the matter at any time afterwards called my attention to the event until yesterday". "It has not been in my mind in any way for five years until yesterday when I was asked if I saw this document at that time and I said that I did".

These admissions alone practically condemned the testimony to a student of the subject of memory. If a witness in effect makes the above admissions, then it is evident that the necessary prerequisites of memory were all absent, and that the observer, even if he, or she, had been there and a document was there to be seen, would not have known the next week, or in any event the next month, that it had been seen. If by carefully prepared questions admissions of this kind are obtained, they furnish practically positive evidence that after a period of five years the memory of an observation of a trivial event, even if it had been witnessed, would be buried in oblivion. In order to show this fact, however, the hearers must be informed on the subject by questions and answers so that they become qualified to reason on the question. The whole question must also later be reviewed and enforced in argument.

The desired result in a cross-examination of this kind can only be obtained by the use of a series of questions leading to a climax resulting from the several admissions that justify only one conclusion. Each admission is an added reason for the conclusion. Memory testimony is often unsuccessfully attacked by asking the witness offhand what should have been the final question of a series. Another ineffective method of attacking memory testimony is to ask about some other trivial incident that must have occurred at about the same time, and when the witness cannot remember another nearby event, the attempt is made to draw the inference that because the observer cannot remember everything at a certain time that he cannot remember anything. If this method was correct it would be possible to show that nobody could remember anything. When the final question is asked first, the witness will deny, or explain, or "side-step", and the whole effect is lost because the hearer who is to pass upon the accuracy of the evidence has not been informed by the admissions that the desired conclusion is justified.

The important requirement in order to show the unreliability of the testimony is to show clearly the fundamental prerequisites affecting memory. When a cross-examination first skilfully brings out the absence of all the circumstances and conditions by which past events are recalled, then it can sometimes in effect be demonstrated that an alleged memory of an event is the result of inference, of confusion, or of conscious perjury.

It can clearly be shown in argument that memory depends, first, upon association of ideas, or events; second, the attention given to the matter; and third, the repetition or subsequent attention given to it by which the "paths of memory" become fixed and distinct. It can be made clear that "the stream of thought" flows on in relation to most events without leaving a ripple on the surface and that without the aid (1) of association, (2) of interest, or (3) of repetition, a past event cannot be recalled.

It is sometimes a pitiful sight to see an employee,

or a relative, or one under some direct or indirect obligation to a litigant, commit obvious perjury by testifying as to the alleged memory of an event that, if true, is an important part of a dishonest defense, or a support of a fraudulent claim on a disputed document. It is often of vital importance that someone should testify to having seen a disputed will, note, contract, or agreement, before a certain date, or at a certain place, or to have witnessed, directly, casually, or accidentally, the execution of the document. The testimony sometimes is only half perjury to the effect that certain persons "were together" and "that writing was done" at a certain definite time. The stories are sometimes ingenious and at first plausible, but when analyzed often are obviously incredible.

The cross-examination of unwilling witnesses of this class is often one of the most important duties of a trial attorney. If testimony of this kind, by an alleged "eye-witness", is not weakened, or destroyed, it may have a controlling effect. On the other hand, when skilfully interrogated, these witnesses, who are unwillingly committing half or whole perjury for friendship, or under real or imaginary obligation to another, often by their admissions expose the fraudulent nature of a claim. As a rule they do not have a bold, assertive manner, but plainly show by their conduct that they are reluctantly performing a most disagreeable act. Their testimony sometimes is partly true, but would be of no value without the untrue part. If dealt with gently but skilfully and firmly these witnesses will sometimes try to remember too much and then, when brought up against a discrepancy, contradiction, or obvious exaggeration, will sometimes practically recant and admit probable error. It is especially important in an examination of this kind that just the proper tone be maintained for, if unskilfully dealt with, a witness may become a dangerous opponent.

Much testimony relates to these alleged occurrences or events, in which the observer at the time not only had no personal interest whatever, but will strenuously deny that he had any interest, and in connection with which he will also freely admit that there was no subsequent reference to the matter, and also that the occurrence was not associated with any other important event by which it is brought up to the surface of memory. The witness who is testifying untruthfully will desire to make it appear that at the time and afterwards, until the controversy arose, he had no interest, and took no interest, in the matter in any way at any time.

Testimony of this kind has to do mainly with alleged visual memory or verbal memory, and in many instances it can be shown that an alleged recollection of something seen or something heard long ago is so improbable that it deserves no credit. The quotation of what are claimed to be the exact words spoken long before is practically conclusive proof of perjury. The cross-examiner must do more, however, than merely state these various facts and ideas. He must, in effect, make the witness state them in response to correctly framed questions. The usual witness, if properly interrogated, must promptly admit that he has forgotten most of the things that have occurred in his life. He will also say that he remembers only those that have been of importance to him personally, that have caused him great pain or great joy, or that are associated with something else that he remembers clearly, or those others that have been so frequently repeated, like the unimportant date of his own birth, that he remembers them without effort.

The untruthfulness of witnesses is sometimes clearly shown by leading them to recite details regarding an invented or imaginary story based on memory. Under the circumstances they hesitate to say they do not remember any circumstance or fact, no matter how trivial, that may have occurred. They hesitate to say, "I do not remember", and often show merely by the fulness of the story that they are not speaking the truth. The truthful witness, if he remembers at all, remembers the occurrence as a whole and regarding its details does not hesitate to say that he cannot recall anything that occurred.

On cross-examination and also in argument the fact can be brought out that what is often related as a report from memory is a mere inference from circumstances. When skilfully led, adverse witnesses will sometimes in effect make the admission. If a temperate and honest man is asked what he did on a certain day several years before, he will admit that of most days that he has no memory whatever, but will not hesitate to say that he did certain things on those days because it was his custom to do them. This statement, of course, is not made as a result of memory, but from pure inference. Much suggested and not quite dishonest testimony grows out of the description of an alleged event to one who is told that he was at a particular place at a certain time. He then assumes by inference that if he was there he would have seen what it is alleged occurred there at that time, and he often testifies that he did see what it is claimed occurred because he thinks he was there, when, as a matter of fact, he has no recollection whatever of the particular event.

One of the most effective distorters of memory is emotion. Excitement, fear, hate, horror, or affection may so influence memory that the report of an occurrence is very far from the fact. Memory may, of course, be inaccurate because observation was not clear, but also because, through bias, imagination and inference are both confused with memory. The biased witness is not wholly untruthful, but reports in addition to what he vaguely remembers of what occurred what he thinks ought to have occurred. Friends and acquaintances often stretch the truth almost to the breaking point when, stimulated by emotion, they attempt to relate what actually took place.

CHAPTER XIV.

CIRCUMSTANTIAL AND FACT EVIDENCE IN DISPUTED DOCUMENT CASES.

A common fallacy in connection with the problem of proof is the idea that every fact or circumstance in a body or mass of evidence is connected with and dependent upon every other circumstance. This fallacy is embodied in the common understanding of the familiar phrase, so dear to the hearts of defense attorneys and to all who would prevent proof, that "A chain of circumstantial evidence is no stronger than its weakest link". This idea is discussed in an illuminating manner by Bentham in Judicial Proof. It is shown that the fallacy lies in the idea that circumstantial evidence can correctly be described as a "chain".

A statement with a very different import, but more nearly true in most cases, would be that "A cable of circumstantial evidence is as strong as the combination of all of its strands". The common refuge of those against the facts in attempting to defeat proof in any matter, of any kind, is to find the weakest element in the proof and then assume that all the other elements are dependent upon it. Proof in a great majority of cases is not a succession of "links" but a combination of "strands".

Of course, when it is a fact that several circumstances, forming a part of evidence, are all dependent upon one other definite circumstance and that circumstance is weak, then the evidence can properly be described as a chain with a weak link, but the common assumption that evidence is always a "chain" is not justified. In many cases what are called the weak links can all be eliminated and yet the main bulk of the proof will still stand, and it is obvious that under these circumstances the circumstantial proof is correctly described as a cable with strands of varying strength.

It would be extraordinary indeed if a series of circumstances, all pointing to one definite conclusion, should all be of equal force. It is simply inevitable that they will vary, and in some instances only one of them by itself is strong evidence of the fact to be proved. The weaker circumstances are merely confirmatory, but in combination with the stronger may all together form irresistible proof, although when considered separately would have but little probative force.

The idea or principle underlying conclusive proof is the combination at one time, place, or occasion of a number of unrelated facts and circumstances of various kinds, each of which has value as proof. As the number in combination increases, the force of the evidence is enormously increased, as any mathematician knows. For example, it would be dangerous to identify a horse from one scar or point of description, which might be found on other horses, but this particular point of description has a value in connection with nineteen other points of varying force, which, if all combined, is so conclusive as proof that practical common sense, as well as the conclusions of the mathematicians, decide that this combination of what singly might be "weak links'' forms a cable of proof that is absolutely conclusive.

Knowledge of this common fallacy regarding this method of measuring evidence by its weakest element furnishes a warning to the trial attorney in sifting and selecting the evidence he is to present, not to include that which is obviously vulnerable, as it is inevitable that this ''chain'' argument will be used. There are attorneys who could hardly practice law without it. Many arguments of counsel by those who are shielding crime, promoting fraud, and preventing the facts from being proved, consist only of attacks upon certain minor phases of the evidence that admittedly are not alone conclusive, with the unwarranted assumption, too often recognized in the law, that if one point of weakness can be shown then this proves that all points are weak. It is incumbent upon the attorney, whose business it is to prove the facts, to expose this fallacy as early as possible in a trial, and it is also incumbent upon those who discuss evidence in printed words to consider the matter from the standpoint of common sense, of logic, and of mathematics.

''In the unbiased search for truth the law has no favorites by presumption. Silent circumstances, without power to change their attitude, or to make explanation, or to commit perjury, may speak as truthfully in court as animated witnesses.'' This was said by the learned judge in a recent notable opinion in a disputed document case, In re O'Connor's Estate (Neb.) 179 N. W. (1920). The comparative values of what is known as personal, circumstantial, and real evidence are old questions in legal discussions, and this quotation from a recent opinion shows that they are still live questions. Circumstantial evidence and also the evidence of tangible things are often in conflict with evidence of alleged observers, or participants, who testify in trials at law relating to disputed documents.

There is widespread misapprehension and unwarranted prejudice regarding evidence other than the direct evidence of witnesses. There are many persons with limited experience and who have thought but little on the subject, who are inclined to think that it is dangerous to depend upon any evidence except the oral evidence of living witnesses. This misapprehension justifies strong statements like that quoted above, for experience teaches, as in this particular case, that "silent circumstances" often have a controlling power as a means of proof that is irresistible.

There are at least three distinguishable classes of so-called circumstances in evidence which, however, cannot safely be interpreted in the same way. One class of circumstances, often referred to in trials at law, includes all outside and related incidents, conditions and happenings which are described by witnesses and necessarily are subject to all of the dangers and defects of oral and memory testimony. There are also circumstances which are admitted, or which arise from the nature of the case itself, which cannot be denied, and lastly there are tangible and visible facts before court and jury which are the basis for a judgment.

This latter class of facts is often erroneously referred to in a critical way in disputed document cases as "merely circumstantial". The law, as well as logic, makes a distinction between surroundings, conditions, and "circumstances" as compared with real and tangible facts. These visible things as an element in the process of proof constitute what is usually called "real evidence". A bungling, overwritten, traced signature, as well as a coat with a bullet-hole in the breast, are both known as "real" evidence. These are the "silent circumstances" that do not commit perjury. Though silent they often are eloquent. To learn their story is the vital part of many trials at law.

All these quite distinct classes of evidence form the basis of legal verdicts and judgments. The great mass of legal evidence consists of the testimony of oral witnesses which has force in proportion as it is believed, but in many important cases a verdict must be based mainly upon the second or the third class of evidence for the reason, as has been well said, that it is not often that a forger or a poisoner invites spectators to witness the act. Circumstances and facts must be interpreted and illustrated in order to show whether a definite conclusion can be based on them. In many cases a particular conclusion is irresistible.

It is obvious that it requires a higher degree of intelligence to reason regarding facts and circumstances than it does merely to believe, or not believe, oral witnesses. The value of circumstantial, or visible evidence, therefore, largely depends upon the clearness with which it is presented and the intelligence of those to whom it is addressed. To stupid observers it means little because the drawing of more than the simplest inferences is beyond their power, while to the intelligent it often is conclusive proof against every kind of opposition.

There has been much partisan argument and loose reasoning on this question of the comparative value of oral evidence, of evidence based on circumstances, and evidence of things as a basis for a judgment. In any testimony that must depend upon human observation, human memory, and human veracity, all the varied human frailties must be taken into account, but with proved, or admitted, circumstances and with tangible things a correct judgment depends in no way upon the mere statements of witnesses. In the absence of the necessary reasoning mind, however, it is true that error may result even if the facts are proved. With the first class of evidence error results from perjury, or human error; in the other cases error, if it results, is due to inaccurate reasoning.

With expert testimony where only bare opinions are given, the credulity of the hearer is what is appealed to; if the hearer believes, then the testimony is given credit. If, however, certain facts and circumstances are admitted or proved, then the facts themselves are the witnesses. This is the point in a disputed document trial where it becomes necessary to emphasize the illuminating idea presented in the quotation above from the Nebraska case. By a kind of perversity there are those called upon to discuss the comparative force of evidence who apparently refuse to reason and who are inclined to exaggerate the comparative value of oral evidence. It is of course easier to listen and believe, or not believe, than to listen and to reason.

It also readily appears that this necessity for reasoning on facts and circumstances has an important bearing on the problem of selecting a jury, and also the wider question whether cases involving difficult technical questions ought ever to be tried by a jury. Where the correctness of a verdict must depend upon the ability to reach a correct conclusion by a logical process it is well understood that there are those sometimes called to decide cases who manifestly are not qualified to perform the act they are asked to perform. Even if the facts are shown, an incorrect verdict may be reached. On the other hand, a narrow view, or an extreme conservatism, or an occasional unwise radicalism, of one individual who is asked to decide a case, may lead attorneys to hesitate to put all questions of this kind before tribunals without juries.

Civil cases involving technical questions are usually tried without juries in Canada and the British Empire generally, and undoubtedly with results that are more often in harmony with justice than in a procedure that puts before the ordinary jury difficult technical questions requiring knowledge, experience, superior intelligence, and reasoning ability. Where it is a question of passing upon the credibility of the testimony of ordinary witnesses, as determined by their appearance and statements, a jury of twelve men in some ways may perhaps be superior to a single individual in arriving at the truth. Eventually, no doubt, when legal processes are perfect, difficult technical matters will seldom be presented to untrained juries.

There is some misunderstanding of terms in these discussions. A fact is freely defined as anything that exists, and it is the same in the law as elsewhere. It may be an idea, a belief, or prejudice in the mind of another, or a visible and tangible thing. Facts are often thought of only as tangible, but many of the most important facts in the history of the world are ideas. Too often prejudice is a fact that cannot be safely overlooked. Some of these facts are susceptible of proof in a court of law, others are inferred from other facts, and still others are admittedly true.

The real facts in a disputed document case in large part are visible, tangible things that can be seen and measured and counted. They must be seen, must be correctly interpreted, and it must be accurately determined what conclusion they justify. These are the facts that are stubborn, that cannot be cross-examined, and that "do not commit perjury". They can be assailed and denounced, and still they remain silent but eloquent. The attorney who can collect, illustrate, interpret and show the significance and the true relation of facts of this kind when they are favorable to his contention, almost compels adherence to his views.

The analysis of nearly any disputed document case shows the unusual extent to which this matter of reasoning enters into the trial as compared with the trials of ordinary cases. In nearly every case there is general evidence which tends to show the probability or improbability of the act and also evidence of alleged eye witnesses, or participants in the actual preparation of the disputed document.

In a trial involving an actual forgery it is almost inevitable that there will also be supporting perjury which attempts to prove the genuineness of the document by direct testimony, and, as a rule, in the trial of a case involving actual forgery there is also testimony of unqualified opinion witnesses who give mere opinions regarding the document, and finally there is the examination of and technical testimony regarding the document itself. It is especially in this latter part of the process that the tangible facts are shown and reasoning must enter, and in many cases the conclusion must finally be based almost wholly upon the interpretation of the visible facts for the reason that the oral and general testimony is in hopeless conflict.

This necessity for reasoning in disputed document cases not only requires an intelligent judge or referee, or an intelligent jury, to pass upon the matter, but also requires somewhat unusual qualities in an advocate which are not so essential in all classes of cases. The necessity for a thorough knowledge of the technical facts, discussed in other parts of this book, is based upon this requirement for reasoning in cases of this kind. If an attorney is not qualified to interpret the facts which he presents, the jury certainly is excusable for failure to make the correct interpretation. It is on these points of reasoning and interpretation that many modern decisions point out the force of real evidence as pointing to a definite conclusion.

In the celebrated Rice-Patrick case, 81 App. Div. 223 (N. Y.), for example, the four disputed signatures all practically superimposed, even to "i" dots in a way that, "from common knowledge and experience", as the opinion said, would not be possible in the writing of an old man upwards of eighty years of age who wrote a very uncertain, variable hand. This tangible fact evidence was before the court and the problem was to determine by common sense and a process of reasoning whether or not four genuine signatures of this writer would be likely to bear this extraordinary relation to each other.

In the ordinary forgery case it is shown how a disputed signature diverges from the average habitual writing of the one whose writing is imitated. These divergences are of various qualities and degrees and differ in number in different cases, and a decision as to the genuineness of a disputed signature, after observing these various characteristics, is the result of a process of reasoning as to whether a genuine signature by the writer would possess all of the peculiar and unusual qualities of the disputed writing.

In a case involving a contract a fold in the paper extended across the body of the document and across two heavily shaded portions of the signature. The fold had broken the paper so that it was almost but not quite separated. Across both the shaded lines of the signature there extended a white broken line where the fold crossed, and the pen strokes were the same width up to the extreme edges of the folded or broken place. At a point only from one-eighth to one-quarter of an inch away a shaded line *of the body of the document* went across the same fold, and where the line crossed the fold the ink had unmistakably run out in both directions into the softened fiber of the paper at the fold. It was contended by those who attacked the document that it would have been physically impossible to write the signature with the shaded lines as it appeared after the paper had been folded, and it was also contended that it was physically impossible that the characteristics of the writing above the signature, where the ink had run into the fold, could be explained in any possible way except that the writing followed the folding. It was shown that it was occasionally necessary for the writer to sign certain documents in blank which were afterwards to be filled out by a clerk, and the contention was that this signed paper had been used for an improper purpose, and this physical evidence was depended upon to show that the body of the disputed document was written after the signature. It readily appears that a conclusion, if based upon this evidence alone, could only be that the contention of those who claimed that the signature was on the document before the body of the document was written was correct.

In another instance the heavily shaded address, on an envelope containing an anonymous letter, consisting of several long and widely separated lines and the letters and word P. O. Box and a number in the corner of the envelope, exactly superimposed an offset, or blotter impression, on an ordinary new blotter which was found in the rooms of a suspected writer. A photograph of the blotter and the envelope was made of the exact sizes of the originals. These photographs were then printed on transparent films and the lines and letters, and even the "i" dots and "t" crossings, and the box number in the corner of the envelope, would all exactly superimpose at the same time when one was put over the other. These were the facts upon which it was necessary to determine whether the letter originated in this particular place, and it was necessary by a process of reasoning to determine whether this exact coincidence would be likely to occur unless that identical writing actually had been impressed on that blotter.

In a handwritten will, not written by the testator but undoubtedly signed by him, an important sentence relating to the disposition of the residuary estate, was manifestly written in a different handwriting from the body of the will and was inserted between the ending of the original writing and the signature. The will was contested on the ground that a sentence had been interpolated after the document was signed. Examination disclosed that one stroke of the last sentence and a stroke in the signature crossed each other, and it was also found that this signature and the apparently interpolated sentence were both written with nigrosine ink, a coal tar product which produces an ink which is described as "black when first used". This ink will dissolve at any time on the paper, and a subsequent line dissolves the first line at the crossing and the edges of the second or last line made are unmistakably continuous across the first line. An examination of this crossing with the microscope showed without any question whatever that the signature was written *after* the sentence above. A greatly enlarged photograph was made and upon being shown at the trial the contest on this ground was at once withdrawn. The visible facts, when shown by the microscope, or in the enlarged photograph, warranted but one possible conclusion.

An alleged copy of a deed, properly witnessed and containing the seal of the commissioner and his signature, was contested. The original document was lost or destroyed, and the pages of the record in the County

Clerk's office had been destroyed. The deed, if genuine, transferred the title to several thousand acres of pine land. The document was dated 1891 and consisted of three long pages of typewriting. It was written on a Smith Premier typewriter. The manufacturers of this machine in the year 1896 changed the width of a number of capital letters. The disputed document contained hundreds of capital letters, and when examined and measured, and illustrated by enlarged photographs, it was shown that the document was unmistakably written upon a Smith Premier typewriter with the narrow capitals. The original model letters themselves were exhibited and measured, and the impressions of them from the date that they were first made. The decision of the case entirely depended upon a comparison of measurements, the differences of which ranged from about 1/100 to 1/250 of an inch. The proof was conclusive that the document could not have been written on its date. The facts were the widths of the capital letters and a correct decision depended upon accuracy of vision and accuracy of measurement of visible tangible facts.

In an important will case involving the writing of an old man with imperfect vision, who wrote with a tremulous hand, an alleged will signature was attacked on the ground that it was a fraudulent imitation. Without magnification the signature appeared to be a continuous writing, but when examined under magnification and in the form of enlarged photographs, the signature showed that it had been repaired, perfected, and overwritten in at least ten different places with a delicacy and skill that the alleged writer did not possess even if disposed to make such additions. The signature was in this condition when it was first produced. It was divergent in other ways and these various questions were the facts from which a conclusion was to be drawn as to whether or not it was a genuine signature.

A signature of a witness upon a contract in controversy, which purported to be eight years of age, appeared to be recent writing. A color reading of the signature with Lovibond Tintometer glasses disclosed that it was exactly of the same color as Carter's Writing Fluid at the end of about seven days in August. A second color examination of the signature at the end of a month showed that the signature had in the meantime (the month of August) turned almost black, or a very dark purple, the color of ordinary iron-gall ink at the end of about a month or six weeks, and a test of this ink showed that it was iron-gall ink. The problem in the case was the determination of the fact whether ordinary commercial ink, which turns almost black in a few weeks, would have remained a bright blue for eight years and at the end of that time would have turned black in a few weeks. These were the physical facts from which to determine whether or not this signature had been on the document eight years.

An important contract, written on a Royal typewriter, contained a postscript which materially changed the effect of one of its provisions. The manufacturers of this machine changed the top of the small "m", making the upward connecting lines at the top nearly straight, so that instead of being rounded the second and third tops of the letter are similar to the teeth of a saw. The purpose of the change was to prevent the filling in at the top of the letter, especially when a fresh ribbon is used. This contract was written and dated before this change in this letter, and examination disclosed positively that the body of the document was written with the small "m" of the old type and that the modifying postscript, although written on the same kind of a machine, was written with a machine carrying the new style of "m", which had not been designed and made until three years after the date of the document. This detail in this one letter, which appeared in many words, was the controlling fact on which to determine whether or not this was a genuine postscript.

In a bankruptcy case a valuable certificate of stock showed a date of transfer in which the last figure of the year was a combination in the same field of the figures "4" and "7". If the year was 1914, then the transfer was made so that it would not be included in the claims under the bankruptcy decision. The writer testified that in writing the year a mistake was made in writing "1917" instead of "1914", and the "4" was immediately made over the "7" with the same pen and ink. Both figures were admittedly by the same writer. The "4" was in the same field as the "7", but as the upper left-hand part of the "4" extended above the "7" it had only one ink, and the "7" extended below the strokes making the "4", so that there were two portions of these overwritten figures where the inks were not mixed. An application of diluted acid turned the upper left-hand portion of the "4" a distinct brick red, and the same acid turned the lower part of the "7" a distinct greenish blue, the two colors being unmistakably different and demonstrating that the testimony regarding how and when they were made was not true. The reaction showed conclusively that one figure was made with logwood ink, and the other with iron-gall ink. These were the physical facts in the case that it became necessary to prove. When the proof was presented the case was discontinued.

A holograph will containing considerable writing was contested on the ground of forgery. Scores of leases with extended writing upon them were available as standards of comparison. This standard writing showed that the writer wrote consistently the Old Round Hand style of writing which, as written by many writers, made the capital "E" without a loop in the middle, but with a continuous curved line instead of a loop or angle. This old writing, as shown in the system and as written by many writers, also finished an "o" at the end of words without the little continuing stroke to the right, but ended with the oval upward stroke of the letter. Both of these characteristics were changed in the systems of writing which followed the Old Round Hand. This disputed will showed three words ending with "o" with a distinct stroke to the right, and two capital "E's" with distinct loops in the middle. There were several hundred words written by this writer in the standard writings ending with "o", and in no instance did he ever end with a stroke to the right, and there were scores of examples of capital "E's" which he always made without the loop or the angle, which was a form entirely foreign to the writing he learned and used. These were physical facts in the case that could easily be seen when clearly presented and properly explained.

A letter, the purpose of which was to prove the genuineness of a deed to several thousand acres of land, was dated in 1892 and was clearly written upon a Remington typewriter. This machine, among other changes, changed the width of the lower part of the capital "P" from .048 to .060 of an inch in the year 1898. This confirmatory letter had several capital "P's" with this portion of the capital "P" .060 of an inch wide. These measurements were the controlling facts in the case.

In two different will cases, one in Pennsylvania and one in Texas, and in a note case in the latter state, upon the trial of the cases the claimants put in evidence in each case as a standard signature the actual model signature from which the disputed signature had been directly traced. This was done apparently on the theory that if the disputed signature was exactly like a genuine signature in the case then this correspondence in exact detail would prove that the disputed signature was genuine. In all of these cases the main fact, after the introduction of the model, was the question whether this damaging identity in size, outline, and exact proportions indicated genuineness or lack of genuineness. In all the cases it was decided that the documents were forgeries by tracing.

A will covering an estate of more than one million dollars was dated the 18th of March, 1912. It consisted of two pages of typewriting, with only six words of the body of the will on the second page followed by the genuine signature of the testator and the names of the witnesses. In the year 1920, after the death of the testator, a careful examination of the document disclosed that the typewriting on the second page, which contained only the six words of the body of the will, was written on an old-style Remington typewriter, and that the first page was written upon a later model of the same machine, which later machine *was not made until 1918.* The work from, and the history and date of, these typewriters were the main facts in the case. After thorough investigation the will was definitely declared to be a forgery by the substitution of a fraudulent first page, and the case ended without appeal.

These various phases and elements of proof in cases of this kind illustrate what is described as real evidence in disputed document cases. It will readily be seen that a correct conclusion in matters of this kind is based upon two separate operations. The first of these acts is the examination of the alleged facts in order to see whether or not they actually exist. The second duty of the one who must reach a conclusion is to examine the facts singly and in combination and determine by employing knowledge, experience, intelligence, and common sense, as utilized in a process of reasoning, whether or not a particular conclusion is justified. In many cases the proved facts compel an honest observer to reach only a certain definite conclusion.

The importance of presenting testimony of this kind with appropriate illustrations and with full and clear reasons at once appears when it is understood that a decision is to be reached by a process of reasoning based upon these various details of the problems as illustrated by suitable enlarged photographs and as observed by the aid of appropriate special instruments. In proportion as testimony is full, clear, and explicit, it naturally becomes possible for those to whom it is addressed to determine whether or not it withstands the test of reasonableness. It is, of course, not alone desirable that testimony of this class be given in full in order that its effectiveness may be shown, but also that its weaknesses may also be seen if they exist.

CHAPTER XV.

THE DESIGNING AND LIGHTING OF COURT ROOMS.

The interests of justice require that trials at law should be held where every word spoken can be distinctly heard, where every piece of visible evidence can be clearly seen, and where every witness can be closely scrutinized by court, counsel, and jurymen. When these requirements are specified, it at once is apparent that many court-houses are not suitable places for trials at law.

The attorney against the facts is naturally inclined to make it difficult to see, to hear, and to understand, and while he may not have designed the court-house, its defects often assist him. There is no doubt that among the allies of fraud and crime can be numbered many unsuitable court-houses. The problem of proof is often affected by various conditions surrounding the presentation of evidence. To be controlling, evidence must be distinctly heard, must be clearly seen, and above all, must be properly understood. It is thus important for one who strives for a verdict based on the proof of facts to realize constantly that his opponent may not only be assisted by error, perjury, and prejudice, but by darkness, disturbing noise, blindness, and deafness.

Many a city in this broad land has spent hundreds

* A few paragraphs of this chapter were included in an address before the eighth annual convention of the Illuminating Engineering Society, at Cleveland, Ohio, September 21–24, 1914. This matter was reprinted in Law Notes, November, 1914; and in Scientific American Supplement, October 17, 1914.

of thousands of dollars on a court-house in which there is not one properly arranged, furnished, and lighted court room where comfort, clear seeing, and distinct hearing are all attainable. Modern laws of some states happily require a certain amount of properly placed light in every school house, but it appears that the laws have not yet been applied to law houses.

Brief experience in many a court room is sufficient to show how such a room should not be arranged and should not be lighted. In many cases artistic and architectural considerations have apparently been the only ideas followed in the matter of design, arrangement, and lighting. These buildings look well on picture post cards, but are not good places in which to try law suits. There are also the big, old barn-like court-houses, from fifty to one hundred years old, that were never either practical or beautiful. They should be remodeled at once. They would be greatly improved for practical purposes by placing new ceilings at about half or two-thirds the height of the old ones. In many a city of our land the court-house is the one place where it is most difficult to hear and most difficult to see.

No court-house should be built without the active co-operation of at least three experienced trial judges, and the architect should have the assistance of a lighting engineer, an acoustic engineer, and a ventilating engineer. Many a beautiful court-house, standing out in an open square, in God's free sunlight, is so designed and arranged that it is necessary to use artificial light in it in the day time! In the interests of justice, as well as of economy, the "lighting engineer" should use, to the fullest extent, the free and unequaled light of the sun.

Ordinary common sense ought to suggest that a court room should be so designed and constructed as to serve best the use to which it is to be put. It should be a place where words spoken in an ordinary tone of voice can easily be heard by jury, by court, and by counsel, and it should be properly and adequately lighted by the sun by day, and by suitably placed artificial lights by night. A room where trials at law are to be held should also have adequate means provided for proper ventilation. If in addition to these essentials it can also be made artistic and beautiful, or even sumptuous if that is desired, well and good, but these latter requirements should not be allowed to supplant the real uses of the room.

There are many of these beautiful court rooms, finished in marble and lavishly furnished, which do not adequately answer the purpose for which they were built. In many of them the natural and artificial lighting are both bad; in others there are constant disturbing echoes, and, worst of all, the various parts are so big and so distant from each other that it is difficult for the participants to hear anything distinctly.

Furthermore, because of lack of ventilation in many of these rooms occupants are inclined to go to sleep, or to become irritable and quarrelsome. It is quite possible that bad air has had a considerable influence in the producing of bad legal precedents and in defeating the interests of justice. An impractical architect should not thus be allowed to punish thousands of citizens of a community for a hundred years or more by an improper design and faulty arrangement of a building intended for public use.

In the first place, rooms designed for this purpose

should have much more window space than is usually supplied, and judge's desk and jury box should be so placed that full advantage can be taken of this daylight. Equally as important as the matter of lighting is that of the size and arrangement of the various parts in relation to each other. This arrangement is often, if not usually, entirely dependent, not upon the practical convenience and comfort of those who are to use the room, but upon its size, its shape, and its architectural balance and appearance.

An excellent practical requirement would be, and this is of first importance, that the furniture and fixtures should be of such a size and should be so arranged that judge, jury, witness, and examining counsel are near enough together so that they all would be included within an imaginary circle not larger than sixteen feet in diameter. Think what comfort and efficiency this one change in arrangement would at once give to hundreds of court rooms! The various participants could then all hear and, if properly arranged in relation to the sources of light, could all see. The change would improve voices, manners, and dispositions. Some of the ponderous furniture would be eliminated and the room would be fitted for practical use and not for show purposes. Judges should take this matter into their own hands and not be passive victims of the mistakes of their predecessors. A few carpenters in a few hours could, in many court-houses, make a decided contribution to comfort, to convenience, and to the interests of justice. These carpenters should be employed without further delay.

Intelligent thoughtfulness would also put the main

court rooms as far away as possible from disturbing street noises, and ceilings would not be made so high that the ordinary tones of the human voice are lost in the stellar spaces. Another help would be the putting of the jurymen close together in three short rows of four, instead of two long rows of six, so that juryman number six, and juryman number twelve, are not too far away from the important proceedings. In many court rooms one of the ridiculous duties of the clerk, or even of the presiding judge, is to say to every witness, "Now speak up so that farthest juryman out there can hear you". This difficulty could be permanently corrected by moving the juryman up into the zone of activity and this change might also assist in keeping tired jurymen awake.

The completely equipped court room has a permament, properly placed chart, or exhibition board, for maps, drawings, and illustrations of various kinds. Crayons and suitable paper are available for instant use in illustrating testimony. The absence of such an exhibition chart points back to the time when testimony was all oral and it was considered dangerous to show anything to a jury. In many places a chart apparently has never been seen in a court room.

When proof in court must be based mainly upon the correct interpretation of delicate, but what may be highly significant, visible evidence, it is simply impossible to prove the facts in some court rooms. Court and jury in a few instances have left their accustomed places in a big, dark, unsuitable room and, in an informal and sensible manner, have gathered close together near some low-placed, clean windows in a small room where all could see clearly and all could hear easily.

When the necessity arises for proving by visible evidence any delicate physical fact this whole question of human vision, with its defects, its limitations, and its aids, becomes a question of vital interest. In the first place, it is important to realize, as more fully discussed in a preceding chapter, that seeing ability is not by any means the same with all observers and that there is such a thing as a kind of unconscious form-blindness.

The blindness and deafness in court rooms in the past has in some measure, no doubt, been a mental blindness and deafness, due in large measure to the ancient legal procedure that by its unwise restrictions threw a twilight gloom around legal investigations and too often made it difficult, if not impossible, to prove the facts. Hampering restrictions in some courts in effect still darkens the windows, and a nervous, unwise insistence on haste sometimes does not allow enough time to prove certain facts that require careful, sustained observation. In the trial of cases in certain courts the conduct of the proceedings sometimes suggests that something in that court of real importance is to be done as soon as the case on trial is out of the way.

The aids and conditions that perfect and intensify human vision are naturally closely related to the question of discovering the physical evidence that points to fraud of various kinds in connection with disputed documents, and the subject is of special importance in connection with the task of actually showing and proving these facts in a court of law in an actual trial. The difficulty is greatly increased if the testimony must be presented to untrained men who must be made to see clearly and understand fully in order to decide correctly. It is therefore highly essential that sense impressions of all kinds be intensified in every way possible. One practical way to intensify all sense impressions is to put the participants into a suitable room.

Anything relating to the subject of illumination that affects the quality of human vision is necessarily of importance in all investigations relating to forged handwriting or disputed typewriting, in which delicate differences in form, proportions, size, or color are the questions of importance in the case. Justice has been defeated many times in these cases because, like cathedrals, court rooms have been lighted with a dim, if not with a religious light, perhaps in harmony with some of the hampering old legal precedents.

Partly because of poor illumination, judges and jurors in many closely contested cases, where the decision has depended chiefly upon visible evidence, have not been able to see well enough to reach a correct conclusion. They not only became weary in trying to hear in the big, lofty room amid the echoes, but became so fatigued in trying to see in the dim, remote light, that in a kind of despair they gave up trying to hear and trying to see and finally made a petulant, desperate guess at the facts, and guessed wrong. There are but few efforts more annoying, or more wearisome, than straining hour after hour to hear and to see under difficulties.

The quality of any mental conception, or comparison, based on sight sensations, and the final accuracy of sight, not only depend upon the force and clearness of the sensation that reaches the brain, but the knowledge and experience which the brain already possesses. The necessity for seeing clearly is that one may be able to interpret correctly. This whole question is discussed more at length in the chapter on form blindness and is here considered only in connection with this discussion of the proper construction of court rooms.

Another important reason why court rooms should be properly arranged and adequately lighted is to enable judge and jury, not only to see the visible evidence and hear what is said, but to see the witnesses with distinctness as their testimony is being given, as well as to hear what they say. That this result may be attained it is highly desirable, as already suggested, that witness box, jury box, and judge's bench be arranged in proper relation to each other, near together and in good light. Fortunately, there is in all of us a kind of instinct, enforced by conscious or unconscious training, by which we determine, at least with some degree of accuracy, whether or not those who speak to us are telling the truth. This important faculty is dependent upon both the sense of sight and the sense of hearing. We constantly thus judge each other in a kind of mysterious and unknown manner. We often at once catch the insincere tone and also recognize the suspicious gesture, manner, or attitude. There are many little things in conduct that we at once interpret as suspicious, or, on the contrary, that are evidences of frankness and honesty. By the use of the eye, as well as the ear, we unconsciously interpret all messages that come to us as sincere, or as deceitful; as true, or as false.

That ancient requirement of the law, written into the charters of liberty, that "the accused be confronted by the witnesses against him", was no doubt partly based upon a recognition of this important faculty by which truth is separated from falsehood. Successful perjury is undoubtedly more difficult out in the light than in a darkened chamber. A witness should, therefore, be placed close to the jury, where he and the jurymen can easily look into each others' faces, or where the witness can directly face the judge, if he alone is to decide upon the truth or falsity of the testimony. The room should be so lighted that every movement and changing expression of the witness can be distinctly seen. Few of us have ever tried to analyze the evidences of sincerity, or of untruthfulness, as shown by tone, by emphasis, by appearance, and by actions, but we all understand that these evidences do exist. It is not uncommon to hear it said, "I was greatly impressed by the sincerity of the witness", or again, "I could see clearly that he was lying".

As has been pointed out heretofore in discussing other topics, expert testimony regarding forgery and disputed documents, under the old legal practice now happily passing away, was mainly the giving of bare oral opinions on a contested question often involving technical interpretations of delicate, but vital visible evidence. This practice, which has justly been much criticised and discredited, still continues in certain cases relating to insanity, medical questions, and some other subjects that the ordinary man, no matter how assisted, is unable to pass upon intelligently. Fortunately a new practice has developed in many jurisdictions in connection with proof of physical facts relating to disputed documents. Under the new procedure referee, judge, and jury are shown the actual basis for whatever opinion is given. These highly important changes in legal procedure regarding visible evidence make still more necessary a suitable arrangement and proper illumination of court rooms.

Vital evidence is sometimes based upon the interpretation of erasures, of indistinct stains, and of delicate tints and colors, which, under dim light, all become a dull and indistinct gray. Unfortunately every day is a gray day in some court rooms. In cases involving chemical erasures certain indistinct yellow stains are of vital significance, but are practically invisible in the dim light of many court-houses. In many rooms where cases are tried the effective use of the necessary microscope is impossible. In certain cases involving the identification of paper, where it is contended that a sheet has been fraudulently interpolated in a disputed document, the facts could be positively proved out in the court yard under the trees, but under the light conditions provided, often intensified by the bad acoustic properties, the bad air, and the petulance and air of haste resulting therefrom, fraud is successful and the guilty escape.

Another class of cases under which the question of good illumination is of vital importance are those involving all ink investigations, either to determine age, or to discover whether two or more ink writings are identical or different. Some of these questions can no more be answered under the illumination of certain court rooms than they could be answered in the light of the average cellar, while the same investigation, if conducted under properly diffused daylight, often shows a result that can be appreciated by any intelligent man with average eyesight. If it becomes necessary to show that writing is not as old as it purports to be, or to prove that an addition or interlineation in ink is the same, or different from other parts of the same document, good light is absolutely essential in order to show the fact. In some court rooms facts of this kind cannot be proved.

By the use of the special color microscope and the Lovibond tintometer glasses it is possible to match and record changing ink colors with great accuracy and the proof of this fact is sometimes the controlling evidence in a disputed document case. Most persons can recognize colors under favorable conditions, but the recognition and matching of colors of this kind in a court investigation in many court rooms is entirely impossible. The lighting engineers have now provided artificial lighting for special purposes that is almost, if not quite, equivalent to daylight, and it is obvious that a completely equipped court room should have available the means for providing artificial lighting of this kind when it is needed. There are times when this provision in a court room is more important than marble walls and mahogany furniture.

All of these desirable methods or processes that diverge somewhat from the usual routine in a court of law are at once objected to, as has been discussed in other connections. Violent objections are usually made to showing things to jurymen. It is argued that all except the ancient and conventional aids that assist in discovering and showing the facts are improper. Strenuous objections are made to the making of illustrations on a chart, to the use of microscopes, and to the admission of enlarged photographs, and these objections, even in these progressive days, are now and then sustained! With rulings of this kind it does not much matter whether a court room is lighted or not. The interests of justice manifestly are not furthered by a procedure that seems to imply that if constant precaution is not exercised the jury will find out exactly what the case is about.

Those against the facts naturally object to more light, more information, more clarity, more sanity, more reason, more common sense in a trial at law, and the more difficult it is to hear and to see, and the harder it is to understand, the better it is for their contentions. Sad to say, there still are men who seem to love darkness rather than light, not necessarily "because their deeds are evil", but evidently because their contentions will not bear clear illumination.

Many court-houses, old and sometimes new, are so designed and lighted as to assist the client and his attorney who are endeavoring to prevent the facts from being shown.

CHAPTER XVI.

THE NEW AND THE OLD PRECEDENTS.

The constant but slow tendency of the new precedents in the law relating to the proof of documents is unmistakably towards a procedure which aids in promoting justice. As has heretofore been pointed out, progress is marked by the removal of certain of the ancient restrictions which made it difficult, if not impossible, to prove the facts and later further advance was made by the adoption of a freedom of interpretation of the facts in testimony not permitted in the old days.

The most important progressive change of procedure in modern times was the admitting of standards of comparison, which began with the English statute in 1854 and is not yet quite completed in this country. There had been some progress, however, before this later advance step because in the still earlier days no comparison of any kind was allowed, even if there was genuine handwriting in the case available for comparison with an alleged forgery.

For many years the old precedents positively prohibited what was called the "Comparison of Hands", and it availed but little to suspect, or even to discover, that a document was forged unless perchance some one actually saw the criminal act performed. Even after comparison was allowed, for many years, as we have seen, no standard genuine writing whatever could be admitted for purposes of comparison, but only that could be used that was accidentally "in the case for some other purpose".

The ancient term, "Comparison of Hands", is still quoted from the old books with a kind of veiled suggestion that there is something improper about the proceeding. In large measure the early violent opinions against "comparison of hands" grew out of the unfortunate Sidney case tried in England in 1683, and the subject from that time for many years was surrounded by a powerful political prejudice. This notorious case by a mere accident had a restrictive effect on handwriting testimony for a long time. The brutal Jeffreys, who exercised a judicial tyranny in England at the time, was so hated that any procedure that he happened to employ even incidentally was condemned, and this old prejudice, because of its emphasis and reiteration in the old books, continues even down to this day.

As is well known, in the early days the great illiterate majority could not write even their own names, and this inability of the average juryman to write no doubt brought about some of the peculiar old legal precedents regarding proof of documents. "What purpose will it serve", it was asked in at least one old legal opinion, "for a jury to 'compare hands' if they cannot read writings?" It seems strange, however, that some of these ancient practices should have been so long maintained after the reason for their adoption had passed. Because of their praiseworthy respect for the law, members of the legal profession sometimes look upon some of these old and outgrown precedents with a toleration, if not an actual fondness, that can hardly be understood by progressive men in other fields.

To their credit let it be recorded and heralded, a few

American states, Connecticut leading the list in 1791, never followed at any time the English precedents on this point of not admitting standard writings, but adopted the sensible rule that mere recollection of a thing was not a more accurate and reliable method of securing knowledge than direct, sustained study and comparison. A sensible judge in a later Connecticut case, Lyon v. Lyman, 9 Conn. 55 (1831), where it was still sought to exclude standards, says of witnesses who had testified, "A fair paraphrase of their testimony is, that they *believed* (italics by the judge) it to be his handwriting from having seen him write. This, according to the second position would render the testimony admissible. But they *knew* it to be his by comparing it with his other writings. * * * But I forbear. It has always appeared to be a very feeble objection; and I rejoice to see it overruled."

The progress from the old practice regarding proof of documents has been substantially in the following order: (1) Testimony only by eye witnesses of the actual act of writing; (2) Expression of opinion by those only who, from having seen a party write once or more, were said to have a "knowledge of the handwriting", but, as pointed out by Professor Wigmore, perhaps only in civil cases involving "forty shillings" or less; (3) Comparison of hands by experts in civil cases only, but not by other witnesses, but of those documents only which were "in the case for other purposes", (4) Admission of genuine writings for the specific purpose of comparison; (5) The use of magnifying glasses and microscopes and scientific appliances permitted in court; (6) Use of diagrams, charts, blackboard and enlarged photographs permitted; (7) Comparison of writings in testimony before the jury and the opportunity to give detailed uninterrupted reasons for the opinion expressed on direct examination in both criminal and civil cases.

The statute in the Federal Courts of the United States, allowing standards of comparison, was not enacted until fifty-nine years after the enactment of the English statute on the same subject, an example of delayed progress in this country not to be proud of. The new law was finally enacted by Congress through the efforts of George W. Wickersham, Esq., then the Attorney General of the United States. Following the enactment of the Federal statute, a number of the belated states passed a similar statute permitting the admission of standards of comparison. In some states the law on the subject is still in confusion, and in some trials no genuine writing whatever can be admitted for the purpose of comparison either to prove genuineness or forgery!

The United States Federal statute was approved and became a law February 26, 1913. The same year North Carolina and Indiana passed substantially the same statute, and in 1915 Alabama, Michigan, and Illinois adopted the new practice. In the great state of Texas standards of comparison are not admitted in civil trials.

Thus it will be seen that the really scientific examination and proof of the facts relating to disputed handwriting in many courts is a comparatively new thing. Most American states, the large majority of which had followed the English restrictive practice, continued to follow the old practice long after 1854. The change was not made in New York till 1880-1888, and Pennsylvania courts continued the old practice till 1895.

When the numerous restrictive conditions were universal, the interests of justice were no doubt defeated in thousands of instances. Very many of the frequently cited old opinions in the books that severely criticised handwriting testimony grew directly out of this bungling old practice now almost entirely discarded. Notwithstanding the notable progress in the procedure, as exemplified in the trials of many cases of this kind, there still are hundreds of court-houses where a case involving a disputed document has never been properly prepared and tried under the new practice with the aid of effective illustrations and helpful instruments and especially with a witness prepared and permitted to give detailed, reason-giving testimony on the point at issue. In these courts neither judge nor attorneys have ever seen a case of this kind properly presented.

During much of the period of this gradual change there was a continuous controversy over the question as to whether even a magnifying glass could be used and, strange to say, it has been necessary many times to answer this question in legal opinions. A similar controversy arose over enlarged photographs, illustrations on a chart, reasons for an opinion, or anything in connection with such testimony by which it was made more clear, more convincing, and more effective. It has been soberly argued in hundreds of cases that anything that differed from the old practice was not only improper but dangerous. Naturally the old decisions are full of criticisms of the weak and inconclusive testimony which inevitably grew directly out of these unwise restrictions and exclusions. Many of these old opinions, defending and justifying the old practice, contain inaccurate and unscientific ideas, applying to the questions as then presented, which have trickled down through the decisions muddying the stream of justice for more than a hundred years.

In attempting specifically to justify the exclusion of standards of comparison, Justice Coleridge in an old opinion advanced the unscientific view that standards of comparison were not necessary because the most reliable means of identifying handwriting was from a recollection, or memory, or impression, of the "general character" of the writing, by which statement he undoubtedly meant its general appearance. This incorrect principle thus established gave the testimony of the opinion witness who had simply seen a person write, perhaps only once, more weight than any conclusion that could be obtained from careful, extended, scientific study and comparison of the writings *even by the same witness.*

The ancient idea that recollection was superior to observation, although utterly unscientific and refuted numberless times, has continued down to the present day and is still quoted with approval in briefs and oral arguments. It has been directly appealed to time and time again for the purpose of discrediting scientific handwriting testimony. It has been necessary in numerous modern decisions specifically to refute the old fallacy. In the case of Green v. Terwilliger, 56 U. S. Fed. 384, as late as 1892, the writer of the opinion felt obliged to say, in combatting the old error, "In many cases it is more satisfactory to allow a witness to compare the writing in issue with other writings of unquestioned authority as to genuineness, than to compare it with the standard which he may have formed or retained in his mind from a knowledge of the party's handwriting."

Another erroneous idea formulated long ago in one of these old opinions has for years been quoted in defense of forgery. The contention was, solemnly presented in the old language, that "similitude has more significance as indicating genuineness than dissimilitude has in indicating forgery". The fallacious argument thus presented was that genuine writings for various reasons necessarily differed somewhat from each other, therefore differences in a questioned writing as compared with a standard had little significance. No consideration whatever was given to the exactly opposite but equally reasonable contention that an imitation of a writing would, according to the skill exercised, undoubtedly be like the original in certain particulars and especially in general appearance, and therefore mere resemblance ought not to be considered as conclusive as indicating genuineness. That general appearance is not a safe basis for an opinion, just the opposite of the old formula, is more nearly accurate as a general principle, and it is not simply "similitude" or "dissimilitude" but their character and extent that is of significance.

This general resemblance doctrine has been the basis for hundreds of thousands of pages of weak, and often erroneous, testimony by lay witnesses "who have seen the person write". It can easily be understood that if an investigation is taken up with the idea that any resemblance indicates genuineness, and no kind or amount of difference indicates forgery, there is no question as to what the conclusion will be. This ridiculous contention about the force of similitude naturally permitted the forger to succeed. Many if not most fake claims based on forged documents are bolstered up by the testimony of incompetent lay witnesses who say the forged writing "looks like" writing they have seen and therefore they say it is genuine. Some of the precedents of this kind in certain great states, and the permitted charges to juries, make it almost impossible to prove the facts regarding a disputed writing. In these states forged wills are probated, fake contracts and agreements are put in force, and vicious "black-hand" writers carry on their nefarious business almost unmolested.

In an introduction to a technical book treating of forgery, Professor John H. Wigmore discusses briefly and clearly this conflict between forgery and society: "Amidst these new conditions, the falsifier again outstrips society for a while. A Chatterton and a Junius can baffle a community. Well down into the 1800's the most daring impositions remained possible, but society at last seems to have overtaken the falsifier once more. Science and art, in the mass, are more than a match for the isolated individual."

Soon after the invention of photography, when the science was new and naturally undeveloped, a few legal opinions outlined the possible dangers surrounding the use of photographs in court and these old opinions are still quoted at great length even though photography has for years been carried to a very high point of accuracy. Although scores of important decisions by the highest courts have said that enlarged photographs have greatly assisted the court and jury, the old restrictive opinions seem to have a longer lease of life and are more frequently quoted. There still are several states where the question whether enlarged photographs are admissible is still undecided. In nearly every trial these helpful illustrations are objected to, and in a few courts they still are excluded.

The new precedents, however, have gradually developed conditions surrounding a disputed document trial which, when followed, make it in effect a legally supervised scientific investigation in which all of the old hampering restrictions are swept aside, and the problem is taken up in a sensible, scientific manner with full permission to use instruments and enlarged illustrations, or any aids that will throw light upon the inquiry. The especially noteworthy change is the opportunity now given the technical witness to give detailed reasons for the opinion expressed.

Without precedents and codes established as authority in the law, nothing, of course, could be fixed, and all would be confusion, but, on the other hand, as is well understood, a too rigid adherence to precedent prevents all progress. This conflict between precedent and progress is inevitable and continuous and slowly changes the law. The legal profession, like society in general, has two parties each constantly criticising the other. One advocates strict adherence to precedent in the interest of stability, and the other leans toward change in the interest of improvement.

The advocates of change in legal procedure in the interest of progress contend that a mere legal opinion should not take on an immutable and sacred character when a head note is written for it and it is printed and bound in a book. They call attention to the fact that the great mass of the law, reposing as it does in hundreds of thousands of these opinions, upon great numbers of subjects, by thousands of authors, unfortunately was not all written by experts. Gross errors, due to ignorance, carelessness, laziness, and prejudice were and are inevitable. Some of the authors, it is reasonably contended, were not qualified at any time to write law, but did write it. What is more serious, once written it has become an inseparable part of the great legal mass. Those not in the legal circle are surprised to know that this great collection of matter, of widely varying quality, is in its entirety printed and bound in books in order of dates, with all kinds of mixed subjects following each other as they happen to come, without arrangement or classification.

With justifiable alarm, attention is now and then called to the fact that many judges, of many courts in forty-eight of our states, and also in the various Federal courts, are industriously writing more and more of this legal opinion law each year and confirming and qualifying what has gone before, and agreeing and disagreeing with each other. This new matter is all bound into new books, thus day by day adding to the quantity, to the complication, and to the confusion. It is estimated that at least 175,000 pages of new matter are added each year! Think of any other profession printing its reference material and literature in such a manner, in such a form, and in such a quantity! It is not surprising that a recent compilation of laws required eight fine print pages with elaborate footnotes to *legally define the word "and"*. Nor is it surprising that legal reasoning is clogged with this mass of inconsequential stuff.

It is easy to understand what confusion there would be in the medical world if there was an authoritative, continuous mass of mixed printed matter on colds, catarrh, and cathartics, on boils, biliousness, and blood-letting, being printed all the time in order of dates, some of it erroneous, a great part of it unimportant, but all of it forced upon the attention of the doctor, who, with the aid of elaborate indexes, was obliged to go through and try to find what might possibly have been said by someone about his particular kind of a case! Both he and the patient might die before his task was done.

The unfortunate thing about the matter is not the loss of time, and paper, and printer's ink, but the fact that those arrayed against the facts are greatly aided in many kinds of cases by certain of these old decisions, combed out of the old books by diligent advocates, and cited without dates. Incidentally it needs to be said that the requirement that every legal citation must include the date would contribute to the interests of justice.

Let us suppose that somewhere in seventeen hundred, or eighteen hundred and something, some unscientific man is called upon to discuss in a legal opinion a scientific subject. He is perhaps hurried and overworked, or because of a possible unfortunate individual experience he may be prejudiced on the subject he discusses, or, because of lack of experience, he may not be informed on the question he considers, and under one or more of these conditions writes out in an opinion some unjustified positive statement, comment, or inference, not necessarily on a strictly law question but on some phase of legal proof. In spite of all progress, that statement will stand fixed, one with tables of stone and tablets of brass.

If perchance the precedent is actually erroneous, or even overdrawn, its immortality is all the more positively assured. It then becomes a beacon of hope for the zealous advocate who is struggling in deep water against the facts. By its aid and the help of other errors and exaggerations, he may not be able to show that black is white, but he is aided in his effort to show that it is at least well streaked with gray. Among some of the eight pages of "and" definitions, he is quite likely to find one that will help him.

Error thus embalmed will be quoted against other opinions, against technical experience, against scientific investigations, against logical testimony, against reasonable argument, against common sense, until perhaps some great calamity, some Alexandrian catastrophe has destroyed all of the libraries. Many of these erroneous, or distorted, ideas live on and on and are used over and over again, year after year, and generation after generation, in the effort to befog, to delay, and to defeat justice. In some way they should sooner be properly discredited and rendered harmless.

The law books contain discussions of phases of an almost endless variety of subjects connected with litigation. When the lawyer sets about preparing a brief on one of these subjects, incidental to the law, the too frequent practice is not to make an intensive study of the question itself, with all the help available from the great outside world, but rather simply to find what has been said about it in the law books, most of them old and many of them incorrect and out of date.

This practice certainly is not in accord with the methods of science. When scientific subjects are investigated and discussed in the law the discussion and investigation should be conducted in accordance with scientific principles. A method which is directed entirely to finding out and slavishly following what has been stated at some former time makes no new contributions and corrects no errors. The method of science is wholly directed to finding the fact and only incidentally to determining whether what has before been said on the subject is correct. The law too often assumes that the question has been investigated and definitely settled, while science begins with no assumption except that ancient pronouncements are probably wrong.

The treatment of the question of the desirability of admitting genuine writing as a standard of comparison illustrates the unfortunate method of the law in relation to scientific questions. It was long contended that this admission of standards would introduce confusing collateral issues, and it was also argued that unfair standards might be selected. England, as we have seen, settled the question in 1854, while Connecticut and a few other progressive American states always followed the enlightened practice now becoming universal. When, however, this same question of admissibility of standards was under discussion in numerous other states of this country, as it was for a century, the question was not investigated as to how the practice actually worked in England and Connecticut and other states that had already adopted the new practice.

As late as in 1911 a state court refused to adopt the new practice of admitting standards of comparison and actually cited an old George the Third opinion in support of the action, instead of inquiring whether the new rule had worked successfully across the border in another state only a few miles away, where it had been followed for fifty years! This is an illustration of the legal method of investigating a scientific question. There still are a few courts, even in these late days, happily growing less each year, where the procedure suggests that the date might be sixteen hundred and something, instead of the twentieth century, and that a witchcraft case might actually be on trial.

In law the question has arisen hundreds and hundreds of times whether enlarged photographs should be used. A scientific investigation would undertake to answer the following questions: What are their purpose and what is the argument for their use? Will they aid in showing the fact? How will they aid? Can they be made accurately? May they mislead or deceive and are they objectionable in any way? Can these objections be overcome or avoided? Finally, have enlarged photographs been used and what has been the result of the experience in other cases?

The tendency of the law in too many jurisdictions has been to do no such sensible questioning, but rather to ask, "What did George the Third's judges say about it?"

There seems to be no good reason why scientific methods cannot be applied in greater measure, in connection with some of these subjects. The vital question in law finally, as in science, is to discover and prove what is true. The investigation ought to be unhampered and free where everything is considered that may safely throw light on the question. What has before been said should be used for what it is worth and only for what it is worth, and should be tested as all else is tested. There is no doubt that too rigid dependence upon precedent has retarded progress by making legal discussions unscientific and legal investigators lazy. There is, however, an awakening on the question, stimulated in large measure by certain able leaders who have the courage to attempt to put into the law the methods of science, and who argue and prove that the law is alive and growing.

There should be much more use made of the books that discuss the reasons and logic of the law prepared by trained and able men who are qualified to consider the conflicting opinions and emphasize the best and weed out and discard that which is archaic and erroneous. More and more progressive courts are citing not merely old opinions but definite pronouncements on, and valuations of, legal opinions by legal experts. This practice is in conformity with the methods of science and is a long step in the direction of desirable reform.

Legal discussions that quote and comment with courage and intelligence are of great value, but pages, chapters, and books full of comments that only say, "A says this but B says this, while C presents this view, and D is somewhat original in what he holds", and so on page after page and volume after volume, do not materially help forward the course of progress. What is useful is a report by one with ability and frankness who says, "A's statement is well reasoned and logical, B's pronouncement is plainly incorrect and not justified by the conditions out of which it arose, C's view is superficial and erroneous, while an analysis of D's view shows that it is practically in harmony with that of A."

At least as frequently as once in every ten years the "new laws" should be analyzed and appraised in an authoritative manner by competent and fearless men and much of the old junk discarded. One of the bars to progress and reform is an unfortunate, hesitating attitude of mind that tends to overlook, if not to excuse, error. Of all things an illogical, erroneous legal precedent should at once be characterized exactly as it deserves. Able and courageous men are all the time needed who will promptly call things by their right names. Fortunately there are men who are doing it and they should be upheld and encouraged. No field of human endeavor more needs this important service than the field of the law.

Under the ancient severe restrictions regarding the introduction of evidence, cases relating to handwriting and documents were necessarily surrounded by violent prejudice that weakened all technical testimony on the subject involved. The decisions themselves with their restrictions, as described above, made testimony on these questions weak and inconclusive and thus perpetuated and intensified the weaknesses that actually grew out of the procedure imposed.

This retention of ancient ideas is discussed in an illuminating manner by Professor Roscoe Pound, Dean of Harvard Law School, in a book review in Harvard Law Review, March, 1911, in these words:

"The dogmatism of many really competent experts, the obvious limitations of the crude empiricism of bank tellers, the extravagances of graphologists, and the unhappy operation of over-technical rules of evidence in many jurisdictions, which preclude the use of sufficient data on which to base a sound conclusion, have given rise to a distrust of expert evidence as to writings which to-day is not justified. Mr. Harris's account of the expert in handwriting, written, it is fair to say, over thirty years ago, but unaltered in the current edition of 'Hints on Advocacy' has no application to the fair, temperate, and reasoned statements of what may and what may not be discovered and determined with respect to the authorship and authenticity of documents which is given us in this book. Modern experimental psychology has furnished a sure foundation, confirmed in its application to handwriting by abundant experimentation and experience, and the ingenuity of the optician has provided standard instruments, giving results that speak for themselves to the layman as well as to the expert."

The striking contrast of the new legal precedents with some of the ancient rules in the proof of documents is conclusively shown in numerous recent American opinions. Two notable opinions in the courts of the State of New York show this change in a striking manner. In Venuto v. Lizzo, 132 N. Y. Supp. 1066 (1911) this is said:

"While the testimony of expert witnesses is carefully weighed and accepted with caution, the law allows such evidence. The conclusion of a handwriting expert as to the genuineness of a signature, standing alone, would be of little or no value, but supported by sufficiently cogent reasons, his testimony might amount almost to a demonstration. While the court in this case did not directly refuse to allow the experts to state their reasons, as was done in the case of Johnson Service Co. v. MacLernon, 142 App. Div. 677, 127 N. Y. Supp. 431, the effect of allowing constant trivial objections and of the erroneous rulings was virtually equivalent to such a denial. * * * We might not reverse this judgment for a particular ruling, standing alone; but the cumulative effect of all the rulings and of the constant interruptions of counsel on trivial grounds is such as to induce the belief that the defendant has not had a fair trial, and that, in the interests of justice, she should be permitted another opportunity to present her defence. The order should be reversed and a new trial granted, with costs to appellant to abide the event. All concur."

In the opinion referred to in the foregoing opinion, Johnson Service Co. v. MacLernon, the court says:

"The witness was then asked to state the reasons for his opinion. An objection to this question was sustained, and the plaintiff duly excepted. This was an error. It is a rule of general acceptance that an expert may always, if called upon, give the reasons for his opinion."

"'Whenever the opinion of any living person is deemed to be relevant, the grounds on which such opinion is based are also deemed to be revelant.' Chase's Stephen's Digest, (2d ed.), 156.

"'On direct examination, the witness may, and, if required, must point out his grounds for belief in the identity of the handwriting on the principle already considered. Without such a reinforcement of testimony, the opinion of experts would usually involve little more than a counting of the numbers on either side.' 3 Wigmore on Ev. 2014.

"In this state the practice of permitting a handwriting expert to give the reasons for his opinion, and even to illustrate upon a blackboard, has been distinctly approved. McKay v. Lasher, 121 N. Y. 477, 483; 24 N. E. 711. The reasons for the expert's opinion, if he had been permitted to give them, might, and probably would, have added great force to his testimony; for the mere expression of opinion, standing alone, has little probative force. For these errors, the judgment and order appealed from must be reversed and a new trial granted, with costs to appellant to abide the event. All concur." Johnson Service Co. v. MacLernon, 127 N. Y. Supp. 431 (1911).

The words ". . . even to illustrate upon a blackboard" in the foregoing opinion are an unqualified expression of the fact that testimony of this class may now be presented in the most effective and convincing manner. It is of course understood that the making of such illustrations would accompany a detailed exposition of the reasons for the opinion expressed. This is certainly a long way from the mere opinion testimony of the old days.

On the general question of allowing experts to give reasons for the opinion expressed, the Court of Appeals of New York has spoken very clearly in People v. Faber, 199 N. Y. 256 (1910):

"As has already been expressed by others, from which expressions we have quoted, it is competent for a person offering an expert as a witness for the purpose of showing the strength of the opinion which he is about to express, to specify in detail the observations upon which the opinion is based.''

When these new revolutionary precedents, established, as it will be seen, by unanimous courts, are compared with the old rulings on these subjects, it can be understood what progress has been made, and the result of this progress is shown by numerous surprising verdicts in cases of this class. Two recent New York cases will serve as conspicuous examples. In the first, six witnesses testified that they saw a certain contract signed, and a jury decided that the document was a forgery, and in the second, a jury convicted a distinguished member of the bar of a forgery of two words in typewriting that by comparison were connected with his own typewriter.

With the use of the microscope and enlarged photographs (Frank v. Chemical National Bank, 37 N. Y. Spr. Ct. 5 J. & S. 34; affirmed 84 N. Y. 209, 1874) the assistance of the chart or blackboard (McKay v. Lasher, 121 N. Y. 477, 1890) and especially with the help of the new precedents, quoted on the preceding pages, a prepared attorney and a competent witness are able, in most cases, to prove the facts in a disputed document case in the New York state courts at least, and the truth will often prevail against what may at first seem to be great odds.

Numerous attorneys and certain judges know that important cases of this class, in several different states, have been discontinued and hastily taken from court calendars before trial, but not till after the documents had been photographed and the physical evidence had been arranged in a formidable and conclusive manner for presentation in court. A few years ago many of these cases would have been won against the facts and in favor of fraudulent claimants.

A conspicuous example of a case of this kind, Oles v. The Macky Estate, was tried a few years ago at Boulder, Colorado. After the case had been on trial for five days the first witness for the defense, a document expert, was called. At the close of his direct testimony, and without cross-examining the witness, the attorney of record for the claimant arose and stated in open court:

> "I have felt all the way through the justness of the cause until yesterday afternoon, when the scientific expert, through the magnifying glass, showed the condition of this contract. I felt at that time—and there arose in my mind a serious doubt as to the genuineness of that document. That was the first time that I had any doubt. I felt then that possibly an imposition had been practiced upon me. I don't propose to practice an imposition upon this court or upon any other person. I therefore ask at this time for a dismissal of the case, or a judgment be entered that will end the case."

A judgment was entered for the defendant by consent and the trial ended. The defendant in the case was the University of Colorado. An attempt was afterwards made to reopen the case but this the judge refused to do and in his opinion said emphatically that if the case had been submitted to him he would have decided it in accordance with the judgment as originally entered.

In certain particulars the most notable opinion on

the subject that has been issued by any court is the opinion, by Mr. Justice Ellis, in Boyd v. Gosser, 82 Southern 758, by the Supreme Court of Florida, 1919. In this opinion, reversing a lower court on the facts alone, the position is distinctly taken and clearly stated that handwriting expert testimony, when given with reasons and illustrations, is not merely opinion testimony but is "demonstration testimony" and is not an appeal to credulity but to the senses and the intelligence of the hearer and the observer. The opinion says:

"It was something more than the mere opinion of the witness. It was a detailed statement of facts relating to the questioned signature of W. T. Boyd which was appended to the two documents; facts which were revealed by the use of mechanical instruments, and scientifically established to the degree of demonstration. * * * 'Preponderance of the evidence' is a phrase which in its last analysis means probability of its truth. In a cause where there is conflicting moral evidence, the jury in the one case, the chancellor in the other, is required to decide accordingly as the weight of the evidence preponderates in favor of one proposition or the other. That is to say, having no personal knowledge of the transaction under investigation, they must, by the application of common knowledge and experience, decide which set of witnesses or line of evidence raises the greater probability of its consistency with truth.

"In the use of demonstrative evidence one relies upon the evidence of his own senses. It is therefore evidence of the highest rank. It is the ultimate test of truth. To this class belongs mathematics, because a proposition in mathematics may be established by the evidence of one's own senses. Moral evidence depends for its value upon veracity on the one hand and credulity upon the other. So in testing the truth of a witness' statement one must therefore draw upon his fund of common knowledge and experience of men and affairs, if, like a prudent man who 'looketh well to his going,' he would decide in accordance with that which seems most probable.

"In the case at bar we have the uncontradicted evidence of the expert on handwriting. The questioned signatures and photographs of them are before the court, as well as signatures admittedly genuine and photographs of them, some enlarged for convenience of comparison; and the means were at hand for measurements and other comparisons embracing the whole field of examination. So that the facts to which the expert witness testified concerning the characteristics and construction of the signatures are matters within the field of demonstrative evidence. * * *"

In another notable recent case, Baird v. Shaffer (Supreme Court of Kansas), 168 Pac. 836 (1917), the question of the weight of testimony of witnesses regarding disputed handwriting is specifically discussed. The opinion, by Mr. Justice Dawson, says:

"There were three witnesses to the will, and they all testified positively that Mary A. Baird had signed the will in their presence, and that they signed it as witnesses at her request, in her presence, and in the presence of each other. The plaintiffs' evidence discrediting the will was partly that of expert testimony and opinion evidence which tended to prove that the signature to the will was not genuine, that it differed materially from other signatures of Mrs. Baird, the authenticity of which was admittedly genuine or sufficiently proved. * * *"

"The testimony of attesting witnesses to a will may be overcome by any competent evidence. Ginter v. Ginter, 79 Kan. 721, 738, 101 Pac. 634, 22 L. R. A. (N. S.) 1024 (syl. par. 5); 2 Wigmore on Evidence, §§ 886, 1514. Such evidence may be direct, or it may be circumstantial; and expert and opinion evidence is just as competent as any other evidence. Indeed, where the signature to a will is a forgery, and where the attesting witnesses have the hardihood to commit perjury, it is difficult to see how the bogus will can be overthrown except by expert and competent opinion evidence tending to show that the pretended signature is not that of the testator, but spurious. The rule contended for by appellants would frequently baffle justice and give judicial countenance to many a high-handed fraud.''

This is an example of the correct scientific attitude in regard to the question. The problem is not what has been said on the subject in the past but whether or not the testimony presented is true and correct. Only a few years ago this case would certainly have been reversed on the ground that the decision was against the weight of evidence.

An editorial on this particular case, by Mr. W. A. Shumaker, in ''Law Notes'', Vol. XXI, No. 11, states:

''From this recognition of the possibilities of an expert examination has grown up what may now be regarded as the prevailing rule, that the testimony of a handwriting expert will be given weight according to the reasons which he adduces in support of it. As was said in Gordon's Case, 50 N. J. Eq. 397: 'Handwriting is an art concerning which correctness of opinion is susceptible of demonstration, and I am fully convinced that the value of the opinion of every handwriting expert as evidence must depend upon the clearness with which the expert demonstrates its correctness.' The experts have proved themselves fully able to meet the demands of this rule. * * *''

''But gradually the judges, who had already verified in

long experience with eyewitnesses the words of the wise man of Israel, 'The simple believeth every word but the prudent man looketh well to his going' (Proverbs XIV, 15), began to recognize that in the science of the handwriting expert there was an instrument which might expose the perjurer and confound the plotter of iniquity. Through that science the forger working in the supposed secrecy of his curtained chamber has learned that, in the words of Epicharmus, 'Mind sees and mind hears; all things else are deaf and blind.' As was said in the Burtis Will Case, 43 Misc. (N. Y.) 437: 'Of course, in cases where the handwriting or signature of a person, since deceased, is attacked as a forgery, the party defending it is apt to ridciule the value of expert evidence, because, almost invariably, evidence of this character is the only kind available to the party attacking the signature. He often has no other means at hand to show to the court or jury that the signature may be or is a forgery; while on the other hand the party defending the signature usually has the aid of one or more witnesses to testify to the fact of the signing, etc. If the court were to adopt the view that expert evidence is of little value and disregard it, the party attacking the signature ordinarily would have but little chance of success, and it would create unlimited opportunities for designing persons to forge the name of deceased persons to important documents and then swear it through.''

Another definite forward step taken by the courts is in connection with the proof of disputed typewriting. The New York Court of Appeals in a recent case has definitely settled the question in New York as to the admissibility of typewriting specimens merely for comparison and this now is the law in most of the states. The court says:

"I think it may well be doubted whether typewriting can

be deemed handwriting within the meaning of the existing statute. Nevertheless, I think the law sanctions the reception of the evidence in question, substantially on the theory adopted by the trial judge. If the impression of a seal were in controversy, it would surely be competent to show by other impressions from the same sealing instrument, that the impression was invariably characterized by a particular mark or defect. * * *''

''These several cases base the rulings which have been mentioned upon the assumption or proof that a typewriting machine may possess an individuality which differentiates it from other typewriters and which is recognizable through the character of the work which it produces. Inasmuch as its work affords the readiest means of identification, no valid reason is perceived why admitted or established samples of that work should not be received in evidence for purposes of comparison with other typewritten matter alleged to have been produced upon the same machine.'' People v. Storrs, N. Y. 100 N. E. 731, 732 (1911).

Another recent notable opinion, illustrating the progressive attitude of the courts, is *In re* O'Connor's Estate, 179 N. W. 401, Supreme Court of Nebraska, 1920, by Mr. Justice Rose. A District Court was overruled on the facts and it was decided that a will was a forgery, notwithstanding the positive testimony of the subscribing witnesses who testified that they saw the will signed. This latter point was specifically passed upon. The opinion says:

''The two subscribing witnesses who testified on behalf of proponents that the will was duly executed were not directly impeached or directly contradicted by other witnesses, and for that reason the trial court, in reaching the conclusion that the will is genuine, indulged the presumption that they told the truth. This presumption, after there had been credible proof of the forgery charged by contestants, was entertained throughout the remainder of the trial below and inheres in the judgment, as shown by the opinion of the trial court. After the evidence of forgery had been adduced the entertaining of such a presumption was a serious error. In a civil case, when there is substantial proof in support of the plea that the will offered for probate is a forgery, all presumptions in favor of genuineness fall. Thereafter the truth must be found in the evidence itself, and every item of proof must stand on its own footing in connection with each evidential fact considered in its proper light. In this test presumption creates no advantage one way or the other. In such a situation persons who declare themselves to be subscribing witnesses and boldly speak from the witness stand as such, though not directly impeached, are subject to the same impartial and penetrating scrutiny as the mute instrument ascribed by them to the deed. In the unbiased search for the truth the law has no favorites by presumption. Silent circumstances, without power to change their attitude, or to make explanations, or to commit perjury, may speak as truthfully in court as animated witnesses. When an issue of forgery in a civil case is raised by pleadings and contested by evidence on both sides, there is no presumption either in favor of witnesses or in favor of circumstances. All of the evidential facts which throw light on the issue must be considered in connection with the allegation of proponents that the will is genuine and with the charge of contestants that the document offered for probate is a forgery. If the truth is found in oral testimony, it must determine the issue, but it is equally potent if found in circumstances.''

In all classes of cases, there of course continue to be decisions against the facts, and there still are cases in which it is impossible to prove with sufficient force, against sympathy and prejudice, what is undoubtedly true, but in very many cases involving disputed documents the old despair has passed away. With the new precedents and the practice now followed in most courts the necessity for a practically new profession has arisen, devoted to the investigation of documents and the photographic illustration and scientific proof of the facts in such cases.

In contrast with these progressive decisions are those of some other tribunals, even of this twentieth century, where the old interpretation of expert testimony as a mere opinion still persists, even in cases where the evidence is visible and in which the reviewing court has as full an opportunity as the court that heard the case to see, understand, and decide on the technical question presented. It is discouraging to those who attempt to promote justice by carefully proving the facts in a court of law to be met with a reasoning which practically says that testimony will not be considered on its merits.

In a recent case in a great state, in which a trial judge of a lower court was reversed on appeal and a document which had been declared a forgery was pronounced genuine, the argument was actually presented in an opinion discussing the illustrated testimony, given with full and explicit reasons, that of two opposing sets of witnesses, both sets of which were paid considerably more than the ordinary fees, that special weight should be given to the testimony of the witnesses on one side *because they were paid the least,* although admittedly they were less competent than those opposed to them. The controlling, vital testimony in the case on the point was discussed in no other way. The question of the comparative value of the testimony was utterly ignored. It would be discouraging in the practice of law if this rule regarding compensation should be applied to legal services.

It is obvious that where reasoning of this kind governs the decisions of reviewing courts that advocates and litigants will continue to furnish the kind of testimony that can be used in such reasoning. It is plain that the point of the reasoning is that the testimony is presented not to be looked at, and examined, and investigated, and tested by the reasoning by which it is accompanied, but that it is to be considered merely on the ground of credibility and as though one witness said that over beyond the mountain he saw a certain thing and that another witness said that he also was there and did not see it. It is of little value in the interest of justice to illustrate testimony and explain it, and make it clear and explicit and convincing, if courts will, in a prejudiced way, refuse to examine it. The quality of reasoning presented in this case will no doubt continue in some places for some time, but it will more and more receive that scorching comment by progressive legal writers and higher courts that it deserves. Think of the danger of entrusting the interests of justice to such minds!

There are a few of these courts that are still strangers to all of the modern methods of presenting disputed document cases, but there is progress all along the line. Fortunately it is more and more coming to be recognized that "This kind of evidence, like all other probable evidence, admits of every degree of certainty, from the lowest presumption, to the highest moral certainty''.

All the honest claimant, and the reputable attorney ask is that the testimony offered be taken for what it is worth and without prejudice or unwarranted ''presumption''. More than one ''demonstration'' during these latter years has dazed old practitioners who in the past have won cases, not by testimony, but by objections based on the ancient precedents. In more than one recent case, those arrayed against the facts, when confronted with the evidence, and especially the illustrative photographs, have actually surrendered, paid all expenses, and discontinued the litigation!

With the enlightened procedure, now almost universal, adequate preparation by the attorney on the right side, and the use of the technical information on the subject now available, the facts can usually be proved. In the comparatively few cases in which there is conflict of expert testimony the new procedure makes it possible, if not easy, to show the errors of the ignorant and the vicious pretensions of the corrupt.

CHAPTER XVII.

THE FINAL ARGUMENT IN DISPUTED DOCUMENT CASES.

If counsel has made the proper preparation by his life, by his education, by the reputation he has gained for frankness and honesty, by his conduct during the trial, and by his knowledge of the facts of the case he is trying, then what he says in argument sometimes may have some effect on the verdict of a jury.

If his argument produces no favorable effect, the result is not always due to the fact that the argument itself is weak, but it may be because an atmosphere of distrust has been developed by unwise advocacy and the hearers assume that an attempt is about to be made to mislead them. They unconsciously brace themselves in mental resistance determined not to be deceived by what they anticipate will be an unfair, incomplete, *ex-parte* appeal. With an audience in this frame of mind a speaker must be an artist in words whose argument reaches the high point of persuasion.

In a previous chapter the importance of proper incidental discussion of the case, which is in effect argument, is briefly considered. This incidental discussion should gradually lead up into the final argument. The skilful advocate thus will have prepared not only himself, but the court and the jury, for his final appeal. Piece by piece he will have brought out in evidence that which he will finally put all together in logical order, consider as a whole, and interpret and enforce. But if he has waited to do all of this work until the final appeal is made the delay is often fatal. From the time the first questions were asked the first prospective jurymen, as proper opportunity has arisen, the alert attorney has gradually brought his point of view before the court in preparation for what he will say in final argument. The experienced and prepared attorney who is aware of the atmosphere surrounding the trial can anticipate in some measure what effect any final talk will be likely to have. Sometimes it is very important and warrants the most thorough preparation, and sometimes it should be very brief.

There are many persons who have the mistaken idea that the result of litigation depends in large measure upon what is known as forensic eloquence. Even a few lawyers still have this notion or they would not do what they do. Some of their Patrick Henry performances are pitiful. Real eloquence still is a mighty force in many fields, and an almost unequaled asset to the lawyer, but in most parts of this land in these days, perhaps more prosaic than in the past, ornate oratory has but little favorable effect on verdicts of courts. The bombastic stuff of the old days is now heard but seldom, and the frock-coated, stern pleader, with flat right hand tucked neatly under coat lapel, is quite a curiosity in courts of law. In many courts fervid oratory not only does not win verdicts but is looked upon with surprise, if not with suspicion, as the last resort of one who probably ought not to win.

There is now a somewhat well defined geography of court oratory and what is fitting here is not good there. It behooves the attorney to study this geography and act accordingly. Those who have not been in widely separated fields are not fully aware of these differences. Fortunately more and more trials at law are coming to be practical, common sense proceedings dominated by the idea that their purpose is to discover and prove facts.

This making of an argument in behalf of a client before those who are to decide a controverted question is the distinctively typical act of the advocate. By making the lawyer his attorney, the client says "He speaks for me". The taking the place of and speaking for another is a great responsibility, and the advocate who fully understands its importance performs the act with the most conscientious care and with the utmost skill that he can command. Certainly more than with most work, the attorney, who for the time stands in the place of his client, is bound in a sense by honor to do well what he undertakes. Errors and inefficiency in performing a task of this nature cannot be lightly excused.

The vital question with the advocate is whether or not he can say anything that will be likely to help win a verdict. It is seldom that evidence, especially before a jury, is so clear and conclusive that it cannot be enforced by argument of the right kind. If the lawyer is sure that court and jury are already convinced that his contention is correct then that simple statement may be argument enough, but, as the lawyer is permitted to say as well as he can why his client should be given a verdict, it is a rare case in which it is not advisable to say something. No matter how effective his witnesses have been, he usually does well briefly to clarify, interpret, and enforce their testimony. He will "sum up" the matter, which is simply the adding together in one sum of all of the evidence on which he asks a verdict. Skill in this kind of addition makes the services of a lawyer of great value.

A tired jury, or a somewhat weary and impatient court, may be greatly pleased at a lawyer's apparent self-denial in proposing not to talk, but if this proposition is not agreed to by the opposing attorney then he must make at least a brief argument. Of course, nothing of importance in an argument should be omitted, but trial attorneys are inclined to talk too much, rather than too little, and thus incur the risk of arousing a more or less unconscious resentment that is unfortunate. No positive rule either as to the advisability of making an argument, or as to its length, can be applied except the rule of common sense as governed by the conditions and the atmosphere of the trial.

When the attorney has definitely decided to try to say something he must then determine what to say and how he is to say it. This seems like an unnecessary suggestion, but it is not. Many advocates trust to the inspiration of the moment and unfortunately the important moment is not inspired. It is not to be expected that the attorney can look in a book somewhere and find just what he ought to say in every closing argument he must make, and it is not presumed here to outline just what should be said in any disputed document case, but some general suggestions are offered and some warnings are given that will perhaps be of some assistance.

It is surprising how many persons there are who have a notion that there is some secret method by which goods are sold and juries are convinced, and as long as it is even approximately true that a fool is born every little while who is a possible victim, there will no doubt be business for the charlatans who pretend to teach some secret method by which it is alleged success of all kinds can easily and quickly be achieved. It is quite safe to say that so-called "psychic power"—whatever it may be—cannot be bought by the yard or the quart. Much popular advertising tends to lead one to think that there is some "hypnotic influence", "secret force", or "method of character analysis", or some manner of "fixing the eye" on the prospective customer, or juryman, that gives a controlling power over those operated upon. Many credulous people have paid money for these silly secrets.

It is hardly necessary to say that these superficial tricks and subterfuges weaken rather than strengthen ability to influence others. Like the effect of certain kinds of shallow instruction in elocution, they divert attention from necessary serious preparation and develop only a few mannerisms and a weakening self-consciousness as to when to smile and how to place the feet, that defeat the main purpose aimed at.

In order to make a good argument counsel must not only know what the case is about—he does not always appear to know—but must also know accurately the exact value of each bit of evidence that has been offered and be able to estimate the force of every outside influence that may affect a verdict. This is a comprehensive requirement, but it is what the conditions impose. The judge, the referee, or the jury in a jury trial, have also heard the evidence and a deliberately incorrect, or even a mistaken representation of it and its value, many times is a serious error. What is sometimes called "pulling the wool over the eyes of the hearers", a performance too often attempted, may succeed with part of a jury and perhaps occasionally with all, but often makes antagonists of intelligent and influential jurors who hitherto may have been friendly. No one likes to be considered gullible and unintelligent.

It is inevitable in a legal controversy that there will be some strong points and some at least not so strong, and a troublesome problem in argument is to know just how to handle and where to place the weaker points. An argument may "explain away" and "account for" weaknesses to such a length that hearers strongly suspect that the speaker knows they are real weaknesses. This "skating on thin ice" phase of an argument requires the very greatest skill. As a rule, the positive or affirmative part of an argument ought to take more time than the negative part. One who denounces without affirming gives the impression that there is nothing to affirm. The final effect of some protracted and bitter arguments is that the advocate has a difficult task to perform and is doing the best he can, but is not quite succeeding.

Because they can string words together in sentences on almost any topic, there are talkers who deceive themselves into thinking that they can make anyone believe anything. Like some weather prophets and fortune tellers, they do succeed occasionally and apparently remember only their successes. What is known as the gift of language is not always a good gift, but in the end may be a hindrance rather than a help except as a source of entertainment. The free and easy talker too often tries to substitute his natural gift for real preparation and accurate information, and many times talks too much and not wisely. Many young lawyers have been led to believe that an advocate should be able to talk at any time, about equally well, on either side of any subject. There are speakers who in this way acquire a superficial proficiency—as well as an habitual insincerity—by which they attempt to confuse and overcome an opponent. The shallow dazzler of this sort is no match for the man of solid parts whose thorough preparation and accurate knowledge often give the impression that he necessarily is on the side with the facts and the law.

Its occasional use in courts of law makes it necessary to determine how to meet and counteract this opposing pseudo oratory. By stressing plain and obvious facts the shrewd, logical minded man often is able to make ridiculous the superficial and flowery orator who is always "striking for his altars and his fires", and who cannot make the simplest statement without at least one gesture and one quivering note in his voice. He often talks of the "beauty of Greece and the glory of Rome" and the "pine and the palm" when these matters are not really in the case in hand. The born orator unfortunately is often born lazy. He also may have been too much praised to think it necessary to prepare himself on the facts of a subject which he undertakes to discuss, and at the last hopes for inspiration that does not always arrive. There have been half-orator human failures of this kind in every considerable community who throughout life were just about to do some great thing, but never quite did it.

Its importance in the practice of law, warrants an enforcement and emphasis of the value of effective language, a subject discussed in connection with incidental argument in a preceding chapter. While the weakness and futility of empty oratory is well known, it remains true that the ability to speak with moving eloquence is one of the most valuable qualifications of the advocate. By every means and in every way, early and late, first and last, the man who tries cases should train himself in the use of forceful, apt, moving language. If he has the gift of language he should be humbly thankful for it, try to avoid its weaknesses, and train himself as if he had no gift whatever.

An effective argument usually must have a positive and a negative phase. It must show why a verdict should be given to the speaker, and it should show the weakness, or fallacy, of the claims of the opposition. An erroneous or false claim is usually based either upon perjury, or a wrong interpretation of the evidence. It is the duty of counsel to point out clearly and fearlessly just how and where the error arose. This is the essential point in a good argument.

Effective arguments on these lines are based upon correct understanding of facts followed by their correct and clear interpretation in understandable words. In large measure the act is one of pure reasoning. A good argument must say why a certain thing is true or why a certain action should be taken. Many arguments contain no reasoning whatever, but are simply a succession of unsupported assertions and accusations. To say why in just the right way is one of the most difficult things done in this world, and there are those who never acquire the ability to do it. It is the essential element in an argument.

There are, of course, those who undertake tasks too difficult for them and who cannot prepare to do well what they will never be fitted to do. As with most failures, however, the most common cause of ineffective argument is lack of preparation. If at this critical time counsel is not just clear as to what the controlling points in the case are he may as well sit down at once. It is difficult to state clearly and completely the essential facts and principles of a subject that one understands, and when the attempt is made to discuss a subject about which he is only partly informed, the performance is sure to be a failure. Vague argument that is only partly understood is just a waste of time for all. The speaker who hopes to "pick up" the points at the last moment often waits in vain and aimlessly flounders around. For a time his hearers wait for him to begin and then try to forget that he is there. It is impossible for one to make a successful journey if the road and destination are not clearly in mind. Many so-called arguments consist only of an inaccurate, incomplete, and often unfair, recitation of the testimony, with favorable comments on the testimony of the witnesses on one side, and unfavorable assertions regarding the testimony of the opposition.

The elements of strength in a good argument necessarily vary somewhat under different conditions, but there are some qualities that are fundamental. A good argument must have interest, it must be technically correct, and have direct application to the problem before the court. It must also have a certain quality of vigor and earnestness, and contain, in some degree, an emotional as well as intellectual appeal, and finally it must have a correct order of statement. It also must not be too long. Talk of any kind begins to lose its force when hearers begin to observe the "good stopping places" that are passed by.

An argument must have interest or it will probably be wholly ineffective. Interest is of value, however, only as leading to something else. To tell funny stories alone does not win victories in court. Interest, to be of value, must partly grow out of the subject itself, and if it does not open the mind of the hearer to a serious consideration of the problem under investigation it serves no useful purpose. If what purports to be an argument is only an amusing performance the speaker might with equal result sing to the jury, or give a phonograph concert. In effect, many concerts are given in courts of law.

The opposite of the fault of purposeless entertainment in argument is that of tiresome dulness. The entertainer at least passes the time away as his hearers gradually grow older, but the flat, stale and tiresome bore, who, like the brook, goes on and on forever, produces no favorable effect and is disagreeable besides. This killing monotony is avoided by the intelligent speaker even by taking the risk of introducing irrelevant levity.

Some of the qualities that make talk interesting are imagination, figures of speech, direct statement, terseness, variety, familiar illustrations, clearness, humor, fairness, and reasonable brevity. If properly employed these qualities put life into language and hold attention. A speaker can hardly hope to convince or persuade who cannot hold the attention of hearers as simple indifference is almost worse than active opposition. The entrance to the mind is through this door of interest that at all hazards must be kept open. Brilliant repartee is a kindler of interest as well as a silencer of ill-advised opposition.

But few qualities in argument are more effective, as aids to interest, clearness and force, than appropriate figures of speech and what is described as homely philosophy. No qualities of language are so readily understood and carry such an appeal to the common man as parables and symbols. All great language is filled, not with mere isolated words that convey ideas, but with proverbs and whole expressions that have live messages all their own. As is well known, the simple, sublime language of the Bible is saturated with figures of speech, and the unsurpassed beauty and the force of Shakespeare largely grow out of their skilful use. All great artists in words are skilled in this use of symbols and figures. Lincoln's clear and simple language, like that of the Old Testament, which was his model, is literally permeated with it. The immortal Second Inaugural is a great picture painted by a great artist and its climaxes are illuminating figures of speech.

The lawyer is unwise who on all occasions attempts to rival Shakespeare and the author of the Second Inaugural, but there is no good reason why he should not employ every proper means by which his language is made interesting and forceful. His language should present ideas that can be understood, and a relevant and vital circumstance or thing, if put into an appropriate figure of speech, at once takes on a new interest and significance. "This ragged, dirty, flimsy scrap of paper", he says, "crept stealthily into this court as an ingenious cloak of crime; it now becomes a flaming beacon illuminating the plan, design, and very footprints of crime". "A thing", he says, "a silent, lifeless thing, becomes an eloquent, irresistible witness whose testimony cannot be denied". Language of this sort, when pertinent, itself becomes a flaming beacon. Even comparatively stupid hearers understand it.

There are some general matters relating to argument that deserve thoughtful attention. One of these, discussed to some extent in connection with the subject of persuasion, is this general question as to why we like to hear some speakers and not others. It is certainly of importance to one who is to argue in court to learn, if possible, the reasons for this vital difference. The question is not quite so simple as it appears on its surface.

One reason why we like to hear some speakers is because we can hear them and hear them easily. A clear, pleasant voice is then one of the first requirements. More than one "voice" has been elected governor, or sent to Congress, partly in protest against those mumblers who talk and cannot be heard. It is also true, of course, that the one we listen to gladly usually has something to say and says it in an interesting way.

Another difference between the attractive and the unattractive speaker is no doubt certain qualities of personality, but this personality must in some degree appear in his thought as expressed in spoken words. The first business of one who seeks to persuade by argument is to make us forget him and think of the subject about which he speaks. The ideas of Socrates were so interesting that his unattractive face was not observed, and the physical outline of the lanky Lincoln was soon lost to those charmed by his words.

The skilful pleader first gets attention and then leads up to his goal which he always has distinctly in mind. Every phase of his argument has a distinct purpose and direction and leads on to persuasion. It is usually possible to win shallow and surface applause for that which is not in point and does not win a verdict. There are speakers who unwisely always seek this intoxication of applause and sometimes appear to be almost more desirous of getting a cheer than of getting a verdict.

The speaker who really persuades is serious most of the time and his hearers become impressed with the idea that he not only knows what he is talking about, but realizes the importance of what he is undertaking to do. By every means he keeps the serious, thoughtful attention of the auditors directly on the subject under discussion. He constantly keeps his eyes on his hearers and his mind in direct contact with theirs and drives his points home.

After interest, or as a part of it, an effective argument, as suggested above, must have direct application to the question under discussion. It must help the hearers to decide a definite question and to do this it must analyze the problem to be solved and answer the question why a certain decision should be made. An argument has been successful when a hearer unconsciously thinks, or says, "I see, I see". To secure that conscious or unconscious admission is the triumph of argument.

A good argument must also have a quality of vigor that is a natural characteristic of important statements on any topic. If the thought is allowed to creep into the mind of the hearer that what is being said is "unimportant even if true", then language is vain. The consequence of error and the result of justice can be dwelt upon in a way that properly leads up to an emotional appeal. Voice and gesture and attitude and manner all have effect, but it is mainly by the intellect that intellectual appeals are made effective. The first problem of the speaker is to make hearers think, the next problem is to make them think right.

The emotional appeal, often of vital importance in spoken language and never to be omitted in the attempt to persuade, is a point of danger and requires perhaps greater skill than any other part of the performance. To be effective it must flow out of, and result from, the reasoning that precedes it and be justified by the conditions. The great danger in appealing to emotion is that the suspicion may be aroused that it is being used as an unjustified means to persuade. Natural sympathy may be frozen into the sternest unyielding justice by an obvious and insincere appeal to emotion. This error is one of the most common weaknesses in forensic oratory. Sympathy, if unskilfully "lugged in" and debased into maudlin sentimentality, becomes a two-edged sword that wounds the user. When, however, emotion is employed by a master mere reason compared with it is weak and ineffective.

A dangerous but powerful source of interest in legal

arguments is that which comes from vigorous opposition. This kind of interest, examples of which go back at least to Cicero, is exemplified in many great speeches. An attack at once commands attention. It gives a reason why words are being spoken. The first sentence of some great speeches is both a text and a challenge. An attack may be upon a person, a proposed measure, or an idea. A personal attack on an individual perhaps arouses the keenest interest and, if justified, forms an important part of a forensic argument. The discussion of a subject may be so impersonal and academic that it has interest only for the student who is making a technical study of that question, but the lawyer is not inclined to fail in this lack of opposition and personalities. Much legal oratory has the opposite fault and is infused with a personal bitterness and venom that make it disagreeable and hence lacks one of the elements of successful persuasion.

There are many insincere defense attorneys whose favorite, if not their only, theory of a defense is to make these bitter personal attacks. This method may arouse interest at the start, but it often is the opposite of convincing. It is often recognized as a mere "throwing of sand in the eyes of the jury" so they will not see the real facts. The weapons of these men are sarcasm, irony, and invective and they continually "denounce, challenge, and defy" until their bitter words produce little if any favorable effect.

Plain words need to be said of a limited group of coarse and brutal lawyers, often forceful and sometimes able, who argue cases as they try them with a total disregard for all the courtesies and refinements of civilization. There are odious specimens of these men in certain communities and they cast a discredit on the legal profession out of all proportion to their number. If they were true representatives of the profession decent men would not belong to it. Arguments by a man of this type sometimes produce a spectacle not to be matched elsewhere in civilized communities. In the course of what he conceives is a legal argument this advocate utterly disregards the truth, insults his fellow citizens, if they happen to cross his purpose, violates the decencies of human relations, and resorts to all the deceitful tricks of sophistry to mislead and deceive. Class and race prejudice are appealed to in the lowest way and, where the judge has no power or does not exercise it, this disgraceful and unfortunate performance cannot be prevented. To the sorrow of all good men the sad truth too is that with the aid of ignorance, perjury, and prejudice these men win now and then. Where the judge has little or no power to control law practice these practitioners have a free field, and, in frantic efforts to succeed, can go almost any length without judicial rebuke. They disgrace an honorable profession by conduct more to be condemned than that for which others hear prison doors shut behind them. Fortunately there are many courts where judicial tolerance and legal public opinion do not shield these flagrant violators of the decencies of life.

If the question to be decided by court or jury is a technical one, as in a disputed document case, and clear and effective testimony has been given, it is not usually advisable to undertake to discuss in detail the testimony itself, except to enforce and characterize it as a whole in a clear and connected way. An attorney may weaken his case by an inaccurate argument on testimony with which he is not entirely familiar. He may claim too much or too little. If, however, counsel is thoroughly prepared on the facts in a case of this kind, a powerful argument can often be made that brings back to the minds of the jury in convincing order the significant phases of the testimony. If effective illustrative photographs are before the jury, then counsel has an unusual opportunity to enforce the technical testimony that has been given.

It is, of course, not possible to give here a technical argument on the facts in any specific case, but it may be possible to connect some of the outlines of general arguments given at the end of this chapter to the particular case on trial.

These outlines of arguments of counsel applying to a disputed document case are a composite of ideas, memories, and suggestions from numerous sources. They also emphasize some of the ideas embodied in the charges to juries outlined in the following chapter. Some parts are adapted from actual arguments in litigated cases, and the matter has all grown out of the modern view of evidence relating to the proof of documents. Some of the points came directly from charges of judges who have given scientific study to the subject and other ideas have been derived from discussions of evidence by certain modern law writers. The arguments as presented are original and new in but little more than phrasing, order of statement, and emphasis.

Some of the ideas, however, may be quite new to a certain type of lawyer who apparently studies only ancient law in the cases he tries. Some of the points in the arguments have heretofore been discussed in various preceding chapters but are here put together in connected form not as model arguments but for their possible suggestive value.

Gentlemen of the Jury:—

The interpretation that the opposition has attempted to put upon some of the evidence before you makes it necessary for us to consider for a few minutes its nature and purpose. The court will instruct you in the law of this case, I do not attempt to do that, but there have been some changes made in the methods employed in cases of this character that throw light on an investigation of this kind. These changes, like many technical legal rules, are not known to the general public. I am quite sure that a knowledge of them will not only assist you in your investigation of the facts in this case but will show you that the contention of the opposition regarding this testimony is not correct.

From some of the arguments made here, during the progress of this trial and now at its close, one might be led to think that you had not seen and were not to be permitted to see for yourselves this disputed writing. Strange to say, in the old days in many cases you would not in fact have been allowed to compare it with any standard or genuine writing whatever. There would have been no genuine writing for you to look at, unless it had gotten into the case by accident. It could not have been put in evidence for the purpose of comparison. You will be astonished to know that this old practice continued in our courts down almost to the present day. Jurors were not supposed to be sufficiently qualified to examine certain subjects for themselves and were asked to listen to what others said and then, if possible, determine from the conflicting evidence before them which witnesses were telling the truth. Long ago there was some reason for this practice because many a jury would have had men who could not read writing, but the old practice continued long beyond the time when juries could read.

The evidence in cases of this kind at the present time, as you have seen, and this is the vital point of application in this case, differs from most evidence in trials at law because it appeals to the mind through the eye as well as through the ear. In any case of disputed handwriting, no matter how plain, or how bold, or bad, the facts may be, some witnesses may possibly be found, as in this case, who will testify against the facts. This testimony in the old days would offset the mere opinion of another witness who had given an opposite opinion, and, with a juror who was a hearer only, the condition was practically as if the testimony had not been given. But when the writings themselves are examined, and full and detailed reasons are given for the opinion expressed, then the old order is totally changed.

You have already heard, or will hear, criticisms in this case of expert testimony as expert testimony. The old books have many such criticisms and it is not strange that in the old days abuses of various kinds were common. Up to 1913 it was against the law in every United States Federal Court of this progressive country, to put in evidence any standard writing whatever for purposes of comparison, and, as stated above, this same practice continued in nearly all the state courts up to a recent time and was only changed in this state by a recent statute.

Handwriting witnesses were supposed to remember how a man's writing looked from having seen it sometime, and then were asked to look at a signature on a will, or a note, or a contract, and say offhand, from memory alone, that it was genuine or not genuine. During these old days the abuse of expert testimony regarding documents was common and inevitable, and under the old rules there was no adequate remedy, but the remedy now is to ask for reasons and illustrations and then to ask the jurymen themselves, with their own eyes and their own minds, to review the conflicting testimony with the actual documents before them. The court will tell you that you are not obliged to take anybody's opinion here regarding these documents.

While we think the opinions of our qualified, experienced and reputable witnesses are reliable and correct, you can review all that testimony and determine whether or not it is logical and credible. You have heard the witnesses and have seen the witnesses, and can see the papers and see them in enlarged form in photographs. The appeal then is not to your credulity, as to whether you would *believe* this witness or that witness, but rather to your intelligence as to whether the witnesses have presented the testimony to you in a reasonable and convincing manner and whether their interpretation of the physical facts before you is a correct interpretation. This practice with the illustrations, you see, takes their testimony entirely out of the class of mere opinion testimony, and when my distinguished opponent talks generalities about the dangers of "mere expert testimony", or about old abuses, you will please to remember that he is *not referring to this case.*

He even objected to their admission as evidence, and now seems unhappy, when we use the photographs. Now let us see for just what purpose they are here under the present practice. They show more distinctly than the originals, and put in more convenient form, the physical facts upon which a conclusion must be based. Their value and use, in your hands and before your eyes, are thus perfectly evident and an objection to their use is an objection to your seeing clearly and distinctly the very evidence upon which you must finally base a verdict. Is that fair to you or to the case? To be really consistent, those opposed to us here should endeavor to darken this room so that you could not see these documents clearly, or should attempt to produce some kind of an actual fog here, instead of a mere verbal and mental fog, and thus prevent or make it difficult for you to see the physical facts.

We have asked our witnesses to give full and detailed reasons for their opinions on direct examination. We are permitted to do this by a decision of the highest courts of this state. This procedure also is a result of a revolution in the practice of law brought about undoubtedly by the advance in education and general intelligence. You can readily see that in making an attack upon our case it is a very different matter to attack the opinions of the witnesses instead of the reasons for their opinions. Cross-examination to the point is cross-examination on the reasons given for the testimony presented here. If these reasons are not reasonable to you, and if you cannot follow and understand, and if the interpretation does not seem to you correct, then you are not bound by it in any way. We confidently think that the more you see and the better you understand, the better it will be for our contention.

You see how different all this makes a case involving what we call opinion testimony with reasons from that class of expert testimony relating to the injury, let us say, of some man who fell from a street car. One doctor comes forward and testifies that the man will never be well again, and another doctor, who seems to know as much as the first, says that in a few months he will be as well as ever. When expert testimony of this class is presented to a jury and there is a conflict in the testimony, the jury is helpless. It is practically as though there had been no testimony given on the subject, but this is not true when reasons can be given and illustrations shown that can be understood and appreciated by intelligent men. This, you see, sweeps away all of that fine rhetoric, bitter sarcasm, and inconclusive logic which assumed that a ready-made opinion was being brought in here to be foisted upon you men for your adoption.

When the opposition argues, thus slurring and attacking the testimony of his own witnesses as well as ours, that if there is any conflict then the testimony is all to be of no value, you will see that this is not a good argument. The primary question is whether the physical things are here that we say are here and whether the interpretation of these things is the correct interpretation. You are not to be misled by any of these general criticisms of expert testimony, for here you not only have the opportunity but it becomes your duty to examine this testimony for yourselves and see just what it is and what it signifies. We are confident that you will not be misled but will see and understand as we desire and expect you will see and understand.

Referring again to the photographs it should be said that these illustrations, these tangible, visible enlargements that you can hold in your own hands and look at with your own eyes and reason about with your own brains, are the very effective reasons for the opinions in this case. That is what they were made for, and the real objection to them by the opposition is that they do well just exactly what they are intended to do, that is, make clear and distinct to you the facts in this case. Our opponent has especially objected to the photographs because they are enlarged and this objection exposes the real purpose of the opposition. The illustrations are of course more plain and useful when enlarged, more effective in illustrating the facts, and therefore the more damaging to the claims of those who are against the facts.

All this, it is evident, is far removed from the kind of testimony that is weighed by counting the witnesses. One good witness with good reasons and good illustrations will prevail against a whole omnibus load of those who merely give opinions, or give some incredible, visionary reasons which neither you nor I can understand. We ask you to examine the facts for yourselves in the light of all the testimony we have presented, and then we think you will render a verdict in accordance with the facts which will be in our favor.

. . . . . .

Gentlemen of the Jury:—

You have heard the violent general criticism of expert testimony, but it has not been so much criticism of the testimony in this particular case as of expert testimony as a whole. We desire especially that you should carefully consider this testimony. We have brought this expert testimony here for the purpose of assisting you in seeing, and correctly interpreting the physical facts in connection with these documents. That is its purpose, to assist in showing the facts. In this connection it is highly important that you should not be deceived as to just what this testimony is. From the references made to it by the opposition one might be led to think of it as something brought in here to deceive you or be foisted upon you, and it is suggested at least that you would be helpless in the matter and could not in any way understand the significance of the special testimony, or be able to recognize its value or discover its worthlessness.

What relation does this expert testimony have to this particular case and to the problem that you have to solve? is the real question for us. The deceptive nature of the criticisms of this testimony becomes quite apparent when it is clearly understood just what it aims to do. Let us see what it is.

On this particular subject a qualified specialist comes before you and is permitted by the law to give an opinion for your assistance, but not necessarily for your adoption. In the old days this testimony ended with the opinion, but as education became more general and intelligence increased, the law has said that a witness of this kind can not only give an opinion but he can give the reasons for the opinion to those who are to decide the case. This at once distinguishes this testimony from testimony regarding insanity and medicine and various questions where it is impossible for those of us not technically trained to follow the witness.

When we are told by one witness that the heart of a living man has a thin wall on one side which is gradually growing thinner, or that some valve is defective in some way and that the health of the patient never will be any better, it is impossible for you and me, by looking at this man or even by listening to his heart, to say whether the statements made about him are correct or not. And then when another witness appears, of equally good appearance, and gives his opinion that this heart is really better than the average heart, you and I are not aided by this testimony in reaching a conclusion about the question at issue because we cannot follow and check up the statements of the witnesses.

But this is not the condition in this case where a disputed document itself is before the court and before you. We in fact have, in these disputed papers, as it were, this "heart" under investigation out here before us where we can see it and examine it and test it by these standard writings and the enlarged photographs, which are really the illustrated "reasons" for the opinion here expressed.

It would be perfectly proper for the opposition in this case to attack with all the skill and vigor available the reasons for the opinion expressed here, but his eloquent and ingenious attack has not been against the reasons but mainly against the opinion. We think the opinion of this experienced and reputable witness has force and is worthy of consideration, but you are not asked to take the opinion unless the reasons for that opinion appeal to you as reasonable men. These reasons we contend are conclusive and are given here because the Court of Appeals of this state in a recent case has said that an expert can give reasons for an opinion on direct examination. On this subject the court says, with a good common sense that appeals to any man, that testimony with reasons may be controlling but without reasons may have little weight. Now you see how superficial and deceiving it is to attack this testimony without attacking the reasons and illustrations on which it is based. We want you to see and appreciate the facts as shown by these documents for the reason that the facts themselves argue for our contention.

We are confident that when you have considered the testimony in these three ways, or under these three heads of the opinion, of the physical facts, and the interpretation of the facts, that you will not be misled but will see and understand as we desire and expect you will see and understand.

CHAPTER XVIII.

THE JUDGE IN DISPUTED DOCUMENT TRIALS.

One who goes from court to court in the various parts of the United States and Canada and carefully observes conditions and results cannot but be impressed by the inefficiency and uncertainty of litigation in many courts as compared with conditions in other jurisdictions. Fortunately, in most courts, in a majority of cases, justice is promoted, fraud is defeated, and crime is punished, but in certain jurisdictions the administration of the law seems to be the only remaining legalized lottery. This criticism especially applies to criminal trials and certain important claim and damage cases. In some of these jurisdictions fraud is often tolerated and compromised with because of the cost, the delay, and especially because of the uncertainty, of legal remedies. The long continued abuses have dulled the keen sense of criticism of the legal profession, but there still are members who regret, and do not excuse but strive to improve, the bungling inefficiency of the law as administered in many courts.

Many observers who are fully qualified to speak say with the utmost positiveness that there is less respect for law in the United States than in any other civilized land. This lack of respect has not grown out of the abuse of the law as an instrument of oppression, but has arisen from its uncertainty, its delay, its cost, and especially its ineffectiveness in defeating fraud and in punishing the guilty. In many states guilty claimants on the most palpable forgeries are not even indicted, and in some instances they make the second attempt when defeated in their first effort. It is humiliating to realize that this great country is the safest place in the whole world in which to perpetrate fraud or to commit crime. This pitiful failure of the criminal law is discussed more at length in a preceding chapter.

This variation in degree of certainty in litigation no doubt arises from a number of causes, but one of the most important of them in jury trials is the varying power of the trial judge. The average citizen is wholly unaware of the wide variation in the power of the judge as exercised under the procedure of the different states and courts. Even many attorneys, excepting those who have had experience over wide territory, do not fully appreciate the significance and effect of this variation.

In the United States Federal Courts, which inherited the English common law practice in 1789, it is the privilege, if not the duty, of the judge to assist the jury in understanding the evidence. It is part of his business to see to it that they are not misled nor deceived, but instructed and assisted so that finally they will be more likely to reach a correct conclusion on the facts as disclosed by the evidence.

It is a surprise to many to know that in many state courts the powers of the judge have almost all been taken away. He must not even *refer to the evidence* in the remotest way at any time, and reads to the jury *in advance of the arguments of counsel,* a written charge. He has practically nothing to do directly or remotely with the proof of the facts of the case and merely passes upon bare propositions of law. In certain courts for him to refer to the evidence in any way is reversible error.

In violent contrast with this practice is that of the State of New Jersey, where the trial judge retains all the privileges of judges in Federal Courts, and is also permitted to comment upon the failure of a defendant in a criminal case to testify in his own behalf. A guilty defendant cannot sit silent and thus avoid cross-examination without the penalty of unfavorable comment, and the result is that defendants are practically obliged to testify. Those who through observation and experience are best qualified to judge earnestly contend that this should be the law in every state. More than one criminal has learned the meaning of what is known as "Jersey justice". The varying practice in these various courts in the various states and in the courts in other countries makes it possible to compare the results of litigation under the varying conditions. Generally speaking, fraud will more certainly be defeated and crime will more certainly be punished in the courts of New Jersey and the Federal Courts than in the courts of certain of the states.

Many attorneys, and practically all students of the subject who are not attorneys, who have observed the varying practice in these various American courts, as well as the practice of the Canadian and English courts, as it relates to the participation of the judge in the trial, highly commend that practice in which an able and fair judge is permitted to assist the jury in understanding and interpreting the evidence. Unprejudiced and qualified observers do not hesitate to say with much emphasis that the present drastic limitations in many state courts are undoubtedly against the interests of justice.

The restrictions of the powers of the judge have in large measure grown out of a contest between the legal practitioners and the court. In many courts in America the practitioners have won a complete victory. They are allowed to do practically what they please in a court of law. A serious effort has recently been made, and no doubt will be continued, to restrict the powers of all United States Federal judges and make them as powerless as the weakest judges of the state courts, and thus give the practitioner a free hand in all these courts. A bill to this effect, which almost entirely takes away the powers of the Federal judges, was recently introduced in the United States Congress. To those really interested in the administration of justice this is an alarming fact.

The drastic change proposed in this bill should of course be examined with a view of determining whether or not the change will be likely to promote justice. It is manifest that the change is ardently desired by certain members of the legal profession especially in the states where they now have unrestricted freedom in the state courts. Their main contention is that judges interfere altogether too much with the practice of the law, and by this interference defeat justice by defeating them. It is a serious question whether the bill proposing this change should not really be described as one designed, not to promote justice, but to give advocates a freer hand with witnesses and with juries, and greater comfort and profit in the practice of the law. One significant provision of the proposed bill requires the judge to deliver the charge before the arguments of counsel, thus giving the advocates a free field and the last chance at any meek and helpless jury without any review or interference whatever by the court.

Many trials at law are futile, pitiful performances where powerful advocates are purporting to promote justice through plastic, impressionable, inexperienced jurymen who are victims of all the tricks and methods of the experienced advocate with practically no control by the judge. In these cases under the rules in force the judge in many courts must remain silent and see fraud triumph or the guilty escape. Many criminal trials are thus reduced to mere farces, and as a result, the uninformed public wonders at the weakness of the law without fully understanding one of the principal causes.

The question naturally arises as to which are greater friends of abstract justice, active advocates engaged in litigation, or responsible judges of courts elected or appointed for long periods of time or for life. It ought not to be difficult to determine which group, generally speaking, are more interested in the protection and promotion of the principles of justice. It is obvious that the advocate is desirous of winning a particular case while the judge, as a rule, has no interest in the matter excepting to see that justice is done.

There are but few men, even including active trial attorneys, who will not admit *out of court* that the interests of justice would be better served in jury trials if the jury always could be assisted by a fair, able, experienced judge. With his experience, his knowledge of witnesses and of human nature, and his familiarity with the many phases of the problem of proof, *as well as with the personnel of the bar,* the judge is able to assist an inexperienced, and always a more or less poorly qualified, jury in understanding and weighing evidence. This proposition is so obvious that it would seem hardly to require argument, but unfortunately it does.

The bald fact is that the legal practitioner whose hopes of success are based mainly on the arts of the advocate, and the litigant who looks for victory, not mainly from the merits of his case but through legal restrictions, prejudice or perjury, are both strongly inclined to the belief that the presiding judge should have no part in a trial other than the preserving of order and the passing on the bare propositions of the law. The guilty and those who represent fraud naturally seek the courts where the trial attorney has a free field and they fear and avoid those courts where witnesses are protected, where perjury is made uncomfortable if not dangerous, where intelligent juries are selected, and where the presiding judge is able to exert some influence in directing the course of justice.

If he is permitted to do so, the wise and just judge in effect puts over the door to his court-room this inscription: "Those who seek justice are welcomed and aided, and witnesses who tell the truth are protected". The mere restraint exercised by the judge with power and authority is a constant wholesome influence in court upon those who, in the heat of controversy, are tempted to employ tactics that do not promote justice.

There are, of course, judges who are unworthy and who abuse their rights and opportunities, but it is unwise, in order to restrain these few men, to weaken the whole administration of the law. The problem is to establish a procedure that on the whole will promote the ends of justice and secure greater respect for the administration of the law. The partisan advocates say, take the power away from the judges and give it to us that we may have a free hand in litigation.

The only adequate justification for the taking away of the powers of the judge in jury trials is that it is impossible under the methods in force to secure competent, unbiased, conscientious judges to whom it is safe to give power. If this is true, then it is manifest that the direction of reform should be towards improving the methods by which judges are selected, and the creating of a public opinion that will better ensure the selection of capable, fair, and fearless men for these important positions. It would undoubtedly promote justice if the judicial position in all jurisdictions could be made more respected, more responsible, and more desirable in every way. One practical means to this end would be a decided increase in the salaries of judges in many jurisdictions so that the office, in this way at least, would be made more attractive to the most desirable candidates. Another change that would no doubt promote justice would be the making of the judicial position an appointive office in all courts.

Only those laymen whose rights and liberties have been seriously imperiled in an actual trial realize to what extent the wise and just judge occupies a position of peculiar power and opportunity in administering justice when he is allowed to participate in the proceedings. This participation naturally must usually be against the contention of one advocate who naturally at once is inclined to become impatient with any interference with what he may look upon as "the game of the law". If he can defeat the opposing advocate he thinks it a hardship to be obliged also to defeat the presiding judge. It is true that judges who are permitted to do so sometimes participate in the trial of a case and comment on the evidence to an extent and in a way that is very offensive to attorneys whose plans and methods are thus seriously interfered with. Attorneys of that class who pride themselves on winning "desperate cases", are livid with rage if their tactics are in any way interfered with by the court.

In a fair discussion of the question it must be stated that these unfortunate restrictions of judicial power have in some measure grown out of justified impatience with abuse of power. The overbearing tyranny and the lack of tact of an occasional official, and in some cases the sacrifice of the ordinary rules of courtesy, deserve only the severest condemnation. Dictatorial, arrogant, domineering methods may arouse an enmity that lasts beyond a term of court and is carried into the legislature where laws are passed that, on the whole, certainly are against the interests of justice. Because of advancing years, or possibly because of impairment of health, the harsh and undiplomatic methods of an occasional autocrat may become so intensified that the suffering victims are tempted to advocate the most unwise remedies.

In all of the states, even where the most severe restrictions are in force, there are judges, sometimes reversed by higher courts, who will not be entirely bound by the crime-assisting restrictions. They conceive their courts to be tribunals established to promote justice, defeat fraud, and punish crime, and fortunately these judges are constantly getting more and more support from reviewing courts. They should have the immediate support of legislatures.

It is also gratifying to note that not so many things are now adjudged to be "reversible error" as a few years ago. More and more trifling errors are said to be just what they are, "negligible". Cases are not now often reversed because some word is not begun with a capital letter or because a cow is not described as an animal. There was a time, not so long ago, when in many courts the main attention by one attorney was not given to trying the case in hand, but to the preparing of the "record" for the reviewing court. There have been jurisdictions where a strong advocate has thus used "reversible error" as a club to browbeat and intimidate a judge who is naturally inclined to assist in promoting the ends of justice.

It is not too much to say that there are but few reforms or changes in all of modern civilization more important than improvement in methods leading to the selection of fair, fearless judges, if, by the procedure in force, they are permitted to assist in the administration of justice. Until they are permitted to assist, no matter what other reforms are instituted, the administration of the law will be ineffective and uncertain. Common sense would suggest that comparison of results under the varying legal rules in force should be made and that the best procedure should then be adopted by all.

Fortunately in a government of separate states it is

possible to make comparison of results in many things, including the law, and this same comparison can also be made with conditions in other lands. State and national boundaries do not stop progress in medicine and mechanics, but do seem to be a bar to legal progress. If typhoid and yellow fever were in some way connected with the law, lives might be saved in Connecticut, New Jersey and Tennessee, but not in other states just across a boundary line. If improvements in lighting systems and harvesting machinery did not jump boundary lines and had to wait for legal processes to bring about changes, then candles and old-fashioned cradles would still be in common use in certain localities.

If it is a fact—and it certainly is—that the content of the law and the application of the law are both superior in some states as compared with other states, and in some other countries as compared with this country, then why is it not possible in some way to find the best and adopt it, as would be done in other things? With medicine and plows and mouse-traps one state profits by the advance of another state. Is it possible that free, sensible men in this twentieth century, in this enlightened land, cannot do this sensible thing with the law? Is there any good reason why all states should not profit by the experience of other states? There certainly is not.

Lagging reluctance, or even failure to do some sensible things and make desirable changes, puts the legal profession into a foggy atmosphere of inactivity and hesitation that prevents improvement. The question naturally arises as to whether the inaction is due to indifference as to improvement, or to lack of appreciation of the conditions. Fortunately there are men in the profession fully aware of the faults and the possibilities—there should be more—and they should be supported and assisted by all good men in their efforts toward improvement so that the law may not be the last in the procession of progress or, what is worse, may be absent altogether.

It is obvious that the essential and final test that should be applied to any proposed change in legal procedure is not what the effect may be upon the practice of law, but what bearing it will have on the interests of justice. It should all the time be remembered, by the bar as well as the bench, that courts are not designed to furnish places and opportunities to practice law, but to establish tribunals where truth and justice are promoted and where fraud and crime are punished.

These variations in procedure have an especially important bearing on all classes of cases where it is necessary to show and prove technical visible evidence. A disputed document trial, for example, as now conducted in many courts, is in effect, as it should be, a legally supervised scientific investigation, but this desirable atmosphere of the proceeding cannot be given to a trial in the absence of the modern enlightened rules and laws and without some helpful participation by the presiding judge. This helpful attitude of the judge in many courts shows clearly the radical changes in law practice in this special field.

With the new laws now in force in many jurisdictions, and an attitude toward the trial like that indicated by the judges' charges printed on the following pages, it becomes much more difficult to mislead a jury than under that practice where the court takes no part in the proceedings. These charges here quoted will astonish practitioners in some states where the judge is not permitted to say anything about the evidence. It was much easier to confuse and mislead a jury under the old practice where expert evidence consisted of mere opinions given without illustrations and without reasons, and this confusion and misleading is still possible in those courts where no interpretation of the testimony or assistance by the judge is permitted.

The modern valuation of testimony regarding disputed documents does not consist of a mere counting of the witnesses, but includes a consideration of the weight of their testimony. Recent decisions on the subject, as well as enlightened editorials and textbook comments, have taken this proper view in which it is said that the value of testimony of this character may range all the way from the merest conjecture up to the highest moral certainty. It is easy to understand how important it is in a trial for a judge to state this one fact.

The following excerpts from charges to juries show how important this part of a trial may become and illustrate, by contrast with the old style charges, and the charges in the courts of some states, the all too slowly changing attitude of the law toward expert testimony regarding documents.

Charge to Jury by the late Justice Henry Childs, in the Supreme Court, Buffalo, N. Y., in case of Fidelity Trust Co. v. Boyer Executors. The first part is a condensed recital of the facts, but the last highly significant paragraph is practically verbatim:

"Gentlemen:—

You have seen these disputed signatures; not only the originals have been shown to you but they have been presented to you in the form of enlarged photographs, and you have also examined the signatures by transmitted light to discover, if such condition exists, any damaging identities or similarities in these signatures in size and relations of parts to each other. You have also examined the enlarged photographs in which the various signatures are arranged under ruled squares that you may be able to see by inspection their line quality and any suspicious similarity if it exists.

"Those who are attacking these documents contend that these three checks, each containing three signatures, are forgeries by tracing made from a common model. You will remember the testimony and how it is explained that by this process of forgery a direct tracing is made with pen and ink or a pencil outline in some manner and then the outline is inked over. The testimony of those attacking the document is that this method of writing is apt to show a broken, disconnected and not uniform line and also it is contended that the exact, or practically exact, duplication of these signatures on three different checks, if you find there is a duplication, is an act so improbable that it would not occur in the ordinary process of writing. It is not contended that the checks are microscopic duplicates of each other, but that these, what are described as, damaging similarities and identities in position, beginning points, proportions, alignments and size, indicate that this similarity could not have accidentally happened as it is here shown.

"Gentlemen, you will imagine that one of these three clumsy writers sits down and writes his name on one of these checks. Then the second writer writes his name under the first, and that the third writer writes his name under the second. Then a week later, or upon the date of the second check, the acts of these three writers are repeated apart from and separated from the first check drawn, and that a week or month later, or when the third check is drawn, the three writers write again. Then when these three checks are brought together and the three signatures superimpose each other practically line for line, if you find that this is the fact, it is, gentlemen, for you to determine whether *that thing is likely to happen* with genuine signatures."

By Honorable Henry G. Ward in case of Newcomb v. Burbank, in the U. S. Court, New York City.

"Gentlemen of the Jury:—

. . . The second class of witnesses are the experts, and my own judgment is that their testimony is extremely important. The ordinary man cannot tell by looking at documents if they are genuine or not genuine with anything like the degree of skill of the expert who has seen many forgeries and many disputed documents and who is trained in this business to detect and interpret the characteristics of the writer. I do not think that the witnesses differ very much about the process. It is a question of reasoning altogether. You are to give weight to the testimony and the opinions of those experts just in proportion as you think the reasons they give for their opinions are good reasons or bad reasons. Of course, you will expect anybody who attempts to imitate writing to imitate more or less closely; it is therefore important for you to discover, even where the general pictorial effect is somewhat alike, whether there may not be a violation of certain little but significant characteristics of the writer, of which he may himself have been unconscious, but that he never entirely omitted whether he wrote well or ill, whether he wrote with tremor or firmly."

From charge of Mr. Justice William J. Gaynor, afterwards Mayor of New York City, delivered in Supreme Court, Westchester County, in case of Redmonds v. Manning, et al.

"Gentlemen of the Jury:—

With respect to the testimony of the experts, I took occasion early in the case, so that your minds might be right about it, to speak of the general misunderstanding with regard to expert evidence. The public take their impressions largely from the press, that reports that when these experts come in here, and perhaps testify one against the other, that we are obliged to decide which one we are to believe. Why, not at all. They only come here to instruct us. They come here and they compare before us these signatures with genuine signatures, and they point out the similarity or the dissimilarity, the contrast and the comparison, and in that way educate us and help us more or less to take them ourselves and look them over and see to what extent they resemble each other, and thus educate us sufficiently to be able to say for ourselves whether we think they are genuine or not. If we were all experienced bank tellers and experts we might not need them at all; but we are not, and therefore they can illustrate and explain some things here and put us on our inquiry and enable us to take the signatures ourselves and see, from our own examination with this expert help given us, which testimony we are to follow.

"Of course, it is not, I suppose an easy thing to tell a forgery; if it were, there would not be all this trouble in courts over forgeries where they do occur, not that I intimate that this is a forgery; that is for you. If a person sits down to forge a signature, no doubt he will follow the signature according to his skill and make it as near alike as he can, and he may take twenty different papers for that matter and write twenty forgeries until he gets one to suit him. The best you can do is take the testimony of these experts that have been given here, and wherein they have helped you, why they have helped you, and wherein they have not helped you, they have not helped you. That is all."

The following charge is a compilation from numerous sources and cases. It is given as an exposition of the modern view of opinion testimony with reasons in a disputed document case. It is not here presented as a model but merely as presenting a discussion of document expert testimony as viewed by modern progressive courts. It necessarily has no place in those jurisdictions where the duty and privilege of discussing the evidence and its significance have been taken away from the judge.

Gentlemen of the Jury:—

It will, as you of course understand, become your duty to decide this case when it is finally submitted to you, and according to your oath your decision should be based upon the facts before you and the testimony presented to you. It should not be based upon any prejudice or sympathy, that you may have brought with you, or that may have been developed during the course of the trial.

It is necessary for you to consider the question of what is called the weight of testimony. This expression can be interpreted in plain language by saying that you are to determine which testimony you will believe and act upon and which testimony you will not believe. You may not be able to say outright that you do not believe certain testimony, and regarding other testimony which seems credible you may have some doubt, but the point is that, like sensible men, you are to consider the whole matter as though it was an affair of your own and decide accordingly. You will not be deceived in considering this question of weight of testimony by the number of witnesses on either side but by the effect that the testimony has produced on your minds. If you are convinced that one witness has told the truth it does not matter if twenty have given conflicting testimony.

This testimony regarding these documents, in which an opinion has been given and then reasons for that opinion expressed and illustrations shown, is called expert testimony, but it is not expert testimony in the usual understanding of that term. It is in fact opinion testimony with reasons and illustrations which should appeal to your own eyes and to your own intelligence.

This testimony should be examined under three heads; first, the opinion expressed, second, the physical evidence pointed out to you and illustrated, and third, the interpretation of that evidence or its meaning and real significance.

The most important part of the testimony of this class comes under the third head. If such testimony is ineffective or dishonest, emphasis will naturally be placed mostly upon the first point, the opinion, and if, under the second head, physical evidence is merely pointed out without interpreting it, as by a dumb witness, we may not understand its real significance. When, however, the three things are combined we, as intelligent men, ought not to be entirely helpless before such testimony even if it is in conflict, but should give it just such weight as it deserves as measured by our experience, our common sense, and our intelligence.

The questions to be determined are, first, does the opinion, as tested by the qualifications, experience and conduct of the witness here before you, bear the proper evidences of credibility, and second, is the physical evidence referred to present and has it been effectively and honestly pointed out, and then finally, is the interpretation of the physical evidence a reasonable interpretation?

You are not asked to give this testimony any weight whatever if, under this third division, it does not appeal to your good judgment. In order that we may have the benefit of this interpretation experienced observers in this field may be required, but when the matter is explained and interpreted to us, on a subject of this kind, and we are shown these things and are told what they indicate, then we can ourselves determine whether the evidence appeals to our own judgment and our own common sense.

Finally, gentlemen, I desire to emphasize the importance and dignity of your task. As jurymen you are for the time the sworn guardians of the interests of justice. This is a responsible and solemn duty not to be lightly entered upon nor carelessly performed. You are now a part of this court, and if you fail then the experience of the ages, the learning of the schools, the sacrifices of the past, have come to naught as applied to the administration of the law. You may well pray for that intelligence and courage that will lead you to see the right and to do the right.

CHAPTER XIX.

A CASE BOOK ON THOUGHT AND REASONING*

Superficial thinking, inability to draw correct inferences from more than simple facts and conditions, and a low general quality of reasoning power are common human qualities. Fortunately, in many divisions of human effort plodding industry and a faithful attention to details bring commensurate rewards even to those with dull and mediocre minds. There are many men who are not required to think and to reason except in the most superficial way, and they go through life on the whole happy and contented, doing routine work which requires almost no mental effort. This variation in human ability and the requirements made on men no doubt contributes to human happiness. There are kinds and classes of human labor, however, in which something more is required in order to reach success than plodding industry and attention to details. One of these fields is the profession of the law.

Competent judges, who have opportunity to observe law practice in this country in widely separated fields and in many courts, are obliged to report that much of it is of very inferior quality. Too often and in too many places it shows illiteracy, inaccuracy, lack of preparation, lack of intelligence, and low moral tone. If there is any doubt as to this statement it can be dispelled by attending trials or by reading reports of actual trials in lands where the practice of law is a profession. A prime difficulty, of course, is the fact that there are

---

***Virginia Law Review*, Vol. XI., No. 2, December, 1924. Reprinted through the courtesy of that publication.

many trying to practice law who should be doing something else; one lifetime is not long enough for them to learn how to do it well. There also are many who may have the fundamental qualities, but who have not had that thorough training and vigorous mental discipline necessary to fit them for an intellectual profession. No one, of course, should presume to practice law, or be allowed to practice law, who imperils human rights, honor, liberty and property by stupid inefficiency. There are too many legal practitioners in this land of opportunity who are strangely out of harmony with the ideals and traditions of an honorable profession. Their qualities and their methods do not match the beautiful marble court-rooms in which their bad English, their bad manners, their low culture, and their incompetence are exhibited.

The ability to think clearly and reason accurately are the fundamental and essential qualifications of the lawyer. If he cannot learn, or does not learn, to do well these necessary things, he should not attempt to practice law for he is not qualified. One of the attractions of the profession is that it deals so largely with matters that appeal to the mind. The whole performance, from first to last, when properly conducted, is infused with the processes of thought and reasoning, and the question here under consideration is whether in law study and in law practice these intellectual elements have not been too much overshadowed by the mere task of gathering the materials for law practice. These materials are certain facts, or alleged facts, and certain legal propositions, legal precedents and statutes that have application.

Interpreting materials is something more than the mere collecting of materials. The legal question involved in a law suit may be the important one, requiring close, accurate reasoning and interpretation, upon which the outcome may largely or even wholly depend; but in many cases a contention of this kind has but little to do with the law. A certain procedure is followed and certain rules of evidence are applied now and then, but the performance many times would be more accurately described, not as a law suit, but as a fact suit. The finding, presenting, proving, discussing and interpreting of certain facts make up a large part, perhaps four-fifths or even nine-tenths, of trials at law, so-called.

A law suit usually grows out of a disagreement, either as to the existence of certain alleged facts, or the interpretation of them, as affected by the law, if the law has any direct application. The litigant asks, "Is my contention a sufficient basis for a suit, or a defense, and is there a reasonable probability of my winning?" Thus every law suit begins with an intellectual problem involving an interpretation of a state of facts and, incidentally, an interpretation of the law that applies. The first act is this act of reasoning to determine whether or not there will be a law suit. Many proposed suits end at just this point, and clients are either advised to settle the contention, or told that it is inadvisable to bring an action. The stupid advocate may lead his trusting client into a proceeding that never should have been begun.

The processes of thought or reasoning not only thus begin a law suit, but continue throughout the performance at every point, and an actual trial is quite accurately described as a contest in reasoning. This ability to draw correct inferences is necessary, not only in weighing the story of the client, but in formulating a trial policy and in meeting all the varied problems that arise in an actual trial. More probably than in any other kind of effort, efficient legal work thus requires prompt, accurate, constructive thought and reasoning.

Besides the law and the evidence to consider, there are in nearly every case also problems of personality and other difficult questions and disturbing influences brought to bear. They must all receive intellectual attention. Prejudice, sympathy and ignorance are nearly always present, and skill in coping with all of these difficult problems requires a study of much more than the pages of digests. Much of this special skill, no doubt, can only be developed in the school of experience, but the question here raised is whether even there, as well as during preparation, more emphasis can not profitably be put upon this thought and reasoning phase of the work.

Real education furnishes the handles by which the mind gets hold of ideas. These handles are the facts of accurate, extended knowledge. Any plan or system of education, or of self-discipline, necessarily fails that aims to teach or to develop thinking, if it can be taught, without supplying these necessary materials. Vague and incorrect thinking is due, in part at least, to vague and inaccurate knowledge. While correct thinking thus must be based on correct knowing, and it is impossible to separate the mind from that with which it works, correct thinking and not mere knowledge is the main result sought for. We seek to know not simply to know, but in order to think and to do. More and more education thus aims to train and discipline the intellect as well as inform the mind. If the training of the intellect does not go along with the accumulation of knowledge, then this mass of knowledge in the head is alone of but little more value than that in the books on the shelves. There are walking cyclopedias in one volume whose extended knowledge is worth less than that on the printed pages of the twelve volumes.

Simply knowing is static while thinking is dynamic. When a man thinks, then he is, of course, performing the distinctly typical and the most important human act; and, if any help whatever can be given, the problem of education is to consider what can be done to improve this valuable power. A hundred can be found who know to one who can think, and in every field those who were given, or who have improved and developed, this power that comes through intelligent, constructive thought, are marked men. We describe them as "men of good judgment," and they are sought for everywhere. In the field of the law they naturally are in the front rank.

Deliberate thought or reasoning is defined as a successive association of judgments and a systematic examination and progressive comparison of preliminary or experimental judgments, leading up to a final conclusion. There is no such thing as an isolated fact, and nothing is known until its relations are known. In any field reasoning thus takes facts, ideas, circumstances and conditions, and separates, analyzes and compares them and determines their relative values and proper relations and the correct inferences to be drawn from them. A new inference thus obtained from ideas, as well as from material things, is invention and may disclose a new relation or result not before known. The great inventor is first a keen and accurate observer and then a creative reasoner who is able to see with the mind.

Any discussion looking toward possible improvement of thinking and reasoning ability in general, or in any special field, is naturally preceded by the query as to what extent the doctrine of predestination applies to these human qualities. This is an ever new old problem that still must be considered by all who are interested in human advancement. We know that there is a mysterious something in the amount, or the balance, or the lack of balance, of human qualities that is inadequately described as genius because we have no better word to describe it. No one knows just what it is. While it is generally admitted that it cannot be directly acquired in any school, from any teacher, by any method, it is nevertheless the accepted theory of education that what is called natural ability can at least be improved, if not added to. Who can tell what Plato would have been without Socrates?

No matter what the natural endowments may have been, it is certainly true that all effective reasoning and the skilled use of the mind comes as a result of patient, sustained study and practice. Not to any one does this priceless ability come as a total and free gift from on high. The final quality of the mind absolutely depends upon what is done with the mind; industry must be added even to the highest endowment.

It is of course true that in all educational processes this ability to reason must mainly be developed, not directly but in connection with other subjects of study. Every wise and efficient teacher is a teacher of it, and if in any phase of education any direct attention to the subject should tend to relieve other instructors of their responsibility in the matter then this direct attention would be a misfortune. The question is whether all could not be stimulated and assisted by a general emphasis on this quality in education and especially in legal education. Some of the technical discussion in the books on logic and thinking gives but little direct help in developing the ability to think. Some of it is much like bare discussions of grammar as a science of language which may have almost no relation to the task of acquiring the practical use of language as a means of conveying ideas.

Notwithstanding their difficulty, however, some at least of the "hard" books on thinking must be found by the earnest student and faithfully studied. The thorough reading of them may be a valuable part of the discipline. One who has not acquired, and will not acquire, the habit of faithfully pursuing a difficult mental task for hours at a time will not become a thinker. Modern American education no doubt lacks thoroughness and has been too much tinged with the spirit of the kindergarten. He who must all the time be entertained while he is educated will hardly be educated.

That it is possible deliberately to practice thinking on a selected subject seems to be wholly unknown to many persons. There are many, not altogether unintelligent human beings, who have the notion that when they are not reading or talking, or doing something with their hands, or learning something, that they are doing nothing, and, sad to say, they often are. Many individuals are wholly unable to be busy with the mind alone. Much good thinking is no doubt made impossible by poor reading and poorer talking, although good talk, like good reading, is of course a most helpful stimulator of good thought. Many persons are uneasy, if not almost terrified, to be alone with nothing to do, and when they have thirty minutes or more of free time, they are disposed frantically to grab something from the curious collections of printed matter on view here and there which too often does exactly what it is claimed it will do, that is, shorten life by killing time. This desperate expedient is only necessary to those who have not learned to think. Unwise and persistent reading is a refuge for the unthinking and often is a sign of ignorance and unintelligence.

An interesting habit-forming experiment, for the law student and for the worker in many fields, would be the definite employment of a short period each day, perhaps at the beginning half an hour, to be used for deliberate thought. If possible, this thinker should then be strictly guarded, the desk cleared, the papers put out of sight, and the intellect alone put to work. Preferably he will be alone; he will read nothing; he will make no marks on paper, but will simply use the contents of his mind, which ought to be sufficient for use in real thinking for at least thirty minutes! If during this period this man's secretary, or roommate, can truly say to inquirers that he is busy, and if by persevering practice he can make this one of the busiest parts of the day, then it might be the most profitable time. It would no doubt sound incredible, if not amusing, in certain places if the report should be made at this period, "Mr. Blackstone cannot be disturbed; he is busy thinking."

If faithfully followed this new practice might also develop an idea now and then, and one alone for that day might be worth more than all the other work of a great office, or the output of a great factory. The fact is now and then disclosed that there are here and there in positions of some importance those who have not learned to think. As a rule their tenure of office, however, is short, even if it begins at all, and the tragedy of the matter for them is that they can hardly be made to understand in just what quality they are deficient. Some men of this unfortunate class are trying cases and trying to prove things in a court of law, and all they lack is the ability to think.

Simply to read of these matters, here or anywhere, or to listen to them in a class-room, is of but very little use unless the reading and the listening lead directly into definite action. Thinking is not learned by reading about thinking, but is only learned by thinking, and anyone can be set down as a fakir who undertakes to teach any easy method of acquiring this faculty. It is not completely learned by "twelve easy lessons by mail," that purport to "develop personality" or "personal power" or anything else. Certain advertisements would lead one to think that there are many easy roads to wisdom as well as to wealth. The fact that so many become discouraged makes the accomplishment by the few all the more valuable. There is no doubt that defeat in these efforts often is due, not so much to poor brains, as to weak wills. Good intentions are not rare; persistent efforts are.

The adoption of the case method of teaching no doubt was an important step in advance in developing in the student of law the ability to reason. By this method the earnest student becomes able to find for himself ideas and principles in among the words on a printed page. This performance is no mean achievement. This method of study no doubt stimulates thinking when in the main it is a quest for principles and not merely the finding of definite answers to certain definite problems. In any field if one only learns a routine, like a plumber, with no attention to the principle involved, he may become a "practical" man who can find precedents, but he will not be a professional man. It is not likely that he will add anything to that which came to him.

An examination of law books and books for lawyers, and entrance examinations for admission to the bar, discloses what appears to be insufficient attention to these questions of thought and reasoning. A short shelf will hold all the special matter that is available even in some of the larger libraries, and there are many lawyers who do not own a printed page on the subject, nor do they know where it can be found even if they know what it is. It is, of course, true that the total content of the law is now so stupendous that it is easy to omit any phase of the study that may not seem to be absolutely essential. Professor Wigmore's *Principles of Judicial Proof* is a valuable and almost unique contribution to the limited literature in this field of thought development. The book deserves the most thorough study from cover to cover, but is perhaps better suited to the actual practitioner or to the advanced student than to the beginner. Would it not be possible to put together a collection of graded material that would serve as the basis for a course of study and practice in this important phase of legal education, A Case Book on Thought and Reasoning, that would perhaps assist a little at least in developing greater interest in this valuable ability?

A wealth of material illustrating all the varied grades and qualities of thought is on the shelves. Literature and history would also furnish unlimited additional matter. If a book of this kind has not been made, would it not be worth while for some competent author to try the experiment? This course might include certain whole opinions, good and bad, both ancient and modern. Mainly, however, it would perhaps be a collection of excerpts, without comment, ranging in length from a sentence or two, to a series of paragraphs or pages, which would furnish practical problems in thought and reasoning. These problems could range in difficulty from those involving the most intricate and abstruse reasoning down to examples of stupid argument, erroneous inference, and incorrect statement. Examples from the highest sources could, of course, be included for study and comment, illustrating the highest type of reasoning and the use of accurate and forceful language as its vehicle.

These excerpts would furnish examples for study, for argument, and for written criticism and commendation. Carefully written discussions would no doubt provide the best method of developing the subject and of discovering whether or not the student is able to solve the problem in hand, for what one cannot express he only feebly knows. One who says he knows a thing but cannot express it usually is either deceiving himself or is not quite telling the truth. When on a given topic words refuse to flow off from the point of a pencil it is because there are no definite ideas back of the words. These various problems of thought could, of course, be made to include those which would involve the necessity of drawing inferences from and judging a great variety of material, including illustrations of inherent improbability, of partially hidden exaggeration, of extravagant statement, of bare-faced perjury, of plain bias, of contradiction, of unsupported assertion, of unwarranted inference, of double meaning, of confusion of ideas, of hidden and of obvious fallacies, of false analogies and of convincing truth and sincerity. Investigation has clearly shown that those familiar with the various phases of law study would be able to furnish concrete examples illustrating the best and the worst in legal reasoning on many phases of the facts as well as of the law.

Thought stimulating exercises and a developing discipline in reasoning could no doubt be provided for the student to wrestle with for perhaps an hour a day for at least part of a school year, or for perhaps for a longer period of time. He could at least thus develop intensity of attention and learn by example the difference between illuminating language and jargon by developing the ability to test all language by the thought and reasoning test. One even might thus be led to make the discovery that the purpose of language is to convey ideas.

This thought study might also be useful to more than mere beginners for unfortunately legal reasoning by those who did not begin yesterday is not always accurate, logical and scientific. Fortunately there have been many legal reasoners who have furnished illuminating examples for study. They possessed logical and scientific minds that not only did not become warped, but were strengthened by the difficulties and diverting influences, until they worked with almost mathematical precision. This Case Book on Problems of Thought and Reasoning might assist in developing more minds of this class.

CHAPTER XX.

THE DISPUTED DOCUMENT PROBLEMS.

A disputed document inquiry sometimes suddenly arises in the midst of the trial of another issue when some paper is offered in evidence and is at once attacked. A will is brought under investigation because of its tardy appearance, its surprising contents, its suspicious character, or sometimes simply because the names of some of the relatives were not among the beneficiaries. Then again, out of some old cupboard, or under some old carpet, or in some old Bible, is found, with much real or assumed surprise, an agreement, note, contract, deed, or other document which becomes the centre of a protracted and bitter controversy. In criminal cases a question may arise over a writing that is evidence against, or an alibi for, the accused.

The progress of civilization has brought about a great increase in the use of documents. A few hundred years ago many a home contained no pen and ink for the reason that no member of the household could write. In those days a document was a rare and mysterious thing that was looked upon and handled with a feeling of awe. It is difficult fully to realize the change that has come about from that day to the present. We now live in a world of documents, and with this increase has come the opportunity for their fraudulent production and use.

Some of the more important questions that are considered when a disputed document gets into court are: whether the handwriting of a will, deed, contract, or note, is genuine or forged; whether material erasures or alterations, by chemicals or otherwise, have been made in a document; whether a fraudulent note or contract was written over a genuine signature; whether there has been a fraudulent substitution of pages in a document; whether writing was continuously written in the order in which it appears, whether the paper was made before the date of the document which is written upon it; whether ink writing is as old as it purports to be; whether typewriting is genuine or forged; whether the typewriting of a document is consistent with its date; whether a document was written on a particular kind of typewriting machine; whether anonymous, blackhand, obscene, or threatening letters, or other letters, or writings of any kind, were written by a certain suspected writer.

A great variety of other questions arise regarding documents, and trials involving these inquiries are now much more frequent than under the old rules. These cases are often of great importance. Only eight disputed signatures in certain contested will cases represented more than twenty-seven millions of dollars. A few pen strokes or, in these days, a few words in typewriting, often furnish vital evidence affecting property, liberty, or even life.

One of the duties of the qualified attorney is to inform litigants and their representatives that there are many questions that arise regarding documents that cannot be answered. Prompt and accurate information of this kind often is of great value. Careful trial attorneys do not formulate definite trial policies until they secure reliable information on the facts.

The first necessary step in the investigation of a disputed document question is, of course, the accurate determination of what the fact really is. Then, if it appears that the client's contention is correct, and the case is to be tried, comes the task of proving the fact in court. This performance in brief requires that the correct interpretation of the evidence must be put into the minds of the jury, or of the court. That is the main problem discussed in this book.

The proving of a case involving a technical question depends upon the careful preparation of the matter for trial by the trained attorney, the proper marshaling of the evidence as presented by the various witnesses, and the elucidation and emphasis of the evidence by the attorney. The result in some technical cases also depends upon the effective co-operation of the informed lawyer and the trained specialist. By a skilful combination of efforts they together are able to describe, illustrate and interpret a technical subject so that court and jury can see, understand, and become convinced.

Suggestions regarding preparation for trial in these cases and effective co-operation of lawyer and ordinary witnesses, and lawyer and special witnesses, are contained in the following chapters. Some of the discussions relate only to certain general phases of the subject, others are devoted more especially to the definite part to be performed by the lawyer, and others to the work of the witnesses. A few other incidental but important questions are also considered, all bearing on the vital problem of how to prove a fact in a court of law.

Every lawyer sooner or later learns that the most formidable evidence that appears in a court is the silent evidence of things. A letter, a telegram, a postal card, a signature, is that which turns the scales of justice. "I would sooner trust the smallest slip of paper for truth than the strongest and most retentive memory ever bestowed on mortal man", said the learned justice who wrote the opinion in 5 Ga. 341. The fact that a mere scrap of paper is so vital as evidence makes the intelligent scrutiny of documents an essential part of the practice of law. If a document is so controlling, it is important to know, and to be able to prove, that it is genuine.

The preparation and interpretation of documents have always been important parts of the lawyer's business, but, no doubt partly because of the old restrictive laws, this scrutiny of documents on the question of genuineness has not received so much attention as it deserved. Genuine papers have no doubt been successfully attacked, and great numbers of fraudulent papers have undoubtedly wholly escaped suspicion. It is unfortunate to develop an unwise suspicion, but every document that comes to a lawyer's attention should receive intelligent scrutiny.

To instruct the untrained, and sometimes the indifferent and the prejudiced, to see, understand, and solve a new and difficult problem is the apparently impossible task given to one called to make preparation for trial in these various classes of technical cases. This result must be attained against adverse testimony which is sometimes corrupt or mistaken, in the face of the frequent interruptions by opposing counsel, under the exacting restrictions of the rules of evidence, and frequently with a jury of only average men. Under these conditions it might seem that a just verdict would be simply a matter of chance, but in most courts under modern procedure this is not the fact; even much abused jurors usually decide cases right.

It is the fashion to find fault with the administration of the law, and there certainly are faults and abuses, but now and then let it be said that there is more to be thankful for than to criticise. Won by the devotion and sacrifice of thousands through the long years of history, that which we vaguely call "the law" still stands as the citadel of human freedom. Its menace in some lands during these recent days tends to make conservatives of many who, while in favor of reform, are opposed to anarchy.

In spite of over-technical procedure and the great flood of perjury, of incompetent lawyers, and the shortcomings of the bench, of the weaknesses of the jury system, and the abuses of expert testimony, of able attorneys on the wrong side, and the debasing contingent fee, of lying experts, and the great mass of conflicting precedents, justice prevails in the great majority of cases. There are grounds for the belief that the stars in their courses still are in league with justice. It behooves the young and aspiring lawyer to see to it that he is on the side of the stars.

CHAPTER XXI.

OBTAINING STANDARDS OF COMPARISON.

Since the decision on the main issue in a disputed document case depends mainly upon some sort of comparison, the finding of suitable standards is an important part of the gathering of the evidence. In these trials one party alleges that a document is genuine; that certain physical evidence is the same as something else, or is in harmony with it; that there is a natural continuity in a document and that there has been no alteration of it, or substitution of parts of it; or he contends that a certain document was or was not written by a certain writer; or that a document was or was not written upon a certain typewriting machine at a certain time and place. The opposing party endeavors to prove that one or more of these contentions is not correct. In legal phrase, the parties join issue on the existence, or non-existence, of a certain fact or series of facts. There usually is some inherent evidence, or some outside information, that tends to show the truth or falsity of any one of these contentions without comparison with anything, but the final proof requires the bringing forward of something for comparison.

The following case illustrates this matter of proof by comparison. An inquiry arose regarding several typewritten documents, of great importance if genuine, all of which bore dates of the years from 1898 to 1902. Two facts proved that the documents were not written on their alleged dates and therefore were not genuine. The first was that they were all written on an L. C.

Smith typewriter, and the second, that this kind of typewriting machine first appeared in 1904. Comparison proved the first of these facts, and the dated history of this typewriter proved the second.

In another case the basis of a large claim was a long document dated "August 27, 1880", said to have been found in 1915, thirty-five years after its date. The document itself disclosed, as the result of careful examination, that it had been laboriously written, or traced, over a partially removed pencil outline of nearly every word. This condition furnished the first proof of the nature of the document. Later in the official files of a public office a long letter was found which was written by the alleged writer of the disputed contract and bore *exactly the same date* as the disputed document, August 27, 1880. This letter, a perfect standard of comparison, and the condition of the contract itself practically demonstrated that the contract was a forgery and led to the sensational abandonment of the claim in the midst of the trial. Without the standard of comparison it would have been difficult to prove the facts.

The standards of comparison first provided in many disputed document cases are too few in number and not suitable in kind, and the finding of suitable and adequate standards of comparison is one of the first steps to be taken in the preparation of a case of this kind. This task of finding standards is sometimes a simple one, but in some cases, especially if ancient documents must be found, or it is necessary to obtain the handwriting of persons who write infrequently, the investigation requires diligent, systematic attention. It also is sometimes highly important that standards be secured with the utmost promptness. Delay sometimes is not merely dangerous, but fatal.

There are attorneys who think that this phase of preparation for trial is too trivial to require their distinguished attention. They sometimes exhibit a kind of false pride that invites defeat, while the capable man studies every phase of his case from top to bottom and knows that cases have been won through the finding of a single scrap of paper. The discreet attorney does not, of course, do this actual work himself, as he cannot testify, but gives intelligent directions in regard to it and knows when necessary things have not been done. If he does not understand these matters he is not qualified to prepare a case of this kind for trial.

Through excessive zeal, or because of a low standard of ethics, or merely through poor judgment, methods are sometimes employed in seeking written and other evidence that imperil results and deserve severe criticism. Courts of appeal, as well as trial courts, frown upon theft even as a means of proving guilt. It is therefore necessary to urge that this work of securing standard writings be done properly as well as promptly. Restraint is sometimes as important as stimulus, and the attorney is properly in control of the whole operation. Warnings are not presented to discourage thoroughness, but to discourage unscrupulousness. It is often necessary to exercise ingenuity, but the prudent attorney does not permit indiscreet assistants by their methods to render evidence almost valueless that otherwise might have much force.

In making a search for genuine writings, or anything to be used for comparison, it is helpful to write out a comprehensive, detailed list of all of the relations of the party, or the matter, under investigation, and every possible source of information. In many cases it at first seems that the necessary evidence cannot be found, or that a certain writer wrote so little that it is impossible to find any useful writings whatever, but a thorough search often leads to the discovery of just what is necessary.

The extended list of suggestions here given, as to sources and methods in the search for comparison material, may aid in a case where it is difficult to find what is necessary. In any given case there may, of course, be other fields of inquiry than those here suggested. Emphasis is laid on the necessity for this special work, the importance of thoroughness, as well as the importance of putting the matter into the hands of one capable of doing the work promptly and well.

Standard writings of a person that grew out of ordinary business connections are naturally first sought, and if sufficient writings of this kind cannot be found then all of the writer's relations to his town, city, state, or nation, which might require writing, should be investigated. Permits of many kinds require writing, and writing is necessary in connection with the collection of taxes and registering and voting. Then there are possible writings of many kinds that have resulted from the social, religious, political, and educational relations of the party. It is difficult for one to live in a civilized community without being called upon to write now and then.

Application for all kinds of insurance and for memberships of all kinds, also requests for installation of gas, electric, telephone, and other apparatus, all require writing. In connection with the search for all possible business and legal papers it is important to look for leases, building permits, checks, deeds, mortgages, notes and drafts, also telegraph, express, and store receipts, registered letter receipts, and originals of telegrams. When payments by checks have been made to a party whose writing is sought, these vouchers can sometimes be obtained for the written endorsements they contain. Letter files of business houses or of individuals who are friendly often contain excellent examples of the writings sought for.

Ingenious investigators sometimes obtain desirable standard writings from those who will not write willingly by having sent to them registered letters or packages. A signature only may sometimes be worth much more than unimportant articles which may be delivered and for which a written receipt is requested. In some communities specimens of handwriting have been obtained by these investigators by asking suspected writers to make out a list of all the inmates of the house, or of all taxable property. Writing can sometimes be secured from women in connection with inquiries regarding health conditions where those under suspicion of having written something are asked to make out in their own handwriting a list of all occupants of the house and sign statements that no one with a contagious disease is living there, or has lived there for a certain length of time. Gas, electric light, plumbing, sidewalk, and other inspections sometimes require signed inspection slips which can be secured by someone with the proper authority. Those who have been arrested, from whom it is desirable to obtain writing, are sometimes asked to make a detailed inventory of their personal belongings that are taken by the jailor.

Ingenious inquiries (always from outside investigators and never by attorney or by a technical expert who is to testify) regarding property, employment, lost articles, servants, possible rich or distinguished relatives, or attractive business propositions, may obtain replies that are useful. In some instances specimens of writing have been obtained by directly asking one to assist in the preparation of written work.

It is sometimes possible to obtain specimens for comparison by openly requesting the suspected party to write. If a person is suspected, or has been accused, and will write in response to a request, it is then important to arrange the details so that the writing thus obtained will be free and natural and especially that it be sufficient in quantity. An innocent person will not be inclined to refuse to write, and one under suspicion of having written something objectionable, who is denying it, may not dare to refuse. Writing done by request should include matter covering all of the characters in a disputed or suspected writing, and it is important that writers be kept at the task until an ample amount of writing is secured. If each separate piece of the writing is at once taken away from the writer as soon as it is completed, it becomes more difficult to maintain a consistent disguise through an extended writing.

It is usually desirable that the suspected writer be requested to write at two sittings, either at a first interview with a short interval intervening, or on different occasions. In some instances, especially in anonymous letter cases, it is important that the writer be kept at the task of writing for thirty minutes, or even longer. If a suspected writer did not write the disputed matter this thorough procedure will usually at once demonstrate the fact. If the suspicion is correct this extended writing will often furnish material sufficient to prove the fact, or even lead to an immediate confession.

One who writes by request is inclined to write self-consciously and somewhat unnaturally, even when no attempt is made to do so. To a considerable extent this undesirable result can be prevented by putting the writer at ease. It is also, of course, desirable that the writing be done under conditions that will, as far as possible, prevent the writer from effectively disguising his writing, and in a manner that will expose the disguise if disguise is attempted. In the interest of efficiency, as well as of justice, a suspected writer will be treated fairly, and it is necessary to emphasize the fact that the rough and even brutal methods sometimes employed defeat the very ends they aim at.

It is important to make such arrangements as shall not embarrass, frighten, or hurry the writer. It is important that the writer be under attentive observation during the operation of writing, and while the extended specimens are being written, and this is especially important if the same matter is to be written more than once, in order that the time required to write each specimen be carefully noted. If ten minutes is required to write a specimen once, and then it is written in five minutes, this will show that both specimens are not free, natural writings. If a writer is suspected of disguising he can be asked to write at least one extended specimen rapidly. Consistent disguise is practically impossible if the matter dictated is written in one-half the time required for the first writing.

When a suspected writer copies, or writes from dictation, a connected discourse which arouses some interest in the matter itself, he is much more likely to write naturally than if he writes simply a series of disconnected names or words. Below are given two examples of prepared matter which will usually secure the attention of the writer to the matter itself. It will be observed that each of these paragraphs contains all the small letters, capital letters, and figures in English writing, together with certain frequently used words, abbreviations, and punctuation marks.

Dear Sam:—

From Egypt we went to Italy, and then took a trip through Germany, Holland, and England. We enjoyed it all, but Rome and London most. In Berlin we met Mr. John O. Young, of Messrs. Tackico & Co., on his way to Vienna. His address there is 1497 Upper Zeiss Str., care of Dr. Quincy W. Long. Friday, the 18th, we join C. N. Dazet, Esq. and Mrs. Dazet, and leave at 6:30 A. M. for Paris on the "Q. X." Express and early on the morning of the 25th of June start for home on S. S. King.

Very sincerely yours.

Dear Zach:—

Well, the old class of "'16" is through at last. You ask where the boys are to be. Val Brown goes on the 24th to Harvard for law. Don't forget to address him as "Esq". Ted Updike takes a position with the N. Y. N. H. & H. R. R., 892 Ladd Ave., Fall River, Mass. and Jack McQuade with the D. L. & W. at Jersey City, N. J., 400 E. 6th St. Wm. Fellows just left for a department position in Washington; his address is 735 South G St. At last accounts Dr. Max King was to go to Johns Hopkins for a Ph. D. degree. Think of that! Elliott goes to Xenia, Ohio, to be a Y. M. C. A. secretary. I stay here for the present. What do you do next? How about Idaho?

Yours truly, and Good bye.

If careful preparation is not made when a suspected writer consents to write by request, the result may be valueless. It is usually desirable to have the suspected writing written on paper like that on which the suspected writing was written, and also on smaller paper, and then finally on a larger sheet. White paper and black ink, or black pencil, are best for writings to be photographed, especially those written with a pencil. If some of the request writing is written from dictation, habits of punctuation, spelling, use of capital letters, and arrangement will be shown that may have distinct evidential value.

If the disputed writing was written with a pen, the first writing by a suspected writer should be written with a pen. After the two letters given above are first written with a pen, and the first writing is removed, the writer can then be asked to write the same matter with pencil. Then if he is led to write the matter a third time, but somewhat smaller or somewhat larger than the first pen writing, and finally with a finer or coarser pen, or more rapidly, as may seem desirable, this will furnish four specimens of the same matter. What is especially desirable is that a sufficient quantity of writing and a succession of specimens *of the same matter* be secured as a means of testing disguise. It is practically impossible exactly to duplicate from memory a series of disguises of the same extended written matter.

Finally, if a series of words, sentences, names, and paragraphs are dictated which include all the important words and letters that are in the disputed writing, the request writings thus obtained will usually be sufficient. It is not usually advisable to disclose to a suspected writer just what the disputed writing is or what it contains, although in certain cases it is desirable that the suspected writing itself be written from dictation several times following the suggestions given above. A stub pen should be used for part of the writing if the suspected writing was written with a stub pen, and if the suspected writing was written with a copying pencil it is important that both copying pencil and ordinary black lead pencil be used in writing the request writing.

Specimens of writing are often valueless as standards of comparison because of improper methods followed in obtaining them, or because they are too limited in quantity. In some cases request writings of this kind, improperly obtained, are of distinct advantage to a guilty party. It is of course improper to ask a suspected writer to copy the disputed writing directly from the original, and, as a rule, the writer should not even be shown the suspected writing. If it is not shown then it cannot later be claimed that the writer imitated the forms because he was asked to do so.

In connection with the great variety of questions that come up for judicial settlement the necessity arises for finding evidence of the most diverse character. There are scores of questions that have a direct or indirect connection with the proof of documents that may require investigation. Among these are inquiries regarding pens, pencils, ink, paper, erasers, erasing fluids, tapes, ribbons, seals, sealing-wax, paste, mucilage, glue, seal presses, carbon paper, press copies, copying presses, typewriters, typewriter ribbons, paper fasteners, eyelets, eyeletting machines, punches, envelopes, post cards, postmarks, postage stamps, cancelling machines, cover papers, legal forms and their printing dates, lithographs, printing, ruling machines, numbering machines, bookbinding, watermarks, and letter-heads. The possible bearing of any one of these various things on a document under investigation should first be determined and then the matter should be thoroughly investigated. It is often necessary to find other "standards of comparison" than handwriting. Light is sometimes thrown on a problem from a most unexpected source.

Typewritten standards of comparison are now often required in typewriting investigations, and in some cases it is desirable to secure a certain machine. In an inquiry regarding a disputed typewriting it is often incorrectly assumed that it is of first importance to secure the actual machine upon which the writing was done, no matter what the date of the writing may be. In some cases it is desirable to secure the machine, but in most cases it is much more important to obtain proved specimens written on the machine of the exact, or approximate date, of the disputed typewriting. The work of a typewriter is constantly changing as a result of use, and the dated work of a machine is therefore usually preferable to the machine itself. In case the typewritten document is of current date, or very recent, then the possession of the machine is desirable.

To many it at first appears to be a hopeless task to discover the origin of a typewritten document, but in many instances it is not so difficult as it seems. A specimen of any considerable length usually discloses the kind of machine used to write it, and often shows its model and approximate number, and with this information in hand, and the co-operation of the typewriter manufacturers, the location of the machine can often be found. As a rule typewriter manufacturers and dealers lend every aid in these important inquiries. Even in large cities the sources of important typewritten documents are often discovered when at the beginning of the investigation the task seemed utterly hopeless.

Caution suggests that in all of these quests the proper approach to those who may be able to furnish valuable assistance be carefully planned. Through misunderstanding arising from lack of forethought, or even as a result of ordinary discourtesy, a source of information may be closed and a valuable supply of material evidence may be unobtainable. If requests are made by the proper persons at the proper time, and in the proper manner, material can usually be obtained if it is in existence. Unnecessary obstacles sometimes block the course of an inquiry because of the lack of that cheap, but sometimes highly valuable, human quality called tact.

CHAPTER XXII.

PHOTOGRAPHS IN DISPUTED DOCUMENT CASES.

Photographs are almost indispensable if the facts are to be proved in a legal controversy involving the genuineness of a document. Many attorneys who have not had experience in this matter do not appreciate the evidential value of photographs. In order to make adequate preparation for trial one who is to try a case of this kind must understand in just what way they are useful. This knowledge is also desirable in order to qualify an attorney to argue in court the question as to their purpose and their value.

The great variation in the seeing ability of different individuals is a fact not fully appreciated, and even a slight enlargement of certain evidence actually makes it visible to some observers who otherwise could not see it. There are a few partially blind men on many juries, and there are others, not jurors, who must decide cases, whose vision should be intensified in every possible way. A suitable enlargement often presents a matter so conclusively to a court and jury that this evidence alone at once carries conviction and cannot be denied.

An enlargement of a disputed signature of only two diameters—twice each way—makes it four times the actual size of the original, and the physical evidence is thus made four times as distinct as in the original. No stronger argument than this ought to be necessary to show the importance of enlarged photographs in a case the proof of which must partly depend upon visible evidence. An intelligent attorney would not long hesitate to take any reasonable action that would make his general testimony four times as effective as it otherwise would be.

If a controversy is of sufficient importance to be taken into court, it is of sufficient importance to be properly prepared and it is not too much to say that an attorney who seeks to prove the facts in a disputed document case and does not secure this valuable photographic aid is either negligent or uninformed. It is far better that he overlook some few remote legal precedents in his preparation than omit this important assistance. If he knows nothing of the methods employed by competent specialists in doing this work, the careful man will at least understand the importance of securing competent assistance on the subject.

The attorney against the facts will, of course, strenuously oppose the use of photographs of any kind, and this is good evidence of their value. He will argue that they are dangerous, misleading, and useless and he will no doubt read some legal opinions on the subject, probably without giving their dates. It is true that good photographs often are dangerous to an erroneous contention. If it were within the power of some advocates they would darken the room and would not enlarge, but would reduce in size the documents in dispute. Restrictive and hampering procedure sometimes does in effect darken the room.

Correct enlarged photographs are sometimes fiercely attacked in good faith by those whose interests they imperil, for the reason that at first sight they seem to contain what is not in the original documents. Certain things that can be seen must be made of a certain size before their real significance is recognized by some observers, and enlarged photographs, on first view, sometimes seem to be inaccurate because they clearly show what in natural size was not recognized. Their purpose is to make plain this partly hidden evidence, and they do this so effectively that they are attacked as incorrect. These attacks, often sincere as well as fierce and protracted, are the most eloquent testimonials to the value of illustrations of this kind.

Photographs also make it possible to put things to be compared close together in enlarged form. The only way certain visible things can be correctly interpreted is by bringing them close together within the angle of vision. This grouping is necessary because the average eye, or brain, retains an image but a very brief period of time and cannot carry it over even a very short distance, in order to compare it with something else. Most observers cannot compare two characters on opposite sides of the same card. By dissecting the photographs and grouping the parts to be compared desirable side-by-side comparisons can be made that otherwise it is impossible to make without mutilating the original documents.

Against sympathy, prejudice, perjury, and skilful opposition, the proof of a fact in court is a much more difficult operation than the discovery of that fact, and certain instruments are as necessary to the examiner of questioned documents who is to prove a fact as other instruments are necessary to the surveyor. The photographic camera, the microscope, and suitable instruments for making accurate tests, measurements, and illustrations are the charts and compasses of the document examiner. In many cases only by their use can effective testimony be presented.

The qualified specialist may not always need these instruments or illustrations in order that he himself may discover the fact, but they are often indispensable if the inexperienced and untrained, who are called upon perhaps for the first time to decide a difficult question, are to be assisted to appreciate the significance of the evidence upon which a correct verdict must be based.

Illustrations and reasons take document testimony out of the class of mere expert opinion testimony, with its inevitable conflicts, and put it into the class of demonstrative testimony. Modern procedure in relation to proof of documents is being revolutionized by these methods which make testimony visible and understandable. The appeal in this testimony is not merely to the belief, but to the intelligence of the hearer. This enlightened practice that makes evidence appeal to the eye as well as to the ear is each year becoming more generally adopted.

This important part of the preparation of a disputed document case is often delayed until almost the last hours before the case opens, when it is too late to do the work properly. To rush into an ordinary portrait gallery the last Saturday before the trial begins to have illustrative document photographs made usually leads to unsatisfactory, if not useless, results. A few poor 5 x 7 negatives, made on the wrong kind of plates, or two or three poor, fuzzy enlargements, are sometimes made to illustrate a case involving an amount in controversy sufficient to buy out the whole photographic shop a hundred times and over! Many good portrait photographers are not equipped with the proper lenses, color filters, and other apparatus necessary to make suitable document photographs, but in nearly every city there are photographers who can do this work properly if they are given time and proper directions.

The designing of photographs suitable to illustrate the various kinds of disputed document problems necessarily requires a clear understanding of the evidence to be offered and the particular problem to be solved. Perfect document photographs tell their own story and by themselves and without testimony make a rational appeal to the observer. As a rule the ordinary photographer is not qualified to decide what photographs are desirable in a particular case and must be definitely told what is wanted. Intelligent operators, however, who possess the necessary technical skill, soon understand what is wanted and then can render valuable assistance.

In these matters the careful attorney will, of course, not attempt arbitrarily to substitute his judgment for that of an experienced specialist, but he should, in some measure, be able to understand what is desirable and, if necessary, offer some criticisms. Time is well spent carefully considering what photographs will most effectively illustrate the particular evidence to be presented. It is well to make a few extra negatives rather than fail to provide the particular one of special value and importance. It is, of course, desirable to gather all the standard writings that are to be used before photographs are made as otherwise it may be necessary to make them the second time in order to include the additional writings.

In connection with the preparation of photographic illustrations it is well to consider:

1. The number and dates of standard signatures to be photographed in connection with the disputed document, or the disputed signature.

2. The degree of greatest enlargement of the disputed document, or of the disputed signature, and of the accompanying standard writings that are to be enlarged.

3. The classification, or grouped comparisons, of words, or parts of extended writings, or portions of signature or other writing.

4. The advisability of transmitted light photograph of disputed document or disputed writing with similar photograph of a standard writing similar in kind.

5. In traced forgery cases the photographing of disputed signature with the model from which it was traced, if model is found, and the printing of photograph of forged signature and model signature on separate transparent films, or oiled paper, and also photographing these signatures under ruled squares slightly enlarged to show suspicious identity by this method as well as by the use of the transparent films or prints.

6. Possible use of stereoscopic illustrations showing retouching, overwriting, mark of nib points, line crossings, erasures, or writing over folds in paper, or any third dimension characteristic.

7. The size of photographs to be used, whether 8 x 10, 10 x 12, or 11 x 14, and also whether they are to be

arranged in loose-leaf album form or separately in portfolios.

8. The use of large bromide enlargements.

It is usually advisable to photograph both sides of the sheet upon which a disputed signature appears. If the document consists of several pages it is usually advisable to photograph them all, and also the backs of all pages if they may possibly contain anything evidential.

A disputed signature should also be photographed in natural size with all the standard signatures nearest in date arranged with it in order of dates. It is surprising how the common characteristics of a series of signatures are brought out by placing them close together in a vertical column. It is not usually necessary to enlarge all these signatures, although in some cases it is advisable to enlarge all the standard signatures. In most cases it is only necessary to enlarge a number of the standard signatures nearest in date to the disputed signature. Justified criticism will be avoided when standards for enlargement are selected with absolute fairness and when the disputed signature and the standards are enlarged on exactly the same scale.

For the effective illustration of suspicious line quality, retouching, or minute changes, and other delicate characteristics, an enlargement of the disputed signature, and a few representative genuine signatures, to a considerable degree, in some special cases as much as from five to ten diameters, may be desirable.

Enlargements are more perfect when made directly on the plate from the original documents. This can be accomplished by the use of a suitable short focus lens and a camera bellows of sufficient length. If a very long signature is to be considerably enlarged a part can be photographed on one plate and the remainder on another, or two exposures can be made on the upper and lower parts of the same plate by using a cut-out in front of the plate, and then the prints afterwards can be suitably attached.

In many cases enlargements of the disputed signature and the standards nearest in date up to only from three to five diameters is all that is necessary. Even if numerous suitable standards are available it is not usually necessary to use for photographic illustration more than twenty to fifty, except in unusual cases. In cases where only a few signatures are available it is often advisable to photograph them all in suitable enlarged form as well as in natural size.

It is important that just the right quality of negative be secured. In order to insure this it is sometimes advisable to make two or more negatives, with varying lengths of exposure, of the most important illustrations. The negative can then be used that shows most accurately and clearly the detail of the original. The general photographer is inclined to make all negatives of this kind with too much contrast and he usually must be cautioned on this point. Search should be extended until a photographer is found who has the suitable lenses and apparatus necessary to do the work well. It is necessary that prints be made with as much care as the negatives, using a paper with a degree of sensitiveness, or contrast, suited to the particular negative.

Before standard signatures are photographed it is advisable to write the date of each one, in very small pencil figures, about one-eighth of an inch below the signature. If figures are made very small and dates indicated by number of month, day, and year (3-26-'58) these marks will not deface the original documents and will identify the photograph as having been made from the particular paper so marked. In order to avoid marking the documents of the opposition, figures indicating dates can be placed on small separate slips of paper which are then photographed opposite and close to the signatures.

In order to avoid the possibility of defacement, no initials, dates, or ink, or pencil marks *of any kind whatever* should usually be put on the disputed document itself. The crude manner in which the zealous, but inexperienced investigator often covers a disputed document with pencil marks in the form of arrows, stars, underlining marks and even comments, shows his lack of understanding of the fact that the evidential value of a document may thus be weakened, if not destroyed. It sometimes may be advisable, as a defensive precaution, to put an identifying microscopic small mark, or device, of some kind, in some inconspicuous place on the standard writings of the opposition, and an accurate record should be made of all of these documents examined.

Accidental defacement, or injury, of a disputed document will be avoided if it is at once put between celluloid covers. These covers can easily be removed when photographs are made. It is especially important that a document of this kind be kept in these covers during a trial so that it will not be injured or soiled by much handling.

An unwise economy sometimes limits photographic preparation just at the point where it would become most effective, that is, the final side-by-side comparison in parallel columns of the visible evidence which in reality are the illustrated reasons for the opinion expressed. These illustrations are particularly effective in typewriting cases, or in anonymous letter cases in which it is necessary to compare the forms, sizes, and characteristics of small things that many persons do not easily perceive.

In all this preparatory work it is necessary to keep in mind the widely varying quality of human vision already referred to. Things must be made so plain that "he who runs may read". There is little danger of presenting things too clearly. Provision must be made for those who cannot see well and for others who perhaps may not much care to see. By suitable illustrations certain evidence can be forced on the attention even of unwilling observers so that it cannot easily be ignored.

In order to avoid the objection that the photograph is a mere duplicate of the original, the preliminary photographs of a continued writing, as in anonymous letter cases, which afterwards are to be cut apart and arranged for comparison, may be slightly enlarged, perhaps twenty-five per cent. When the grouped comparisons are finally arranged the prepared exhibit itself can then be enlarged two or three diameters. In typewriting cases it may be desirable to make the first enlargement two or three diameters and then enlarge the exhibit, as finally arranged, two diameters more, making the final form at least equal to a four, or six, diameter enlargement. Photographs are sometimes excluded unless they are enlarged.

The degree of enlargement desirable in order that a delicate physical fact may be properly appreciated naturally depends upon the characteristics of the thing illustrated and the seeing ability of the observer. Not only may a thing be too delicate for its real meaning to be understood, even if it is visible, as already pointed out, but it is also true that too great an enlargement may have a tendency to confuse or hide that which it is desired to illustrate. Skilled workers with the microscope are well aware of this fact and are always careful to provide the degree of enlargement most appropriate to the particular thing illustrated. One who seeks to confuse an issue may contend, or the uninformed may think, that the greater the enlargement the better in all cases, but this is not the fact. In enlargements that are too great some unessential element may obscure the vital evidence.

It is impossible to specify just what the most desirable degree of enlargement for different subjects, or different observers, should be, but where only the design of script letters is under consideration, as in the identification of handwriting in anonymous letter cases, an enlargement of two to three diameters is usually sufficient. To properly illustrate some special point, as heretofore suggested, an enlargement up to five, or even ten, diameters is sometimes necessary. Where only the forms of letters are being considered enormous enlargements are not usually desirable. Unless for special purposes like the illustrating of broken letters, slight deviations in slant, the sequence of strokes, or some relation of minute parts to each other, it is not often advisable to make enlargements of typewriting larger than about three to five diameters.

There are certain qualities of human vision utilized in the comparison of things that it is well for the attorney to keep in mind in order that his preparation and his discussion of the subject will be correct and effective. In examining enlargements of small objects, like typewritten letters or minute characteristics of writing, it is helpful to accompany the enlargements with photographs of the same objects only slightly enlarged, or of natural size. This is desirable in order that the examination of the enlargement may be made directly in connection with the examination of the same matter in natural size. If close attention is directed to a small object and then attention is immediately directed to an enlargement of the same object, the characteristics as shown by the enlargement will appear with special distinctness and the connection between the two objects will be clearly recognized. The principle is the same as that relating to certain physical exertions. For example, after handling a heavy weight a light weight can apparently be handled with greater facility and skill. In the same way the eye comes from the greater difficulty of observing the small elements to an enlargement with an intensity that makes the enlargement all the more distinct and significant. The late Dr. Gross, the eminent criminal psychologist, observed that it is comparatively easy, even for an untrained observer, to begin to see characteristics in natural size, that would otherwise be invisible to him, after these same qualities have been observed in enlarged form.

Reversed photographs, white on black, made with the photographic machine, are not desirable for illustrating a disputed document. To be made like the original they must be rephotographed, and this method, as well as the first operation, covers up some of the detail which often is the vital evidence. Photographs of this kind sometimes quite effectively hide some of the most significant evidences of forgery.

Enlarged and grouped photographs are now usually admitted and marked in evidence. If they are not admitted such exhibits, under the rules in some jurisdictions, can be offered as "illustrative charts" and used even when not admissible as separate photographs. In order that photographic comparisons of this kind may become admissible certain definite questions must be asked, to which the witness gives affirmative replies:

Q. Does this photographic chart illustrate your testimony?

Q. Will you describe just what it consists of?

Q. Did you prepare the chart?

Q. Are the photographs from which it was made accurate photographs?

Q. Is it made up entirely from exhibits in the case?

Q. Does it correctly represent these various writings in evidence?

Q. Is it necessary to a clear and complete presentation of your testimony?

If, after this definite testimony, the illustration is excluded, this exclusion in some jurisdictions is reversible error. In order, however, to constitute error it must definitely be shown that the enlargement or chart is necessary to a full and clear presentation of the evidence. If the questions are not asked properly the record may not exactly cover the point.

The new film plates now available have numerous advantages over glass plates for the making of document photographs. They are light and portable and can easily be taken into court, if this for any reason is desirable, and they also have some technical advantages. Prints for court use to be perfect require as much care as plates and if printed on glossy paper of the right degree of sensitiveness will show the utmost detail. They are more easily handled if not mounted on ordinary heavy mounts but backed with backing paper and hinged in album form. In cases of alleged forgery it is advisable to make separate prints of the various sizes of the disputed signature which can be placed in an attached pocket of the album. These detached prints make it possible to put the disputed writing next to any part of the standard writing for more effective comparison.

For convenience of the jury and the saving of time, the use of duplicate photographs and sets of photographs is usually permitted. At least ten sets of photographs are provided in important jury trials. With this number available there will be a set for each two jurymen, one set for the court, one set for the witness, and a set for each of the attorneys. In some cases a set is provided for each juryman, in which event sixteen sets are required in all. In a case without a jury four full sets of photographs are usually sufficient.

In a jury case enough prints of at least one important photographic exhibit should be made so that every juryman can hold the photograph in his own hand and look at it as much as he pleases while certain parts of the testimony are being given. This one important exhibit to be provided in every case, no matter how unimportant the case may be, should perhaps include the disputed signature and the nearest standards, suitably enlarged, and the same signatures in natural size. In an anonymous letter case, or one involving the identification of a continued writing, this one photograph should perhaps include the entire disputed document in natural size, if it is suitable and not too large, and the various characteristics from the disputed and standard writings cut out and arranged in columns for comparison and suitably enlarged.

In some trials, even where good photographs are supplied in limited numbers, the jurymen on the "back row" do not see them except by a hasty glance as they are passed from one to another. There is a distinct value in examining visible evidence by a sustained view at just the right distance from the eye until the evidence "sinks in". Many observers will hastily say they have seen a thing, when in fact they have only half seen it. The less important illustrations can be put in albums, or in a portfolio, and passed around. In important cases, however, it is highly desirable that all the photographs should be put into the hands of every juryman. Unwise economy in this phase of the case may be a serious error.

Large bromide prints made from small negatives often show no detail accurately and every part of the image exhibits ill-defined, fuzzy margins which tend to conceal the physical facts contained in the original writing. If a print from an ordinary photographic negative is made by projection, and enlarged beyond a few diameters, the result usually shows an image which, in photographic language, is not "sharp". As the enlargement is increased the contrasts and gradations of the original are diminished until finally all parts appear ill-defined and of about the same depth and quality. If, however, the original negative is made with a suitable lens and an enlargement from it, of not more than two or three diameters, is made on glossy paper, a good print can be made. There are conditions under which these large bromide prints are desirable for use in court.

In cases where a disputed signature shows unnatural tremor with a hesitating, uneven line and with varying pen pressure, and especially if fraudulently retouched or overwritten, it is sometimes important to show these qualities in a large bromide print so that court and jury can all see the illustration at the same time. In order to make perfect large prints of this kind the original signature should first be enlarged from two to five diameters directly on the plate, and then from this negative the enlarged bromide print can be made. Not many photographers have equipment for making enlargements from negatives larger than 8x10 inches, but at commercial centres enlargements can be obtained from large negatives. If a signature two inches long is enlarged four diameters, or to eight inches, and then from this negative a bromide enlargement is made thirty-two inches in length, or four diameters, a good clear print can be obtained if proper lenses are used for both operations.

In order to show the utmost detail the enlarged print should be made on glossy bromide paper. When put on an easel a print of this size is visible to all the members of the jury at once and in some cases is very useful in proving the facts as there is a cumulative effect resulting from a continuous view that has much force.

Many presumptuous fraudulent documents are brought forward with the confident expectation that the claim will be settled out of court. There is nothing that so frightens a fraudulent claimant, who is attempting to loot an estate, or perpetrate some other kind of a fraud by means of a fraudulent document, as the insistent demand, to the proper court if necessary, that opportunity at once be given to photograph the document and "make such enlargements as may be necessary". Fraud is usually if not always cowardly, and prompt and vigorous steps looking toward the discovery of the facts about a fraudulent document will often lead to a withdrawal of the claim. As has been explained, photographs are often a most effective means of showing fraud, but those who are presenting a fraudulent claim often imagine that they will show more than they really do, for "The thief doth fear each bush an officer". Prompt, vigorous procedure often puts a quietus on a fraudulent claim that, if taken up in a mild and apologetic way, may end in a dishonorable compromise.

CHAPTER XXIII.

CROSS-EXAMINATION FROM THE STANDPOINT OF THE WITNESS.

Whatever its theoretical purpose may be, even brief experience in a court room shows that the too frequent, if not usual aim of cross-examination is to destroy adverse testimony. The witness faces the cross-examiner, not with the thought of being tested, but of being attacked, and naturally assumes that the performance about to begin is designed to break the force of his testimony. This attempt is made in a great variety of ways, but the effort is usually made to make it appear that the matter of the evidence is unimportant, erroneous, unwarranted, or exaggerated, or that the witness is not worthy of belief.

The witness who becomes impatient with searching but fair cross-examination should, however, always remember that there are witnesses who testify who are honestly mistaken, others who consciously or unconsciously exaggerate, and still others who for friendship, for spite, or for pay, commit deliberate perjury. The interests of justice require that ignorance and corruption should be exposed, and for this purpose, it should be clearly understood, cross-examination is a necessary and important phase of law practice. Under its privileges the testimony of the honest and competent witness is often unfairly assailed, but this action is an unwarranted abuse of the right to cross-examine.

The abuses of cross-examination are well known and their correction is one of the necessary but difficult reforms of law practice. When the whole bench and bar are more earnestly devoted to the cause of promoting justice the only purpose of cross-examination will be to test the truth and accuracy of testimony. It requires no argument to show that the too common practice which aims to destroy all opposing testimony, irrespective of its quality, is a serious menace to the interests of justice. There is an indifference to certain of these well-known abuses on the part of numerous members of the legal profession that cannot be understood by honorable men in other professions. The plain fact is that many attorneys never think of cross-examination excepting as a means of destroying opposing testimony. This is the view of the subject as understood and practiced not only by many lawyers, but tolerated, if not actually praised, in too many legal discussions. Naturally this effort to destroy testimony becomes especially strenuous and bitter if an adverse witness has given important and convincing evidence. The time will surely come when public, as well as professional, opinion reacting upon court procedure, will not permit the honest witness to be unfairly and often shamefully attacked whenever it becomes his duty to give testimony in a court of law.

The first and most important part of the preparation of the witness for cross-examination goes back to that fortunate time when he learned to tell the truth. The other and later phases of the preparation came when he gained accurate knowledge of the particular matter that he tells about in his evidence. These are the two essential requirements of a good witness, that he be truthful and that he be accurate. With these qualifications he is prepared to face any cross-examiner, not always without dread but without fear of being successfully attacked. The witness who says only what he knows and knows what he has said can say it in as many ways and as many times as is required. He may be unfairly assailed, but his testimony itself will not often be weakened if he speaks the truth and knows what he pretends to know.

The inexperienced witness, uninformed regarding the rules of evidence and a stranger in the court room, naturally is at great disadvantage when opposed by the experienced, astute cross-examiner, familiar with all the tricks and methods by which the force of correct evidence is weakened if not destroyed. There are many reputable, self-respecting persons who all their lives remember with hot indignation their one experience on the witness stand, and many deserving cases are defeated because of the absence of important witnesses who under no conditions can be induced to testify because of their terror of cross-examination. By almost any means they will avoid being called as witnesses. The far-reaching general effect of this grave abuse in the administration of justice is not fully appreciated. It is difficult to devise an effective remedy, but it is through the judge and an extension of his powers that this abuse can perhaps most effectively be corrected. An impartial judge in every court should have the power to prevent the interests of justice from being sacrificed through the deliberate destruction of correct testimony of honest witnesses.

The witness need not always meekly submit to unwarranted attack and undeserved abuse, although under some circumstances his testimony is enforced if he allows himself to be unfairly treated without attempting to retaliate in any way. The honest witness will naturally resent insulting insinuations, and if the nature of the attack upon him is openly unfair a fitting rejoinder will receive immediate sympathetic approval. The deliberate purpose of unfair cross-examination in many instances is to lead a witness, under the bitter sting of attack, to attempt to retaliate in some way and thus perhaps be led into indiscretion or error that will weaken or nullify his testimony.

On account of his duty to the court, for his own protection, and as a means of making his testimony more effective, the most important advice that can be given to a witness about to be cross-examined is that he maintain an attitude of fairness and frankness toward the cross-examiner exactly the same as his attitude toward the lawyer for whom he has just testified. When the lawyer, through excess of zeal for his client's interest, or now and then perhaps in his own interest, forgets that the purpose of testimony is to elicit the truth, the witness should not also forget this fact. By his abuse of the right to cross-examine, an attorney often seems to gain a temporary advantage, but is in fact sometimes thus defeating his own effort by losing the confidence of court and jury. Testimony is often made more damaging when the witness who has given it is unfairly assailed.

The conduct of a good witness at all times is that of one who is seeking to assist in proving the facts. If this attitude is in distinct contrast with the acts of an unfair opposing advocate, the testimony of the witness is thereby further strengthened. If the examiner makes a slight or serious technical error in a question, as is almost inevitable, or does not say just what he intended to say, the witness should not try to take advantage of his opponent, but should respond exactly as if the attorney was favorable to him instead of against him. In a respectful and unobtrusive way he should either answer the question as it is apparent the lawyer intended to ask it, or ask to have the question reframed. This act on the part of the witness is that of the fair and honest man, and especially after repetition, the attorney himself, unless he is much hardened, cannot but be somewhat disarmed by this unexpected conduct. The judge and the jury will certainly approve this proper attitude of the witness, which is maintained, not for any advantage that will arise from it, but because it is the attitude that befits an honest man.

As the bringing about of belief is the purpose of testimony—some advocates hardly seem to understand this—naturally anything that affects this result is a matter of interest to attorney and to witness. Belief is undoubtedly strongly swayed by our estimate of the frankness and fairness of one who seeks to convince us. A full appreciation of this important truth will influence the conduct of both attorney and of witness on direct as well as on cross-examination. Neither witness nor lawyer should, however, be led to think that credit will be secured by the self-serving declaration of an intention to be fair and frank. Good intentions in any field have little value until translated into acts. Hypocrisy and deceit are always asserting their fairness and candor, but credit for fair dealing only arises from conduct. One instinctively suspects the shopkeeper, who in his window advertises, "Only honest goods sold here", and is inclined to think that he will cheat in the quantity or the price, if not in the goods. The solemn claim of unassailable virtue is to be expected from the sharp practitioner, and the lying witness is also inclined to assure his hearers of his undying devotion to truth. It is clear that insincere attempts to enlist fairness and truth in behalf of a contention are the strongest evidence of their force as a means of winning favor.

The capable witness who has testified correctly and truthfully will of course defend his testimony. There is now and then a flabby-minded witness who, in an eager desire to be thought fair, and in order not to give offense, is not honest with himself. Witnesses of this class are the despair of the trial attorney. They will not say on the witness stand what they said in the office, and under hard pressing on cross-examination will modify and weaken anything they have said. Witnesses who are not sure of anything should not be allowed to testify. This attitude of surrender is, however, not the usual effect of cross-examination. Unfortunately many witnesses under the ordeal at once assume an unwise attitude of antagonism and resentment that often exposes them to attack and throws a shadow over their whole testimony.

The qualified technical witness must be prepared for unfair, as well as fair, cross-examination. He must consider all the various kinds of attacks that may be made upon his testimony. He especially keeps in mind that he may be asked on the witness stand about anything that occurs in connection with the presentation of the case, the investigation of the problem, or any reports thereon. In view of these contingencies the technical witness has a right to insist, and should insist, that if a matter is to be presented to him that it be presented properly and as he desires. Preparation for cross-examination by the prudent technical witness begins from this first moment that a matter is brought to him for examination and is then continued up to the time he goes on the witness stand and all the time he testifies. The prepared witness must consider step by step in his preparation all of the various possible vulnerable points in testimony and prepare himself accordingly.

One point of attack that can sometimes be avoided, as suggested above, is that regarding the manner in which a case is presented at the first interview. If a disputed document problem can be presented without disclosing the contention of the party presenting it, it should be thus presented. It is sometimes impossible to submit such a problem without some natural inference being drawn from the documents themselves, but an effort should always be made to secure a nonpartisan presentation, if this is possible under the circumstances. The witness can usually at least prevent the relating of other evidence, outside of the technical question to be asked, that might influence an opinion. It is often difficult to induce the attorney trained in advocacy to restrain himself on this point, but the attempt should be made.

As in any investigation, it is proper in a disputed

writing case for the examiner to know the alleged circumstances surrounding the act including anything about the preparation of the document that, if true, might have affected it in any way. It is also usually desirable in investigating a disputed writing to know the approximate age and general physical and mental condition of the alleged writer. It is also entirely proper to receive information regarding the care or custody of any document under investigation, handwritten or typewritten, that in any way may have affected its appearance or condition. There are, of course, many disputed document problems in which, in presenting a case, it is necessary to relate the details of the problem.

A witness should not examine any papers in a case which cannot be put in evidence, that may have a bearing upon an opinion he may be called upon to give. As already suggested, the experienced witness knows that he may be asked about anything that he has seen or examined, or anything that occurs. A lawyer is sometimes inclined to forget this requirement that can be made of a witness that cannot be made of him. If from the beginning the witness keeps in mind the three possible general sources of error, with their various subdivisions, as classified in detail in the later chapter on errors in the identification of handwriting, this precaution may relieve him from much embarrassment on cross-examination.

An attack upon technical testimony often begins with a question regarding some trivial error in the testimony, or a possible slight error in the use of a word. The indiscreet, or the belligerent, witness, or the one who is not quite candid, may be led to deny that he has made an unimportant wrong statement, or he may unwisely defend a slight inaccuracy that cannot successfully be defended. A heated controversy then sometimes arises over a trivial point and the effect of the whole testimony is perhaps somewhat weakened. The competent witness will of course endeavor to be accurate and will endeavor to use words correctly, but if he has made an error, small or great, he will instantly and cheerfully admit it.

In case of actual error the frank witness says at once, "If I said that then I did not say what I intended to say", or "I should have said habitually instead of infallibly", or "Possibly I may have over-emphasized my statement", or "You may be right but it does not seem so to me", or "I will try to answer the question again if you will state it just as you wish to put it". It is highly important that the witness be fair, candid, and prompt in admitting any actual error, and not lose his temper, or become impatient and petulant under the sting of the sharp, and perhaps slightly unfair, questions of an experienced advocate. If the witness becomes irritated, tense, and resentful, he is in danger of getting himself into a vulnerable state of mind that may lead to disaster.

It is always very bad policy, as well as highly improper, for the witness to attempt to punish the cross-examiner by injecting into the record any answers not fully justified by the questions. Punishment can sometimes be inflicted, but it should always be fair. Certain questions cannot properly be answered without an explanation because of the danger of conveying a wrong impression, but it is best that the explanations follow the answer. It is the deliberate, and often unfair, effort of some cross-examiners to get erroneous impressions of this kind before a jury. The well-known question, "Have you discontinued beating your wife?" is an example of a question that cannot satisfactorily be answered by yes or no. The careful witness is at all times on his guard against these double meaning questions, or those that cannot adequately be answered without an explanation, but also carefully avoids giving the impression that he is in constant fear of being trapped because he has made an error. It is entirely proper for the witness to say calmly, "I cannot properly answer the question by yes or no".

The competent and alert witness can do something to control an examination by the character of the answers given to certain questions which do not admit of a simple yes or no answer. If the question is asked, "Is it not true that, etc., etc.," and the unqualified answer, "Yes", leading up to another question, is hoped for by the examiner, the answer, "Under certain conditions", will usually bring as the next question, "What conditions?", whereupon the witness can make the desired explanation. Questions of this kind can also be answered by "That may be true", or "Sometimes", or any reply that will lead the examiner to say, "Under what conditions?" The witness then is allowed to explain the answer. The skilful technical witness carefully studies this phase of cross-examination and also becomes sufficiently familiar with the rules of evidence to know, at least in a general way, what his rights are.

One frequent line of examination is that which attempts to show that testimony regarding the authenticity of documents is usually in conflict with opposing testimony on the same subject. As a matter of fact, such testimony is not as often in conflict as so-called fact testimony, or testimony based on observation of an alleged occurrence. There is, as a rule, no conflict except in sensational cases. In one instance an actual count of ordinary litigated cases in which technical testimony of this character was given, showed fourteen cases in succession without conflict. The opportunity to state this important fact can be secured by answers something like the following:

Q. Handwriting experts often disagree, do they not?

A. Occasionally, but not often.

Q. Would you not say more frequently than occasionally?

A. Such testimony as a rule is not in conflict as often as so-called fact or observation testimony.

This positive statement will usually bring out the inquiry, "What basis have you for such a statement?", and then the statement can be made that in many consecutive cases there was no conflict of testimony on the subject. This brings out facts just the opposite of those the attorney was seeking to bring before the jury.

The attempt is sometimes made, in an improper way, to discredit the technical witness because he receives pay for his services. This line of questioning may be something like the following: "Are you paid to testify?" It is obvious that the purpose of this question is to create the impression that the compensation is a sort of bribe which has improperly bought the testimony. In order to counteract this effect the fact can be brought before the jury that the honest witness does not always agree with those who seek to obtain his services and, of course, in such cases he will not be paid as a witness, but simply as a specialist who gives an adverse decision.

A good answer to the above question is, "I am paid for my services, but not always as a witness, as I am not called to testify when I decide against the lawyer who brings a case to me for investigation". A prompt answer of this kind properly brings a relevant fact before the court and jury bearing upon the honesty of the witness. In response to further questioning on the point the answer can be given that the witness is paid to discover and to prove a fact, which is another idea that the opposing counsel does not desire to have brought before the court.

By forethought, alertness, and a sufficiently thorough knowledge of the subject, the witness can, as suggested, in some small degree, guide an examination by his answers so that he will be asked certain questions, the answers to which will give to the proceeding a tone that the witness desires to give to it. There are a few courts strongly inclined to favor the advocate rather than the witness in contests of this kind, but, as a rule, the fair witness is treated fairly.

The competent witness acquires the habit of answering all questions as promptly as possible so that court and jury will wait for the examiner rather than for him. One of the common indications of lack of frankness in any witness under cross-examination is undue hesitation, and the competent technical witness acquires just the opposite habit and answers instantly every question that can thus be answered. The most convincing testimony by a specialist, on either direct or on cross-examination, is that which is given in a clear, prompt, decided, straightforward, unimpassioned manner. Such a witness makes his testimony definite and positive, but without excessive emphasis, and without giving the impression that he is an unfair partisan. Testimony should not be hesitating and weak, but technical testimony is not so apt to be weak as to be dogmatic and overemphasized.

The tone or general effect of testimony is in some degree the result of many of these little things which in combination become important. The use of one unfortunate word will change the whole tone of testimony. In attacking a document it is usually advisable deliberately to avoid the use of the word "forgery" or any expression which charges crime. The most convincing evidence is that directed to the impersonal facts before the court and jury. The witness can say that he has compared a signature with the standard writings and has reached the conclusion that the signature was not written by the writer of the standards, instead of saying that he has reached the conclusion that the disputed signature is a forgery, or still worse, "a rank forgery". The first statement is that of the scientist; the second, or the third, that of the zealous advocate.

In reports and in testimony it is usually advisable not to use names, but to describe the writer as "the writer of the standard letters", or "the writer of the disputed document". One improper answer like, "The anonymous letter was written by Mr. Brown, the defendant'', will at once put the witness in the undesirable and unnecessary position of a direct accuser. The correct method of description does not weaken emphasis, but enforces it by giving a fair and proper scientific tone to the testimony. The matter under discussion should always be considered as a scientific problem which is being illustrated, explained, and solved without any regard to the effect that the outcome may have upon any particular person.

In giving assent one word, yes, is sufficient and usually it is better if spoken with a falling inflection. For a negative, nothing is better than the simple word no, also spoken with a falling inflection. The answers often heard, ''Yes, I am'', and ''Yes, it is'', are not so good answers as the one word. The witness who apparently is eager and aggressive and indulges in personalities, overemphasis, and accusations, thus weakens his testimony instead of enforcing it.

CHAPTER XXIV.

CROSS-EXAMINATION FROM THE STANDPOINT OF THE LAWYER.

The cross-examination contest between the examiner and witness has a moral as well as an intellectual phase. The court and jury sit one side and observe the contest and draw conclusions therefrom. The cross-examiner often seems to be wholly unaware of the fact that on the moral side he, as well as the witness, is being tested. Is he fair and honest and sincere, or, when the performance is finished, has it been to the jury a spectacle in which a wily, experienced advocate has taken advantage of one who cannot defend himself?

The success of cross-examination is measured by its final effect on the problem of proof. When it is finished the members of a jury have many times partly forgotten the intellectual pitfalls that the witness may have fallen into, but clearly remember that the contest was not a fair one between equals. Their unconscious sympathy often leads them to give an importance to the assailed testimony that it does not deserve. The advocate is sometimes inclined to take pride in an apparent success when, if he could read the minds of the jury, he would learn he had failed.

The shrewd attorney never forgets that he too is on trial. By every proper means he endeavors to reverse the unfortunate effect of cross-examination in which the examiner appears as an unfair aggressor and tries to show that he, who is seeking to prove the facts, finds it difficult to do so against a "smart" witness who will not answer questions and who, by his mental agility and lack of fairness, puts himself under suspicion.

Notwithstanding the opportunities for practice and observation, cross-examination is that part of law practice which is most unskilful and ineffective. In too many instances the attempt is made to make up for lack of ability by violating common courtesy and by an unnatural emphasis which in effect is little more than an increase in noise. Many competent observers say that the usual cross-examination enforces the evidence already given. It is certainly true that in many instances the real significance of testimony is not understood until it is repeated and emphasized on cross-examination. A combination of ignorance of human nature and ignorance of the technical questions involved often insures the failure of the cross-examiner.

Cross-examination is one of the most important phases of the administration of the law. Under no conditions should it be dispensed with and, when proper, it should not be restricted. Much of that which passes as cross-examination, however, can only be accurately described as an inane, futile, waste of words. In an expensive public trial, held perhaps in a marble court room, it is a distressing spectacle to see precious hours of life wasted with the kind of cheap performances that are called cross-examinations. For an unprepared man to accomplish nothing, and waste the time of perhaps a hundred people, as is often done, is but little short of an outrage. In no other phase of law practice are the deplorable conditions resulting from ignorance, pretension, discourtesy, unpreparedness, and a low moral tone, so clearly shown as in cross-examinations.

The necessity for cross-examination arises, as is well understood, because testimony may be untrue, or exaggerated, or presented in a way that produces an erroneous impression.

A few of the common ways in which testimony varies, as presented by different witnesses, are as follows:

(a) A witness tells the exact truth and only the truth, (b) A witness testifies honestly, but is mistaken, (c) A witness testifies correctly as to the essential facts, but exaggerates either consciously or unconsciously, (d) A witness confuses two events or two circumstances so that an erroneous conclusion is reached, (e) A witness observes incorrectly, (f) An expert witness draws wrong conclusions from observed facts or draws positive conclusions from inadequate data, (g) A witness has an unreliable memory or confuses memory with inference, (h) Through bias or friendship a witness exaggerates, or feels justified in testifying to a partial untruth, (i) A witness commits outright and deliberate perjury.

Ordinary intelligence suggests that it would be unwise to cross-examine all of these witnesses in just the same manner, but many cross-examiners do this unwise thing. When properly interrogated an honest witness who is mistaken will often admit the reasonable possibility of error, and under skilful questioning a witness who has perhaps unconsciously exaggerated will make this same admission. The witness who has testified through friendship will sometimes, when properly led, freely admit his earnest desire to assist a friend by giving favorable testimony. When a witness has actually committed outright perjury, a direct, emphatic, intelligent series of questions will sometimes uncover it, but certainly it is bad policy, as well as bad ethics, to cross-examine every witness as if he had deliberately committed perjury. Many lawyers fail to understand how completely they lose the sympathy of court, jury, and spectators by these unwarranted attacks upon honest witnesses who have given the impression to everyone except to the lawyer that they have told the truth.

To determine how much to cross-examine, and what attitude to assume towards each adverse witness, are the important questions to be answered by the trial attorney. The atmosphere of a trial is greatly affected by the attitude of an attorney toward opposing witnesses and especially toward an opposing party if such party testifies as a witness. The lazy, usually ineffective, and sometimes brutal attitude toward opposing witnesses is to act on the assumption, as suggested above, that they have all lied and then treat them accordingly. This method is sometimes deliberately followed when client and advocate apparently act on the idea that a law suit is brought, not principally to get a verdict, but for the low purpose of taking advantage of the opportunity thus offered to abuse and humiliate the opposing party and his witnesses. Courts are sometimes used for this contemptible purpose and there are here and there men, a disgrace to their profession, whose services are available for work of this kind. They should be disbarred.

The conscientious attorney who is trying a suit to

secure a verdict often eagerly wishes he had command of some power that would infallibly detect perjury. His task as a cross-examiner would thereby be greatly simplified. He could then avoid this often unwarranted assumption that perjury has been committed, or, on the other hand, could avoid letting the perjurer go scot-free who, if he escapes uninjured, may have done irreparable damage to a case. It is only by experience, coupled with intensive study and accurate knowledge, aided also by a sort of cultivated intuition, that the attorney becomes qualified to recognize certain indications of perjury, as well as certain quite well-marked evidences of truth.

The mere appearance of certain witnesses, with their furtive, hang-dog, unnatural manner, sometimes quite clearly indicates the intention of being untruthful, although this unattractive attitude must be carefully distinguished from ignorance and possible embarrassment resulting from unusual surroundings. It is dangerous to assume that there are any infallible indications of perjury, but there are certain of these tell-tale symptoms that have some value in weighing the testimony of one who has sworn to tell the truth and only the truth.

Perhaps the most frequent indication of a tendency towards untruthfulness is the repeating by the witness of perfectly audible and plain questions. This is an unconscious act growing out of the desire to gain time to remember just what the testimony was and to consider what the hidden purpose of the question is, and also to think out an unassailable answer. Repeated and obvious indications of a lack of frankness of this kind are usually a proper basis for assuming that a witness is not wholly truthful.

Those who are experienced and observing also say that the perjurer, as a rule, is inclined to avoid looking at the questioner except by an occasional quick glance, but often keeps the eyes fixed in an unnatural manner on some distant part of the ceiling, or some remote point in the room. These acts, however, must all be considered as possible indications of embarrassment or, in some instances, simply as exhibitions of bad manners.

One who is testifying untruthfully who is not a hardened and experienced liar, and who may be committing perjury only as a reluctant act of friendship, sometimes persists in talking in an almost inaudible voice and often shows in a number of ways a desire to be somewhere else and to be through with the disagreeable experience. These witnesses also sometimes seek in a sort of protective way to shield the face with the hands or even to cover the mouth while speaking. A witness of this kind often can be effectively cross-examined. The unwilling witness, who has been teased to testify, will, under skilful handling, sometimes expose a whole conspiracy. If intently observed a proper opening can usually be discovered and it is highly important that the proper approach be developed and the proper tone maintained. A witness of this kind will often admit in response to kindly but searching questions that he did not want to testify, that he was urged to do so, and that he may be mistaken.

One of the most infallible evidences of perjury, when it can be detected, is unnatural emphasis. This emphasis is not only improperly placed, but unskilfully graded, and also often takes the form of double positives and double negatives. The answer, "No, I did not", is not usually as convincing an answer as no, and may indicate perjury, but this, of course, may sometimes be a mere mannerism, or a particular question may warrant this emphasis. The repeated effort, however, to emphasize some alleged fact in the case that has much evidential value is sometimes alone adequate basis for suspicion that the witness is not truthful.

In addition to listening to testimony for possible discrepancies with known facts and also for inherent improbabilities in the story itself, the alert attorney observes the eye, the face, the actions, and the posture of the witness and gives the closest attention to his emphasis, his inflections, his gestures, and the quality of his voice. Excepting with hardened and experienced sinners this task of lying on the witness stand is a difficult and unfamiliar piece of acting, and there are not many who can do it perfectly. Close scrutiny often detects a lack of frankness that, when skilfully probed, exposes exaggeration if not wilful perjury. This intent observation should not be interfered with by the unwise attempt to take voluminous notes.

There are some perjurers who carry what may be described as the defensive smile, and who indulge in the nervous laugh, not in any way warranted by the circumstances, but apparently employed unconsciously with the desire to cover deceit. This is the same kind of irritating smile that is put on by certain unskilful salesmen and solicitors, who are endeavoring to persuade, as well as by some unctious advocates who are attempting to deceive.

Another indication of perjury that sometimes appears is an unnecessary, affected, minute accuracy which by its insincere quality shows that the witness suspects himself and is trying hard to demonstrate to all hearers that he is telling the exact truth. When asked if the incident occurred at about 3:30, he will say, "I think possibly a little later, perhaps from 3:30 to 3:35 P. M." The honest man says, "Yes, about that time". When asked his opinion as to whether or not an ink written signature is just twenty years old (a question that no one can answer) he says, "In my opinion it is from eighteen to twenty-two years old", and adds, with a self-righteous yawn, "That is as close an approximation as I can make".

Another occasional indication of perjury in the more or less hardened liar, as with a certain type of advocate who has a difficult task to perform, is the volunteered and repeated statement of a burning desire to be especially accurate and truthful. This statement, sometimes accompanied by appeals to the Deity, is also a self-defense statement by one who thus unconsciously confesses that his evidence needs the strongest kind of enforcement. All these attempted enforcements are inconsistent with a plain, sincere statement by a truthful person. The witness who says, "I want to tell only the truth", or "I want to be perfectly frank", or "So help me God, that is true", by these very statements often shows that to speak the exact truth is not in every instance his, or her, principal desire or intention. There are, of course, skilful liars who appear to be frank and honest and who thus deceive, but to act a part successfully is usually beyond the ability of one who undertakes it before keen and experienced observers.

In order to avoid error it is, of course, just as important to be able to recognize credible evidence of truth as of untruth and not be deceived on either phase of the problem. There are certain qualities of frankness and sincerity, often observed in the testimony of the young and the inexperienced, that are at once interpreted as indications of truth. The skilful cross-examination is guided by these various qualities that suggest the proper direction and tone of the examination.

There are certain common weaknesses of cross-examination that the thoughtful attorney endeavors to avoid. He does not ask every witness to repeat the testimony already given. About the poorest cross-examination is that which asks the witness to repeat in detail all the damaging testimony that has just been heard. If a story is inherently improbable it sometimes can effectively be attacked by this method, but not otherwise. The damaging effect of repetition is also heightened if, as is too often the case, the examiner sarcastically, or unconsciously, repeats each answer of the witness while he is thinking out the next unimportant question. If some cross-examiners could hear themselves, they would either change their methods or never cross-examine again. They should be punished by the official stenographer by being reported verbatim.

The most serious, as well as the most frequent, error

by the cross-examiner, however, is that referred to above, in which the attempt is made to render valueless the evidence of all opposing witnesses, irrespective of its character. To exhibit this phase of law practice to a jury of fair-minded men is often fatal to an attorney's contention. In the first place they see in it a standard of ethics in violent contrast with that of any other profession. The indiscreet and unwise attorney, sometimes led on by the spirit of advocacy, thus not only loses the confidence of a jury, but, because of his venom and his brutality, is looked upon with actual scorn by those unfamiliar with court practices. This conduct of course deserves condemnation simply from an ethical standpoint, but it is also usually unwise from the standpoint of efficiency. Some cheap applause may be won by these methods, but at much too high a price. This conduct is recognized as that of the partisan who takes every possible advantage and gives the impression that he is trying hard to prevent the truth from becoming known.

This cross-examiner, who brings discredit upon the profession, indulges in certain stock phrases that he shouts at the witness. He comes close to the victim and reiterates, in an accusing and intimidating tone, "Will you *swear* it was after three o'clock?" If permitted to do so, he lectures the witness and, often without reproof, admonishes him in advance to pay attention and tell the truth and fiercely asks, "Do you want this jury to understand, etc., etc.," with the intimation that not he but the witness from the beginning has had a set purpose to deceive the jury. These disgraceful methods perhaps recommend the advocate to guilty criminals and to those who desire to conceal the facts and defeat justice, but to no one else. The efficient cross-examiner is insistent, and, when necessary, severe, but many times produces his results in the record and before the jury so skilfully that it is not always at once seen that he has greatly discounted, if not destroyed, the unreliable evidence of an opposing witness. He always aims at something and all witnesses are not treated in the same manner.

Naturally with its usual weaknesses, cross-examination often becomes still more ineffective when it relates to a technical subject which the witness understands and the examiner does not. The intelligent attorney either qualifies himself or declines to cross-examine a qualified technical witness on his own specialty. An examiner sometimes eagerly and foolishly leaps into such an examination because his ignorance has led him to the unwarranted conclusion that the witness has made a mistake when, in fact, the examiner has not understood the testimony.

It is, of course, not possible for the lawyer to make himself an expert on every subject upon which he cross-examines, but he will make some preparation before attempting to cross-examine a technical witness. If wise he will not hope to be able to absorb the knowledge of a technical matter through the pores of his skin without effort and without assistance. The better qualified the attorney is the more eager he will be to secure assistance from any source, but the bunglers do not know that they need assistance. The specialist who has heard hundreds of witnesses cross-examined in his own field, and who has himself been cross-examined many times, ought to be able to make some helpful cross-examination suggestions in a particular case.

It is of course desirable that, as far as possible, all suggestions be made in advance and that courses of procedure be outlined out of court. To directly suggest question after question as they are asked is less effective and naturally somewhat embarrassing to the attorney who is thus made the mouthpiece of another who is furnishing the ideas. It is generally understood, however, by experienced attorneys and judges that trial counsel will consult technical specialists and secure assistance in a trial involving a technical subject.

It is quite possible that some of the suggestions here offered may be distorted and improperly used in the effort to weaken or destroy the correct and honest testimony of reliable witnesses. It would be difficult to furnish any definite suggestions of any kind that could not, by the unscrupulous advocate, be twisted and diverted to his own improper use.

Those who are arrayed against the facts often, if not usually, present some fantastic theory in the form of testimony, or make some improbable claims, that can be shown to be untrue or ridiculous by a carefully prepared line of questions based on a clear knowledge of the subject under consideration.

Some of the attacks made upon expert testimony regarding the genuineness of documents are:

1. That the technical preparation and experience of the witness do not properly qualify him to testify on the subject.

2. That the witness has not given sufficient study to the particular problem presented.

3. That the case was improperly presented to the witness.

4. That the personal record or character of the witness casts suspicion upon his testimony.

5. That in the presentation of his testimony the witness has been unfair, (a) by using misleading illustrations, (b) by unfair selection of examples, (c) by improper emphasis or exaggeration, (d) by drawing inferences not justified by the facts.

6. That the particular subject itself is not one permitting a really scientific inquiry that leads to a conclusion deserving serious consideration.

7. That the opinion expressed is not justified by the alleged reasons given.

8. That the vague and trivial facts upon which the opinion is based do not afford a sufficient basis for any opinion whatever, and that the conclusion arrived at is a mere guess.

9. That the witness has been unfair and biased in his attitude and treatment of the whole question and has tried to make the most of a doubtful case.

10. That the problem is a difficult and unusual one regarding which even a conscientious and competent witness may be mistaken.

11. That the witness has been influenced by other things than the technical evidence on which he purports to base his opinion, and consciously or unconsciously has reached a conclusion for other reasons than those which he gives.

12. That the witness has made technical errors in his testimony.

13. That the witness has made serious errors in other cases.

14. That the witness is corrupt, is committing perjury, and has been employed to do so.

If the alert and technically prepared attorney listens to erroneous, or corrupt, evidence with these various points of attack in mind, he will be likely to find an opening which he can follow up to advantage.

Most writers on the subject wisely advise the lawyer not to attempt to cross-examine the technical specialist in his own field. Generally speaking, this advice is good, but the advisability of cross-examination always depends upon the quality of the testimony given, the competency of the witness, and the preparation and experience of the examiner.

If the effect of corrupt, or erroneous, adverse testimony can be destroyed by opposing testimony which is to be presented later, then any extended cross-examination may be unnecessary. If convincing opposing testimony has already been given and the court, or the jury, are already in some measure instructed on the subject, a cross-examination is perhaps unnecessary except to bring out clearly the conflict. If the opposing evidence is strikingly in contrast with testimony already given that has favorably impressed court and jury, it is sometimes a good plan on cross-examination to lead a witness to repeat his testimony in a way that will still further bring out and emphasize the contrast.

When examining counsel is technically qualified and has had competent assistance it is, as a rule, advisable to make a vigorous direct attack upon mistaken or corrupt technical testimony. As a rule it is unwise to attempt to make a witness directly admit that his conclusion is wrong, but that the physical facts, or the reasoning upon which his opinion is based, might warrant a different conclusion. A witness, under skilful leading, will often decidedly modify and weaken the basis for a conclusion when he will not change the conclusion.

The unqualified witness and also the corrupt witness are usually called in the attempt to show that a forged writing, showing many fundamental significant defects as writing, is genuine. Occasionally, but not often, witnesses of these classes testify that genuine writing is forged. An unqualified witness may testify that a disputed writing and a standard writing were written by the same writer when they simply contain certain general features, or characteristics of the system of writing learned, which are found in many handwritings. Cross-examinations which clearly develop the obvious sources of the error in these various cases can often be made very effective.

If correct testimony has not yet been given, it is not usually a good plan to cross-examine in a way that will anticipate the points to be made and thus weaken the effect of positive testimony to be given. Generally speaking, it is not wise to try to prove any case by adverse witnesses. If, however, mistaken or corrupt testimony is first given in the trial it is advisable to lay the foundation on cross-examination for subsequent testimony by securing certain important admissions from the witness. In order to do this effectively the cross-examiner must, of course, understand the facts of the case and the exact significance of the testimony that he is to offer on the point.

The skilful cross-examiner keeps an examination confined to a definite line of inquiry and conducts it in a snappy, vigorous manner during which any considerable delay in the proceedings is caused by the witness who takes time to frame his answers. If the conditions are reversed and the witness answers quickly and clearly in response to bungling questions, the effect produced is just the opposite of that desired by the examiner. The skilful cross-examiner persists in developing the exact "point" he has in mind and does not allow the subject to be sidetracked. His tone and manner are also adapted to the particular witness under examination.

By following the Socratic method, cross-examinations can be conducted so that nearly every question must be answered by yes or no. An examination of this kind is in effect an argument by admissions in which an adversary assents to every succeeding reason for a final embarrassing conclusion. If a lawyer has never read the Dialogues of Plato he will do well to discontinue reading law reports and everything else until he has read some of them. A thorough study of these immortal dialogues will help a trial attorney in every case he tries.

If a witness will not answer questions which clearly call for direct answers, this evasion itself exposes him to criticism, especially if he is directed by the court to answer. Any lack of frankness always produces an unfavorable impression, but a witness is, of course, not compelled to answer by yes or no double meaning questions. The witness may destroy the favorable effect of direct testimony by irresponsive and evasive answers on cross-examination. The cunning or "smart" witness, who appears to be too wary to be trapped, often seriously discredits himself. The able cross-examiner makes the most of all these vulnerable weaknesses of the untruthful or insincere witness.

The cross-examination outlines here given, when expanded and adapted to the existing circumstances, will often show clearly the error or the unreliability of testimony of the following types of witnesses.

(1) The bank clerk or business man who, testifying positively that a forged signature is genuine, has based his opinion entirely upon the general appearance of the disputed writing and not upon a careful analysis.

(2) The unqualified witness who undertakes to give reasons for an erroneous opinion, based upon an incorrect interpretation of the characteristics of the writing.

(3) The adverse expert witness who is mistaken or who is corrupt.

(4) The lay witness who has seen a person write at some time and who assumes "to know a handwriting".

The most common error in document expert testimony is made by the bank clerk or ordinary business man, who testifies that he can look at a signature and at once decide that it is genuine from its general appearance alone. Witnesses of this class can often be effectively cross-examined by a series of questions like those here given. If the questions, however, are not given with accuracy and the witness is not held strictly to a definite line of inquiry, the whole effect is often lost.

It is entirely proper for the examiner to have in hand a series of questions fully written out. He can properly say, "This is a technical subject and in the interest of accuracy and also to save time I have prepared a short list of questions that I will ask you. If there are any of them that you do not clearly understand I shall be glad to make them clear to you if I can do so".

First Series.

The following examination will sometimes decidedly weaken, if not entirely destroy, the testimony of a witness who is mistaken and depends only on general appearance as the basis for an opinion:

Point: Writing can be skilfully imitated, especially by the tracing method, and when so imitated may so resemble genuine writing that the witness who judges by general appearance alone is easily deceived.

Q. You have said that this signature is in your opinion genuine?

Q. Is there such a thing as forgery of signatures?

Q. Have you ever seen a forgery?

Q. Is it possible for one person to imitate with some degree of success the form and general appearance of the handwriting of another?

Q. In your opinion some imitators would be more successful in this than others, would they not?

Q. And if this was done well enough it would be difficult to detect, would it not?

Q. It might be done well enough, could it not, so that

from the general appearance alone it would be dangerous to say positively that the writing is genuine?

Q. You know, do you not, that, because only this general appearance test was applied, that hundreds of thousands of dollars are paid on forgeries every year by banks and business men?

Q. You have said that this signature is genuine because its design and general appearance are the same as your memory of the genuine signatures of this writer?

Q. Are we to understand that your point is that when you look at this signature it looks to you like a genuine signature and your opinion is based upon this view of the signature as a whole?

Q. Have you ever seen what is described as a forgery by tracing?

Q. Do you understand what a traced forgery is?

Q. What is it?

Q. If a tracing was well made, would it not show the same form as the model followed?

Q. If it was accurately traced would it not show exactly the same form as the model?

Q. If then the design was correct would it not have the same general appearance as a genuine signature, and, according to the method you have applied in this case, would you not be obliged to say that it is a genuine signature?

Q. Then is it not true that this very signature itself may be such an imitation?

Q. As a matter of fact (to a bank clerk), you would not pay out money on handwriting alone, would you?

Q. With a check payable to bearer, endorsed and

presented by a total stranger, with this signature on it, would you pay it if the check was for $5?

Q. Would you pay such a check payable to bearer to a total stranger if it called for $500 of your money or your bank's money?

Q. How about paying a $5000 check under these circumstances?

Q. Would you pay it without requiring identification?

Q. Why would you require identification?

Q. If this disputed signature, as it appears, was attached to a letter ordering you to send $5000 of a depositor's money by express, would you send it without investigation?

Q. You would not, of course. Now, why would you not send it?

Q. It is because, it is not, that you would not depend upon your opinion regarding the handwriting alone?

Q. This being true, would you think it safe to depend upon your opinion here in this case?

Q. Have you ever paid a forgery?

Q. Has a forgery ever been paid by your bank?

Q. Do you know of a forgery ever having been paid by any bank?

Q. If a forgery was so paid it was because the paying teller thought the signature was genuine, is not that true?

Q. And now finally, do you think it would be safe here to depend upon your opinion?

If the questions of this first series are asked of an uninformed witness and it is shown that he is not qualified to testify, other incompetent witnesses may thus be kept off from the witness stand. In some cases a whole troop of similar witnesses have been assembled to give similar testimony. It is very important that the questions be asked accurately and in the proper order. As they can all, or nearly all, be answered by yes or no, a yes or no answer should be firmly insisted upon. The witness should be kept strictly within the line of the questions and not allowed to wander.

Second Series.

This series of questions are intended to show that the ordinary untrained witness is not qualified to give an opinion as to the identity of a handwriting and is not qualified to give technical testimony as to the genuineness or forgery of a disputed signature. The problem is a scientific one and uninformed and inexperienced witnesses cannot furnish reliable assistance. With one who is not a bank clerk the examination should begin with the eighth question.

Point: To show that the witness has made no study of the subject, is posing as an expert, and is not qualified.

Q. As a paying teller (if the witness is a bank clerk) or as a business man passing on handwriting, did you, or do you, make a careful study of every check presented to you for payment?

Q. There would not be time for this at a teller's window, would there?

Q. What you do is to look at the check, look at the one that presents it, and if the circumstances are regular and the check is not too large, you pay it, do you not?

Q. You, in fact, pay if all the surrounding circumstances are regular, do you not?

Q. Have you ever paid a forgery?

Q. How many forgeries has your bank paid?

Q. Was the general appearance of that forged signature good?

Q. Have you made a study of the subject of handwriting identification?

Q. Do you know anything about the various systems of handwriting?

Q. Would not two writers of the same system be more likely to write in a similar way than two writers of different systems?

Q. Two writers of the same system might write much alike, is not this true?

Q. Would you say that a signature is genuine or not genuine from one characteristic in it or one thing about it?

Q. Is there anything about this signature that causes you to hesitate at all in reaching the conclusion that it is genuine?

Q. Is it as good to you as any of these standard signatures?

Q. How long did you examine it before you said it was genuine?

Q. Did you compare it with any signatures or give an opinion from recollection?

Q. What signatures did you have?

Q. How many were there?

Q. Were there some particular qualities in this disputed signature that led you to think that it was genuine?

Q. What were they?

Q. Would the characteristics you have described as

indicating that this signature is genuine be likely to be imitated in a careful imitation?

Q. Would they be likely to be reproduced in an accurate tracing?

Q. If so reproduced, you would then think the signature genuine even though it is not?

Q. It is true, is it not, that you may be mistaken in your opinion regarding this signature?

Q. You would advise other means of determining whether or not it is genuine than merely your opinion alone?

Q. If the question involved $10,000 of your own money would you still depend upon your own judgment?

Q. You, of course, do not hesitate to say that you may be mistaken in your opinion?

Q. What special instruments for use in this work do you possess?

Q. Have you at any time made any serious study of the subject?

Q. Do you know there are special books on the subject?

Q. What books on the subject have you read?

Q. Have you ever read or seen (showing book) Osborn on "Questioned Documents"?

Q. Have you ever read or seen (not showing book but having some book in hand) Ames on "Forgery"? (There is such a book.)

Q. Did you ever hear of it?

Q. Have you ever read or seen (not showing book but having some book in hand) Hagan on "Disputed Handwriting"? (There is such a book.)

Q. Have you ever seen or read (have some book in hand) Farnsworth on "Forged Documents"? (There is no such book.)

Q. Have you ever even heard of any of these books on this subject before to-day?

(As a rule these men will admit not having read any books on the subject and it will thus appear they have made no real study of the question. If the witness says he has heard of, or read, "Farnsworth", this point should at once be followed up by mentioning other fictitious books and authors, and then finally telling him which are real and which fictitious.)

Third Series.

If the corrupt witness who has testified against obvious facts has not himself exposed the unreliable character of his testimony he may be asked the questions given below.

Point: To show that the witness has misinterpreted or ignored significant evidence, has exaggerated certain details by which he has attempted to befog the question and mislead the jury. In some cases it is advisable to make a witness still further emphasize the incredible testimony he has given.

As already suggested, it may be bad policy to cross-examine a witness of this kind on the technical question involved, except under the conditions already outlined in this chapter. If, however, a witness of this class has defended a crude and obvious forgery, saying that it is genuine, some of the following questions should be asked:

Q. Is there anything of any kind about this disputed

signature that requires excuse, apology, or explanation?

Q. Did you find about it anything of any kind that was suspicious in any degree?

Q. Do you consider it an average, normal, genuine signature of this writer of this date?

(If the witness says the signature is not suspicious in any way the question can be followed up as follows):

Q. Comparing the disputed signature with the signatures nearest in date to it, do you find any differences that even remotely suggest that the signature may not be genuine?

Q. You see none?

Q. You do see differences though, do you not?

Q. If there were twice as many as you find would you still say the signature is genuine?

Q. If there were four times as many differences of this same character, would you still say the signature is genuine?

Q. Have you simply ignored the differences you have found or excused them?

(If the witness says there are no differences whatever and that the disputed signature is an average, normal signature, he then should be asked):

Q. If this disputed signature, apart from the document on which it appears, was submitted to you with three or four of the standard signatures nearest in date, would you be able to tell which signature was under suspicion if you were not told?

Q. You would, of course, know at once which was disputed, wouldn't you?

Q. Do you think your judgment on the subject is

based on such reasons as to make it reliable and trust-worthy?

(If the signature is a palpably divergent one and this divergence can be seen by the jury, and has been minimized or ignored by the witness, the following questions should be asked. During this inquiry and the preceding one the photographs should be in the hands of the jury):

Q. How long did it take you to reach the conclusion that this is a genuine signature?

Q. Who submitted the matter to you?

Q. What standards did you have?

Q. Did you make a memorandum of what standards you examined?

Q. Have you that memorandum?

Q. Did you make a report in the case?

Q. To whom was the report made?

Q. Was it oral or written?

Q. Did you ask for any additional standard signatures?

Q. Was your first report the same as your latest?

Q. Do you have a copy of your report with you, and if so, are you willing to submit it or are you willing to submit the original that you submitted in the case?

Q. Did you not say at the beginning that there were some suspicious qualities in this signature that needed explanation?

Q. Have you your notes of the examination with you?

Q. Are you willing to submit them?

Q. Has your testimony been practically in accordance with your first report and your notes?

Q. In what way, if any, does it differ?

The cross-examination of a witness who has made a mistake in the identification of handwriting, either as genuine or not genuine, can be conducted along lines suggested by the chapter on errors in identification of handwriting. There are those who sometimes testify regarding handwriting, some of them penmen, who are able to see and describe the peculiarities of a writing but are not qualified to reason regarding its qualities and characteristics. The chapter on errors points out three general classes of errors, and a cross-examination may be outlined under either one of the three divisions or on a combination of all of them.

Fourth Series.

In identifying handwriting, as in anonymous letter cases, error is sometimes made by ignoring differences and basing a conclusion upon a few similarities. An uninformed or incompetent witness can be attacked by showing that he is not technically qualified, and by bringing out the fact that if he is ignorant on the subject he may be mistaken in his conclusion. In a case involving a handwriting with foreign characteristics, or the handwriting of a particular system, the fact should be developed that the witness cannot recognize or interpret the differences between these various nationalities and systems. The witness sometimes is sincere but misled because of his ignorance, and in a skilfully conducted examination the candid witness will admit that he is incompetent.

Point: That the witness is not qualified to reason on the question and is unable to estimate the significance of evidence upon which a conclusion must be based.

The following questions may be asked:

Q. Is there about this disputed handwriting anything which indicates that it was written by a foreigner or by one who wrote a particular system of handwriting?

Q. The writer must have learned some system, is not that true?

Q. What was the system upon which this handwriting was based?

Q. Do you know the handwriting distinctions among the different nationalities?

Q. For example, can you tell whether a writer first learned to write in Germany, or in England, or in Italy?

Q. Can you tell us the qualities by which you distinguish between one who first learned to write in England as compared with one who first learned to write in Germany?

Q. What are the various American systems of writing?

Q. Is it not a fact that a system of handwriting or a national style of handwriting would be likely to leave a general impression or appearance in a handwriting?

Q. This general appearance would be due to certain characteristics or peculiarities, would it not?

Q. Now, if you cannot tell what these peculiarities are would there not be danger of your concluding that any writer whose writing contained these peculiarities might have written a certain disputed writing in which they appeared?

Q. You would be in danger, without any intention

on your part of doing so, of interpreting a system characteristic or a national characteristic as an individual characteristic, would you not?

Q. Do you know the distinctions in American handwriting between those who learned to write in 1840, in 1875, and one who learned to write in 1895?

Q. When was what is called the Old Round Hand system of writing last taught in American schools?

Q. When did what is called the Vertical System first appear in American schools?

Q. What is the Angular System?

Q. Can you tell the distinctions between the various styles of handwriting that have been taught in America?

Q. There would be certain similarities, would there not, between two handwritings of the same class even though written by different individuals?

Q. Now, if you cannot tell what constitutes or produces these similarities would you not be in danger of identifying certain general characteristics as individual characteristics?

Fifth Series.

The witness who has ignored or overlooked certain repeated, significant, individual characteristics and has given the opinion that the writings are not by the same writer because they are to some extent disguised and necessarily contain certain minor differences, should be interrogated directly on the subject of disguise.

Point: What is disguise in handwriting, and how is it detected and what will it probably include?

The following questions may be asked:

Q. What is disguise in handwriting?

Q. Have you ever seen a disguised writing?

Q. If writing is disguised by changing the slant, or size, or design of some of the letters, is it impossible to identify it?

Q. Would you expect a disguised writing to differ somewhat from the regular, genuine writing of the same writer?

Q. How would you tell whether or not a writing is disguised?

Q. If you find in it numerous repeated inconspicuous characteristics, probably unconscious to the writer, would you take this to be disguise?

Q. Such repeated small peculiarities would probably be the writer's personal characteristics, would they not?

Q. Would one be likely to disguise the delicate, inconspicuous characteristics of a writing and leave undisguised the conspicuous and evident characteristics?

Q. Would not the effort probably be in just the opposite direction, that is, the disguising of the general features and the overlooking of the delicate and inconspicuous features?

Q. Would a disguised writing be likely to be rapidly and freely written?

Q. If then, parts of a writing are rapid and free, and repeated in practically identical form many times, would this indicate that the characteristics thus shown are the natural characteristics of the writing or the disguised characteristics?

Q. Two writings by the same writer are bound to differ somewhat, are they not?

Q. If the writer attempted to make them differ he could do this, couldn't he?

Q. Would you say that if he did it well enough that nobody could detect it?

Q. Now, if it is only partially disguised how will you be able to say that it is by the writer who thus attempted to disguise?

Q. You would look, would you not, for those things which the writer would be likely to be unconscious of or overlook and see if there were a sufficient number in combination to indicate personality?

Q. If you find such identities you must either conclude, must you not, that it is the same writing or that the identities are due to accidental coincidence?

Q. Have you examined this writing with these various ideas in mind?

Q. If you have not, is it not true that you may be mistaken in your conclusion?

Q. Would you not say that it is possible that you are mistaken?

Q. It is possible, is it not, for one to learn something of this subject and know the history of handwriting and the various systems, and if one has learned in this way and such a student was intelligent otherwise, you would say, would you not, that he would be more likely to reach a correct conclusion than you might reach?

Q. You would say, wouldn't you, that with study one might learn more of this subject than he would otherwise know?

Q. You would say this of yourself, wouldn't you?

Unskilled lay witnesses who testify wholly from recollection as to the genuineness or identity of handwriting in many cases can be effectively cross-examined if a definite method is followed. This is especially true of cocksure witnesses who testify that disputed signatures are genuine and who assume to have an ability that they do not possess.

Attempted fraud is often bolstered up by bringing forward a flock of incompetent witnesses, relatives, friends, neighbors, and even casual acquaintances, who have been gathered together to testify that a forged signature is genuine. These witnesses sometimes have been led to think a claim is justified and, having seen the alleged signer of a claim paper write at some time, no matter how little or how long before, they are thus legally qualified to give an opinion on the handwriting. Witnesses of this class are often ingeniously led to think they really can accurately identify a writing when in fact they are not qualified to do so. It is solemnly argued that because these persons knew the party, or lived in the neighborhood, they are therefore qualified to testify regarding the disputed handwriting.

Numerous of the questions given heretofore can to advantage be asked of these lay witnesses, but it has seemed desirable to put in one group a series of questions especially prepared to show the unreliability of the testimony of that class of witnesses that are assumed, in legal phrase, "to know a handwriting". These questions have been tested, and if propounded in the proper manner and spirit will show the unreliability of the testimony of the incompetent witness who is attempting to do what he is not qualified to do.

Sixth Series.

Point: The usual lay witness, wholly unskilled, is not qualified to say whether or not a disputed writing is genuine; has made no study of the subject, and has had no experience whatever in identifying disputed handwriting.

In this particular examination a friendly, inquiring tone should be maintained.

With a witness who is probably sincere and honestly mistaken, ask:

Q. You haven't, I suppose, made any special study of the subject of disputed writings and forgery?

Q. Did you know there are special books on the subject?

Q. Have you ever seen any of these books?

Q. You do not consider yourself an expert on the subject?

Q. You think, do you not, that if you studied it you could learn more about it than you now know?

Q. Have you ever made a study of the various systems of handwriting?

Q. You know, do you not, that there is such a thing as forgery?

Q. Have you heard of forgeries being paid?

Q. Did you know that in this country several millions of dollars are paid on forgeries each year?

Q. You do not think, do you, that all these payments were due to gross carelessness?

Q. Do you think you would have paid any of them?

Q. Why do you think the forged papers were paid?

Q. It was because, was it not, that those who paid them were deceived?

Q. You would not assume, would you, that you would not have been deceived by any of these papers?

Q. You would probably have paid most of them, wouldn't you?

Q. Have you ever seen one forgery?

Q. Had it been paid?

Q. Was it a clever imitation?

Q. You do not, of course, assume to be an infallible judge of handwriting, do you?

Q. If a signature was imitated with skill it would look like a genuine signature, would it not?

Q. And you would probably say it was genuine?

Q. Is it not a fact that you could be quite easily deceived?

Q. You would consider it unsafe to decide this case on your opinion alone, would you not?

Q. And this signature may in fact be a clever imitation?

Seventh Series.

Point: The cocksure or more positive witness who assumes to possess skill, who is not committing perjury but has been led to think he is qualified on the subject.

To the witness: Please take this pen and these three pieces of paper and write your own signature three times, once on each paper, as you usually write it and let me have the three papers.

Q. Has your signature ever been successfully forged?

Q. Do you think it could be forged by anyone so your bank would be deceived and pay it if it came to them in a manner that did not lead them to suspect it?

Q. Do you think you could infallibly detect an imitation of your own signature?

Q. Do you think there is a person in America who could imitate this signature of yours so you could not tell whether you wrote it or not?

Q. Do you think there is anyone in this city who could imitate it so well as to deceive you?

Q. Do you think there is anyone in this room who could do it?

Q. You think it is possible, do you not, that you might be deceived?

Q. Why, in your opinion, are forgeries paid?

Q. Do you think in every case they would not be paid if presented to you?

Q. You wouldn't consider yourself proof against forgery, would you?

Q. You do not consider yourself an expert on the subject, do you?

Q. Do you know how many hundreds of thousands of dollars are paid out each year on forgeries?

Q. You would not say that all these paying tellers and cashiers and business men are grossly careless, would you?

Q. They paid on signatures that looked genuine, did they not?

Q. You might have been of the number, is not that true?

Q. Have you ever really studied the subject of disputed handwriting?

Q. Did you know books have been written on the subject?

Q. Have you read any of them?

Q. Do you think you could learn more about the subject if you did study it?

Q. Then is it true that those who have studied the subject are probably better qualified than you are?

Q. What would you expect to find in a forgery as compared with a genuine signature?

Q. If it was a fairly good forgery would you expect it to look like the signature imitated?

Q. You would, wouldn't you?

Q. If it was well imitated you would expect to find it much like it, would you not?

Q. If it was carefully and accurately traced from a genuine signature its form would be just like it, would it not?

Q. You say this signature looks like the signature of Mr. ————?

Q. And an accurate tracing, or a skilful imitation, would look like it, would it not?

Q. And you would probably say, would you not, that such an imitation is genuine?

Eighth Series.

Point: A series of questions for the witness who, when carefully interrogated, will freely admit that he is not qualified on the subject. Many lay witnesses will also admit that without an examination of the standard signatures in the case they would not be able to give an opinion, and some of these witnesses will admit that their testimony is in fact based on the standard signatures and not on their recollection. If a lay witness makes this latter admission his testimony sometimes can be excluded, and if he is one of the first witnesses of a series called to prove a fraudulent document, this exclusion often is a disaster to the proponents of a forged will or note.

To the witness: Will you please step here and observe me carefully as I write my signature. You have now seen me write my name in the manner in which I habitually write it. I fold up the paper and will ask you to take the witness stand again.

Q. Do you consider that you now know my handwriting?

Q. Do you think that a week from to-day you would be able to decide whether or not a document bearing my signature had actually been signed by me?

Q. How long ago did you last see the writing of the decedent in this case?

Q. Do you think, having seen me write my signature, that after as long a time has expired as you have just mentioned, you would be able to give a reliable opinion as to a disputed signature of mine?

Q. You would not, of course, would you?

Q. Can you tell now within five minutes after you have seen it how it was written?

Q. What was the form of the first letter?

Q. How many times was the pen taken up?

Q. Were the capital letters all shaded?

Q. Is your recollection or memory of form in writing good or bad?

Q. Do you remember the decedent's writing in this case with special clearness and accuracy?

Q. Without attempting to imitate the signature, can you illustrate in a general way how he made the letters in his signature?

Q. Or do you have only a vague recollection of it?

Q. Now I wish to ask you a somewhat extended but, I think, not difficult question. There are two recognized methods by which writing is identified. The first method is that pursued by witnesses who have seen a party write, but without necessarily paying special attention to the act, and afterwards, perhaps five or ten years, they are called upon to identify a writing alleged to be by the same writer. By the second method, genuine, or so-called standard, signatures are found as near as possible to the date of the disputed document, sometimes signatures written on the same day, and with ten, or twenty, or fifty of these genuine signatures an observer, like yourself for example, or one who has made a special, scientific study of the subject, takes all these genuine signatures and examines them carefully and studies them and compares them with each other as to form, proportions, connections, pen-lifts, slant, shading, pen pressure, smoothness of line, roundness or angularity of connections, speed, carelessness, and then in all these particulars compares the disputed signature with this group of genuine signatures. This is the second method of identification of writing. Which method, in your opinion, would be more likely to be accurate if followed by the same observer?

Q. Do you have a recollection of this decedent's signature independent of any standards that you have seen in this case?

Q. Did you examine the standards?

Q. Did you say at the beginning when you were consulted that you did not remember the writing well enough to testify regarding it, and were you afterwards shown the standards in preparation for your testimony, and without the standards you would not have a definite opinion on the subject, is that true?

Q. If you had not seen them would you have been unable to testify?

Q. You would not, then, have had an independent recollection or knowledge of this signature without comparing it with the standards?

(If this admission is made, the testimony of a lay witness can sometimes all be excluded for, if he is not an expert he is not allowed to compare the signature and reach a conclusion, because this the jury can do as well as he. If the admission is not made, then the examination should be continued.)

Q. Do you now have a distinct recollection of the outline and form of the signature of this decedent?

Q. Could you describe it in the dark without illustration?

Q. Will you be kind enough to close your eyes for a moment. Do you now have in your mind, or memory, a mental outline of this signature?

Q. Is this the mental outline which you have compared with this disputed signature?

Q. Is it clear to you?

Q. Will you describe the first letter as you see it in your mind?

Q. Please keep your eyes closed and say how the first letter begins and where in relation to the base line?

Q. How many times is the pen taken up in writing the signature?

Q. I am referring to the mental outline of the signature which you say you recollect. Will you describe the second capital letter in the signature?

Q. What part of the letter is the highest and where is it shaded?

Q. I am not going to ask you a question in law, but I want to read you a sentence from the case of Green v. Terwilliger, 56 Fed. 384, and ask you a question relating to your testimony. In this case the court said, "In most cases . . . it is far more satisfactory to allow the witness to compare the writings with other writings of unquestioned authenticity than it is to compare it with the standard he may have retained in his mind." Do you not think that direct comparison, by yourself for example, or by the members of this jury, would be a more satisfactory way to determine the genuineness or lack of genuineness of this signature than for you to compare the signature with this vague recollection of what you saw some years ago?

Q. You, of course, do not claim that you cannot be mistaken?

Q. Do you think anybody in America could imitate this signature well enough so that you could not detect that it was not genuine?

Q. Do you think anyone in this city could do it?

Q. Do you think anyone in this room could do it?

Q. As a matter of fact, you do not attach much importance to your opinion in this case, do you?

If these examinations of the lay witnesses are given in the proper manner and spirit it can usually be shown that the testimony of the usual witness who is supposed "to know a handwriting" deserves no serious consideration whatever. The witness himself will often, if not usually, make the admission. These witnesses should not be assailed in a fierce and accusing way, but should be firmly kept to the point and made to answer the questions. This subject of testimony by lay witnesses is discussed more fully in a separate chapter, and that discussion should be considered in connection with this subject of cross-examination.

Ninth Series.

There occasionally appears on the witness stand an almost totally unqualified witness who is, however, called as an expert. Ignorant and presumptuous witnesses of this kind should be thoroughly cross-examined in order to show the general ignorance of the witness as well as his ignorance regarding the special topic on which he presumes to speak. These witnesses are often conceited as well as ignorant, and do not themselves realize how their testimony is rendered valueless by proper cross-examination.

Point: To show that the witness is ignorant on general subjects as well as the special subject on which he pretends to speak; that he is in fact a pretender and not an expert, and does not even understand the terms and words relating to the subject on which he speaks.

Q. You consider yourself an expert on this subject on which you have testified?

Q. You understand, do you not, that you have been called here and have testified as an expert witness?

Q. What do you understand by the word expert?

Q. Does the definition "especially skilled" apply to you, in your opinion?

Q. In your work in this field do you distinguish between an inference and the report of an observation of an actual fact?

Q. What is your understanding of inference?

Q. Is it your opinion that your testimony is based on scientific principles?

Q. What do you understand by scientific principles?

Q. Are there principles that apply to this special subject on which you testified?

Q. Just how do you define principle?

Q. Would you say that it is an established rule applying to a subject?

Q. Are there characteristics in this handwriting?

Q. According to your understanding, what is a characteristic?

Q. Do you distinguish a characteristic from an attribute or general quality of a thing?

Q. There are certain general ways in which handwriting, or other things, resemble each other, are there not?

Q. Would you call these general ways or qualities, characteristics?

Q. The characteristic of a camel would be his hump, would it not?

Q. A quality or attribute of a camel would be that he has four feet. Is that not so?

Q. Now, have you distinguished characteristics from attributes or general qualities in your examination of the question here on which you testified?

Q. Have you actually studied this subject in detail as a means of identification?

Q. How do you understand that a thing is correctly identified?

Q. It is by comparison of its characteristics and its general qualities, is it not?

Q. And error may result, may it not, if you confuse these two things?

Q. Have you considered in examining handwriting the distinction between characteristic and general qualities?

Q. Did you do this before you knew how to define the word characteristic?

Successful cross-examination is persistent, severe if necessary, and is kept strictly to the special point under inquiry. This latter requirement is perhaps the most difficult to maintain and enforce. Unless the attorney is alert and technically qualified, and constantly keeps in mind his main purpose, he is likely to be led off into a side issue that usually defeats the end he is aiming at. No matter what excursions the examination may lead to, the witness each time must be brought back again to the exact line of inquiry that has been marked out.

If the witness is inclined to be fair he should be dealt with gently, but with a firmness and persistency that leads the witness to understand clearly that sooner or later he must give attention to the exact point under inquiry. It is important that the examiner should not become petulant, but simply persistent.

Again it is necessary to emphasize the fact that if a cross-examiner is only half prepared on the facts of the case, the alert, side-stepping witness will soon get him far afield and lost. He becomes dazed and forgets what he started out to do, and is unable to tell whether or not the witness has really answered the questions. A perfect series of cross-examination questions in the hands of an unprepared attorney is as useless as any perfect tool in the hands of one who has not learned to use it.

CHAPTER XXV.

DISPUTED TYPEWRITING PROBLEMS.

"What actual, individual machine was it written upon?", "What kind of a machine was it written upon?", "Was it all written on the same machine?", "Was it written continuously?", "Is it possible that it could have been written in the typewriting it contains on the date it bears?" These are a few of the most frequent questions asked about a suspected typewriting. Sometimes they cannot be answered and then again the answer is unmistakable.

This identification of typewriting, and the determination of the date of a typewritten document from the typewriting itself, still are rare performances and to the uninformed the writing machine seems to afford an excellent opportunity for concealment, and, it is altogether probable that, in very many instances it has in fact been an effective ally of fraud. Many typewritten "Exhibit A's" and "Exhibit B's" that grew out of conditions that at the time aroused justifiable suspicion are no doubt lying uninvestigated among the records of old cases in court houses and in private law offices. The whole question is so comparatively new that even many lawyers and public officers are not aware of the possibilities of the subject and the extent to which the investigation of typewriting has been carried. More and more as the years go by, the typewriting of fraudulent papers is becoming the key that unlocks the secrets of clever conspiracies.

As is well known, typewriting itself is a comparatively new thing in the history of documents. The first practical writing machine came into limited use in 1874, but the machine was in a crude and experimental state until 1879 when the first practical machine was put upon the market. It is common knowledge that from that time there has been a constantly increasing use of the typewriter in the business and legal world. As the great bulk of business correspondence and of legal documents came more and more to be written on the typewriter, it was inevitable that the machine would be employed for fraudulent purposes, and these questions have more and more been arising regarding the condition, origin, and date of suspected typewritten papers. Although there have been quite a number of important cases of this kind in American courts, and a considerable amount of legal literature relating to disputed typewriting cases already exists, there are many hundreds of court houses where such a case has never been tried and there are thousands of lawyers who have never seen, or at least have never recognized, a piece of fraudulent typewriting.

It is quite surprising how many different kinds of questions arise in relation to the typewriting of a document. It is often of vital importance, for instance, simply to learn where a document originated. Fraudulent wills and contracts are sometimes "found", according to the testimony, with no history of their preparation, and the discovery of their origin through the typewriting of the document is sometimes a most important first step in the exposure of an ingenious fraud. More and more the typewriter is also being used to write anonymous letters, usually with this common assumption that typewriting cannot be identified and traced to its source.

One of the most important questions that arises regarding a typewritten document is whether or not the typewriting of the document is consistent with its date. Many fraudulent wills, contracts, and other documents are dated back to a certain desired date in order to fit in with some actual event, or ingenious story regarding the alleged preparation of the document, and are written on some old typewriter which it is either assumed will not indicate by its work the date when it was made, or this question is given no thought whatever. It is practically impossible for one without a thorough knowledge of the history of typewriting to select an old machine, the work of which may not prove that a document of this kind is fraudulent.

Mistakes of this kind also are sometimes made because of the superficial and incorrect information obtained from typewriting men who have never had occasion to investigate this particular problem. Naturally these changes and improvements, especially in type faces indicating date, some of them of a delicate character, are not generally known unless the improvement happens to have some distinctive commercial value. One of the reasons that the fraudulent character of many typewritten documents is not at any time discovered is, no doubt, due to the fact that many of these men, interested in typewriters only in a commercial way, have never had occasion to investigate the question of typewriting individuality. Typewriter salesmen, and others who have some direct or remote connection with the business, when asked about a particular document, or a particular problem in typewriting, will often say at once and without any investigation whatever that it is impossible to tell anything about it, and an inquiry regarding a suspected document sometimes ends with this misinformation. There are now, however, not only qualified specialists who have made an exhaustive study of the whole subject, but numerous technical men in the typewriter business who have given careful attention to the question and can give reliable information.

Any intelligent person would know that a document in typewriting of the period of the American Revolution would necessarily not be genuine, but it is not generally known that a document purporting to have been written only a year or two ago may in its typewriting characteristics prove that it is fraudulent and could not have been written on the date it bears.

In determining the date of a typewritten document it is, of course, necessary that the history of the typewriting machine should be known and its work illustrated by actual dated specimens. The first machine began with an experimental set of type, made to print an equal number of letters to the inch (ten in ordinary typewriting) no matter whether the letters were narrow or wide. This uniform spacing, a new requirement in letter designing, and the requirements of legibility and the artistic development of the work of the engraver have produced many progressive changes in type faces down to the present day. Fortunately some of the oldest and most popular machines have made many changes which mark definite dates in the history of the typewriting of those particular machines.

It would manifestly be in the interests of justice if all manufacturers made certain slight changes from time to time. In the work on certain machines a particular design or size of letter indicates that the typewriting cannot be older than the year 1921, in others than 1916, in others 1912, others 1906, 1896, 1892, 1888, and so on back to 1879.

The importance of this question is forcibly illustrated by a will case in New York in which the first page of a will covering a million dollar estate, which page contained all the bequests, was written on a typewriter that was not made until five years after the will was signed and witnessed, and also by an important patent case in Washington, in which a fraudulent page in an application was substituted. In this latter case the fraud was also discovered and the guilty parties sent to prison. Postscripts on old letters, or additions to receipts, contracts, and agreements, are sometimes written on machines that were not made on the date of the document to which these additions are attached.

In other cases the problem presented is that of determining whether the typewritten document is a continuous writing which was completed without being taken out of the typewriting machine, and in other cases it is desirable to determine whether or not the document was all written on the same typewriting machine, or whether a word, or sentence, or line, or paragraph, was written at a different time and on a different machine. In still other cases it is desirable to determine, if possible, whether a document was written on the same machine but at a different date than it purports to have been written. There have been a number of important cases of this kind in which it was possible to demonstrate conclusively by the progressive changes that a particular document, admittedly written on a particular machine, could not have been written on the date it bore. Still another problem that occasionally arises is whether a carbon copy could have been made through a particular weight of typewriting paper, and in other cases it is asked whether a certain ribbon, or a ribbon in a certain condition, was used to write a document. By this latter test it is sometimes possible to show conclusively that a document was written on a particular machine, but not on the date it bears for the reason that the typewriting does not match the condition of the ribbon of that day.

To many persons this particular problem of identifying the typewriting work of a certain individual machine naturally seems to be somewhat of an assumption, if not actually impossible. It is known that machines are made as nearly as possible like other machines of the same model, the type especially all having been made from the same originals, and it is incorrectly assumed that the work of such a machine will show no individuality. This would be true if the machines could be made perfectly and continued to write perfectly. As a matter of fact, however, it is not commercially necessary to make the machines so that they will write with absolute perfection, and it is mechanically impossible to make them so that they will continue to write perfectly. Their individuality begins from the very beginning. Even the alignment of the machines, as a rule, is not entirely perfect, and the work of twenty entirely new machines can be differentiated in a number of ways if sufficiently clear and extended specimens are available. The usual typewriter carries eighty-four characters, any one of which may be individualized in many different ways, and this combination of characteristics is of almost infinite variety.

It is true that many problems arise that are too difficult for solution, but in other cases the question can be answered with such certainty that testimony on the subject with illustrations amounts to a demonstration that cannot successfully be denied. In an important case in Wisconsin a document was produced bearing the signature and seal of the official register of deeds of the county, who himself testified as to its date and genuineness, but notwithstanding this testimony it was conclusively proved and definitely decided that the document could not have been written until more than six years after its alleged date. From these various facts it is easy to understand how important it is in preparing a case for trial involving a typewritten document to give prompt and proper consideration to every phase of this question of typewriting.

The proof of disputed typewriting in an actual trial often requires somewhat more careful preparation in certain particulars than the proof of the facts in other classes of disputed document cases, but in many instances the proof as finally made is more conclusive than proof regarding many other questions regarding documents. The differences in the width of the impressions of two typewritten characters may not be more than one one-hundredth of an inch, but when properly illustrated, especially with properly enlarged photographs and definite enlarged measurements, this proof, which may show a fraudulent date of a document, often becomes unmistakable. It is especially necessary to keep in mind in the presentation of proof on this subject that there are observers, as suggested in the chapter on form blindness, who cannot recognize delicate divergences, or similarities, and that it is essential in connection with typewriting proof that suitable enlarged illustrations be supplied.

It is particularly important in connection with the proof of the facts regarding a disputed typewriting, especially in a jury case, that one or more of the principal illustrative photographs be put into the hands of each juryman, in accordance with the suggestion in the chapter dealing with photographs. Evidence of this kind is of a somewhat delicate, as well as unusual, character and with many observers its significance is not properly understood unless ample time and full opportunity are given for study and consideration. Where the facts are to be proved to a judge or a referee it may also be important that every point receive full consideration and thorough explanation. In considering a new question there is a natural tendency to say hastily that a thing is seen and understood when this is only partly true. In proving the facts in a case of this kind it is not usually sufficient to hand photographs around from one observer to another for a mere momentary glance.

As necessary as the matter of careful observation and study is that of bringing out fully and clearly the principles, as well as the facts and conditions, that enforce proof in matters of this kind. It is not usually sufficient simply to point out the evidence on which a judgment is to be based. In order to become qualified to show another, it is of course necessary that the attorney himself should first become thoroughly acquainted with the theory and principle of the proof as applied in a problem of this nature.

The identification of a typewriting as having been written by the same machine that wrote other specimens is the result of the same process of observation and reasoning as is required in the identification of anything containing many varying qualities which are the real evidence of the fact and which can be seen, described, and understood. The principle underlying this kind of proof is that it is the result of a combination of evidential matter which, according to the calculus of probabilities, makes it practically impossible that it would have thus combined if it had not come from the same source and that this combination proves a certain fact.

It is well understood that the proof of a fact, when positive and conclusive, is carried to that degree of certainty when it is unreasonable to reach any other conclusion and that common sense, as a result of human experience, compels one to decide in a certain way. It is readily understood how even with the manufacturer's numbers filed off, or obliterated, it is possible for one to identify an automobile, which he has driven for some time, by certain qualities, conditions, marks, and scars. A few unimportant and inconspicuous accidental marks in certain definite places, the exact history of which are known to the driver, are often alone sufficient to insure unmistakable accuracy in identification. The principle is the same as that applied to the identification of a horse, or of a person, by a general description and by a combination of distinguishing general and individual qualities, and especially by certain of these accidental or unusual characteristics.

The advocate who hopes to prove facts of this kind, especially to a jury, must be able to explain these matters clearly and simply and make it understood why with a combination of certain kinds of evidential matter it is reasonable to reach a certain decision, and why a decision is approved by common sense. Any advocate who endeavors to prove facts in a court of law will be greatly assisted in these phases of the subject by the study of the question as discussed by Mill, and Bentham, and Whately, and by the writers in the cyclopedias, especially in their discussions of the "calculus of probabilities", which is described by one of these writers as the combination of mathematics and common sense.

Where the problem is to prove the identity of two specimens of typewriting, actually written on the same machine, it becomes necessary to show definitely why it is reasonable to reach the positive conclusion that they must have been so written. With eighty-four characters upon a typewriter, any one of which may show numerous divergences from normal, there naturally arises a possibility of variation, as already suggested, of almost infinite extent, but these facts must be brought home to the mind of juror, referee, or judge, by proper descriptions, analogies, and illustrations, until it comes to be clearly understood why a certain decision must be reached.

Under the present contentious method in trials at law part of the business of the advocate is the disparaging of the alleged proof presented by the opposition, and this requirement of the advocate has naturally led to many discussions of the subject of proof that are filled with error. Many legal discussions of this subject are characterized by a sophistry, and by certain unwarranted assumptions, that have been developed by this effort of at least one advocate in every legal controversy who aims to prevent proof. For example, it is contended by those who are injured by proof that it must always be absolute, and violent objection is made to anything in the process that is described as inference, or of any proof whatever short of absolute mathematical certainty. This requirement would make it impossible to arrive at any decision in the usual trial.

As is well known, most so-called proof is the result of some measure of inference regarding the evidence of persons, of events, or of things. We are informed by the writers on evidence and by students of logic that knowledge of an unknown, or a bygone fact is obtained either from those who have direct knowledge of that fact, or by means of inference or conclusions drawn from other facts more or less directly connected with the fact that it is necessary to prove. Even when positive oral testimony is given it becomes necessary to infer whether or not the speaker is telling the truth and was qualified to observe, and is reporting correctly. When the evidence is offered it then of course becomes necessary to decide whether it is reasonable to reach a conclusion as to the fact which the evidence is supposed to prove. It is also important to keep in mind that one can hardly be convinced by evidence unless the evidence in some way or ways is related to the experience and knowledge of the one who is asked to decide. The final conclusion based upon evidence of almost any kind is necessarily the result, in some measure, of a process of reasoning, or a combination of all the various inferences drawn from the evidentiary matter. In identifying anything a sufficient number of evidentiary facts must, of course, combine so that one is justified in concluding that the evidence is sufficient to prove the fact which it is desired to prove.

In many, if not in all, kinds of proof there necessarily is a theoretical possibility of error. An argument to this effect can be made in relation to almost any kind of evidence. As suggested above, where the most positive oral proof is given there still remains at least a remote possibility of error in observation or report. Where several witnesses testify positively that a certain thing occurred at a certain time, there is necessarily the possibility of incorrect observation, as well as of perjury on the part of any or of all the witnesses. It is therefore necessary in acting upon any testimony to determine, in the first place, whether the witness is truthful, and in the second place whether the witness is qualified to report on the fact which is reported. Belief in all oral testimony, therefore, in some degree, must be based on the inference that witnesses are truthful and competent observers. Necessity requires and human experience leads observers to act upon evidence of this character which appears to be reasonably accurate and reliable. Ordinary human judgment and common sense must finally decide.

Underlying the whole theory of proof, by oral testimony and by tangible evidence of things, is this question of probability, a word the use of which tends to throw into a fit the insincere advocate who is seèking to prevent proof of any kind. It is, of course, always necessary to consider the possibility of error and determine whether under the circumstances it is reasonable to say that this possibility makes it dangerous to reach a conclusion, or that the possibility is so remote that it is reasonably safe to decide in a certain way. The advocate against the facts will always argue strenuously that if there remains the most remote possibility of error in any proof that a definite conclusion is not warranted. The qualified attorney must be able to discuss this question so that it can be understood by the ordinary juryman or one who must decide a mooted question.

The general principle underlying proof by real or tangible evidence can be illustrated, for example, by the process of identifying a certain person from a general description and by measurements, and by certain identifying marks and scars. Even if this person is looked for in a city containing six millions of people, it can be shown how he can be identified with reasonable accuracy. For purposes of illustration let it be assumed that these people are all available for examination. The description calls for a young man with black hair, of about thirty years of age. It is obvious that all the inhabitants who do not answer these two general descriptions can at once be dismissed. The next, or third, and more definite description, is that he is exactly five feet eight inches tall. All of the remaining possible candidates who do not answer approximately this description can then be dismissed. The next, or fourth, point of description, still more definite, is that he has a scar two inches long on the back of his left hand beginning opposite the little finger and extending toward the base of the thumb. It now becomes obvious that all but a few of all the remaining candidates for identification can be dismissed, and there would be remaining only a few with peculiar scars on the back of the left hand. The last, and fifth, point of description is that he has a brown birthmark on the inside of the right wrist, one-half inch wide and one inch long. This requirement, in combination with the preceding points, would no doubt eliminate all the other candidates of the six millions excepting the one man who was sought, if he was present in that city. Common sense and human experience, as well as mathematics, lead to the positive conclusion that it is reasonably certain that there are not two persons out of the whole six millions who will exactly answer only these five points of description.

The proof of a disputed typewriting is based upon exactly the same principles as those described above. For example, if it should become necessary to identify a typewritten letter of twenty lines, containing most of the ordinary written characters, and written upon a typewriter which had become individualized by use, this same process of elimination could be followed. As in the previous example, let it be assumed that all of the typewriting machines in this city of six million people were available for examination.

In the first place, in the operation of identification all machines could at once be eliminated excepting those that wrote exactly the same size and style of type which appears upon the disputed letter. A disputed letter containing only the six distinctive individualities here described, in combination with the sixty or seventy other characters which write on this machine in a normal or correct manner, can be positively identified.

In the specimen of typewriting the letter "l" appears with the lower left-hand extension missing, constituting an unmistakable defect. It is obvious now that all of the machines can at once be eliminated which do not have this particular letter writing in this particular way. Out of a million machines, more or less, it is entirely possible that there may be a considerable number that would contain this same defect. The next, or second, identifying quality in the typewriting is in the small "u", which shows that the right-hand staff of the letter prints with a blank portion in the exact middle of the stroke, showing that there is a broken part, or saw tooth, in the letter at this point. Now out of the remaining machines all can be eliminated excepting the machines with this peculiar characteristic in this particular letter, in this exact place, and it is obvious that out of the hundreds, or even thousands, of machines remaining that only a few would be left. The next, or third, characteristic is that the capital "I", which, like the other characters specified, appears numerous times, plainly slants two to three degrees to the left of vertical. Out of the remaining machines all could be eliminated excepting those with a capital "I" showing this characteristic. The next, or fourth, identifying quality, as shown in the typewriting under investigation, is found in the small "e" which has been worn off on the right-hand side of the letter until it prints in a distinctive manner with two open portions or spaces on the right-hand side. The fifth characteristic is a small "n" printing heavy on the right-hand side, and the sixth characteristic is in the small "t" which prints high, out of true alignment, and all the machines except those that show these identifying qualities are eliminated. Now, assuming that the machine that wrote the letter under investigation was actually present with the million or more typewriters in that city, with only these few specified identifying characteristics in combination with the perfect characters on the machine, this particular machine would at the close of the investigation no doubt be the only one left out of the whole number of typewriters examined.

The mathematical statement of the improbability of the concurrence of various events, each of which is itself improbable, is illustrated by the throwing of a six-sided cube, or die, which, if marked from one to six, would, in a large number of throws, fall with the one upward approximately one-sixth of the times. If another die of the same kind is added and both are thrown, the probability of the concurrence of the two ones is one-sixth of one-sixth, or one-thirty-sixth. The mathematical statement of the probability of concurrence is that the continued product of the fractions presenting each separate event represents the probability of the concurrence of all. With eight cubes, or dice, thrown at once, the mathematical probability of concurrence would be once in 1,679,616 times.

It is obvious that the possibility of development of a defect in typewriting would be much more remote than one in six. In many cases, like those specified above, it would be one in not less than five hundred or a thousand, and with a half dozen events or characteristics *to be combined* it would hardly be possible to express in figures the remote probability, and it is easy to see that the possibility of an exact accidental concurrence of all the characteristics in two different machines is so utterly remote that it can be dismissed as a practical impossibility.

It is, of course, well understood that testimony as to mere conjectures is properly objectionable, and the courts criticise or reject all testimony that does not have a proper basis. It is proper, however, to base testimony as to probabilities upon actual experiments, or investigations, the basis of which forms an actual part of the testimony. In a typewriting investigation, for example, where there are ten or twenty characteristics by which it is sought to identify typewriting, it is proper to base testimony upon the examination of twenty, fifty, or one hundred machines of the same kind which show how frequently or infrequently a certain characteristic will appear, and it is of course proper in testimony by a skilled witness, qualified as a mathematician, to say how often the separate events will be likely to coincide when it is known how frequently each event will occur.

All matter of this kind, however, is mainly valuable

as a basis for argument, incidental and direct, by which the force of the actual testimony in the case is measured and shown. As is well understood, argument permits illustrations and analogies which would be improper in testimony. The foregoing illustrations of the identification of a person, and of a typewriter, could hardly be put into the form of testimony, even by a skilled witness, except when based on actual experiments, but can properly be put into the form of argument. The important point is that the juror or referee, or one who is to decide, should thoroughly understand the significance and force of the testimony presented. As stated above, it is a common fallacy to suppose that it is unsafe to reach a conclusion if there remains what is accurately described as a theoretical possibility of error.

An event can properly be described as "practically impossible" when it is actually theoretically possible. This idea can be illustrated as follows: If twenty-five soft lead balls are thrown all at once against a white wall by one standing ten feet away, each one will make a small mark. If the balls are then gathered and from the same spot they are all thrown at once in the same way a second time, it is theoretically possible that every mark made at the first throw will be duplicated at the second, so that as a result of both throws there will be only twenty-five small marks on the white wall. Although it is a fact that it is theoretically possible that every one of the balls will exactly hit a spot made by the first throw, the probability is so utterly remote that common sense says that this result would be practically impossible.

It is not here urged that decisions should ever be based on uncertain or inadequate evidence, but it is contended that the subject of proof should be divested of the fallacies and sophistries that have become attached to it like hindering barnacles. The tendency of the law has too often been towards a procedure that hampers proof by restrictions, exclusions, and unwarranted assumptions that have been developed by advocacy. Common sense requires that common sense be applied to the whole operation and that inherently improbable evidence be properly scrutinized and weighed, or entirely rejected, and that logical and reasonable evidence be given due and proper weight. All these legal restrictions and exclusions have special force when applied to a comparatively new question like disputed typewriting. Under the imposed conditions it is sometimes impossible to prove in a court of law what could be proved anywhere else.

CHAPTER XXVI.

ANONYMOUS LETTERS AND THE LAW.

In the natural course of events many anonymous letters find their way into law offices, and sooner or later nearly every lawyer will gain more or less experience in connection with such investigations. There are some facts and particulars about these cases which become of special interest to the attorney called upon to give advice or render assistance in an inquiry of this kind, and some general knowledge of the subject is of practical value to the general practitioner.

But few people are aware of the enormous number and the strange character of these curious manifestations of unkindness, jealousy, envy, hate, greed, and insanity. Many of them well deserve their popular newspaper name, "poison-pen letters". Many of these communications are unspeakably vile and vicious, and the accusations they make, in a great majority of cases, do not have the slightest foundation. Investigation discloses that the motive in many cases is of the most trivial character, and it is impossible to understand why the letters were written.

Persons of prominence and those holding important executive positions are the most frequent victims of the anonymous letter writer. Superintendents of great business establishments, managers of estates, employers of labor, judges, public office holders, corporation managers, prominent society women, school teachers and school officers, ministers and their wives, and many private persons are persecuted by the anonymous letter writer. A new and especially vicious class of writings has recently been added to this great flood, called Black Hand letters. These communications, named from a foreign secret society, usually ask that certain specified acts be performed or that money be left at a certain place, under penalty of bomb attack, kidnapping, incendiarism, disfigurement, or death. To allay unwarranted anxiety, it should be known that very many anonymous letters falsely purport to be of this dangerous class simply to frighten those receiving them. Many anonymous communications are merely petty, annoying exhibitions of spite, envy, or jealousy, and are comparatively harmless, while others are of a character that warrants the most rigorous investigation. Letters of this class have led to suicide and not infrequently whole communities are oppressed and brought almost into a state of frenzy over a series of horrid letters, and it becomes of great importance to find the writer.

It is not usually wise to destroy an anonymous letter at once, as is often done, as it may be followed by others, and it is always easier to find the author of several letters than of only one. Recipients should be advised not to be unduly disturbed or depressed over these unwarranted attacks and can be somewhat appeased by being told that prominent people are getting them constantly. Many letters of this class grow out of unhappy or improper relations of men and women, and very many of them contain matter that it is unlawful to send through the mails. Love and gold are perhaps the two chief causes of anonymous letter writing, although envy and spite are close seconds. It is a surprise to many to know that the great majority of these anonymous communications, except the real Black Hand letters, are written by women.

A careful examination of a collection of anonymous letters, as fully outlined later in this chapter, often will at once throw light on the investigation and point to the possible writer, specimens of whose writing can then be obtained. It is remarkable how similar to each other the various classes of letters of this kind are in many ways and how they fall into one of a quite limited number of groups. The human mind under similar stimulus works in similar ways, and, given certain general circumstances, it is often possible to find the cause and anticipate the result. The class of the particular letter tends to point out a possible writer. When properly examined the contents alone will often point quite clearly to the probable author, and usually there are in these strange missives many unconscious and unsuspected things, outside of the handwriting, that are at once apparent to one with experience, which tend to identify the letters as probably coming from a particular source.

It is important and reassuring to know that a scientific study of the handwriting, and of all these other various elements, features, and circumstances surrounding a particular case, makes it possible in very many instances to find the writers of these letters. Even if not successful, such an investigation sometimes shows conclusively that a certain suspected writer did not write the letters, a result which often gives much relief to those who, for other reasons, may have been led to suspect some friend or associate. More and more during recent years anonymous letters are typewritten, and, strange as it may appear to many as outlined in a previous chapter, their source in many instances can be positively proved. The highest courts have now decided that specimens of typewriting may be admitted simply for purposes of comparison, and typewriting individuality is often so unmistakable that confession at once follows accusation.

A frequent disguise, back of which the anonymous writer seeks to hide, is some style of partial or complete pen or pencil lettering, which, however, often has a most surprising individuality. Habit enters into the act the same as in all writing, and many significant elements may combine to make up individuality. An "exhibit" in an important case were some letters cut with a knife on a barn door. A peculiar kind of ink, or the work of a peculiar pen, may be the means of calling attention to the possible author of a disputed writing, and paper and envelopes and watermarks have exposed many hidden writers. An impression left on an ordinary blotter has been the means of locating the source of a disputed writing, and a study of postmarks sometimes throws helpful light on an investigation. A careful study of language, as outlined later, of the use of capital letters, of spelling, and of style of expression, may be important steps in an anonymous letter investigation. Sometimes a single word or one expression is the key that unlocks the mystery.

One common and surprising circumstance, well known to those of experience in this field, and that always should be given attention, is the fact that when a number of persons have received similar anonymous letters, that in approximately one case out of five, the actual writer will be one of those who has received one or more of the letters. The explanation of this is simple. A natural defense from suspicion in such a case is the apparent persecution with others of the actual writer of the letters. There are those also who write and send letters of this kind to themselves in order to gain sympathy or merely to draw attention to themselves.

The subject matter and language when critically examined usually indicate very clearly whether an anonymous letter was written by a man or a woman, and in any extended communication, or series of communications, the approximate age, sex, education, and often the occupation of the writer, is more or less clearly indicated. It should be understood that this information is the outcome of an application of principles and knowledge radically different from what is ordinarily understood as graphology, or the attempted determination of character from the handwriting alone. If graphology could actually do even a small part of what it pretends to do, it alone in many cases would disclose the writer of an anonymous letter, for letters of this kind frequently are not disguised in any way but are natural, free, unconscious writing, but not signed.

It is usually possible by a careful study of the language employed and the thought expressed, to make a fairly accurate estimate of the scholastic ability and general qualifications of the writer. This is a preliminary step of importance that should receive early attention, following the outline given at the end of this chapter. It is, for example, very difficult for an educated person to simulate illiteracy with success in all ways, and it is, of course, entirely impossible for the illiterate writer to assume a disguise which suggests education and refinement. A careful analysis of the ideas presented, the selection of words, the use of adjectives, and particularly the choice of idioms, will usually indicate quite clearly the educational status of the actual writer.

A thorough knowledge of handwriting, especially covering its recent history, its distinctive systems, and its many characteristics showing nationality, often indicates at once the probable authorship of such letters. When the impetuous man who has rashly accused his sister-in-law of having written certain vile communications, is informed that the letters were undoubtedly written by one who had first learned to write German, he exclaims in dismay, "My God! Then it is the nurse as my wife thought." When it is shown, as it often can be, that a letter was actually written by one who first learned Italian, or German, or French, or had learned to write in England, Ireland, or Canada instead of the United States, this information alone may be of sufficient importance to solve the problem.

Many errors are made by the uninformed who attempt to identify such writing, and for the protection of the innocent it should be known that usually the one first suspected is not the guilty party. When a series of anonymous letters are written in English by one who first learned to write Italian, the average uninformed investigator suspects, and may even accuse and arrest, the first Italian whose handwriting he sees.

This same mistake may be made with writing containing French or German qualities although written in English, when examined by those who are not qualified. Erroneous conclusions may also be reached by the uninformed regarding writing closely following any distinctive system of writing. Those under suspicion, but not guilty, whose writing seems to be similar because its national or system characteristics are the same, are sometimes accused first and the investigation made afterwards.

As with forgery, but few of those who write anonymous letters have made any study of the subject of handwriting, and the disguises usually employed are of the flimsiest and most transparent character. The most common disguises are a change of slant or a change of size, or the making of certain grotesque letters. Frequently the small letters are not disguised in any way, which is a most serious error for, with the great number of forms, varied proportions, modifications, and peculiar connections, they make up the chief characteristics of a handwriting. Occasionally, however, anonymous letters are so effectively disguised that it is impossible to identify them, even if the writing of the actual writer is available for comparison, but such letters are very unusual and are perhaps the work of those who have had considerable experience in this strange work. The most difficult writing to identify is that of young persons whose handwriting is immature and undeveloped. Letters that come out of schools should be examined with special caution and thoroughness.

An interesting and often most important phase of

the subject, always to be considered, is that anonymous letter writing may be one of the first indications of insanity, and the writers of such letters are sometimes found simply by investigating peculiar individuals in a community, or among a group of possible writers, who may not be under the slightest suspicion in any way of having done the writing. There are those who seem to have an uncontrollable desire to be the centre and cause of that which brings about a conspicuous disturbance, or attracts great attention, and apparently for this reason alone letters are circulated containing strange tales which, let it be said in defense of humanity, usually are not true. This abnormal mental state, called megalomania, is sometimes first disclosed by a series of anonymous letters of a nature that is likely to attract attention.

One of the first and most important duties of the attorney who is consulted about anonymous letters is to warn a recipient not to make premature accusations. More than one "defaming of character" suit has grown out of hasty and erroneous charges of this kind. It is often at once assumed that someone who is unfriendly, or who for other reasons is disliked, wrote the letters, and when a hasty examination shows a few similarities in the writing, even in the most common qualities, the incorrect conclusion is jumped at that the suspected person is the writer and an accusation is made. It must be remembered, as pointed out in the chapter on errors in identifying handwriting, that handwritings in the same language are bound to be alike in numerous ways.

It is especially important in all anonymous letter

investigations that suitable and adequate standards of comparison be supplied before any definite opinion in the matter is given. The careful specialist will positively refuse to give any opinion whatever until suitable standards are supplied. Those who have been cruelly persecuted, and in some cases their impetuous legal representatives, may be impatient with a proper caution that experience teaches. As is well known, it is unlawful to send obscene and threatening letters by mail, and cases of this kind are often taken into the criminal courts, and it is particularly important that the preliminary steps in cases of this class be taken with extreme caution. Before formal charges are made in any instance the matter will naturally be submitted to someone who is technically qualified to report positively on the question, and if there is reasonable doubt as to the fact, no action whatever should be taken. Some very regrettable results have followed hasty action in these matters.

At the beginning of an anonymous letter investigation it is important to learn how many letters have been written and to how many people and for how long a time. All the letters with the envelopes should be collected, and all who have received the letters should, if possible, be interviewed separately in the most thorough manner. It is usually unwise to do anything in a public way that will disclose that the letters are causing annoyance or fear, unless it is desired to get more letters written. As a rule, specimens of writing of all those who have received the letters should be obtained, but this should, of course, be done without arousing any suspicion or making, even by inference, any accusations. To even suspect an innocent person of having written a vile anonymous letter may be an almost unforgivable offense.

Not infrequently those who receive anonymous letters are not quite frank and open in giving information regarding events or conditions the knowledge of which may be of great value in an investigation. A recipient should frankly be told that if it is really desired that the writer be found that every shred of information that by any possibility may throw light on the matter must be given. To one with experience in these matters certain information often is very important.

An examination of any document for the purpose of discovering its authorship should, as suggested, always include a careful examination of its language, subject matter, and general and special features and qualities. The following outline directs attention to some of the many points to be considered. This phase of a preliminary examination will sometimes at once eliminate a suspected writer, or direct attention to matters which will lead to the discovery of the actual writer. Every idea or statement of fact, or alleged fact, in a communication of this kind should be considered in connection with the personality, history, qualifications, age, and conditions of any possible writer or of any suspected writer. In some cases by this study of the document the writer can be located as probably coming within a comparatively small group. In this connection it is often very helpful to have full and detailed information regarding all the conditions.

Unless the contents are so bad as to make this undesirable, one of the first steps to be taken in the examination of the language and subject matter of a document is to read aloud the matter to be considered, in such a manner as to bring out clearly and forcibly all the ideas contained in the communication and the style and form of expression. This oral reading discloses the tone and character of such a communication much more forcibly than a silent reading. The trivial, artificial, disconnected, or childish character of the document may be recognized in an oral reading, or, on the other hand, the actual sincerity and seriousness of the communication may thus be shown. Certain idioms and expressions in an oral reading of a document of some considerable length also usually show quite conclusively evidences of masculinity, or of femininity, which are not so easily recognized by sight as by sound.

After this oral reading the general quality as a whole of the document, in ideas and expressions, should be considered in order to determine whether or not it is consistent with the educational qualifications and general ability of a suspected or possible writer, and finally, a complete analysis of the whole document should be made covering the various points in the following outline. A careful examination often clearly discloses that an anonymous letter positively is not the work of a writer of the class that it purports to be, and a careful examination of its ideas, idioms, expressions, errors, and technical terms often shows that it is not the work of the one first suspected.

One of the most important parts of this analysis is the determination of the real purpose of the communication, if it has a purpose, and also any secondary or hidden purpose. It is also important to determine whether or not the communication exhibits in any way evidence of an unsound mind as indicated by fixed ideas, incoherence, or the repetition of irrelevant matters included with no apparent purpose.

Analysis of Subject Matter, Language, and Style of a Written Communication, and the Determination of its Motive, Purpose, or Purposes, as a Means of Discovering its Authorship.

(I) *Subject Matter and Purpose.*

(1) Central idea and related secondary ideas, (2) Wholly disconnected or irrelevant ideas, (3) Are sentiments real or assumed? (4) Main purpose and partially concealed or indirect purpose of communication, (5) Does it contain suggestions, charges, advice, information, warning, threats, requests, demands, commands? (6) Are threats real or only to terrorize? (7) Are demands made with expectation of response or primarily to annoy or frighten? (8) Is there any known basis for charges? (9) Are allusions possibly designed or names actually included, in order to cast suspicion on an innocent party as probable writer of document?

(II) *Motive, Cause, or Conditions Which Led to the Writing.*

(1) Jealousy or attempt to arouse jealousy, (2) Spite, (3) Envy, (4) Antipathy, (5) Anger, (6) Hate, (7) Revenge, (8) Self-defense, (9) Ambition, (10) Love, (11) Fear, (12) Pride, (13) Malice, (14) Cupidity, (15) Childish prank, (16) Practical joke, (17) Blackmail, (18) Megalomania, (19) Sensational or sug-

gestive newspaper reports, (20) Insanity, (21) Politics, (22) Racial, religious, class, professional, or sectional prejudice, (23) Sexual immorality, (24) Social ambition, (25) Is letter written to advance the interests of a friend or relative?

(III) *General Qualities or Features.*

(1) Analysis and interpretation of all technical words, terms, or expressions, (2) Investigation of all references to persons, places, incidents, or occasions, (3) Are there evidences of masculinity or femininity in expression or subject matter? (4) Childish statements or indications of youthfulness, (5) Evidences of intelligence or of ignorance and stupidity, (6) Hysteria, (7) Incoherency, (8) Indications of delusions, (9) Illiterate or educated, (10) Fixed and repeated ideas, (11) Literary quality, (12) Assumed illiteracy as a disguise, (13) Obscenity as a disguise, (14) Style of handwriting, or form of any character, pointing to a foreign nationality, (15) Handwriting of a particular system.

(IV) *Rhetoric, Composition.*

(A) Tone or general effect: (1) Dignified or lofty, (2) Insulting, (3) Respectful, (4) Menial, groveling, or obsequious, (5) Imploring, (6) Commanding or overbearing, (7) Informing, (8) Accusing, (9) Vehement or restrained, (10) Penitent, (11) Childish, (12) Inconsistent, (13) Trivial and unimportant.

(B) Figures of Speech: (1) Character, frequency, infrequency, (2) Slang, profanity, (3) Nicknames, (4) Insulting epithets, (5) Interjections.

(C) Order and Logical Character of Statements: (1) Logical and progressive, (2) Faulty and illogical, (3) Omission of basis of conclusion, (4) Interpolated irrelevant ideas, (5) Reference to matter, alleged facts, or ideas, not specified, (6) Vague allusions, (7) Veiled threats, (8) Alleged reminiscences, (9) Anti-climax.

(D) Emphasis and Control: (1) Method of emphasis, (2) Exaggeration and use of superlatives, (3) Straining for emphasis, (4) Restraint, (5) Repetition, (6) Underscoring, (7) Justified climax from evidence and reasoning.

(E) Diction: Skill or lack of skill in the choice of (1) nouns, (2) adjectives, (3) adverbs.

(F) Construction: (1) Long or short sentences, (2) Simple, complex, or compound, (3) Frequency and location of relative clauses and modifying words, (4) Weak or strong ending of sentences, (5) Disconnected statements, (6) Smoothness and continuity, (7) Frequent or rare use of connectives.

(G) Style: (1) Educated or illiterate, (2) Vigorous or mild, (3) Clear, vague, or ambiguous, (4) Argumentative or assertive, (5) Elegant or slangy, (6) Natural or affected, (7) Plain or flowery, (8) Terse or discursive, (9) Original or conventional, (10) Refined or coarse, (11) Cumbersome and heavy, or flowing and easy, (12) Masculine or feminine, (13) Foreign, (14) Literary, (15) Journalistic, (16) Childish, (17) Ecclesiastical, (18) Sporting, (19) Theatrical.

(H) Manner: (1) Hurried or deliberate, (2) Studied or precipitate, (3) Careless, slovenly, precise or careful, (4) Courteous or disrespectful, (5) Brusque or suave, (6) Dictatorial or obsequious, (7) Threatening or appealing, (8) Sincere or affected, (9) Sad, gay, injured, dejected, crazy, insulting, belligerent, (10) Cold or passionate.

(I) Individual Habits in Language or Expression: (1) Underscoring, (2) Omission of letters from words, or words from sentences, (3) Excessive division of words at ends of lines, or no divisions, (4) Use of interlineations, (5) Overwriting of words, letters, or figures, (6) Marking out or obliterating words, (7) Favorite expressions, (8) Favorite words, (9) Postscripts, (10) Excessive punctuation, (11) No punctuation, (12) Use of interjections, (13) Use of quotations, (14) Divulging alleged secrets, (15) Writing across or at right angles with other writing, (16) Blots and offsets, (17) Margins and paragraphing.

(V) *Errors in:*

(1) Spelling, (2) Capitals, (3) Punctuation, Division of words, (4) Paragraphing, Arrangement, Margins, (5) Titles, (6) Person, (7) Number, (8) Case, (9) Pronoun and antecedent, (10) Verb and subject, (11) Mode, (12) Tense, (13) Voice, (14) Possessives, (15) Omission of subject or of predicate, (16) Repetitions, (17) Incorrect abbreviations, (18) Incorrect use of words, (19) Errors in names, initials, places, or titles, (20) Erroneous statements and incorrect information, (21) Incorrect addresses, (22) Unsuitable or improper materials.

(VI) *Inferences and Conclusions.*

(1) Are all facts stated positively within knowledge of a suspected writer? (2) Are perfections or imper-

fections of document those reasonably to be expected from a suspected writer? (3) Is the document superior in any way to work of a suspected writer? (4) Is it inferior? (5) Are errors of places, facts, and events such as would be made by a suspected writer? (6) Are errors purposely made? (7) Do materials used have any identifying significance? (8) Does place, or hour, of mailing have significance?

The foregoing outline may be of but little use unless it is intelligently applied directly to the problem in hand. An examination of a suspected writing often accomplishes nothing because the writings are looked at only in a superficial manner that does not disclose what they contain. With one short, simple letter this detailed study may not be necessary but with a long letter, or a series of letters, a careful analysis will almost certainly disclose valuable ideas and suggestions that will either relieve a suspected writer of suspicion, or point toward the actual writer. Finally, of course, if a particular writer is suspected, the handwriting should be examined and compared with the utmost thoroughness.

An extended technical discussion of the subject of Anonymous Letters and other disputed document subjects, with illustrations, appears in the author's work, "Questioned Documents", published in 1910. A Second Edition of this book is now in process of production, September, 1926. The book can be found in most Bar Association Libraries.

CHAPTER XXVII.

HANDWRITING TESTIMONY BY LAY WITNESSES.

The attempt is sometimes made to prove the most glaring and clumsy forgeries to be genuine by unqualified lay witnesses, a whole troop of whom have been led to think that a document on which a claim is based ought to be genuine whether it is or not. In the interests of justice it should be better known that about the weakest and most inconclusive testimony that is ever presented in a court of law is the usual opinion testimony of lay witnesses regarding handwriting.

It is an unwarranted assumption of the law, established by long practice and recorded in numerous opinions, that a knowledge of handwriting can be gained by superficial observation of the mere act of writing. More than this, the old legal precedents even go to the unbelievable extreme of assuming that an observer is qualified to give an opinion under oath as to a disputed signature, even in a controversy of great importance, who has seen the alleged writer sign his name only once many years before. It is not easy to imagine anything more unscientific than this rule. It would be but little more ridiculous to allow a man to testify as an alienist because he lived less than a mile from a lunatic asylum.

The law solemnly declares that in some mysterious way a casual glance at the act of writing years before gives to an observer what the law calls "a knowledge of a handwriting". It should be understood that no particulars or details of the act of observation are asked for. Necessarily most views of this kind would be from a considerable distance and usually with the writing wrong side up as observed. These important facts and conditions receive no consideration. The legal requirement is not an observation of the forms and qualities of the writing itself, but simply of "the act of writing", which forever afterwards qualifies this uninterested observer to testify in court under oath regarding an alleged writing of the person he thus saw in "the act of writing".

The almost unbelievable extreme to which the courts have gone on this matter is shown by two cases here described. In an old New York case, Wilson v. Betts, 4 Denio, it was shown that a proposed witness had seen a person write "more than sixty years before and not later", and yet the ruling was made that the testimony "might properly be submitted to the jury for whatever it was worth". And in a case in Pennsylvania, 127 Penn. St. 371, a lay witness had seen a person write "two or three times" thirty-two years before, when the observer was only ten or eleven years of age, and had not seen the writing of the person since that time, and yet the witness was allowed to give an opinion as to the disputed handwriting and it was said, "but the matter was within his [the judge's] discretion and his conclusion was, as already said, within the limits of the authorities".

These precedents still stand as "authorities", but New York has taken a step in the right direction in connection with testimony of this class in at least one case, People v. Corey, 148 N. Y. (1900), in which case it is said of a proposed lay witness, "He should have an intelligent acquaintance with the handwriting of the party so that he can determine with a reasonable degree of certainty whether the writing offered is his genuine handwriting''. This is exactly the requirement that should be made of every witness in every case. It should be said that in the case referred to the proposed witness could hardly read or write, so the ruling is not as valuable as it otherwise would be.

The assumption that technical knowledge that is of any value can be acquired by a mere glance is simply absurd and would be so considered by all sensible men had it not been dignified by long usage. It is gravely said in some of the old opinions, in a somewhat apologetic way, that objection to a performance based on so slender a foundation ''goes to the weight of the testimony rather than to its competency and the court does not undertake to say how much observation is necessary in order to qualify a witness to testify''. The court certainly should have the courage and the good sense to undertake to say that testimony given under conditions like those specified in the above two cases, has no weight whatever. The refusal to say it indicates that hesitating mental attitude that is the despair of those who attempt to correct the errors of the past and put the methods of science into the administration of the law.

This whole question of the necessary qualifications of a witness is almost entirely within the discretion of the trial court and a stop should be put to the unscientific, ridiculous practice by which in cases of importance anyone who can read writing is permitted to give an opinion on the subject. It is to be hoped that some courageous judge in every jurisdiction will take the first step and make a ruling on the subject to the effect that no witness will be allowed to give an opinion on handwriting, who is not qualified by having an "intelligent acquaintance" with it.

It should also be understood that much of the undue emphasis on this testimony of unqualified lay witnesses has grown out of a few frequently cited old legal opinions which went to the absurd point of contending that testimony based on this kind of casual recognition was peculiarly reliable. The exactly opposite view is, of course, the scientific fact and it should be understood that these unscientific arguments were brought forward long ago in opposition to the effort, then unsuccessfully made, to secure the admission of genuine writings as standards of comparison. These old opinions illogically contended that standards were not necessary because the casual observer of the act of writing was better able to pass on its identity or genuineness than one who actually compared it with genuine writing. The attempt was thus made to justify the ruling then made that no standard writing could be admitted.

It is possible for an occasional lay witness to become familiar with a particular signature by seeing it often and under conditions that enable the observer to gain a knowledge of its features and qualities. But even this knowledge in almost every case covers only an acquaintance with the general appearance of the signature as a whole. As every imitation takes on some elements of this general appearance, and a tracing, if well made, very closely approximates the general appearance of the genuine model from which it was traced, a dependence on general appearance alone on which to base an opinion that a signature is genuine is always dangerous. A forgery, however, is sometimes so palpably bad that it does not require much skill to decide that it is not genuine.

One of the most unreliable kinds of evidence that is ever presented in a court of law is that of personal identification based upon the recognition, from features and general appearance alone, of a person seen long before, or perhaps only once. Exactly the same danger of error arises when it is assumed that the recognition of a handwriting by recollection in this same manner is a simple and easy task. There are certain classes, systems, and schools of handwriting, and a writing in any system even by different writers is bound to show many general similarities, like the similarities in race, complexion, and general appearance in persons, and error is likely to follow in depending alone upon recognition from mere general appearance in identifying a handwriting exactly as error may thus arise in identifying a person. These facts are so obvious that it would seem that they ought to be admitted without argument, but unfortunately the procedure in many jurisdictions has tended to dignify testimony of this class and give it an importance that it does not deserve.

Many of the discussions of this subject of handwriting identification are pervaded by the false idea that the ordinary unscientific observer who knows a person, and lives in the same town, but has seen his writing only infrequently and perhaps only once, in some unknown way has developed an intuition, or a sort of occult power, by which he is able to identify the handwriting of this townsman or mere acquaintance. It is not true that ability to identify handwriting correctly is thus casually, or accidentally, acquired. In the interests of justice it should be understood, especially by prosecuting officers, that it is always dangerous to bring about a conviction, or even base an indictment, upon the unsupported evidence of unskilled observers who attempt to identify a person from a few lines of handwriting.

Intuition and what is sometimes described as natural ability certainly are not alone sufficient on which to base handwriting testimony that charges crime. It is doubly dangerous to depend on this evidence if the handwriting is disguised. If all differences are explained as disguises and all similarities are construed as proof of identity, then error is almost certain to follow when the witness is not able to understand the comparative force and the real significance of the qualities upon which an opinion is based. One who attempts to identify handwriting who is not able to discover, understand, and interpret dissimilarities, when present, is always in danger of committing grave error. A dissimilarity may be a common and frequent variation in handwriting, or it may even point conclusively to a member of a different nationality or race.

In the ordinary proof of uncontested documents, witnesses are called to prove signatures who are assumed by the law to "know the handwriting". This proof usually is of the most perfunctory character and it is not assumed to have much, if any, technical value, as no one disputes the contention and every natural inference tends to prove the fact. This use of this testimony in uncontested cases has no doubt led to its use in cases of importance.

It is not always understood by hearers that many times the real purpose of this testimony by lay witnesses in trials involving disputed documents is not what it purports to be. It presumes to give help in solving a scientific problem, but in many instances testimony on the subject is in fact simply an expression by the witness of his judgment on the case as a whole as possibly affected by personal interest, prejudice, or sympathy. Especially in a community where all the various citizens are known to each other, at least by reputation, this testimony often has considerable force. A prominent citizen, who consents to testify, really gives his formal opinion on the merits of the whole controversy when he testifies as to the handwriting. He is a thirteenth juror.

Proof of handwriting by lay witnesses would be better understood and less dangerous if given in response to a question something like the following: "From what acquaintance you have with the contending parties, and from what knowledge you have of this case on trial and the circumstances surrounding it, and from your general opinion of the merits of the case as a whole, and finally from what feeble and shadowy knowledge of the handwriting that you possess, is it your opinion that this handwriting is genuine or forged?" This question would, of course, not be permitted, but whether or not the question is propounded in this way this often is exactly the question that the witness is answering. On the legal presumption that he is qualified he is ingeniously led to think that he is really giving technical testimony when in fact he is brought into court to give his opinion on the merits of the case as affected by his prejudice, his actual interest, or his friendship for one of the parties or for an attorney.

Notwithstanding all its technical weaknesses, there are some conditions under which testimony by lay witnesses has much force. In a case in which a claim against an estate is based upon a forged document, the positive testimony of a widow, or a son, or an intimate and influential friend, that an alleged signature of a decedent is not a genuine signature has value mainly because of close personal relations with the alleged writer and not because of a technical knowledge of his handwriting. The moral value of the testimony in some measure is based on the idea that these witnesses are qualified by a kind of intuition to identify a handwriting of an intimate friend or near relative. When carefully analyzed, however, it will probably appear that the real force of this testimony arises from the partly unconscious thought that these friends and relatives are in a position to know from other circumstances that the writing under investigation is not a genuine writing.

The interests of justice require that a witness called upon to testify on the question of disputed handwriting in any important matter be thoroughly examined in advance by the court as well as by counsel. If in the course of this examination a prospective witness is asked whether he would be willing to risk his own property, or liberty, on testimony based upon a knowledge of a particular handwriting in dispute, no greater than that possessed by himself, the frank and honest man will usually say that he would not dignify his opinion on the question in any such important manner.

Stupid, half blind, unskilled persons are constantly being asked to give testimony on the subject, who are no more qualified to do so than they would be to make a chemical analysis, or to determine whether or not a law is constitutional. When their ability is tested they fail on the very simplest tests, and in most cases are totally disqualified to do what they are asked to do. Some witnesses who actually testify are barely able to read the handwriting they undertake to identify. In an important case an illiterate, tottering old man was called to prove that a presumptuous forgery was a genuine writing. He was asked the usual questions, including the crucial one, "Did you ever see Mr. Townsend write?" He answered, "Yes, I seen him write". He was then asked, "Can you write?" and the witness answered, "I can write some". Then the final question was put, "In your opinion is this signature here a genuine signature?" and this answer was given, "I guess I could read it if I could hold the paper still enough". Many lay witnesses of this class are asked to testify in courts of law.

It is usually possible to secure a number of these witnesses, often perfectly reputable and honorable men, but totally unqualified technically, who will testify that the most glaring forgery is genuine if their friendship or their prejudice inclines that way. The usual mistake by these incompetent witnesses is made by testifying that a forgery is a genuine writing, but the opposite error is occasionally made. Not being qualified to discover forgery, at any time, or in any way, they usually assume that any writing they examine is genuine. These witnesses, who usually are not qualified to give any opinion in the matter, are skilfully led by suggestion to interpret the problem as is desired by those who submit it to them. They are not often dishonest but are uninformed, and usually are unconsciously prejudiced. Success in securing favorable testimony of this kind depends in large measure upon promptness and persuasiveness in presenting the matter. If the technically unqualified witness testifies, he is likely to appear for the one who gets to him first and presents the matter in a favorable light.

It would be a safer and better method of proving documents in court to ask a Clerk of the Court, or a Surrogate's Clerk, or official reporter, or some public officer with a somewhat extended term of office, to qualify on the subject of handwriting identification and testify in place of lay witnesses. There have been a number of notable examples of highly qualified specialists who have been developed in these various fields. A very little practice and study would render witnesses of this kind incomparably superior to the ordinary lay witness. There should be men with this training in every jurisdiction to whom these problems can be referred.

In disputed will cases one collection of relatives, more or less distant, and friends more or less friendly, on one side give testimony that a signature is genuine, and a similar but usually somewhat smaller group give exactly opposing testimony. Both sets of witnesses are wholly untrained, without scientific knowledge, and, as a rule, unconsciously acting under suggestion if not prejudice. It is perhaps practically impossible to dispense entirely with testimony of this class, but it should always be received with caution and should not be given more weight than it deserves.

As has been well pointed out in numerous modern decisions, and in many discussions of handwriting expert testimony by scientific law writers, a question discussed in a preceding chapter, the real value of expert testimony of this kind, unlike most expert testimony, arises, not from the mere opinion itself but from the reasons for the opinion by which this particular class of expert testimony can be greatly enforced. The untrained witness gives no reasons and is, of course, not qualified to give reasons.

The dangers from this unscientific testimony by incompetent lay witnesses can be reduced in considerable degree by skilful cross-examination. Detailed outlines of cross-examinations of these witnesses are given in the chapter on cross-examination. If the first witness of a group is thoroughly cross-examined, the other prospective witnesses may be convinced that they are not qualified and refuse to testify.

If incompetent witnesses are not effectively cross-examined, that might be thus examined, and a denial of justice results, the fault in many cases is clearly chargeable to the attorney who has not prepared himself. Successful cross-examinations of this kind are not usually difficult, but do require some special technical preparation on the part of one who is not familiar with the subject involved. When examined in just the right manner these unprepared witnesses will themselves often freely admit their own lack of qualifications and the consequent danger of accepting their opinion in any important matter.

CHAPTER XXVIII.*

ERRORS IN IDENTIFICATION OF HANDWRITING.

The scientific spirit and the spirit of advocacy, if not exactly opposed, at least have little in common. One seeks to establish a contention, the other seeks to discover whether or not a contention is true. Training as an advocate, therefore, naturally tends to disqualify one as a scientific investigator. The vigilant attorney is aware of this fact, and by its recognition in some measure prepares himself to avoid its dangers. The continued effort to make the best of doubtful contentions develops a tendency, not to find and expose error, but to explain and excuse it. This same spirit tends to develop a tolerance of far-fetched theories and inherent improbabilities that can hardly be understood by those untrained in advocacy. The most ridiculous theories and excuses are all the time being elaborately put forth and listened to in courts of law with a solemn credulity unworthy of a group of grown men.

The method of science gives attention to every phase of a subject under investigation. It considers not only its certainties and its outstanding features, but its mooted points, its difficulties, and its dangers. In contrast with this method is the narrow spirit of advocacy often employed, which, when applied to one side of a scientific problem, either by superficial investigator, by specialist, or by advocate, does not tend to discover truth. Even when a legal controversy arises over a question that must finally be solved by the appli-

* *American Law Review*, Nov.-Dec., 1914.—Revised.

cation of scientific principles, if it is to be solved correctly, this same unscientific method of the advocate is too often applied.

Although the question is certainly open to argument it is not here claimed that the present contentious method of settling disputes is not perhaps the best practical method under present conditions of society, but that its manifest tendencies and dangers should be understood and, as far as possible, avoided.

When the competent and reliable specialist is called upon to consider a scientific problem in court, he does not permit himself to be made a narrow and unfair partisan for either of the opposed contentions, but rigidly continues to follow the method of science. He understands that he owes a duty to himself, to his subject, and to society, and by rigidly following correct scientific methods his subject not only gains respect, but his own assistance in the end is more effective than otherwise would have been possible. Unfortunately the specialist is sometimes forcefully and ingeniously urged to debase his knowledge and skill to low partisan ends, and it must be said that there are those who agree to assist in an attempt to defeat justice.

Like the conscientious specialist, the advocate with the wide horizon does not permit himself to be made a mere messenger of a party who seeks to profit by fraud. He knows the dangers of unwise advocacy and seeks that greater success that comes to the one who thinks of more than the winning of the one case in hand, and who at all times zealously guards his reputation. To the honest specialist and to the high-class attorney, there is only one side to a technical case, and that is the side with the facts, and in the event that either of them is not consulted by that side he does not appear. The contention that any lawyer takes any case is an unwarranted and cruel slander. The contention that any specialist takes any case is equally untrue.

The scientific problems that arise regarding disputed documents are of great variety and of all degrees of difficulty. The answers to some of the problems are almost obvious, while to others no definite answer can be given. The variety and the difficulties of the problems presented afford the opportunities for error and for the exhibition of dishonest partisanship. The interests of justice require that these dangers should, as far as possible, be known. The unfair advocate in his partisanship may even attempt to take advantage of an admission that errors regarding a technical problem are ever possible and contend that if at any time anything is uncertain then nothing can ever be depended upon. Unfortunately, certain old legal opinions almost take this view and, in defiance of the principles of science, attempt to establish general rules by isolated instances.

It is gratifying to know, however, that the slow but constant tendency of courts of law is to treat scientific questions in a scientific manner. More and more it has come to pass that specialists are asked, not merely to help win a case, but to assist first in discovering the fact and reporting thereon, whatever it may be, and then, if the report is favorable, to help in proving that fact in court.

The interests of justice, however, do not anywhere require that when a specialist is endeavoring to prove a fact on the right side of a case that he do this in a half-hearted, hesitating way. After an honest and competent man has made a favorable report, he is not then asked to be non-partisan to the advantage of fraud and of a party and an advocate who are endeavoring to establish it. Right and justice require that he be fair and honest, but also require that he be positive, uncompromising, and fearless in his attack upon error.

The necessity for proof of handwriting in courts of law, as we have heretofore seen, has very greatly increased with the complication of modern civilization. Proof of this kind is now often absolutely necessary and on it often depends property, liberty, or even life. This proof is sometimes very simple, or it may involve complex and difficult problems. In either case it is too often disposed of in the most superficial, perfunctory and partisan manner. The task as frequently presented requires certain technical experience and special knowledge applied in a scientific manner, if the result of the investigation is to rise much above a more or less positive guess. As has been pointed out in a previous chapter, many persons who are called upon to give testimony on this important question are not qualified to do so and the interests of justice are thus seriously imperiled.

One of the final results of knowledge in any field is the ability to estimate correctly the difficulties of its problems, and one of the highest proofs of competency in any subject is shown by a knowledge of its possible sources of error. Many proverbs are based upon this principle, notably that about the danger of a little knowledge. The subject of disputed handwriting and documents is no exception to the rule. The uninformed novice, and the presumptuous charlatan, with equal promptness, give definite answers to the most difficult as well as to the simplest questions. Those who are best qualified in any field promptly admit their own limitations and the limitations of their own specialty.

The principal causes of error in determining whether handwriting is genuine or forged, or in deciding whether a particular handwriting was or was not written by a certain writer, may be arranged in three general classes. The first class of errors is due to incompetence in the observer, either because of lack of ability or lack of experience. The second class of errors results from the conditions of the problem presented, in which internal matters in the problem itself lead to error. Errors of the third class arise from external matters or influences outside of the document or writing itself.

Errors of the first class, or those which result from *Incompetence in the Observer,* are:

(a) Basing conclusion entirely upon general appearance, or upon "general character", of handwriting as a whole; (b) basing conclusion on forms or designs of letters alone; (c) mistaking general characteristics of writing for individual characteristics and basing conclusion thereon; (d) mistaking system features of writing for individual characteristics and basing conclusion thereon; (e) mistaking elements or features indicating nationality of writer for individual characteristics; (f) basing conclusion on accidental or insignificant variation; (g) failing to observe and consider significant divergence in inconspicuous but fundamental characteristics; (h) finally, and most important of all, failure to reason correctly regarding the observed characteristics. This latter phase of the problem is the one on which the unskilled amateur usually fails; he sees the evidence but does not know what it means.

Errors that arise from the nature of the inquiry, or *Internal Matters in the Document,* are:

(i) Basing conclusion upon too limited amount of disputed writing, or upon too limited amount of standard writing; (j) basing conclusion on too few characteristics or characteristics of uncertain, or of unknown, value; (k) reaching conclusion without considering date of writing under examination, or date of standard writing; (l) giving definite opinion on mere marks or illegible scrawls which contain insufficient writing individuality; (m) basing conclusion entirely on poor or inaccurate photographs; (n) reaching conclusion in the absence of necessary observing, measuring, or testing instruments; (o) reaching conclusion in certain unusual cases before helpful enlarged or special photographs are made.

Errors that arise under the third head, or from *External Matters or Influences,* are:

(p) Basing conclusion on facts and circumstances apart from and outside of the handwriting or document itself; (q) reaching conclusion in haste, under embarrassment, or under unfavorable circumstances of any kind; (r) forming conclusion from influence of opinions of others, or reported opinions of others; (s) basing conclusion, in whole or in part, upon antipathy, friendship, or a zealous advocate's advance argument based upon alleged facts and circumstances outside of the writing itself; (t) reaching conclusion, or rendering judgment, against the weight of evidence because of strong prejudice on the general subject of expert testimony.

The result of every handwriting investigation should be tested by a careful consideration of all of these possible sources of error. Incompetent or corrupt witnesses who testify on the subject can be most effectively cross-examined along these lines by an attorney who is qualified on the facts. Some of the above topics require no elaboration as their bearing is obvious, but a few of the principal topics are here more fully considered.

The last point listed above, under "t", has special application to one who is inclined, perhaps unconsciously, to base a judgment, not on the problem before the court, but partly on experience in a previous case. Strange decisions can sometimes be explained only on the ground that the decision was not on the case on trial but on some other case still in the mind of the one making the decision. Outside of the law that human characteristic that bases judgments on preconceived notions is described as prejudice and it sometimes leads to grave error in a case depending upon handwriting identification.

The identification of a handwriting, as to its genuineness or lack of genuineness, or of a continued writing as to whether it was written by a certain writer, is based upon the fact that handwriting embodies various qualities and characteristics which in combination are sufficiently personal to serve as a basis of identification. These many attributes and qualities are of varying degrees of force as evidence of identity, depending upon just what they are and their number. Many of them are totally invisible to the incompetent observer; he does not see what is before him. Other qualities, though perhaps seen, have no significance to the incompetent observer.

There are two main questions, or difficulties, that confront the examiner of an alleged forgery. The first of these is to determine how much and to what extent genuine writing will diverge from a certain type, and the second is how and to what extent will a more or less skilful forgery be likely to succeed and be likely to fail in embodying the essential characteristics of a genuine writing. Here we have the very heart of the problem, for, at least in some measure, a forgery will be like the genuine writing, and there is also always bound to be some variation in the different examples of genuine writing by the same writer. Incorrect reasoning infers forgery from any variation or infers genuineness from any resemblance.

The process of identification, therefore, must include the determination of the extent, kind, and significance of this resemblance as well as of the variation. It then becomes necessary to determine whether the variation is due to the operation of a different personality, or is only the expected and inevitable variation found in the genuine writing of the same writer. It is also necessary to decide whether the resemblance is the result of a more or less skilful imitation, or is the habitual and characteristic resemblance which naturally appears in a genuine writing. When these two questions are correctly answered the whole problem of identification is solved.

It must also be kept in mind by one who is to identify handwriting correctly, that the attributes and qualities of writing are much more than the mere outline or forms of the letters. Writing becomes a nearly automatic and an almost unconscious act and has many physical and psychological qualities outside of the mere forms of letters. The consideration of a writing by all unskilled observers gives attention only to designs of letters. If the general designs are correct the writing is considered genuine, or, on the other hand, if they diverge in any way or any degree, the writing is thought to be a forgery.

One of the most distinctive qualities of writing is that about it which, by its execution as shown in its line quality, indicates whether it was freely and unconsciously written, or whether it was written in a constrained, slow, and unnatural manner. Unconscious writing is not necessarily skilfully written, but is written with a lack of attention to the act. If such unconscious, careless, free writing embodies the significant form habits shown in the genuine writing, this is conclusive proof of genuineness. It should, however, not be overlooked that a forgery by one with more muscular skill than the writer of the writing imitated may fail by showing a higher degree of skill than the genuine writing. As has been said, "One cannot write better than he can".

There often is in handwriting many of these inherent evidences of genuineness, or evidences of lack of genuineness, that can be seen without comparison with any standard writing whatever. Carelessness, freedom, and indications of unconsciousness of the operation of writing, when they embody characteristic forms, are proof of genuineness in handwriting. The opposite conditions, undue care, attention to detail, hesitation, indicating not lack of muscular control but attention to the process, and especially delicate, unnecessary repairs and overwriting, all point to a lack of genuineness without comparison with any genuine writing. A correct, scientific discussion of these points is necessary in effective testimony and should also form the basis of argument on the subject by the attorney.

The problem then, briefly stated, is an analysis of the standard writing with a detailed and thorough recognition and an accurate estimation of the value of all of its qualities, attributes, and characteristics, and a similar examination of the disputed writing. Then a detailed rational comparison of the writings must be made and the value of all the evidence must be interpreted and weighed.

A study of the standard writing should determine what is to be expected in any writing by the same writer, and a detailed study of the disputed writing must answer the question as to whether it does contain what is to be expected in a writing by the alleged writer, or whether it contains qualities foreign to the writing of the alleged writer. A writing that is not genuine will be likely to fail in both particulars, as not containing that which it should contain and having in it what it ought not to have in it.

If the writing under investigation is genuine, then it will have in it a sufficient number of the characteristics of the genuine writing, with the absence of significant divergent qualities, to warrant the conclusion that it is not an imitation and therefore must be genuine. Errors of the incompetent are due to the fact that they do not know how to distinguish the qualities indicating individuality from the general qualities which may point to system, or nationality, and which are found in the writing of many different writers.

From this brief analysis it will appear that the weighing of the significance of the various qualities is the important and difficult part of the problem of handwriting identification. Many look at things and never really see what they contain because they have no power to interpret what is before them. It is easier simply to see things, as it were, with the eyes only, than to see them mentally and reason regarding them with the brain. Many who are both mentally deaf and blind undertake to identify handwriting.

It is apparent that a disputed writing may contain a fundamental divergent characteristic, of design or execution, which alone is very significant as indicating that the writing is not genuine, but as a rule, an opinion must be based upon a sufficient number of divergences in combination so that it is unreasonable to conclude that they all would accidentally combine. If even a few qualities are distinctly foreign to the genuine writing, or are violations of fixed individual habits in the genuine writing, and cannot be explained in any reasonable manner, then the conclusion must be that the writing is not genuine.

Certain comparatively trivial and unimportant divergences can be pointed out when any two genuine writings, or signatures, by the same writers are compared with each other. These signatures will differ in size and will differ also in certain minor particulars in design and execution, due to the fact that the human writing mechanism is not an accurate reproducing instrument like a copper plate, but produces an inevitable variation within a certain field. The degree of this variation varies with different writers, and its degree is to be determined, not by any general rule, but by an examination of the genuine writing in the particular case.

A suspected writing or series of writings may contain so many delicate, unconscious, inconspicuous attributes, qualities, and characteristics that it is altogether unreasonable to reach any conclusion except that the writing is a genuine writing. It is often possible to prove conclusively, even against the most positive denials by the writer himself, that a writing is undoubtedly genuine. Every writer puts into his writing many things which he himself never sees and, unless he is a qualified student of the subject, there are in the writing of others many things wholly hidden from him.

Because genuine writing varies it is of course not proper to assume that all variation is thus explained. It is necessary carefully to determine the amount, extent, and exact quality or character of the variation. A scientific comparison of handwriting thus becomes, in large measure, a distinctly rational process and not merely the visual examination of the writing under investigation. Trivial or expected variation in a handwriting should, of course, not be construed as an indication of a lack of genuineness and will not be if the question is properly considered. If this natural variation was of an unlimited and fundamental character it would then be impossible to identify any handwriting. Divergence in handwriting is analogous to divergence in speech. A man does not always speak in just the same way, but one who talks with an Irish tongue does not all at once break off into a German accent, and habit firmly controls the hand as well as the tongue.

This variation in genuine writing is the basis of the stock defense of forgery by the partisan advocate. The most clumsy and palpable forgery is excused because in some slight ways the genuine writings themselves are not all exactly alike. It is argued that if writings vary in any way then forgery cannot be shown by any amount or quality of variation. By the same logic it could be argued that men cannot be identified because in some ways they look alike. Because of the conflicting evidence in the writing itself, or because of its limited quantity, there are conditions under which it is impossible to reach any positive conclusion as to the genuineness, or falsity, or identity, of a disputed writing. There are other cases in which there can be no reasonable doubt as to the significance of the evidence upon which an opinion is based.

In examining a disguised writing, or a continued natural writing, as in a disputed letter inquiry, for the purpose of determining whether or not it was written by a certain writer, two main questions also arise. In order to avoid error one must know what is natural and habitual in the writing, and what is disguised. With these two questions correctly answered, and sufficient standard writing in hand for comparison, all the rest is easy. The recognition of personality in handwriting, too often assumed to be a simple and easy task, is sometimes easy, sometimes difficult, and sometimes impossible. The capable and conscientious investigator approaches every task as if it was the most difficult, and when the question cannot be answered he does not attempt to answer it.

There are some principles underlying this phase of the subject, and their consideration is necessary if error is to be avoided. In the first place, in order to identify handwriting correctly, it is as necessary to know how handwritings by different writers are likely to resemble each other as to know how they vary. Writings in the same language must inevitably resemble each other in some ways and modifications of these writings must necessarily retain some of these similarities. Handwritings of the same system as taught in the same schools, and writing by different writers of the same nationality, must inevitably be similar in certain ways. As a basis, therefore, of an accurate judgment on the identity of handwriting, one should possess knowledge of these basic facts or error is not only possible but probable. It will readily appear how one attempting to identify an anonymous letter showing the characteristics of an unfamiliar system or style of any kind, will be inclined to say that it was written by any suspected writer who may happen to write that unknown style.

It is a dangerous assumption for one who is unacquainted with the characteristics of the ordinary differing styles of handwriting as affected by use, system, nationality, sex, age, and occupation, to undertake to identify a disputed handwriting. Special technical knowledge enables the observer to recognize, identify, and correctly interpret the great variety of characteristics which must be depended upon to identify a piece of handwriting. Judgment on the subject must finally be based upon a study of similarities and differences as compared with each other, for to some extent there must be both in any two specimens of handwriting in the same language.

The mere statement of these various facts is sufficient to show the danger of asking those without any knowledge whatever of these important principles to identify a handwriting. What safeguards testimony on the subject is a full discussion of the reasons for any opinion expressed. If the reasons are inadequate and confused, the opinion can be dismissed, and on the other hand, if they are clear, understandable, and convincing, then the opinion can be given the weight it deserves.

The accuracy of a conclusion in any identification is finally dependent upon the number and character of the characteristics relied upon, and error may result either because a conclusion is based upon too few characteristics or from a misinterpretation of the characteristics. Error in identifying a person may arise when identification is based upon only one or two characteristics of a general nature, or on the other hand, such identification may become unmistakable if marks, scars, measurements, and other significant characteristics combine in sufficient number. The problem in all identification is the discovery and weighing of all the characteristics.

To one unfamiliar with the personal characteristics of a foreign race, like the Chinese for example, any two Chinamen of about the same age look much alike. The reason for this is that only the pronounced characteristics are first noted and these, being divergent from those with which the observer is familiar, make different individuals look alike. This same error is possible in any kind of identification if based upon characteristics unfamiliar to the observer. It is the principle underlying an identification of this kind that makes it dangerous to identify a writing from general appearance alone.

It is contended that handwriting can be identified as we recognize the face of a friend, and that we gain a knowledge of it incidentally and without effort. It is true that we recognize the usual, undisguised writing of our friends just as we recognize them in their usual dress and character. The difficulty is that a disputed writing may be either a clever imitation of the writing of another, or a more or less skilful disguise of one's own writing, and in either case superficial knowledge of a handwriting, limited to the recognition of only its ordinary, conspicuous, or surface, features may easily lead to error. Under these conditions the very least similarity is often taken as proof of genuineness, or, on the other hand, the slightest divergence from normal may be construed as proof of forgery. The error thus may go in either direction.

Finally, as with every subject of investigation, rules and methods, special knowledge and experience are of little avail in the absence of frankness and sincerity coupled with the true scientific spirit that follows the fact wherever it goes. Unfortunately every profession is debased by some of its members, but every evil carries its own antidote. Truth is its own best champion, and ignorant pretension sooner or later proclaims itself for what it really is.

CHAPTER XXIX.*

FORM BLINDNESS, OR DEFECTS OF SIGHT IN RELATION TO THE PROBLEM OF PROOF.

This inquiry regarding the relation of variation in human vision to the administration of justice grew out of an adverse decision by a judge who, after giving careful attention to the questions involved in the case, wrote an opinion disclosing the fact that he had not really seen in the visible evidence what had been perfectly apparent to those with normal sight. An inquiry of leading psychologists regarding data on this phase of variation in human vision, especially in recognizing form and distinguishing size, disclosed the fact that the subject was one that had not been fully investigated and reported upon. Professor Joseph Jastrow, of the University of Wisconsin, the eminent psychologist, manifested much interest in the problem and at once began a careful investigation of the whole subject. He has now given much thought and experimentation to the question and is to make an exhaustive report.

In some preliminary tests, made and reported by Professor Jastrow, astonishing variation in speed and accuracy was shown in recognizing certain visible evidence. These tests were made with persons of intelligence and approximately of the same age. It was found that seeing ability ranged from one hundred per cent. of accuracy in eight minutes and thirty-five seconds with one observer, to sixty per cent. of error, on the same tests, in nine minutes and fifty-five seconds with

* *Case and Comment,* Volume 19, No. 12.—Revised.

another observer. It is easy to understand in what peril the interests of justice would be if that second observer, unconsciously half blind, was called upon in a court of law to decide a delicate question appealing to the sense of sight!

It is not always as clearly kept in mind as it should be in considering this question, that the operation of seeing is something more than the mere focusing of an image on the retina of the eye. To see is to perceive through the sense of sight, and perceiving is a mental operation, the eye serving only as the window of the brain. This mental quality in the act of seeing has been explained and clarified for us by the psychologists. In the administration of justice this mental phase of the act obviously becomes a matter of importance in those cases in which proof depends in some measure upon visible evidence. In these matters to see really means to understand. Most legal controversies are decided on testimony addressed to the brain only through the ear. There are cases, however, in which evidence appeals to the mind through the eye, as well as the ear, and in these cases the question of the quality of human vision becomes important.

The vital evidence in many important cases relating to disputed documents is that which depends finally upon the correct understanding and interpretation of visible evidence. Evidence of this class often is of an unusual, or of a microscopic character, and to be understood may require, not only clear presentation and illustration, but also correct analysis and description before its real significance can be appreciated, especially by an unskilled observer. If testimony of this kind is hampered by unfavorable surroundings and restrictions, as sometimes is the case, it is sometimes impossible to prove the facts, especially to those who are partly blind and do not know it.

It is well known that in every normal eye there is a small portion described as the blind spot, but it is not generally understood that many eyes are blind all over to many things that other eyes can see. Reference is not made to those who are color blind, nor to the many who need the assistance of the occulist, but to a surprisingly large class of persons who are supposed to have normal vision, but do not have it. These partly blind persons are unaware of certain distinctions, or similarities, in common things, which to others are perfectly apparent.

All eyes are blind to certain microscopic differences and identities in things, as all are deaf to certain sounds above or below the hearing range. Failure to recognize these so-called subliminal qualities is not the defect here discussed, but the failure of some persons to see what is clearly seen by others. The two points that are of special interest in relation to the administration of justice are that this type of blindness varies greatly in different individuals and is to a large extent unconscious. With some persons it reaches a degree of deficiency that makes dependence upon a judgment based on visible evidence a manifest source of danger. Like color blindness and tone deafness, this inability to identify or distinguish form, size, difference, or identity, may be found in those who in other fields possess average, or even unusual, intellectual attainments. This imperfect vision is certainly a kind of blindness.

It is well understood that many observers are wholly unable to distinguish certain colors and many others are unable to recognize certain combinations of sounds which are called tunes. In these fields it is as if one person possessed a forty per cent. ability, another seventy-five per cent., and another one hundred per cent. plus. It is common knowledge that there are those who are said to be "hard of hearing", others who are near-sighted, and still others who are far-sighted, but it is not generally understood that there are those whose sense of sight, in recognizing likenesses or differences, or slight variations in size, is of so low an order that they may be described as "hard of seeing". Many no doubt go through life and never know that others see certain things better than they do.

In the active mental processes involved in visual comparisons it becomes especially apparent that perceiving through sight is wholly a mental operation. This complex proceeding is in fact an intermingled recognition and weighing of identities and differences, and skill in the performance can undoubtedly be cultivated. The savage, like the dumb animal, does not really see with his brain a watch or a steam engine and many of the complicated things that are before him. As has often been said, the visitor to a foreign land sees only what he takes with him.

In many fields we do not even begin to see until we have been trained, although, no doubt, this difference in quality of vision to a considerable extent is a born, as well as an acquired, difference. The person without scientific training, who has little mechanical ability, and who has had but little actual training in working with, or comparing, physical things, is often almost wholly unable to recognize identities and differences that others see instantly. The proof reader will see at once the wrong letter that the untrained reader may never discover, and the sailor or the plainsman recognizes an object on the distant horizon that others may need a telescope to recognize. The unskilled observer receives the same sense impression, but is unable to interpret that impression correctly.

One of the common variations in seeing ability is in the power to measure with the eye or recognize small differences in size. If two fine lines are placed a short distance apart, and one is slightly longer than the other, some observers are unable to say which is the longer, or whether or not there is any difference in them. If the test is one of slight divergences in the parallelism of lines, or of a slight deviation of slant of a short line to the right or left of vertical, many persons are totally blind to qualities that others can see. The artist and the architect see at once a defect or a distortion that is also before others, but which is never perceived until it is carefully pointed out.

The range of difference in ability to perceive actual similarity, or difference, in forms or outlines, as of printed or written letters, is much wider than in some other vision tests. It is in this latter field especially that what may properly be called "form blindness" has a direct relation to the administration of justice, and has special application to many questions that arise in connection with the proof of documents. The disposition of property worth millions of dollars, as well as questions affecting reputation, liberty, or even life, sometimes depend upon the recognition and correct interpretation of certain forms. Those who are to decide cases of this kind certainly should be able to see accurately.

In a lawsuit in which the main issue must be decided in large measure by an appeal to the sense of sight, the physical evidence must necessarily be clearly seen and correctly interpreted if those who are attempting to prove the facts are to succeed. In a case of this kind some general knowledge of the psychology of sight may be very useful to a trial lawyer, perhaps as useful, as affecting the verdict, as a knowledge of the law. When it is complacently assumed, as is usually the case, that the quality of human vision in those asked to decide a case of this kind is practically the same in all men, error may result.

Most men in their selfishness and absorption in other matters are quite indifferent to all these various questions of legal procedure in the administration of justice until they are affected personally. Then the subject takes on a vital importance that leads them to think that everybody ought to be interested in it. When one has a lawsuit in court, and on his opportunity and ability to prove the facts depends his rights, property, or liberty, he becomes vitally interested in the administration of the law. Under these conditions a man wants good laws, sensible procedure, able judges, and intelligent jurymen. If our individual rights and liberties are to depend upon the correct understanding of visible evidence we are interested to have a procedure established that will permit us to show clearly and interpret correctly the evidence upon which a decision depends.

If a decision must depend upon things to be seen then we want only those asked to decide who are able to see.

As is well understood, it is usually to the advantage of one of the parties in a legal controversy to prevent the facts from being proved, and it often appears that this negative phase of legal proceedings has been developed beyond the positive phase. The procedure often seems to favor the party who seeks to prevent proof. Those without experience are surprised that objection is promptly made to the doing of many things in court that apparently any sensible man would approve anywhere else, and they are sometimes still more surprised when these things actually are not allowed. The sustained objection often amounts to a denial of justice, and legal rules themselves often prevent the facts from being shown, and this is especially true in cases involving visible evidence. In order to avoid injustice, injustice is done. In the old days, with even part of the many inevitable objections sustained, a trial at law in which the vital evidence depended upon correct human vision, proceeded in a kind of legal twilight that made it difficult to see, interpret, and prove the facts. A few courts are still under the shadow of the old restrictive practice where apparently it is feared that the truth regarding the matter under inquiry will be discovered.

Another not infrequent producer of fog and confused vision in courts of law is a thick atmosphere of prejudice surrounding court, counsel, and jury. An appeal to prejudice is always a resource of those against the facts and, if the mind is closed in advance, one may indeed have eyes and see not. Inattention and indifference also shut out some of the light, but an unrestrained prejudice may actually envelop a subject in an equivalent of almost total darkness. To present evidence to the prejudiced is like "carrying water in a sieve".

As Dr. Gross clearly points out in his great work on Criminal Psychology, the business of the whole court in a trial at law ought to be "the critical interpretation of the matter in hand, whatever it may be". With proper assistance, it is surprising in many instances how quickly even the untrained can be made to see and understand what at first was not recognized and understood. With accurate interpretation and suitable instruments and illustrations, a flood of light can be thrown on a difficult and entirely new problem. On this point Dr. Gross also says, with a keen insight, "If we have seen something with a magnifying glass we later can recognize details without its help". In some courts a trial at law is a constant fight against objections, based on old legal rules that favor those whose interests are served when the facts cannot be shown.

It readily occurs to those who have had experience in the matter that in a case involving that quite new thing in a court of law, a disputed typewriting, where the decision must depend almost entirely upon the recognition and correct interpretation of delicate similarities and differences, that it may be very unfortunate for those who seek to prove the facts if the one who is finally to decide the case, judge, referee, or juror, is even partially blind, especially if he is not aware of it.

It is also a disaster to the one whose contention is based on a clear understanding of the visible evidence if enlarged photographs and helpful instruments and methods are ruled out as "against the law".

This recognition of the varying characteristics of typewriting is one of the practical tests of seeing ability, requiring, as it does, the accurate recognition of form, proportions, slant, size, parallelism, comparative weight of impression, and defective forms. A few simple tests will show that some observers cannot see distinctions in these things that to others are perfectly evident. This defect of vision is especially apparent when it becomes necessary to examine specimens in natural size. It is easy to understand how a miscarriage of justice may result when important questions of this kind must finally be decided by an opinionated blind man who thinks he can see, or by a jury which has not been aided in every proper manner.

It would promote justice if it were more widely understood in the legal world that this variation in seeing ability is a proved, scientific fact. Such knowledge would tend to repress offhand judgments and lead to greater care in finally deciding questions depending upon accurate vision. The careful reading of legal opinions shows quite clearly that lack of visual discrimination and perception has had an important bearing upon the rendering of judgments. It is especially important, in the interests of justice, that courts of review sit in "lighted" chambers.

It is often true, as was significantly said in one case, "that there are things which to the ordinary mortal are not discernible", but exact accuracy in some of these cases would require that this statement should be not "the ordinary mortal", but "this ordinary mortal". A blind man's judgment on a painting is not worth much, and his judgment on a disputed document is as valueless.

Even if something equivalent to the well-known Binet-Simon tests might serve a useful purpose, it is hardly to be expected that judges and referees, who try cases without juries, or jurors who are called upon to pass upon questions involving the ability to distinguish form, size, or color, can actually be tested as to accuracy of vision. It is possible, however, that it become better known and understood by all concerned in a trial involving visible evidence, especially by judges and by trial counsel, that there is this variation in the quality of human vision. The emphasizing of that idea is the purpose of this chapter. In a case of this class it should be one of the duties of the judge, and of the trial lawyer who is seeking to prove the facts, to see to it that this topic has proper attention. Justice would certainly be promoted by appropriate and timely cautions on the subject by the trial judge, who would be able to give to such a matter its proper emphasis in those courts where the judge is still permitted to assist in some measure in promoting justice. The subject is one that in some cases should receive proper attention in the preliminary examination of prospective jurymen.

It needs to be plainly said that it is with some feeling of despair that delicate, visible evidence of this class is presented to an old man, perhaps almost entirely devoid of scientific training, who has never studied the technical subject involved, but who might resent the slightest suggestion that any living person could see anything that he could not see. Notwithstanding this risk, it is true that in difficult cases involving evidence of this class the interests of justice are probably best served when cases of this kind are decided by a trained judge without a jury. The average combined judgment of a jury can, however, usually be trusted if the legal rules have permitted the matter to be properly illustrated and fully and clearly presented.

Even brief consideration of this subject of proof of visible evidence shows clearly the vital importance, as aids to clearer seeing, of all helpful instruments and appropriate enlarged photographs. Even slight enlargement makes clearly evident to some observers what before they could not see, and a suitable enlargement often makes differences and identities so plain that they can be seen even by those of foggy vision who, in examining the same objects in natural size, would literally be blind. In many cases to exclude helpful photographs is to exclude the evidence. In most courts properly made photographs are now not only allowed, but welcomed.

Ruskin is quoted, by Neltje Blanchan in a book on birds, as saying, "The more I think of it, I find this conclusion more impressed upon me, that the greatest thing a human soul ever does in this world is to see something . . . Hundreds of people can talk for one who can think, but thousands can think for one who can see".

A good book is the precious life-blood of a master spirit, embalmed and treasured up on purpose to a Life beyond Life.

Milton.

No prince fares like him; he breaks his fast with Aristotle, dines with Tully, drinks tea at Helicon, sups with Seneca.

Cibber.

The world has long ago closed the great assize of letters, and judged the first places everywhere. In such a matter the judgment of the world, guided and informed by a long succession of accomplished critics, is almost unerring. When some Zoilus finds blemishes in Homer, and prefers, it may be, the work of some Apollonius of his own discovering, we only laugh. There may be doubts about the third and the fourth rank; but the first and the second are hardly open to discussion.

Frederic Harrison.

Consider what you have in the smallest chosen library. A company of the wisest and wittiest men that could be picked out of all civil countries, in a thousand years, have set in best order the results of their learning and wisdom. The men themselves were hid and inaccessible, solitary, impatient of interruption, fenced by etiquette; but the thought which they did not uncover to their bosom friends is here written out in transparent words to us, the strangers of another age.

Emerson.

It is the education which gives a man a clear conscious view of his own opinions and judgments, a truth in developing them, an eloquence in expressing them, and a force in urging them. It teaches him to see things as they are, to go right to the point, to disentangle a skein of thought, to detect what is sophistical, and to discard what is irrelevant. . . . It shows him how to accommodate himself to others, how to throw himself into their state of mind, how to bring before them his own, how to influence them, how to come to an understanding with them, how to bear with them. He is at home in any society, he has common ground with every class; he knows when to speak and when to be silent; he is able to converse, he is able to listen; he can ask a question pertinently, and gain a lesson seasonably, when he has nothing to impart himself; he is ever ready, yet never in the way; he is a pleasant companion, and a comrade you can depend upon; he knows when to be serious and when to trifle, and he has a sure tact which enables him to trifle with gracefulness and to be serious with effect. He has the repose of a mind which lives in itself, while it lives in the world, and which has resources for its happiness at home when it cannot go abroad.

Newman.

BIBLIOGRAPHY.

There are professional men who by their acts, if not by their words, contend that the education of a doctor, or of a lawyer, or of members of some other professions, should be as severely practical as that of a plumber, and this question as to whether education should be merely practical or something more must necessarily be considered in making a list of books relating even to one phase of a profession. The list of books that follows is made up on the theory that the education of the professional man should not only lead to technical skill but should extend somewhat beyond what will merely "bring grist to the mill". No doubt there are many things that a lawyer or a doctor may not know and still be technically successful, but often the severely practical are impractical in the higher reaches of a profession and of life. There are doors that never open because the steps leading up to them were not taken. It is not necessary to be a poorer lawyer, or worse doctor, in order to be more of a man.

It is generally admitted that there has been a tendency in America to lower the professional standards, but fortunately that tendency seems to have been recognized and partly checked, and more and more students of law and of medicine are being prepared for professions and for life and not merely for business.

Influenced as he is by the conditions that surround him, the professional man is inclined to be a narrow man. The truth is that in many cases his general mental development stops when his practice begins, and of all men he is in special need of intellectual stimulus outside of his narrow technical field. Part of this stimulus he can get from the right kind of books, and, as has been said many times, and needs to be said many times more, the reading of books is that part of education that is never finished and, in effect, is a continuous post-graduate course of study. With all the emphasis on its importance, however, it must be added that it is a course that comparatively few take.

Though a man learns but little that he definitely can catalogue, there certainly is nothing more necessary to his continued intellectual development than this fixed habit of coming into mental contact with other minds. Even if one cannot become intimate with all the great ideas, and may never be able to follow all the conclusions all the way through, it certainly is well, even in a somewhat distant way, thus mentally to meet the best thinkers. It is also desirable that these meetings come when the mind is sufficiently matured to be in a receptive mood. To the professional man this mental widening of the horizon is a requisite of the highest efficiency and a sure means of escape from the slavery of routine.

To their discredit let it be plainly said that there are many men who neither through conventions, current literature, nor technical books by the leaders, keep in contact even with the great minds in their own professions. Many of these men live their little narrow lives all alone on this globe and neither directly nor indirectly contribute one iota to progress. They do not seem to know that there are living thinking men and naturally they have forgotten that great men of the past have put their wisdom into books. These unprogressive men do not "break their fast with Aristotle, nor sup with Seneca".

To buy at least one good book a week is a good habit to acquire in early professional life, and the fact that one is not a *paid subscriber* to at least two technical journals devoted to his own profession is at least some evidence of unprofessional conduct. The man with the wide view will also read outside of his own special field. One will irresistibly be led towards the great books, and will also do his own special work better, whatever it is, by reading what Dr. Osler says of the work of the great physician.

To each one in different degree the great minds inspire and help, depending upon the approach, the mood, and the age. It is a lifelong misfortune if a few scrawled notes and a few forgotten examinations permanently close the mind to the great thinkers of the past whose great works were perhaps peeped into at too early an age. To live in a world of thought without thinking is in a measure to be one with the beasts of the field. Socrates is reported by Plato as relating how the Handmaidens of Thrace laughed at the philosopher who, through looking at the stars, fell into a pit, but, he adds, with one of those immortal flashes, the handmaidens never saw the stars! There are many who are with the handmaidens!

Nor will one who reads for growth read merely the

easy books. Every man who cares to develop his mind will perseveringly read some of the great books that are hard to read. One who will, for example, faithfully work his way through Mill's Logic, or Whately's Elements of Rhetoric and similar books, will ever after have a better mind. Some of these books properly used in effect are intellectual gymnasiums where the girth of the mental biceps can be increased.

There are many men who think and who say they have no time for general reading, who with chagrin perchance learn that others, busier than they, in some way find the time. It should frankly be confessed by those who do not read that either they do not have the taste for it, or are too lazy. There is no excuse good enough to excuse one for not reading good books.

A few good books relating either directly, or somewhat remotely, to the topics discussed in the chapters of this book are here named. The standard works on evidence are not included as it is assumed that they will be in the lawyer's library. The following list could, of course, be greatly extended, and there may be better books for the purpose, but these are good and deserve a place in a course of general reading for the lawyer, and in a course of special study in The Problem of Proof. Many of them ought to be in every lawyer's library.

BIBLIOGRAPHY.

G. F. Arnold, Psychology Applied to Legal Evidence, Second Edition. Thacker Spink & Co., Calcutta, 1913.

A book that should be included in the "required reading" of every lawyer. A book may still be very useful even if its every contention cannot be fully approved.

Jeremy Bentham, Rationale of Judicial Evidence.
In Five Volumes, Edited by John S. Mill.
Hunt & Clarke, London, 1827. (Out of print.)
The brilliant Sydney Smith says of Bentham:

"Mr. Bentham is long; Mr. Bentham is occasionally involved and obscure; Mr. Bentham invents new and alarming expressions; Mr. Bentham loves division and subdivision—and he loves method itself, more than its consequences. Those only, therefore, who know his originality, his knowledge, his vigor, and his boldness, will recur to the works themselves. The great mass of readers will not purchase improvement at so dear a rate; but will choose rather to become acquainted with Mr. Bentham through the medium of reviews—after that eminent philosopher has been washed, trimmed, shaved, and forced into clean linen".

Notwithstanding this forbidding outlook, the earnest student of The Problem of Proof will do well to dig deep into the Bentham mine, where he will certainly find wisdom even if he is not instructed in the brevity and simplicity of language.

Alexander M. Burrill, A treatise on Circumstantial Evidence. Second Edition, J. S. Voorhies, New York, 1859, 1868.
Contains many single ideas worth many times the cost of the book.

Richard C. Cabot, M.D., Training and Rewards of the Physician. J. P. Lippincott & Co., Philadelphia, 1918.
A book, like that by Professor Osler here listed, stimulating to any professional man, whether he makes bridges, prepares briefs, or writes prescriptions.

Orrin N. Carter, Ethics of the Legal Profession. Northwestern University Press, Chicago, 1915.

Julius Henry Cohen, The Law: A Business or a Profession? The Banks Law Publishing Co., New York, 1916.

George P. Costigan, Jr., Cases and Other Authorities on Legal Ethics. West Publishing Co., St. Paul, 1917.
This, and the two preceding books, should be in the lawyer's library of Caution and Restraint.

Benjamin N. Cordozo, The Nature of The Judicial Process. Yale University Press, 1921.
A highly valuable discussion—apparently unique in some particulars—of The Problem of Proof from the *effect* instead of from the cause

side. The book is Mr. Justice Cordozo's answer to the question, "What is it that I do when I decide a case?"

Criminal Justice in Cleveland. The Cleveland Foundation, 1922.
In numerous ways the most valuable contribution to the study of the administration of criminal law in America.

John Dewey, How We Think. D. C. Heath & Co., Boston, 1910.
A stimulating and suggestive little book. Read it all.

Charles Dickens, Bleak House and The Pickwick Papers, 1853, 1836.
The reading of "Jarndyce and Jarndyce", and the case of "Bardell vs. Pickwick" should be a requirement for admission to the bar.

Conan Doyle, Sherlock Holmes Stories, London.
Famous tales emphasizing the development of inference from intelligent observation.

Emerson's Essays, First Series. Houghton Mifflin & Co., Boston, 1841.
Read "Self-Reliance", "Compensation", "Spiritual Laws", "Prudence", "The Over-Soul", "Intellect". From Society and Solitude, 1870. Read "Books", "Success".

Raymond B. Fosdick, European Police Systems, 1915, and American Police Systems, 1921. The Century Co., New York.
Two books by one of the highest American authorities on the subject, and indispensable to the student of criminal law and criminology. These books give some of the reasons why the administration of the criminal law has failed in America.

Benjamin Franklin, Autobiography. Houghton Mifflin & Co., Boston.
A quaint recital that contains much condensed wisdom.

R. Austin Freeman, The Red Thumb Mark, The Singing Bone, and John Thorndyke's Cases. Hodder & Stoughton, London, New York, Toronto.
A series of little detective tales emphasizing in an effective manner the possibility of drawing of inferences from obscure facts.

John Marshall Gest, The Lawyer in Literature. Boston Book Co., 1913.
Interesting and suggestive.

Dr. Hans Gross, Criminal Investigation. Translated by J. & J. C. Adam, Madras, 1906.
A world famous work by a great authority dealing with all kinds of evidence and its value.

J. G. Holland, Seven Oaks, 1875.
An interesting story dealing in a novel way with evidence and proof.

Oliver Wendell Holmes, Collected Legal Papers. Harcourt, Brace & Co., New York. 1920.
Read especially " Law in Science and Science in Law ", " The Path of the Law ", " Learning and Science ", " The Bar as a Profession ".

William James, The Principles of Psychology. Henry Holt & Co., New York, 1890.
Read chapters on " Habit ", " The Stream of Thought ", " Attention ", " Discrimination and Comparison ", " The Perception of Things ", " Reasoning ".

William James, Selected Papers on Philosophy. (Everyman's Library) E. P. Dutton & Co., New York, 1917.
Read " The Will to Believe ", " The Will ", " The Energies of Men ", and then read " On a Certain Blindness in Human Beings ", and then read this last again, and then read it at least once each year.

W. Stanley Jevons, The Principles of Science: A Treatise on Logic and Scientific Method, 3rd Edition, Macmillan and Co., 1879.

B. Jowett, The Dialogues of Plato. Translated into English by B. Jowett. Charles Scribner's Sons, New York, 1871.
Read " Laches ", " Protagoras ", " Euthydemus ", " Apology ". " Crito ", " Phaedo ", " Theaetetus ", and the Introductions by Professor Jowett.

John D. Lawson, LL.D., The Law of Expert and Opinion Evidence Reduced to Rules. T. H. Flood & Company, Chicago, 1900.

A. Lucas, O.B.E., F.I.C. Forensic Chemistry. Edward Arnold & Co., London, 1921.
A valuable treatise in a special field, based on actual experience, and containing many useful suggestions in special investigations.

Sir Henry Maine, Ancient Law, London, 1861. E. P. Dutton & Co., New York.

John Stuart Mill, A System of Logic. Longmans Green Co., London, 8th Edition, 1872.
One of the great books. Good for " hardening the brain ", as William James says. Read especially Books II, III, IV, V.

William Minto, Logic, Inductive and Deductive. Charles Scribner's Sons, New York, 1893.

Read all of Book II and especially "Rational Belief", "Ascertainment of Simple Facts", "Facts of Causation", "Methods of Observation".

C. Ainsworth Mitchell, Science and the Criminal. Little, Brown & Co., London and Boston, 1911.

Contains many suggestions regarding the discovery and proof of physical facts.

Charles C. Moore, A Treatise on Facts. Edward Thompson Co., Northport, N. Y., 1908.

A valuable collection of data relating to the subject.

Albert S. Osborn, Questioned Documents. Lawyers Co-operative Publishing Co., Rochester, N. Y., 1910.

William Osler, M.D., Aequanimitas, With Other Addresses. P. Blakiston's Son & Co., Philadelphia, 1906.

A book by a doctor that lawyers should read. Read especially "Teacher and Student", "As Depicted by Plato", "The Leaven of Science", "Teaching and Thinking", "The Student Life".

Karl Pearson, Grammar of Science, Part I. Physical, 3rd Edition. Adam & Charles Black, London, 1911.

Marcus Fabius Quintilianus, De Institutione Oratoria.

Liber XII. (80-90 A. D.)

English Translation by H. E. Butler, M.A.

In Four Volumes. The Loeb Classical Library, London; William Heinemann, New York; G. P. Putnam's Sons, MXMXXI. Also available in the Bohn Classical Library, 1856.

It is now presented in this new translation in the excellent Loeb Classical Library, described above, in four very attractive little volumes, printed with the original Latin on page opposite the translation.

This is a work that cannot be skipped by the student of the problem of proof. Any trial lawyer will be helped by familiarity with the thoughts of this distinguished schoolmaster and practical trial lawyer, whose words and ideas matched the marble-pillared halls where he was heard. As Emerson says of Plato, he plays havoc with all our originalities.

Like all thorough students, he knew his past as he knew his friends, and no earlier Quintilians were strangers to him. But it is unmistakable that his work did not merely grow out of a library, but is a product tested by the white heat of actual experience. He clearly shows how little has been added to the sum of human knowledge on certain subjects in nearly two thousand years. Quintilian would be a distinguished and sought for member of any college faculty in the world to-day. Professor Wigmore says of the work, "A book on the whole art of a Roman lawyer, including examination of witnesses, addressing the jury, etc., etc. Founded on human nature which has changed little."

Alfred Zantzinger Reed, Training for the Public Profession of the Law. Charles Scribner's Sons, New York, 1921.

Published by the Carnegie Foundation for the advancement of teaching. Notwithstanding the portions that apparently justify the criticisms of Mr. Kales, in the Harvard Law Review of November, 1921, and other critical reviewers, this is a book that the progressive lawyer must read.

James Ram, A Treatise on Facts as Subjects of Inquiry by a Jury, 4th American Edition, 1890. Baker, Voorhis & Co., New York.

A book that deserves a place in every lawyer's library.

Henry Wade Rogers, A.M., LL.D., The Law of Expert Testimony Central Law Journal Co., St. Louis, Mo., 1891.

William C. Robinson, LL.D., Forensic Oratory. Little, Brown & Co., Boston, 1893.

A valuable book hidden under an unfortunate title that gives no hint of its wide scope and great usefulness. No lawyer of any kind or class should be without it.

Sir Walter Scott, "The Antiquary", "Rob Roy", "The Heart of Midlothian".

Containing interesting discussions of phases of law practice by a celebrated author who was a lawyer.

J. Arthur Thompson, Introduction to Science. William & Norgate, London, 1911.

Read Chapters I, II, III. An excellent brief statement of the method of science. Every lawyer should read it.

Arthur C. Train, By Advice of Counsel, and Tutt and Mr. Tutt. Charles Scribner's Sons, New York, 1920, 1921.

Entertaining books by a practical lawyer that are especially valuable as studies of that elusive, delicate, and powerful quality in law practice inadequately described as "atmosphere".

Mark Twain (Samuel L. Clemens), Pudd'nhead Wilson. Harper & Brothers, 1894.

The application of the principles of proof, by a master artist as applied to a special subject, finger-print evidence, and a delightful and fascinating story.

John Tyndall, Fragments of Science. P. F. Collier & Son, New York. Read "Scientific Use of the Imagination".

Francis L. Wellman, The Art of Cross-Examination. The Macmillan Company, New York, 1908.

Contains many valuable suggestions which grew directly out of, and have been verified by, extended experience.

Richard Whately, D.D., Elements of Rhetoric. Archbishop of Dublin, 1828. John P. Morton Company, Louisville, 1912.

Another book with a misleading title. On the whole perhaps the most valuable book on Persuasion. It should be in every lawyer's library and much of it should be in every lawyer's mind.

Richard Whately, D.D., Elements of Logic. Archbishop of Dublin, 1826. John P. Morton Company, Louisville, 1912.

Read especially "Of Fallacies" and "Dissertation on the Province of Reasoning". Contains much that has direct application to the business of the lawyer.

William Wills, Circumstantial Evidence. London, 1838, 1850. Sixth Edition, 1912.

A standard work of great value that deserves a wider circulation in this country. It contains much of interest and value to the trial lawyer.

John H. Wigmore, The Principles of Judicial Proof, As Given by Logic, Psychology, and General Experience. Little, Brown & Co., Boston, 1913.

Contains much stimulating and informing discussion and a wealth of reference material relating to many phases of Legal Proof. Another book that every lawyer should own.

INDEX

INDEX